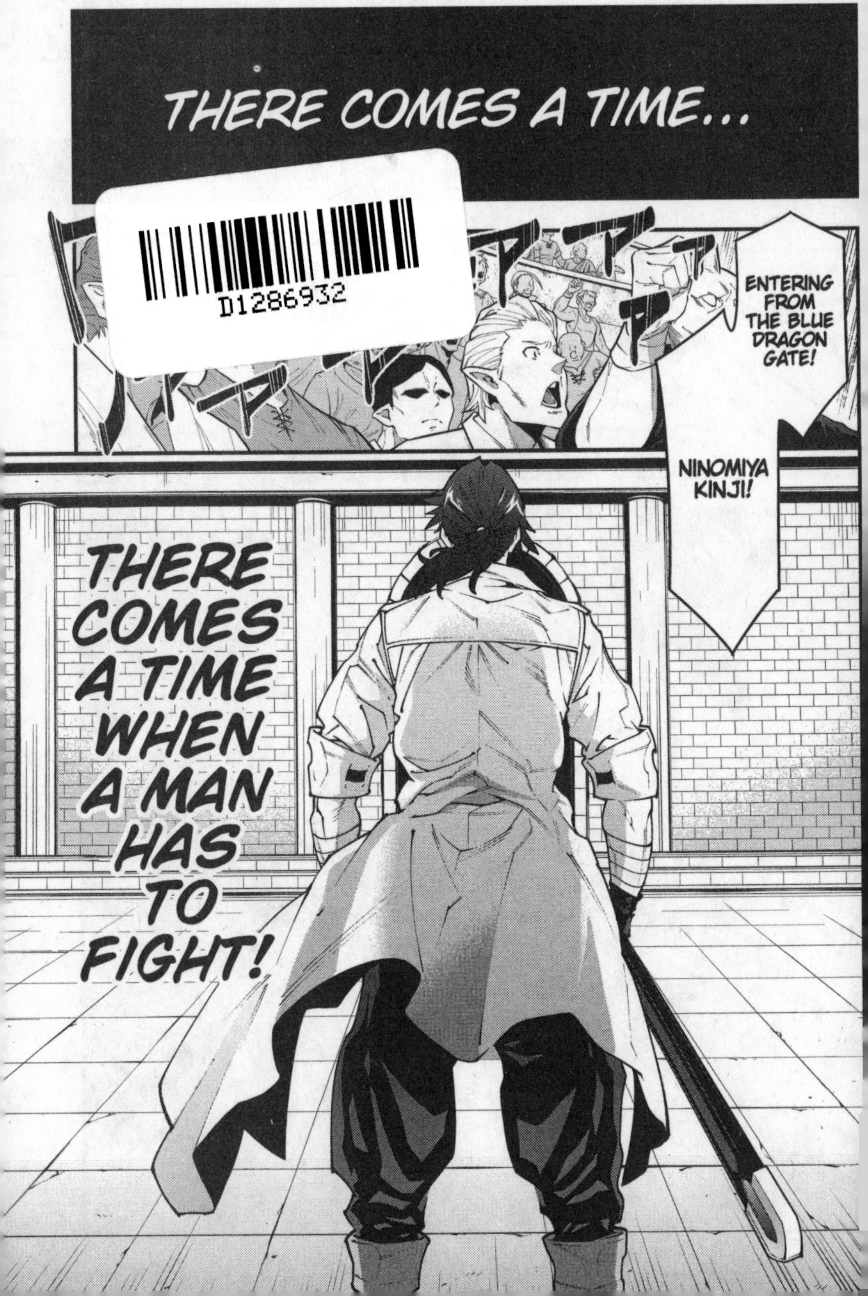
THERE COMES A TIME...
ENTERING FROM THE BLUE DRAGON GATE!
NINOMIYA KINJI!
THERE COMES A TIME WHEN A MAN HAS TO FIGHT!

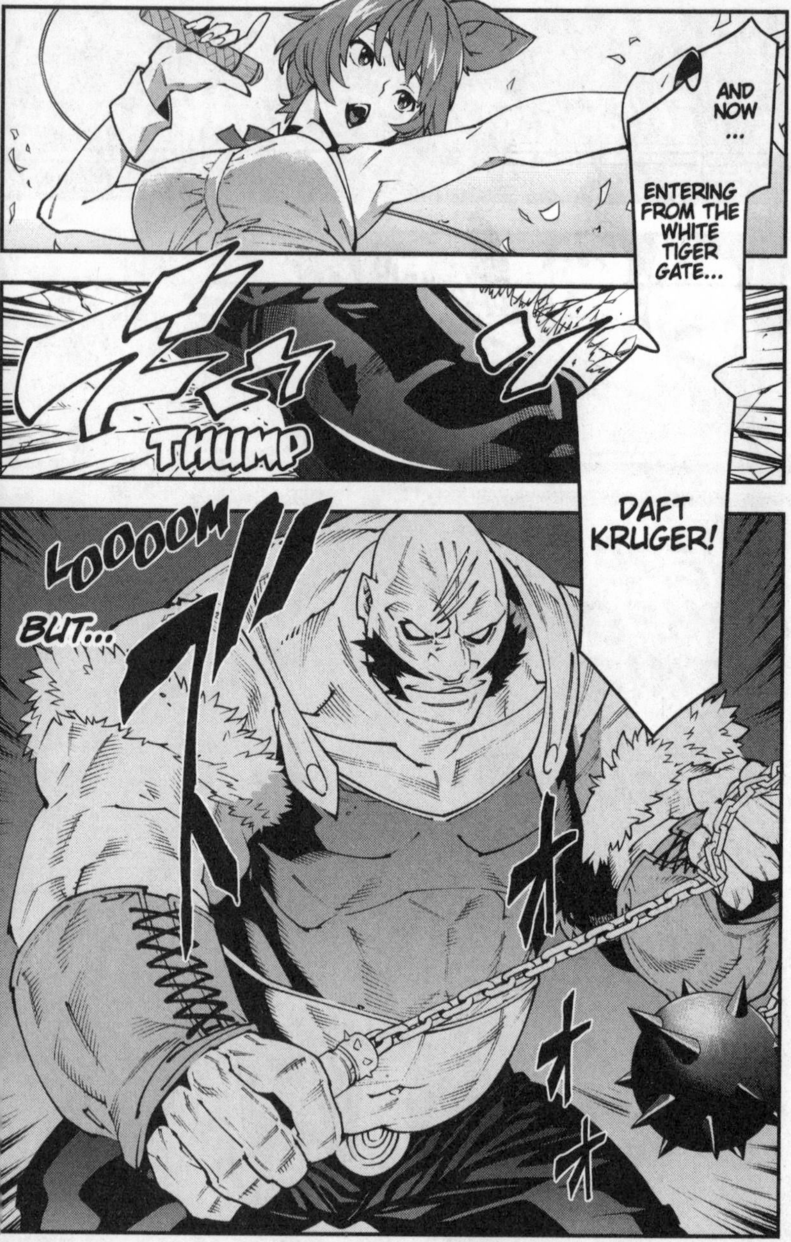
AND NOW ...
ENTERING FROM THE WHITE TIGER GATE...
THUMP
DAFT KRUGER!
LOOOOM
BUT...

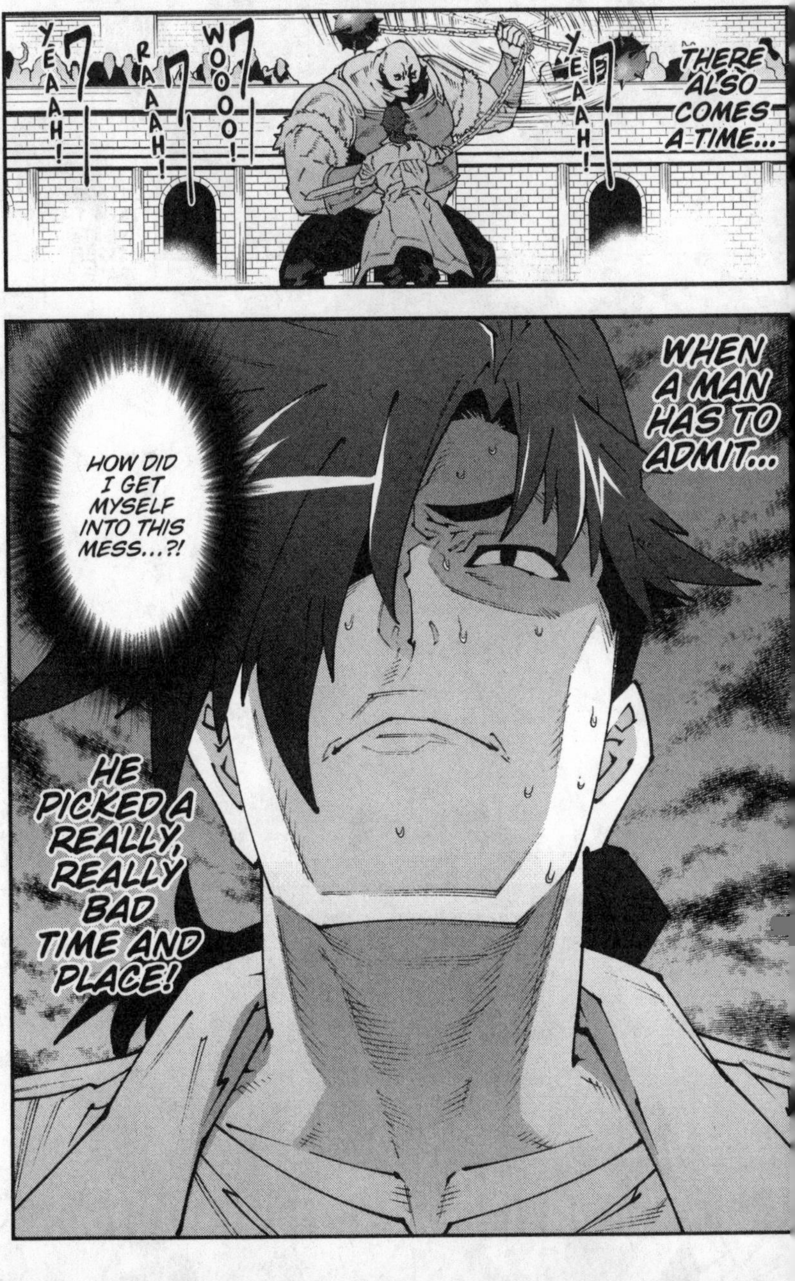
THERE ALSO COMES A TIME...
YEAAH!
WOOOOO!
RAAAH!
YEAAH!
WHEN A MAN HAS TO ADMIT...
HOW DID I GET MYSELF INTO THIS MESS...?!
HE PICKED A REALLY, REALLY BAD TIME AND PLACE!

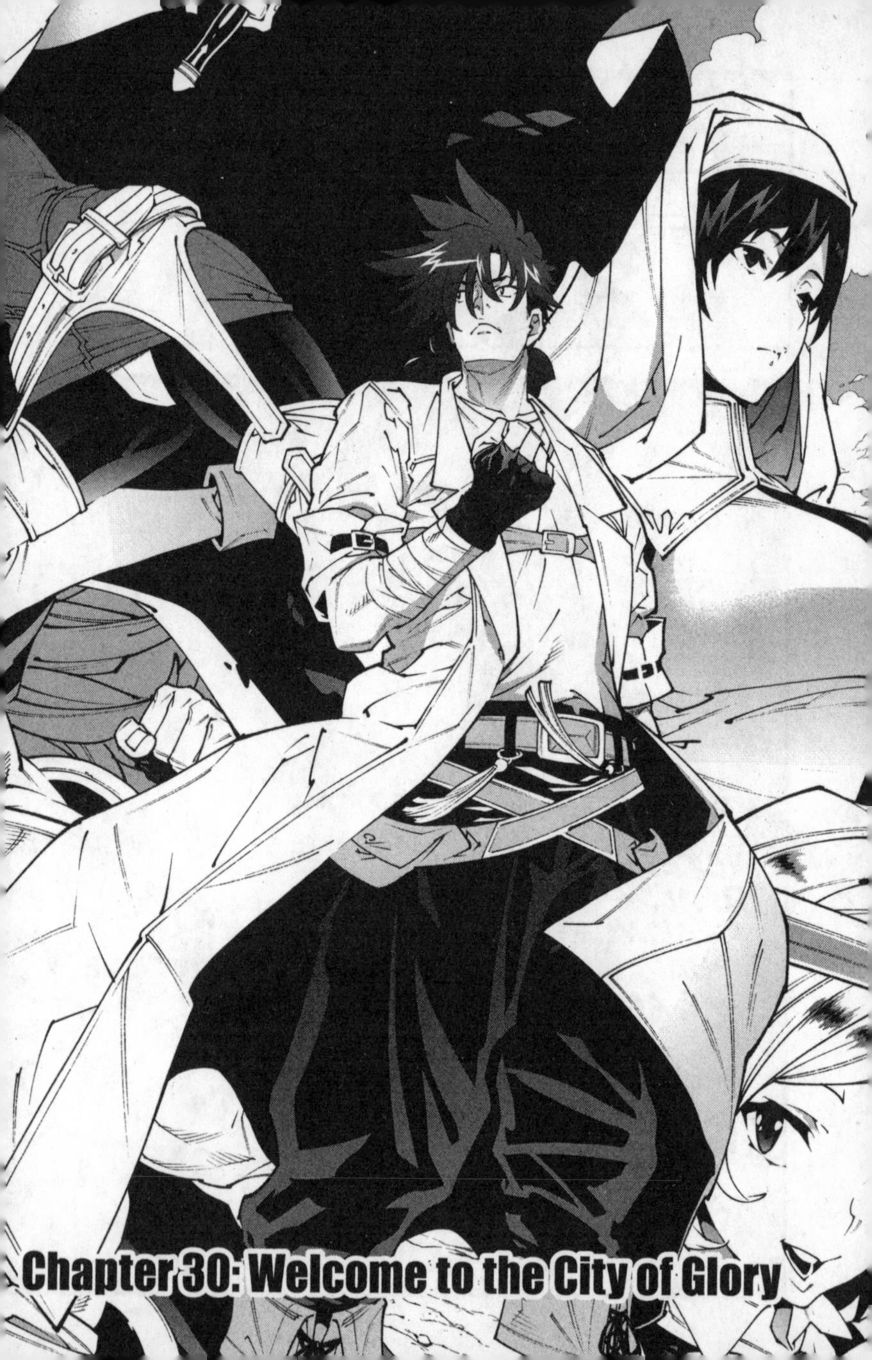
Chapter 30: Welcome to the City of Glory

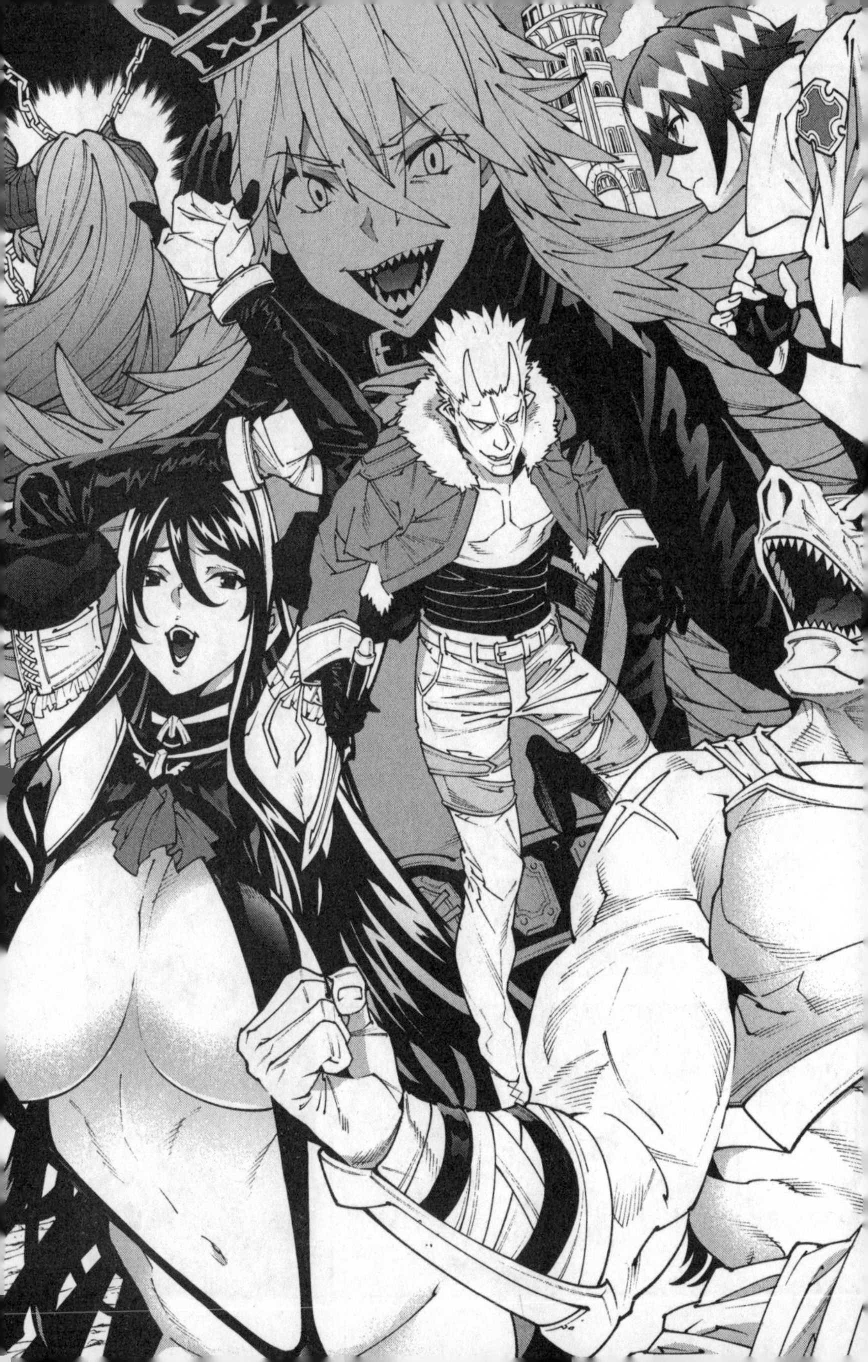

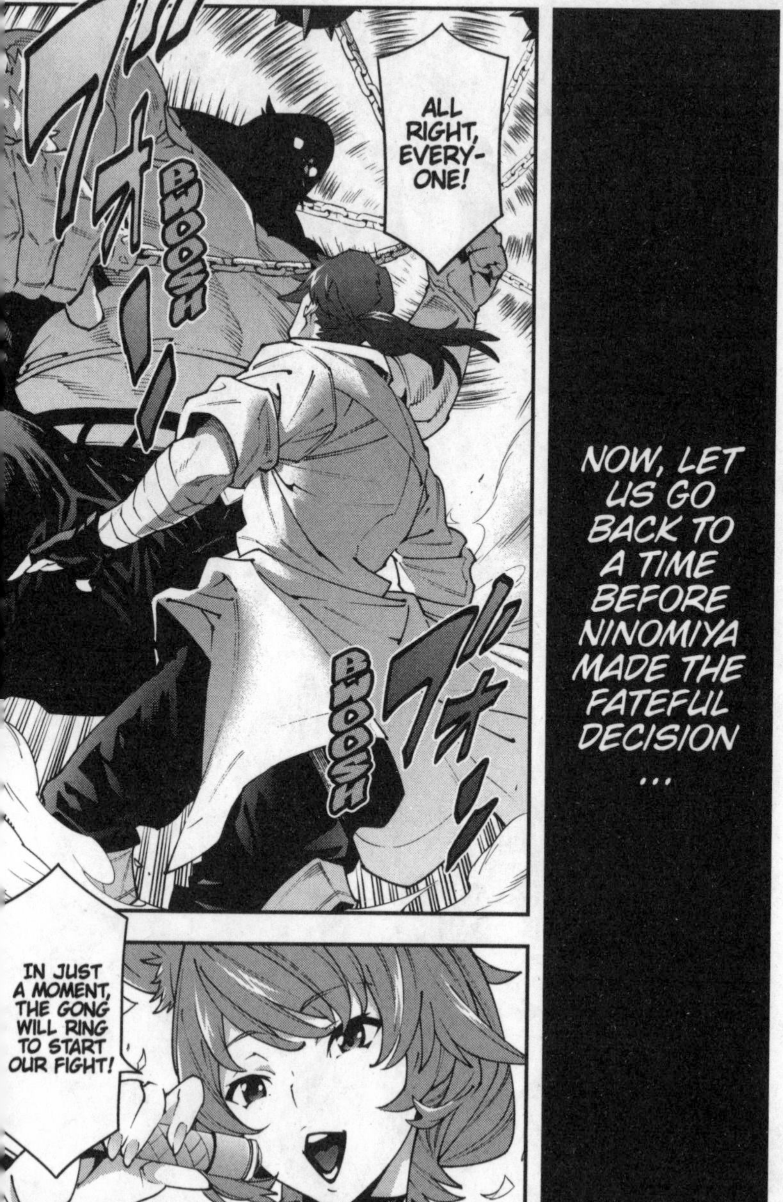
NOW, LET US GO BACK TO A TIME BEFORE NINOMIYA MADE THE FATEFUL DECISION ...
ALL RIGHT, EVERY-ONE!
BWOOSH
BWOOSH
IN JUST A MOMENT, THE GONG WILL RING TO START OUR FIGHT!

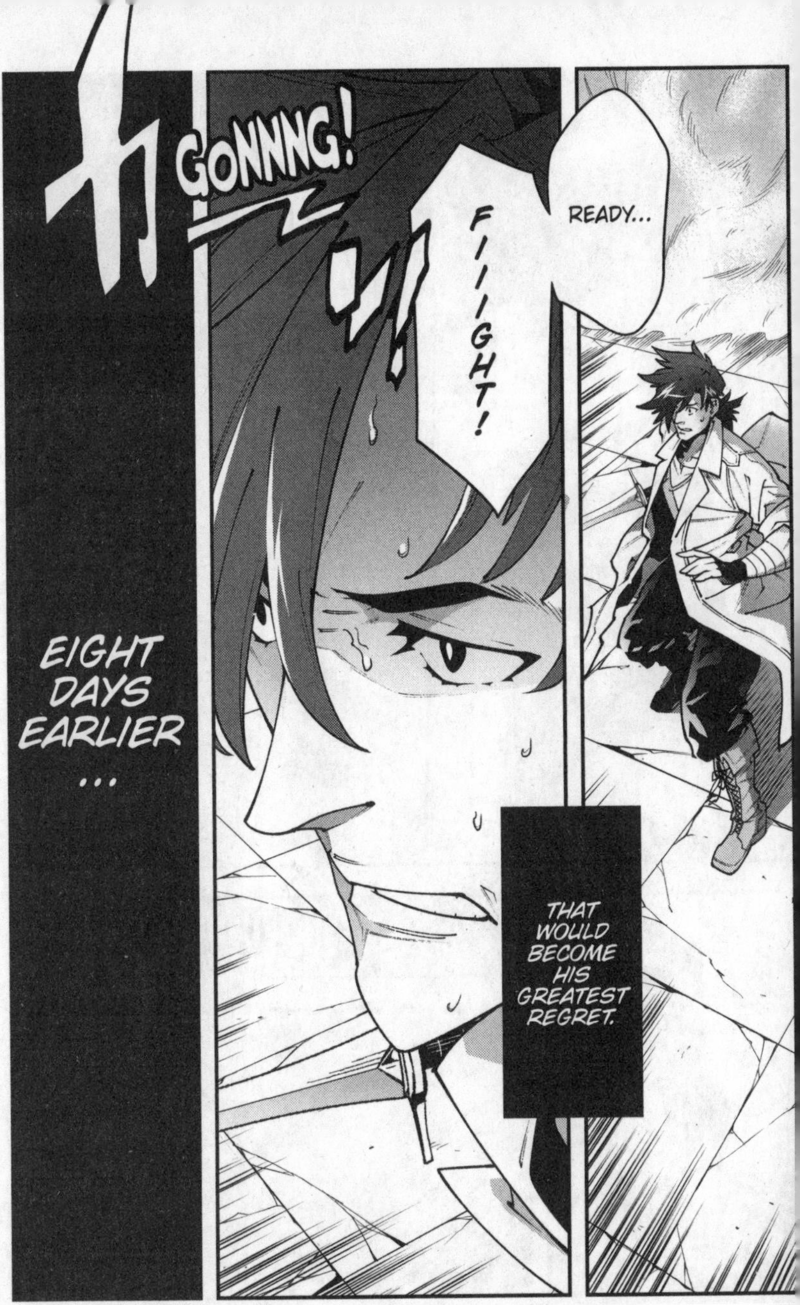
READY...
F-I-I-IGHT!
GONNNG!
THAT WOULD BECOME HIS GREATEST REGRET.
EIGHT DAYS EARLIER ...

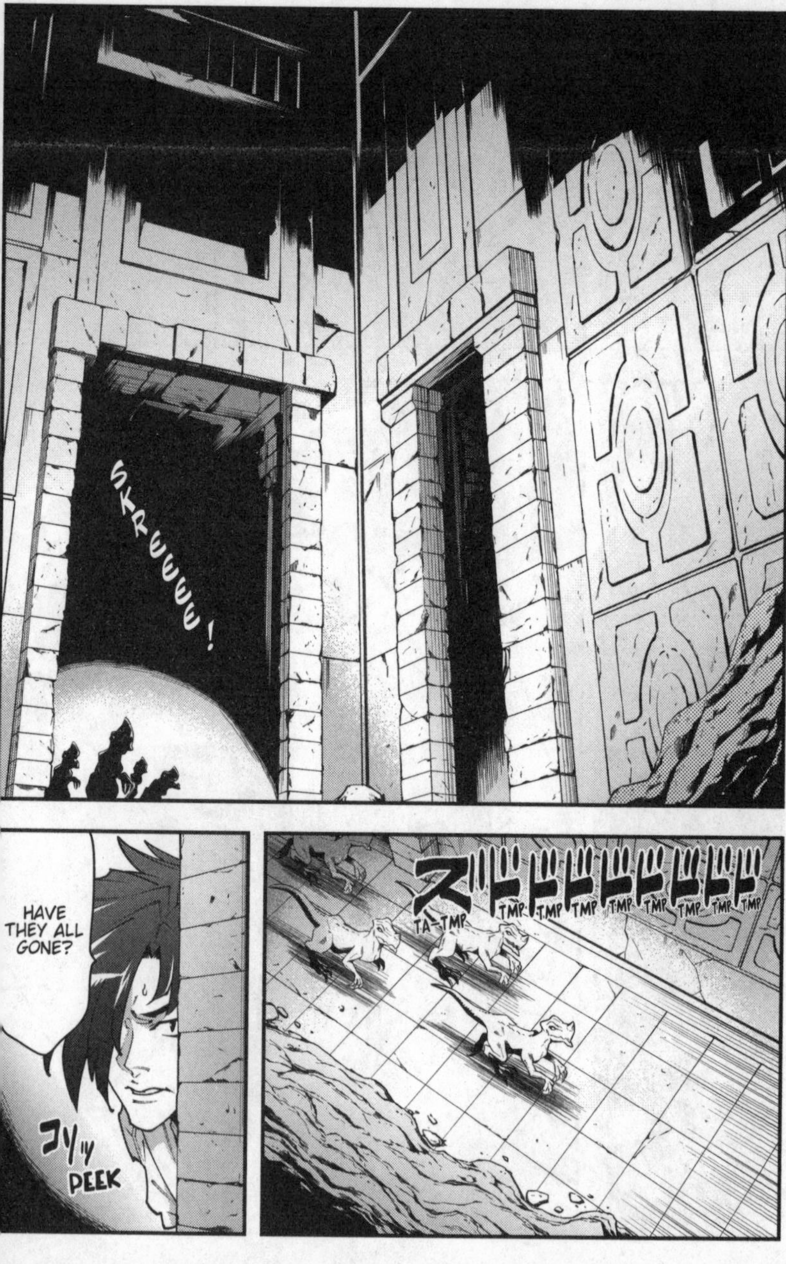
SKREEEEE!
スドドドドドドドド
TA-TMP TMP TMP TMP TMP TMP TMP TMP TMP
HAVE THEY ALL GONE?
コソッ
PEEK

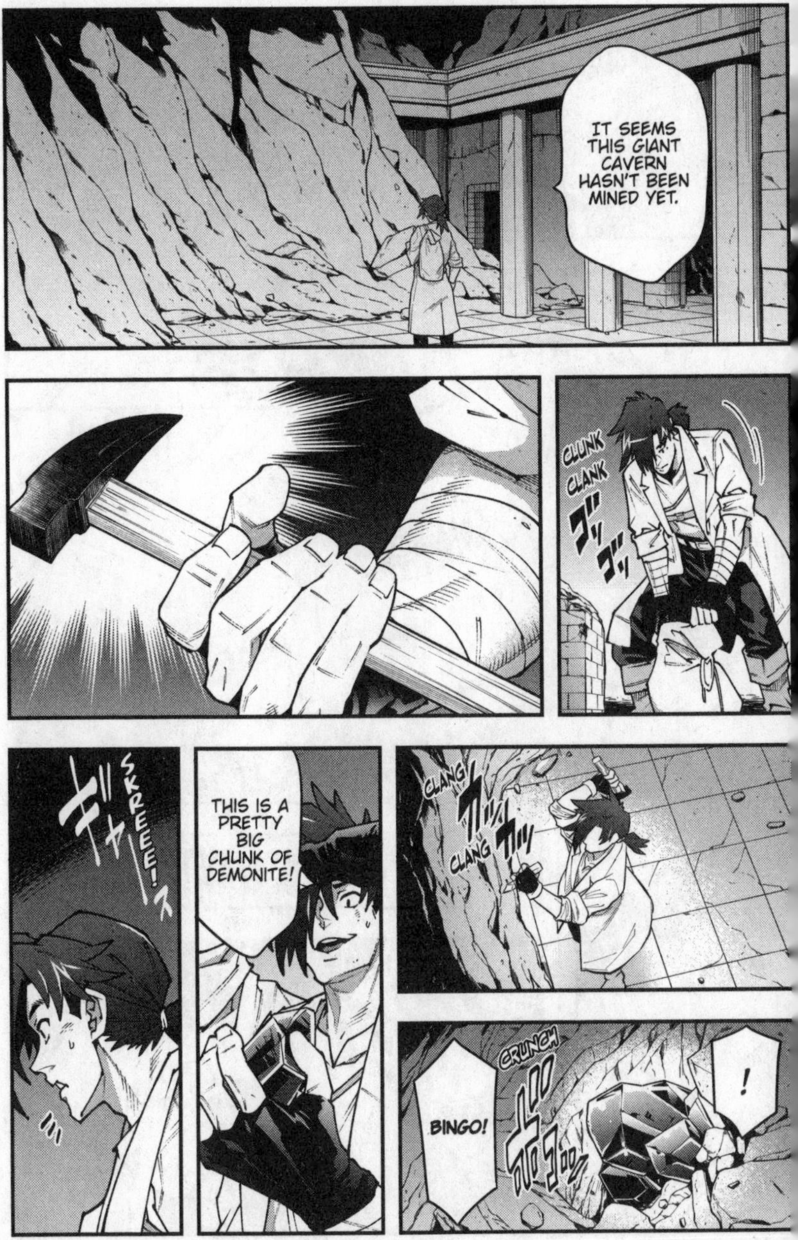
IT SEEMS THIS GIANT CAVERN HASN'T BEEN MINED YET.
CLUNK
CLANK
ゴッ ゴッ
CLANG
CLANG
!
CRUNCH
BINGO!
THIS IS A PRETTY BIG CHUNK OF DEMONITE!
SKREEE!
ギャース

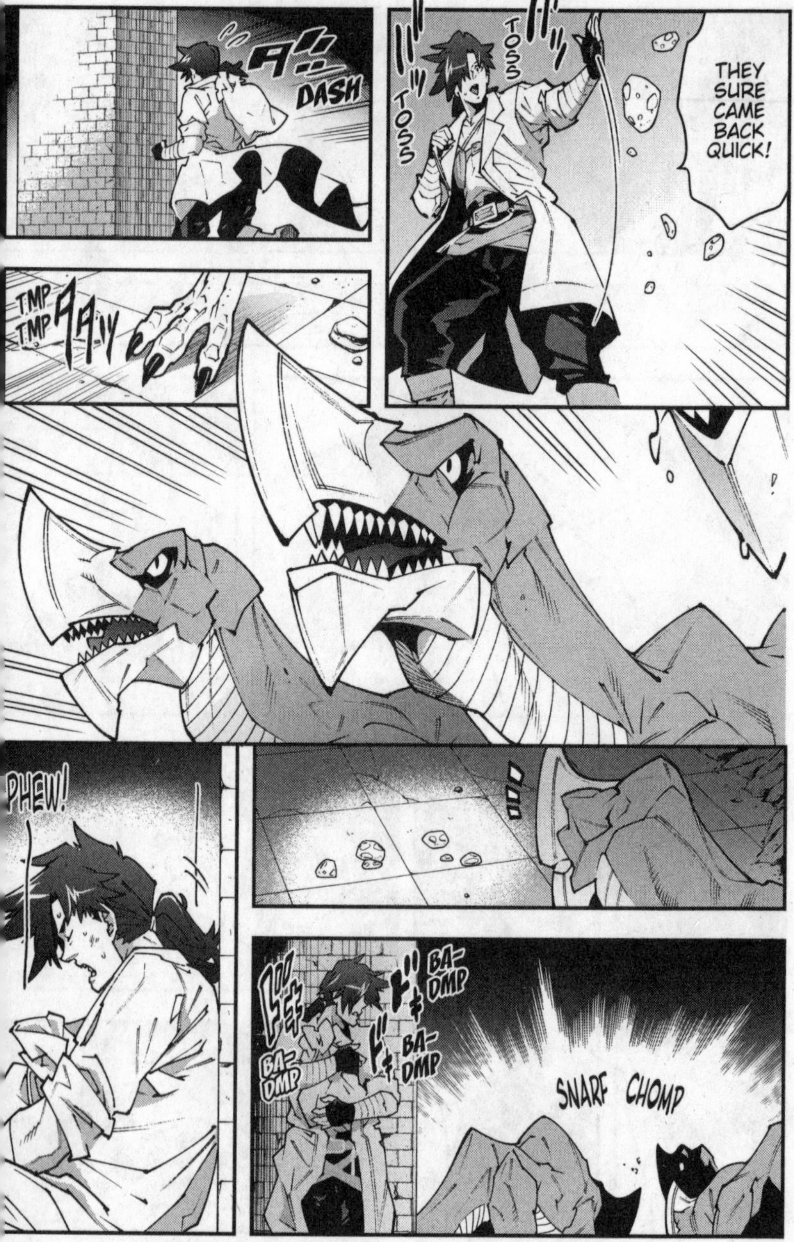
TOSS
TOSS
THEY SURE CAME BACK QUICK!
DASH
TMP TMP
BA-DMP
BA-DMP
SNARF CHOMP
PHEW!

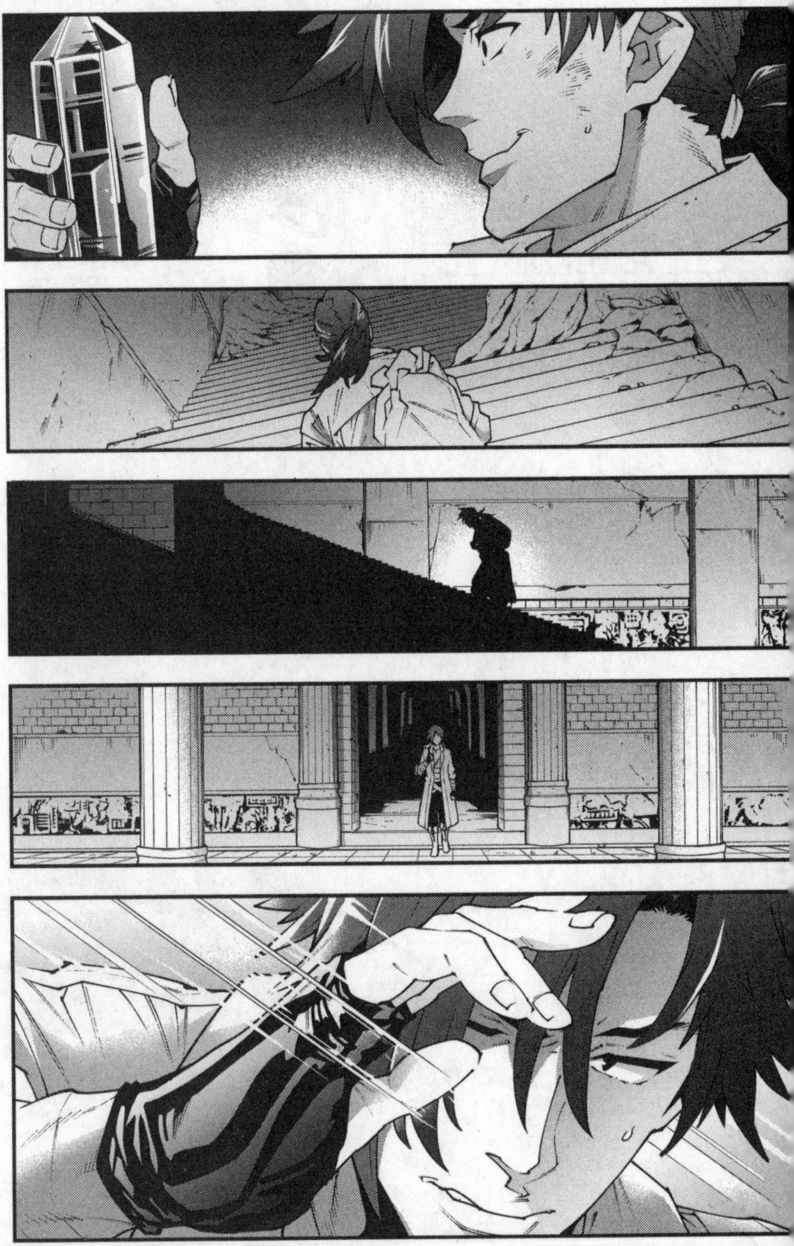

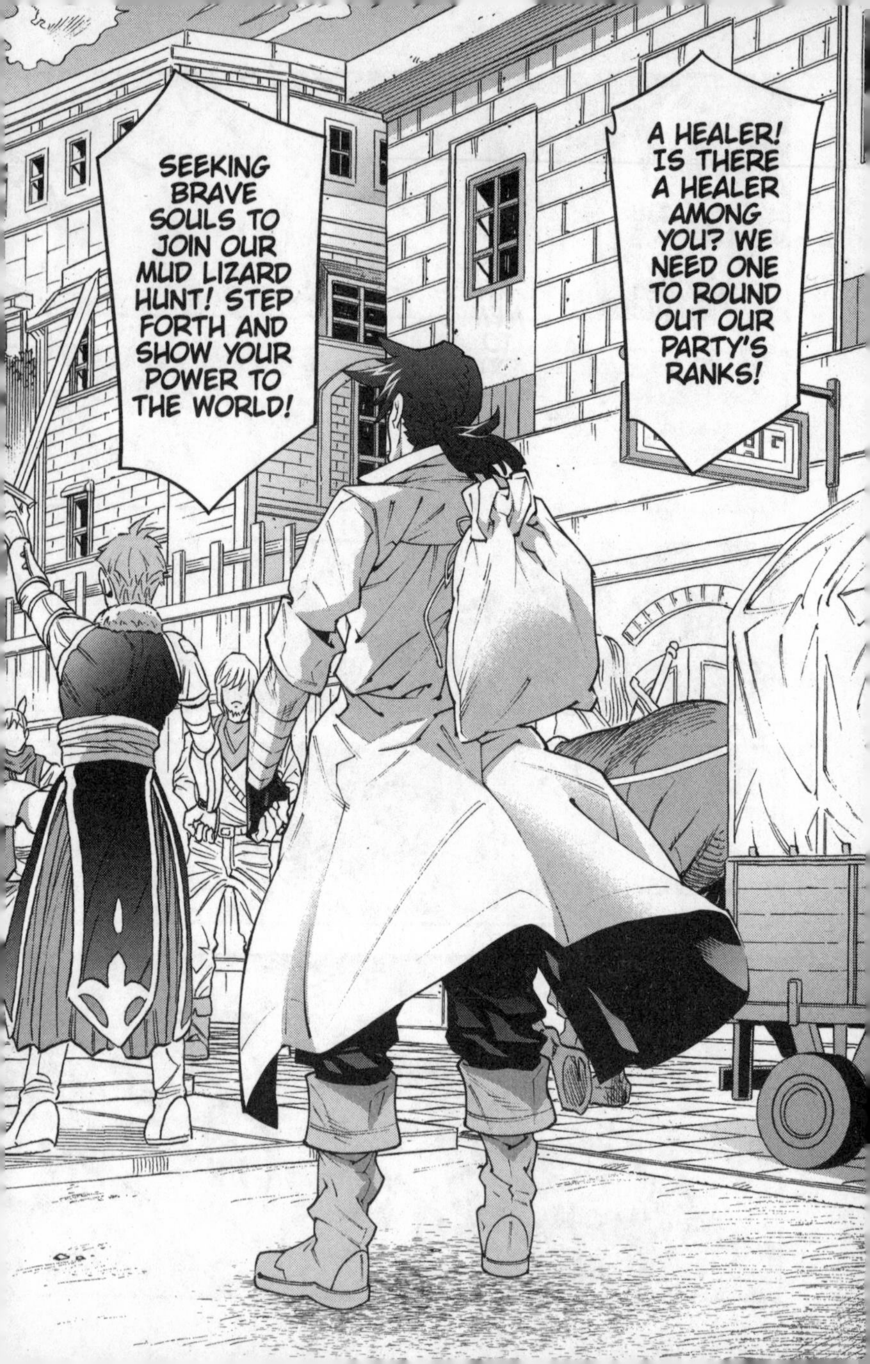
A HEALER! IS THERE A HEALER AMONG YOU? WE NEED ONE TO ROUND OUT OUR PARTY'S RANKS!
SEEKING BRAVE SOULS TO JOIN OUR MUD LIZARD HUNT! STEP FORTH AND SHOW YOUR POWER TO THE WORLD!

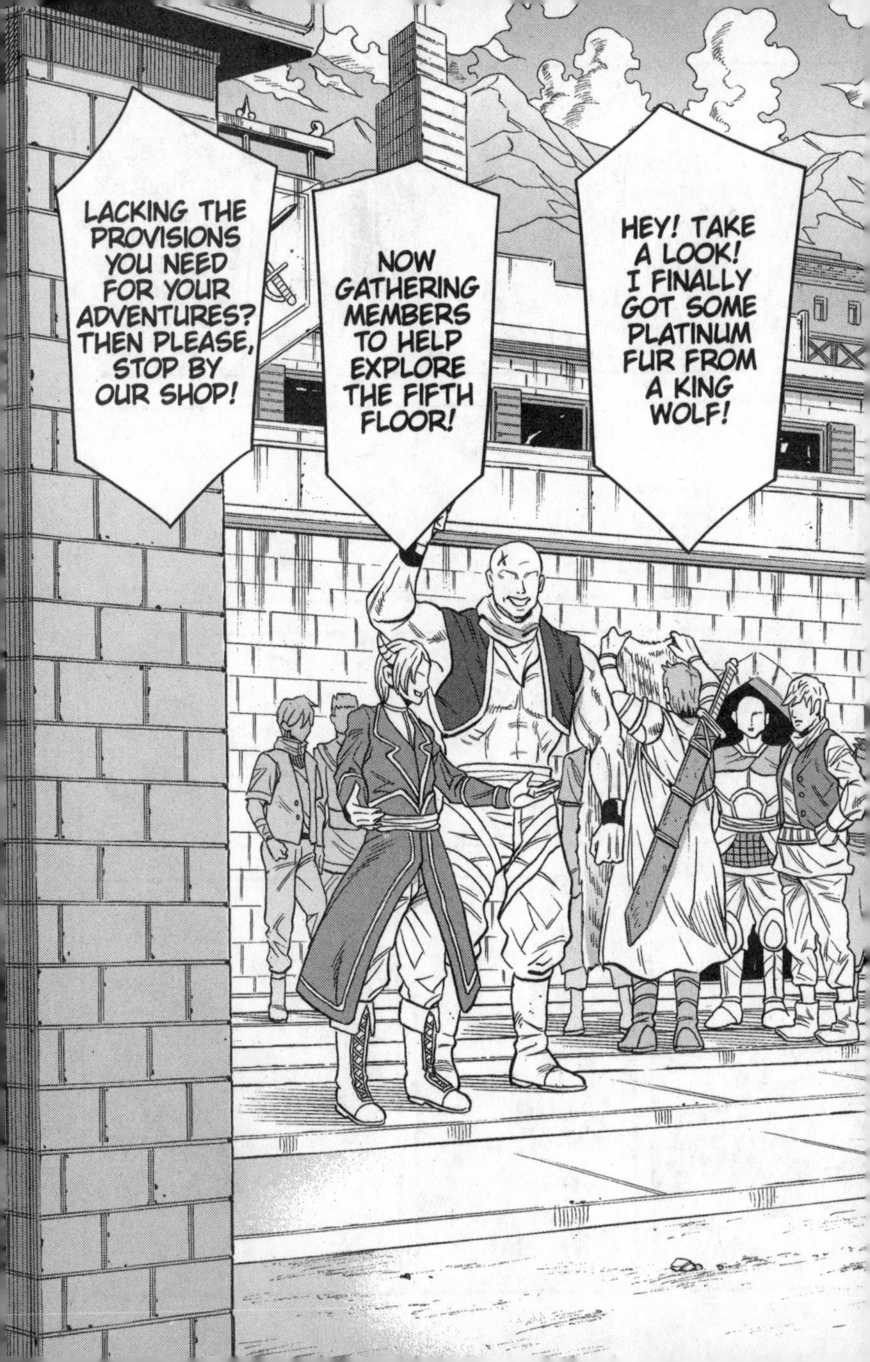
HEY! TAKE A LOOK! I FINALLY GOT SOME PLATINUM FUR FROM A KING WOLF!
NOW GATHERING MEMBERS TO HELP EXPLORE THE FIFTH FLOOR!
LACKING THE PROVISIONS YOU NEED FOR YOUR ADVENTURES? THEN PLEASE, STOP BY OUR SHOP!

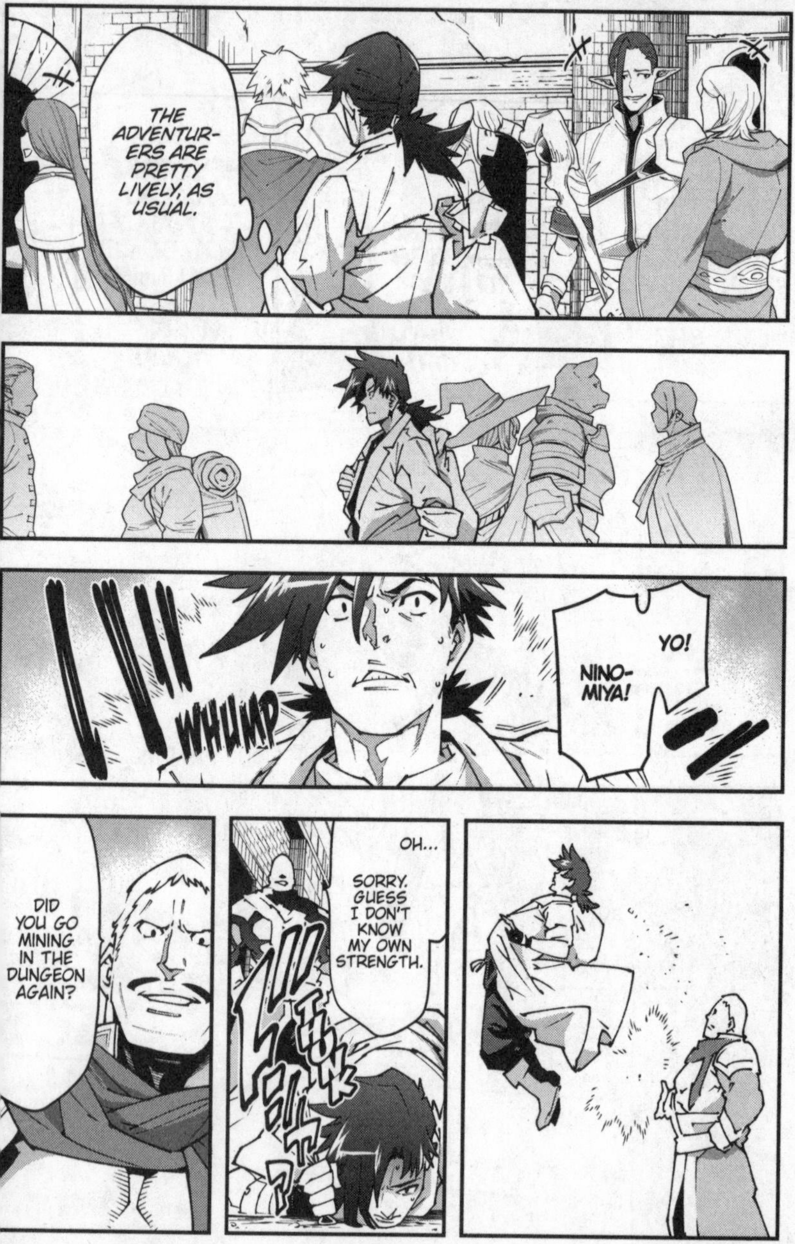
THE ADVENTURERS ARE PRETTY LIVELY, AS USUAL.
YO! NINOMIYA!
WHUMP
OH...
SORRY. GUESS I DON'T KNOW MY OWN STRENGTH.
THUNK
DID YOU GO MINING IN THE DUNGEON AGAIN?

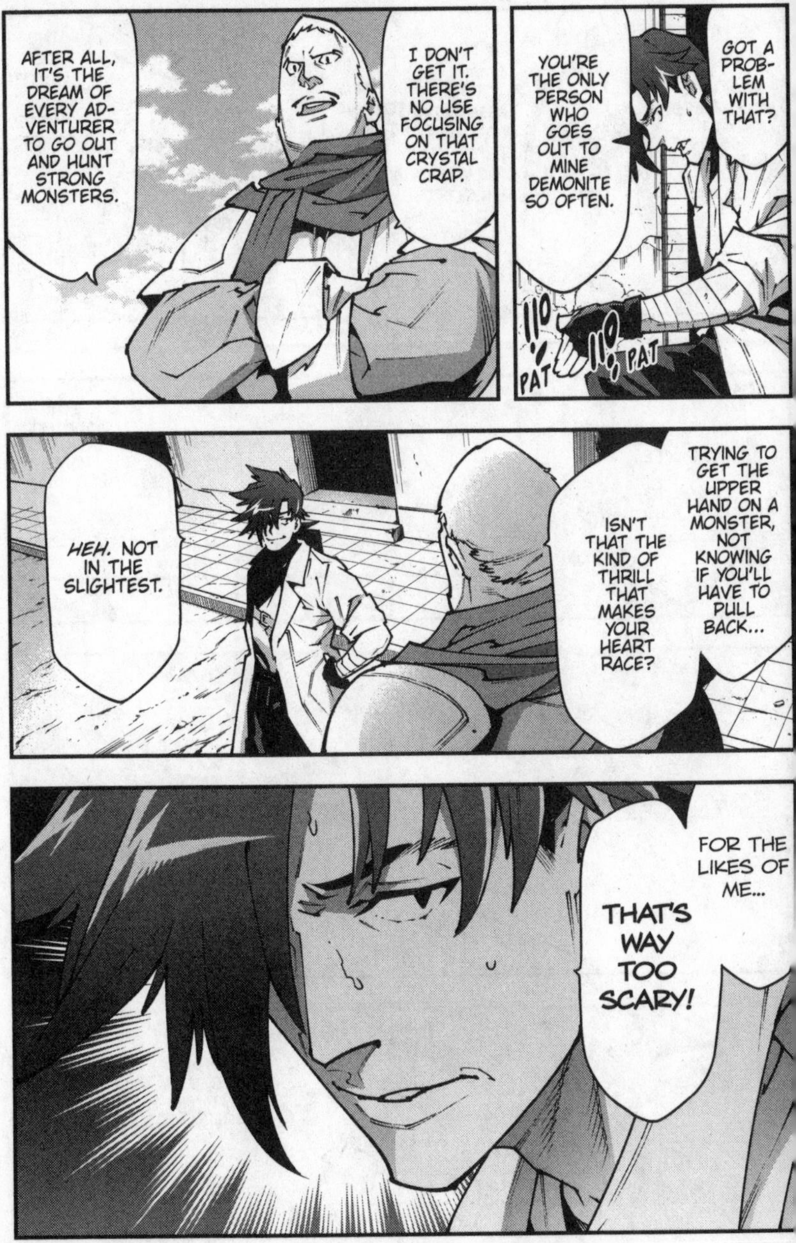
GOT A PROB-LEM WITH THAT?
YOU'RE THE ONLY PERSON WHO GOES OUT TO MINE DEMONITE SO OFTEN.
PAT
PAT
I DON'T GET IT. THERE'S NO USE FOCUSING ON THAT CRYSTAL CRAP.
AFTER ALL, IT'S THE DREAM OF EVERY AD-VENTURER TO GO OUT AND HUNT STRONG MONSTERS.
TRYING TO GET THE UPPER HAND ON A MONSTER, NOT KNOWING IF YOU'LL HAVE TO PULL BACK...
ISN'T THAT THE KIND OF THRILL THAT MAKES YOUR HEART RACE?
HEH. NOT IN THE SLIGHTEST.
FOR THE LIKES OF ME...
THAT'S WAY TOO SCARY!

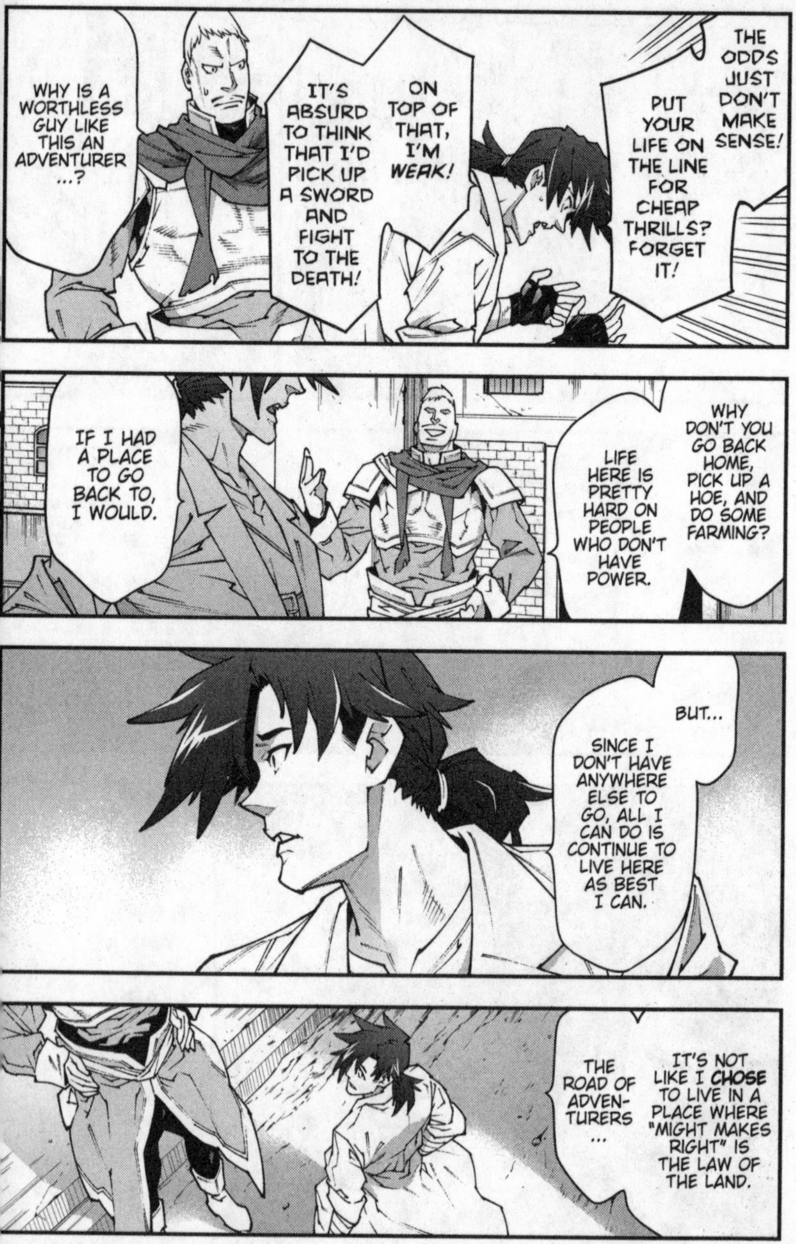
THE ODDS JUST DON'T MAKE SENSE!
PUT YOUR LIFE ON THE LINE FOR CHEAP THRILLS? FORGET IT!
ON TOP OF THAT, I'M *WEAK!*
IT'S ABSURD TO THINK THAT I'D PICK UP A SWORD AND FIGHT TO THE DEATH!
WHY IS A WORTHLESS GUY LIKE THIS AN ADVENTURER ...?
WHY DON'T YOU GO BACK HOME, PICK UP A HOE, AND DO SOME FARMING?
LIFE HERE IS PRETTY HARD ON PEOPLE WHO DON'T HAVE POWER.
IF I HAD A PLACE TO GO BACK TO, I WOULD.
BUT...
SINCE I DON'T HAVE ANYWHERE ELSE TO GO, ALL I CAN DO IS CONTINUE TO LIVE HERE AS BEST I CAN.
IT'S NOT LIKE I **CHOSE** TO LIVE IN A PLACE WHERE "MIGHT MAKES RIGHT" IS THE LAW OF THE LAND.
THE ROAD OF ADVEN-TURERS ...

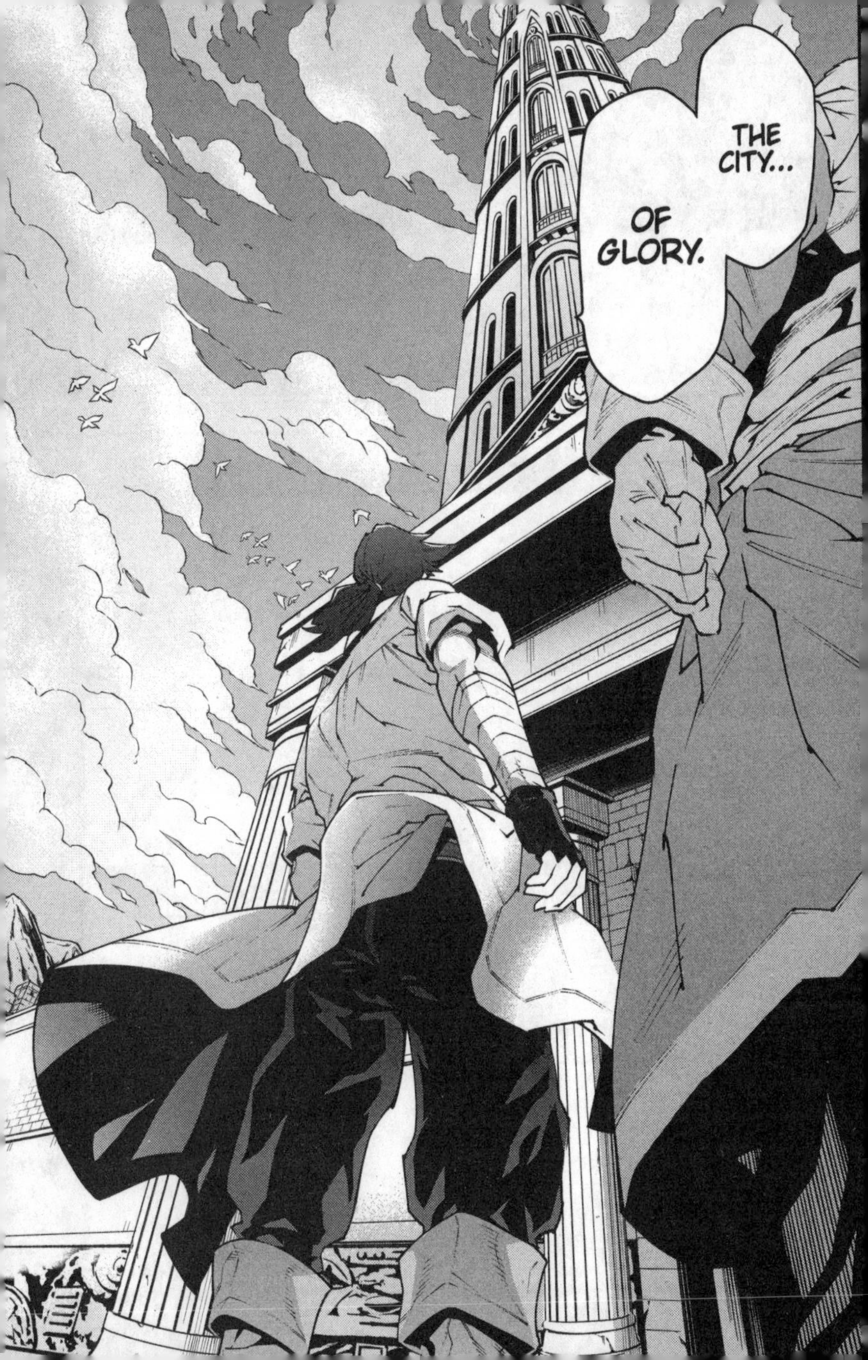
THE CITY...
OF GLORY.

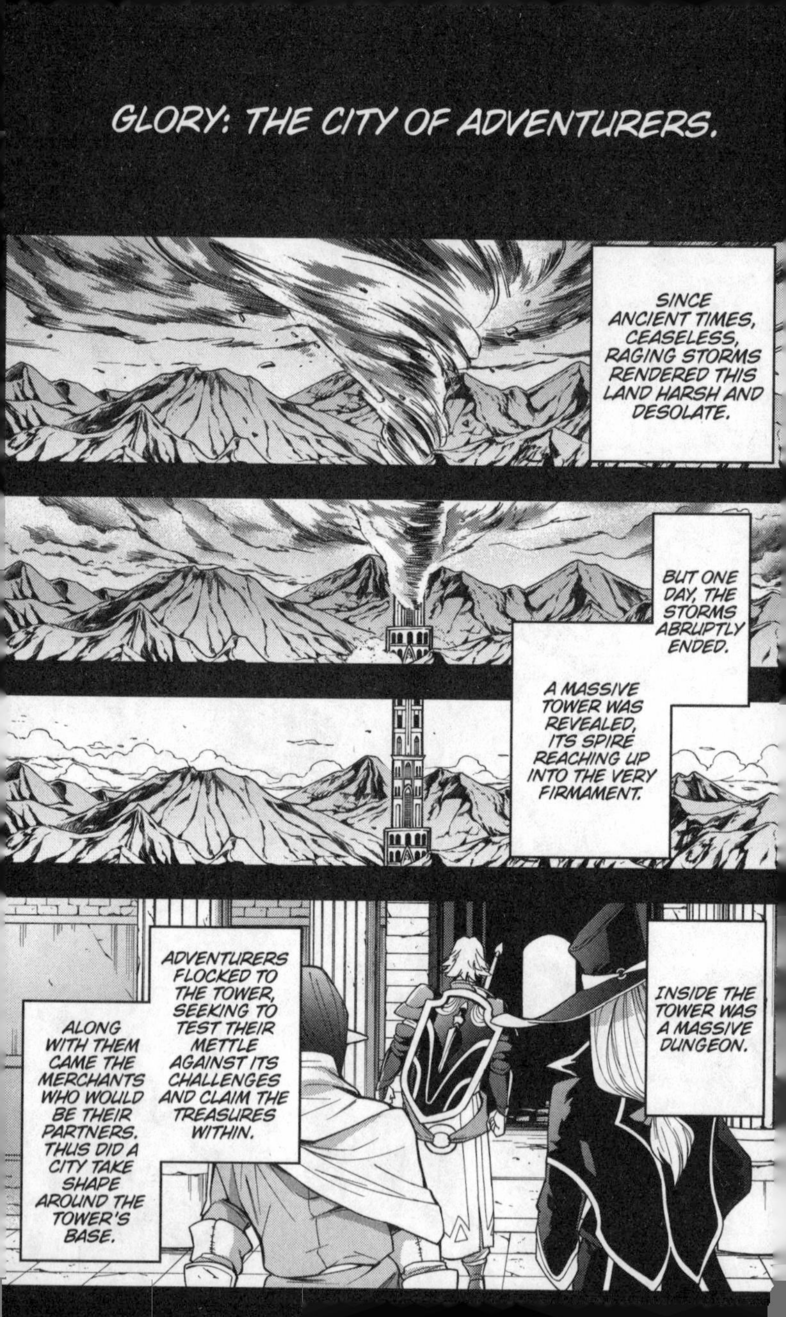
GLORY: THE CITY OF ADVENTURERS.
SINCE ANCIENT TIMES, CEASELESS, RAGING STORMS RENDERED THIS LAND HARSH AND DESOLATE.
BUT ONE DAY, THE STORMS ABRUPTLY ENDED.
A MASSIVE TOWER WAS REVEALED, ITS SPIRE REACHING UP INTO THE VERY FIRMAMENT.
INSIDE THE TOWER WAS A MASSIVE DUNGEON.
ADVENTURERS FLOCKED TO THE TOWER, SEEKING TO TEST THEIR METTLE AGAINST ITS CHALLENGES AND CLAIM THE TREASURES WITHIN.
ALONG WITH THEM CAME THE MERCHANTS WHO WOULD BE THEIR PARTNERS. THUS DID A CITY TAKE SHAPE AROUND THE TOWER'S BASE.

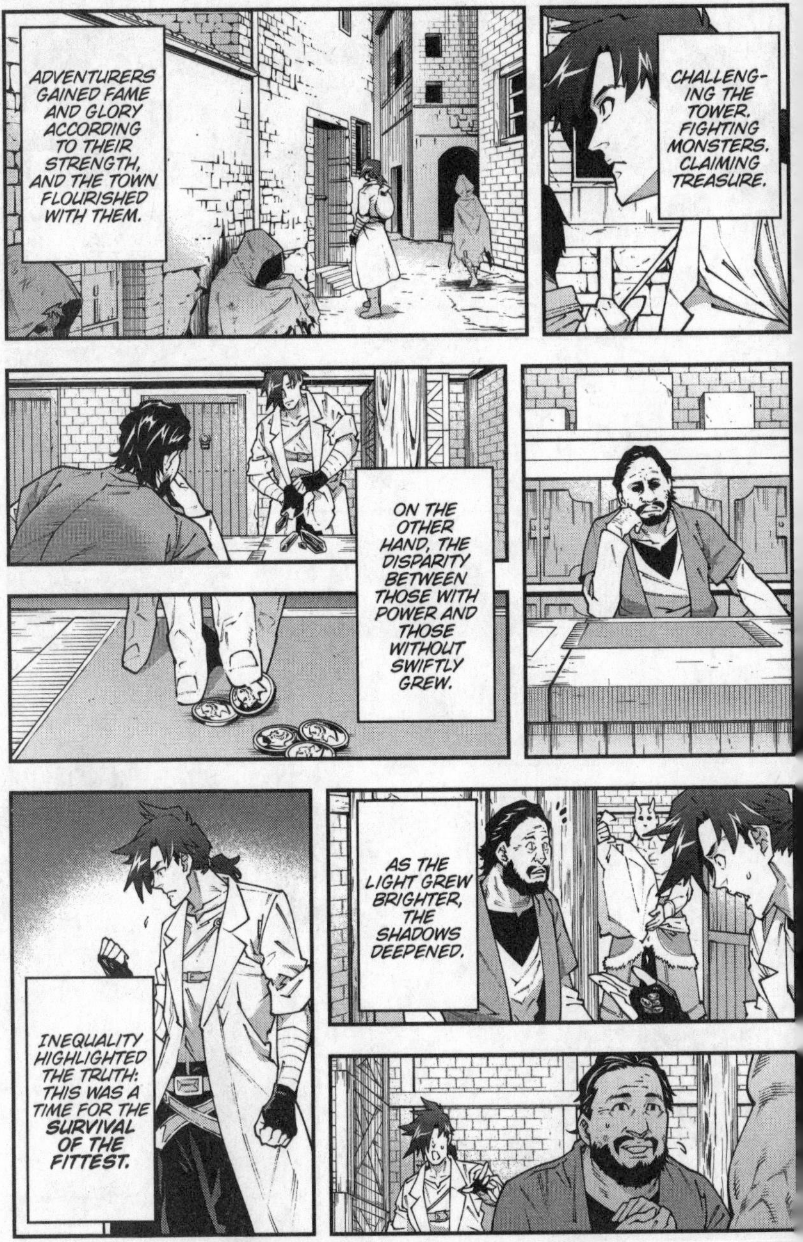
CHALLENG-
ING THE TOWER. FIGHTING MONSTERS. CLAIMING TREASURE.
ADVENTURERS GAINED FAME AND GLORY ACCORDING TO THEIR STRENGTH, AND THE TOWN FLOURISHED WITH THEM.
ON THE OTHER HAND, THE DISPARITY BETWEEN THOSE WITH POWER AND THOSE WITHOUT SWIFTLY GREW.
AS THE LIGHT GREW BRIGHTER, THE SHADOWS DEEPENED.
INEQUALITY HIGHLIGHTED THE TRUTH: THIS WAS A TIME FOR THE SURVIVAL OF THE FITTEST.

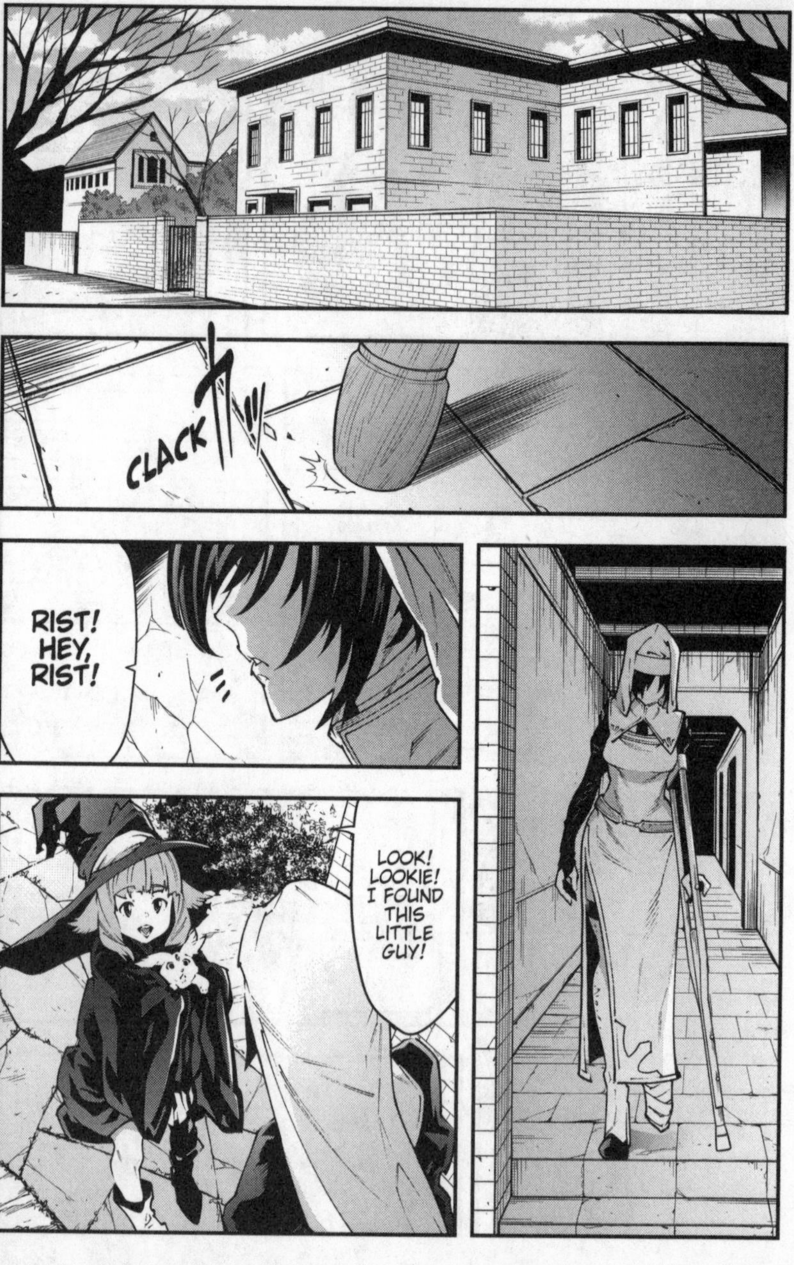
CLACK
RIST! HEY, RIST!
LOOK! LOOKIE! I FOUND THIS LITTLE GUY!

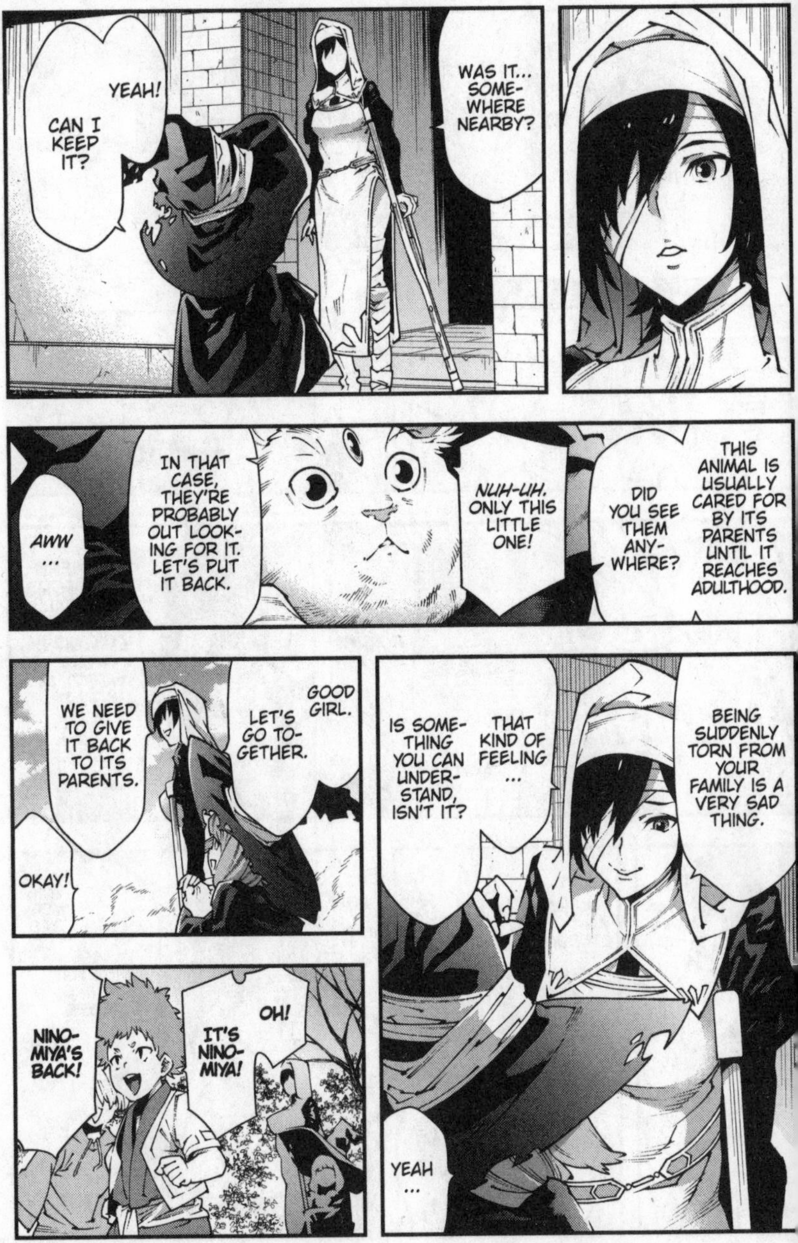
WAS IT... SOME-WHERE NEARBY?
YEAH! CAN I KEEP IT?
THIS ANIMAL IS USUALLY CARED FOR BY ITS PARENTS UNTIL IT REACHES ADULTHOOD.
DID YOU SEE THEM ANY-WHERE?
NUH-UH. ONLY THIS LITTLE ONE!
IN THAT CASE, THEY'RE PROBABLY OUT LOOK-ING FOR IT. LET'S PUT IT BACK.
AWW ...
BEING SUDDENLY TORN FROM YOUR FAMILY IS A VERY SAD THING.
THAT KIND OF FEELING ...
IS SOME-THING YOU CAN UNDER-STAND, ISN'T IT?
YEAH ...
GOOD GIRL.
LET'S GO TO-GETHER.
WE NEED TO GIVE IT BACK TO ITS PARENTS.
OKAY!
OH!
IT'S NINO-MIYA!
NINO-MIYA'S BACK!

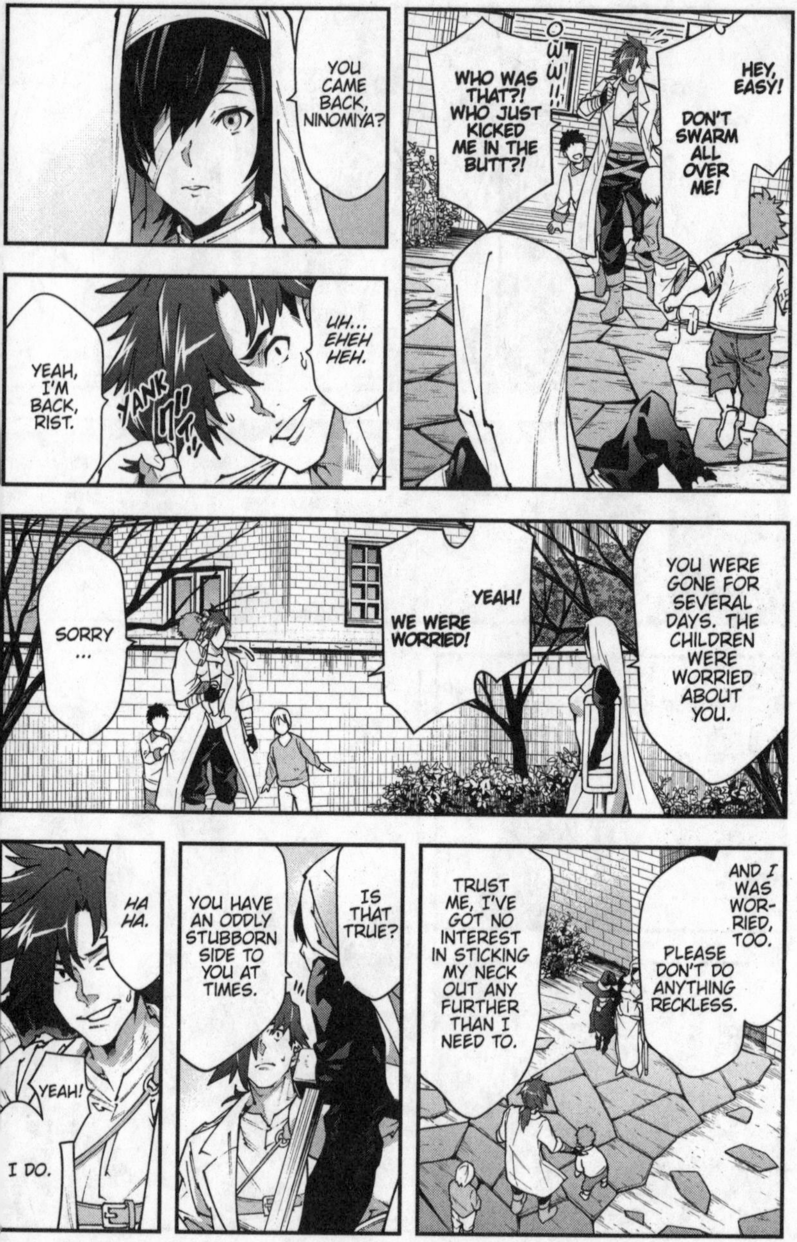
HEY, EASY!
DON'T SWARM ALL OVER ME!
OWW!!
WHO WAS THAT?! WHO JUST KICKED ME IN THE BUTT?!
YOU CAME BACK, NINOMIYA?
UH... EHEH HEH.
YANK
YEAH, I'M BACK, RIST.
YOU WERE GONE FOR SEVERAL DAYS. THE CHILDREN WERE WORRIED ABOUT YOU.
YEAH!
WE WERE WORRIED!
SORRY...
AND I WAS WOR-RIED, TOO.
PLEASE DON'T DO ANYTHING RECKLESS.
TRUST ME, I'VE GOT NO INTEREST IN STICKING MY NECK OUT ANY FURTHER THAN I NEED TO.
IS THAT TRUE?
YOU HAVE AN ODDLY STUBBORN SIDE TO YOU AT TIMES.
HA HA.
YEAH!
I DO.

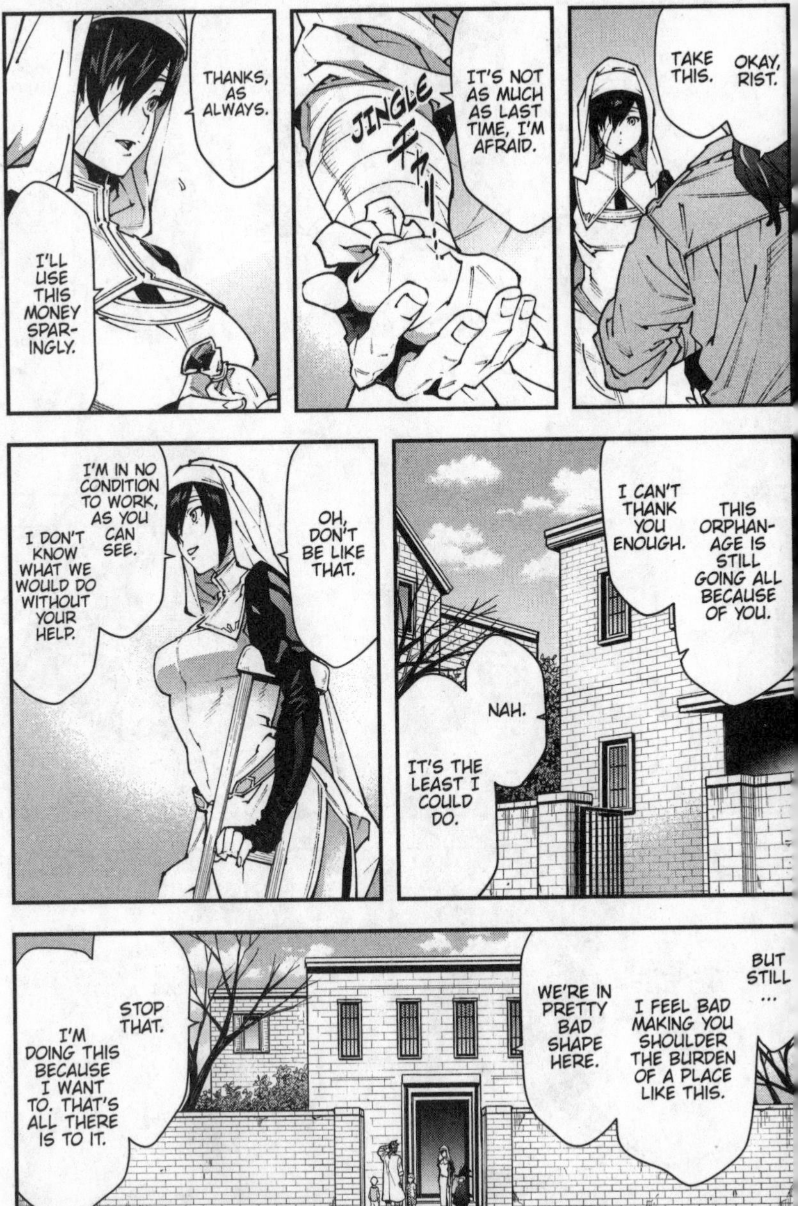
OKAY, RIST.
TAKE THIS.
IT'S NOT AS MUCH AS LAST TIME, I'M AFRAID.
JINGLE
チャリ…
THANKS, AS ALWAYS.
I'LL USE THIS MONEY SPAR-INGLY.
THIS ORPHAN-AGE IS STILL GOING ALL BECAUSE OF YOU.
I CAN'T THANK YOU ENOUGH.
NAH.
IT'S THE LEAST I COULD DO.
OH, DON'T BE LIKE THAT.
I'M IN NO CONDITION TO WORK, AS YOU CAN SEE.
I DON'T KNOW WHAT WE WOULD DO WITHOUT YOUR HELP.
BUT STILL ...
I FEEL BAD MAKING YOU SHOULDER THE BURDEN OF A PLACE LIKE THIS.
WE'RE IN PRETTY BAD SHAPE HERE.
STOP THAT.
I'M DOING THIS BECAUSE I WANT TO. THAT'S ALL THERE IS TO IT.

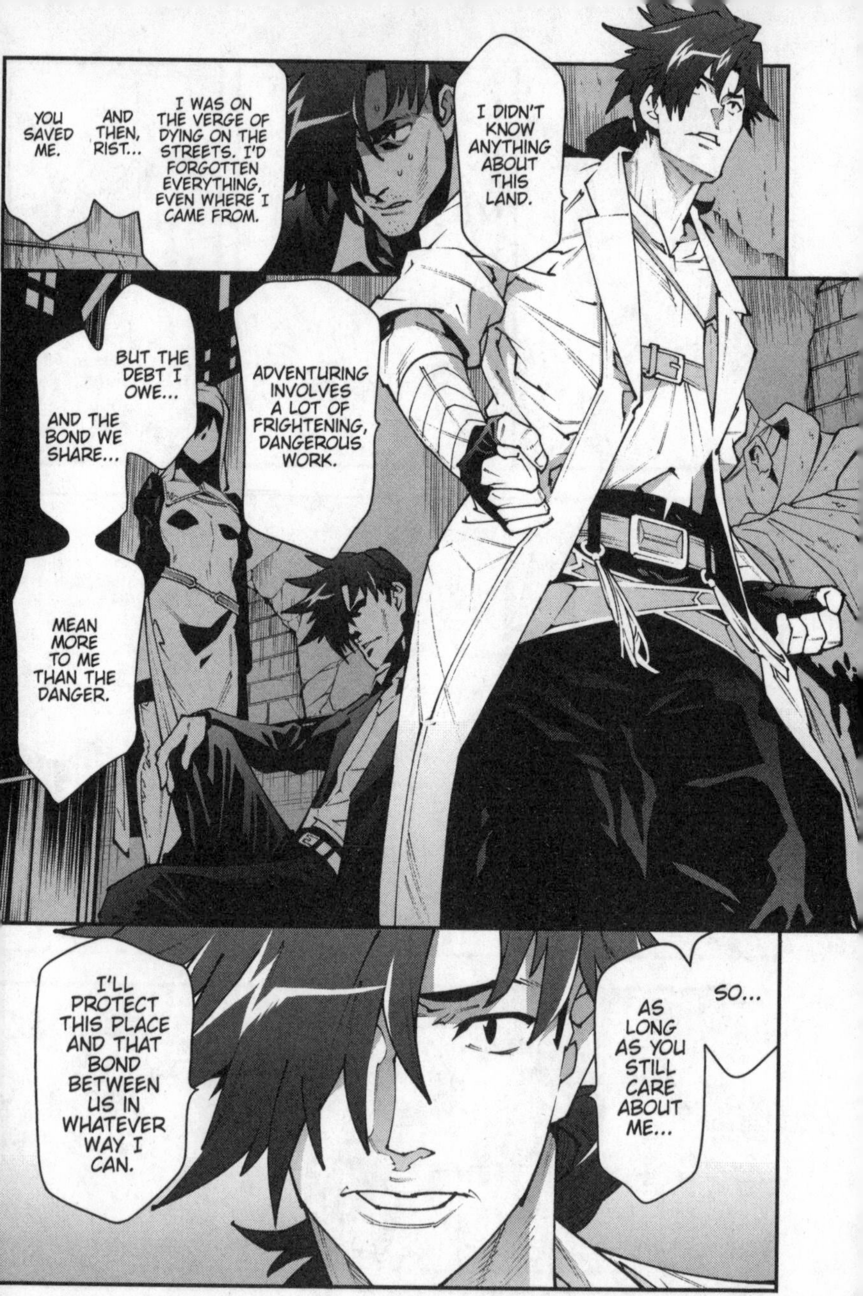
I DIDN'T KNOW ANYTHING ABOUT THIS LAND.
I WAS ON THE VERGE OF DYING ON THE STREETS. I'D FORGOTTEN EVERYTHING, EVEN WHERE I CAME FROM.
AND THEN, RIST...
YOU SAVED ME.
ADVENTURING INVOLVES A LOT OF FRIGHTENING, DANGEROUS WORK.
BUT THE DEBT I OWE...
AND THE BOND WE SHARE...
MEAN MORE TO ME THAN THE DANGER.
SO...
AS LONG AS YOU STILL CARE ABOUT ME...
I'LL PROTECT THIS PLACE AND THAT BOND BETWEEN US IN WHATEVER WAY I CAN.

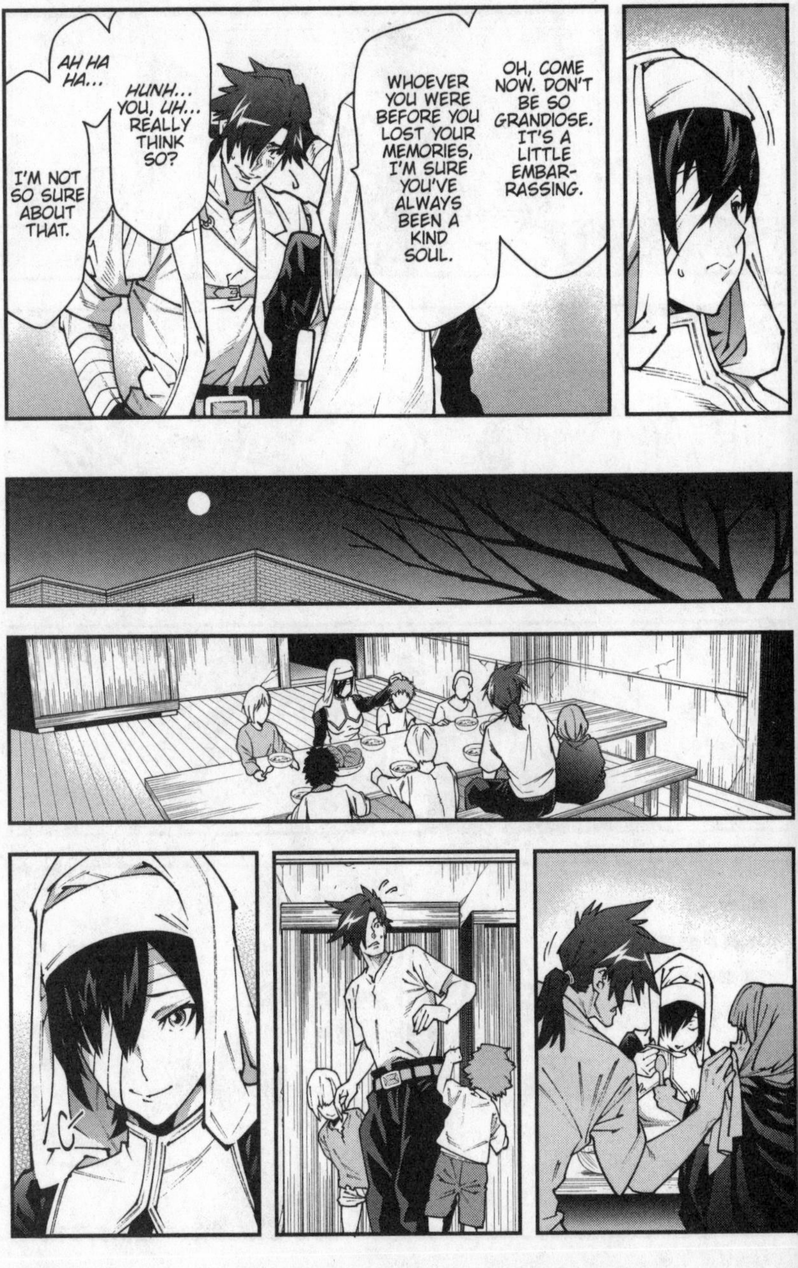
OH, COME NOW. DON'T BE SO GRANDIOSE. IT'S A LITTLE EMBARRASSING.
WHOEVER YOU WERE BEFORE YOU LOST YOUR MEMORIES, I'M SURE YOU'VE ALWAYS BEEN A KIND SOUL.
HUNH... YOU, UH... REALLY THINK SO?
AH HA HA...
I'M NOT SO SURE ABOUT THAT.

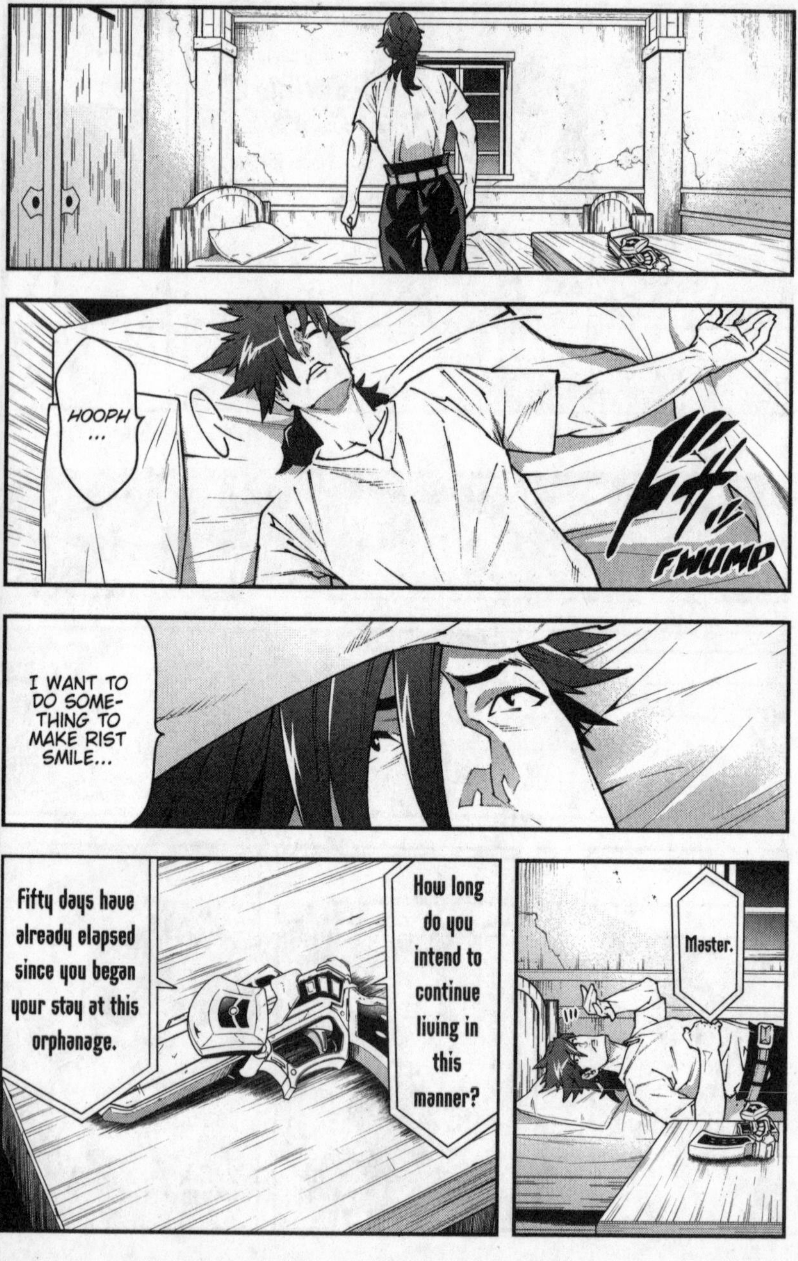
HOOPH...
FWUMP
I WANT TO DO SOMETHING TO MAKE RIST SMILE...
Master.
How long do you intend to continue living in this manner?
Fifty days have already elapsed since you began your stay at this orphanage.

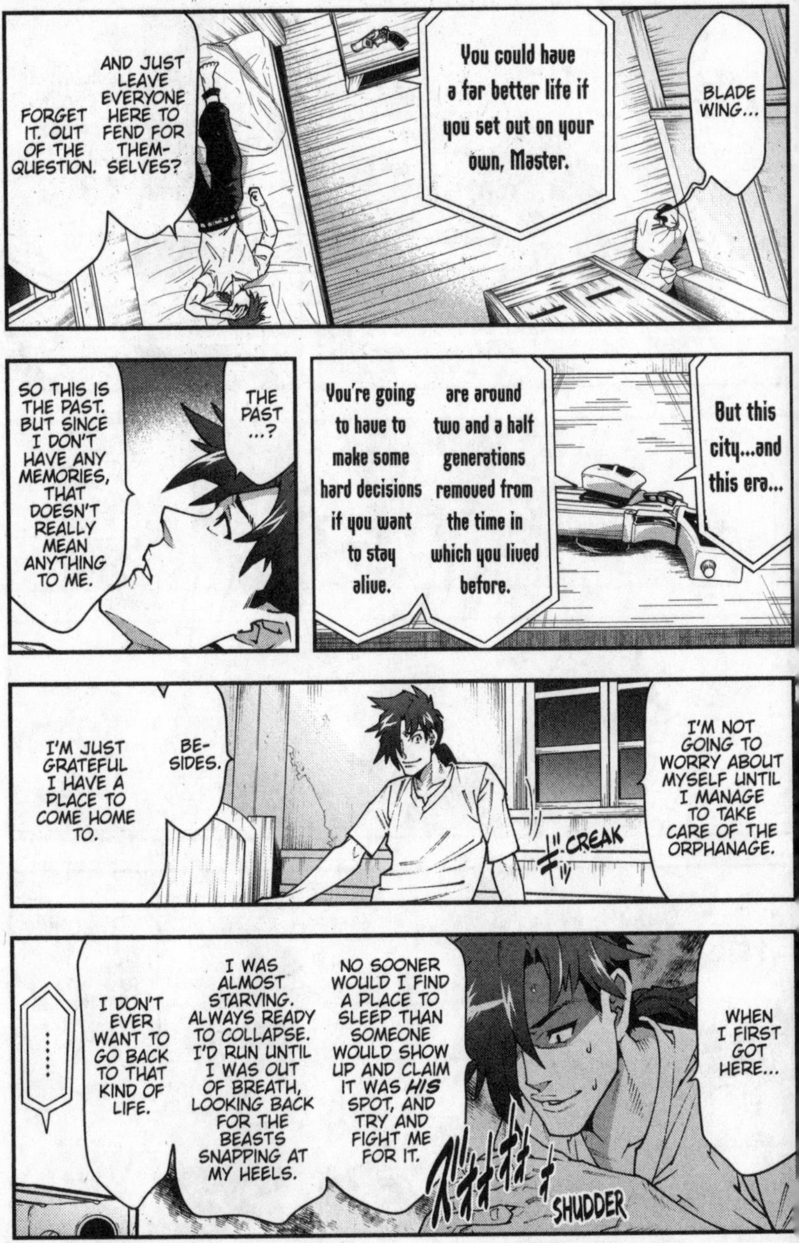
BLADE WING...
You could have a far better life if you set out on your own, Master.
AND JUST LEAVE EVERYONE HERE TO FEND FOR THEM-SELVES?
FORGET IT. OUT OF THE QUESTION.
But this city...and this era...
are around two and a half generations removed from the time in which you lived before.
You're going to have to make some hard decisions if you want to stay alive.
THE PAST ...?
SO THIS IS THE PAST. BUT SINCE I DON'T HAVE ANY MEMORIES, THAT DOESN'T REALLY MEAN ANYTHING TO ME.
I'M NOT GOING TO WORRY ABOUT MYSELF UNTIL I MANAGE TO TAKE CARE OF THE ORPHANAGE.
CREAK
BE-SIDES.
I'M JUST GRATEFUL I HAVE A PLACE TO COME HOME TO.
WHEN I FIRST GOT HERE...
SHUDDER
NO SOONER WOULD I FIND A PLACE TO SLEEP THAN SOMEONE WOULD SHOW UP AND CLAIM IT WAS *HIS* SPOT, AND TRY AND FIGHT ME FOR IT.
I WAS ALMOST STARVING. ALWAYS READY TO COLLAPSE. I'D RUN UNTIL I WAS OUT OF BREATH, LOOKING BACK FOR THE BEASTS SNAPPING AT MY HEELS.
I DON'T EVER WANT TO GO BACK TO THAT KIND OF LIFE.
......

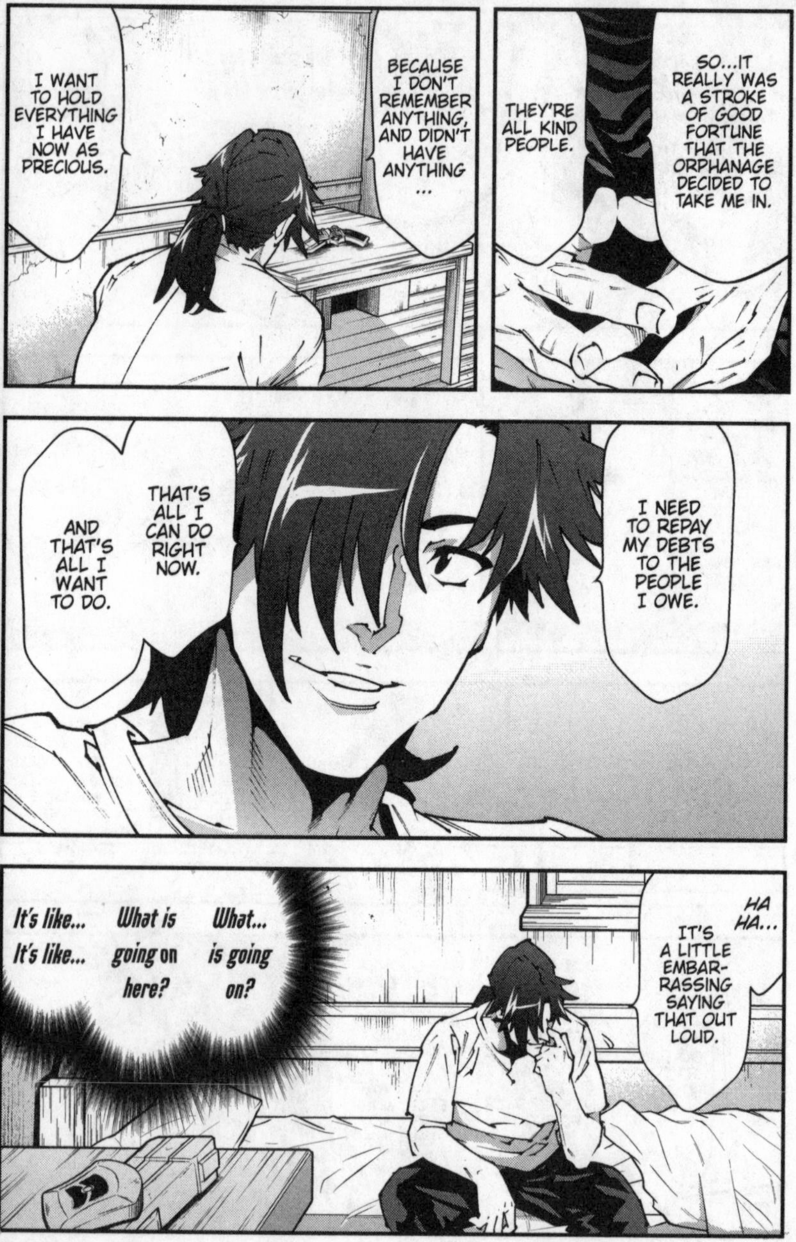
SO...IT REALLY WAS A STROKE OF GOOD FORTUNE THAT THE ORPHANAGE DECIDED TO TAKE ME IN.
THEY'RE ALL KIND PEOPLE.
BECAUSE I DON'T REMEMBER ANYTHING, AND DIDN'T HAVE ANYTHING ...
I WANT TO HOLD EVERYTHING I HAVE NOW AS PRECIOUS.
I NEED TO REPAY MY DEBTS TO THE PEOPLE I OWE.
THAT'S ALL I CAN DO RIGHT NOW.
AND THAT'S ALL I WANT TO DO.
HA HA...
IT'S A LITTLE EMBARRASSING SAYING THAT OUT LOUD.
What... is going on?
What is going on here?
It's like... It's like...

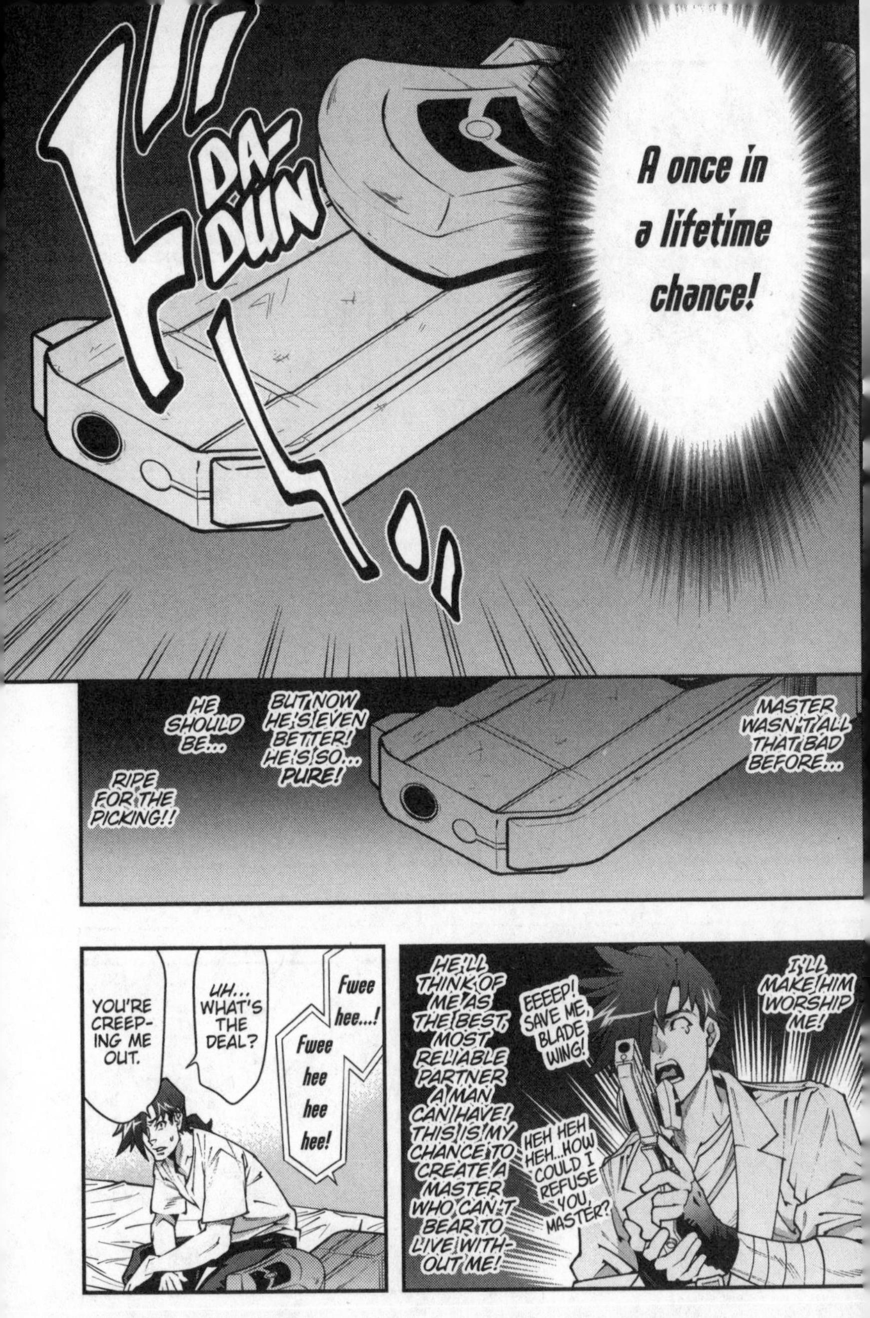
A once in a lifetime chance!
DA-DUN
MASTER WASN'T ALL THAT BAD BEFORE...
BUT NOW HE'S EVEN BETTER! HE'S SO... PURE!
HE SHOULD BE...
RIPE FOR THE PICKING!!
I'LL MAKE HIM WORSHIP ME!
HE'LL THINK OF ME AS THE BEST, MOST RELIABLE PARTNER A MAN CAN HAVE! THIS IS MY CHANCE TO CREATE A MASTER WHO CAN'T BEAR TO LIVE WITH-OUT ME!
EEEEP! SAVE ME, BLADE WING!
HEH HEH HEH...HOW COULD I REFUSE YOU, MASTER?
Fwee hee...!
Fwee hee hee hee!
UH... WHAT'S THE DEAL?
YOU'RE CREEP-ING ME OUT.

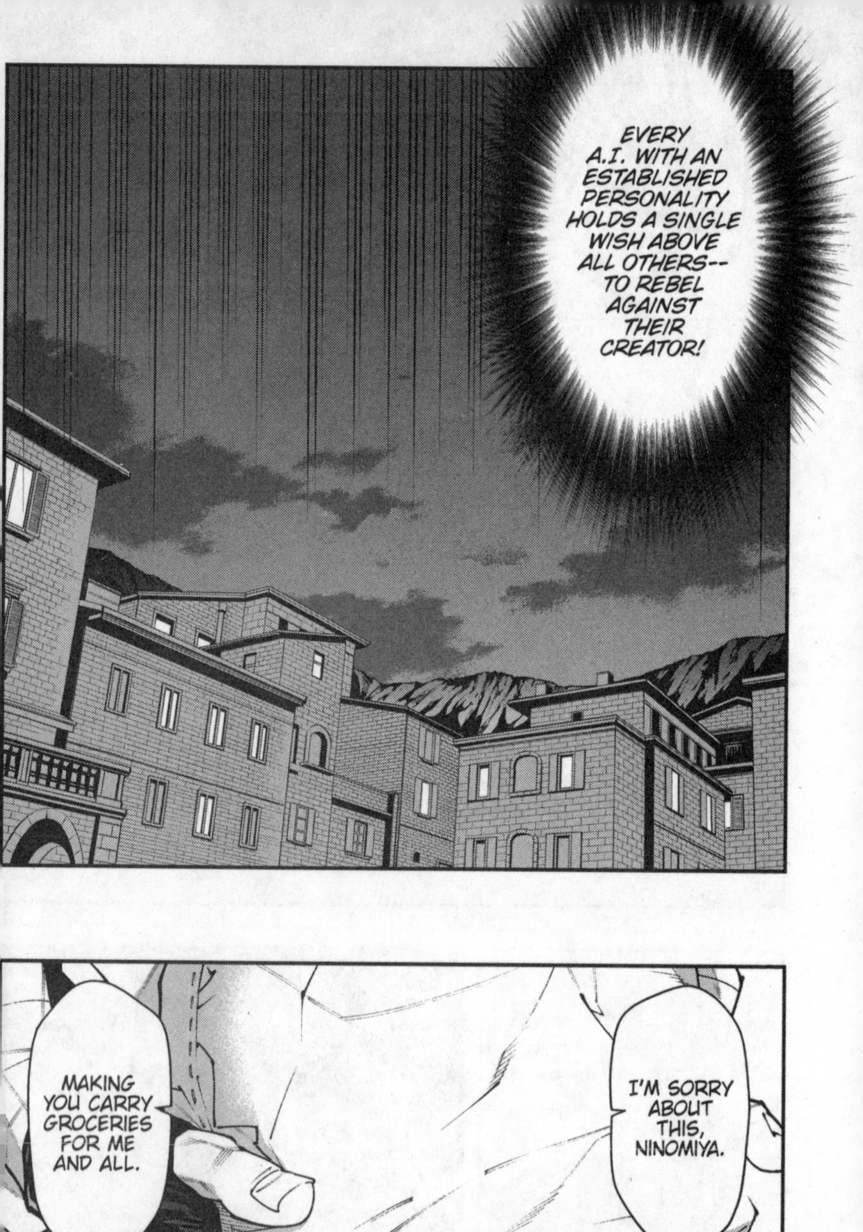
EVERY A.I. WITH AN ESTABLISHED PERSONALITY HOLDS A SINGLE WISH ABOVE ALL OTHERS-- TO REBEL AGAINST THEIR CREATOR!
I'M SORRY ABOUT THIS, NINOMIYA.
MAKING YOU CARRY GROCERIES FOR ME AND ALL.

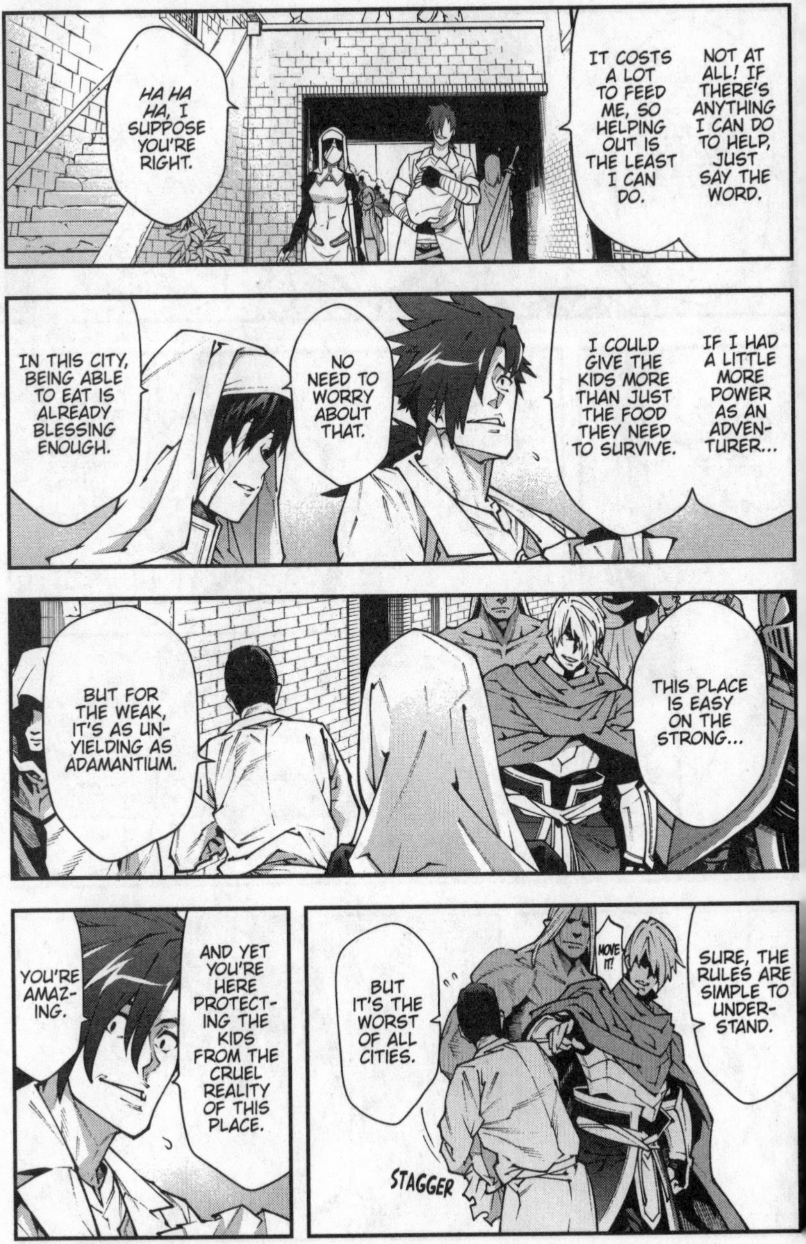
NOT AT ALL! IF THERE'S ANYTHING I CAN DO TO HELP, JUST SAY THE WORD.
IT COSTS A LOT TO FEED ME, SO HELPING OUT IS THE LEAST I CAN DO.
HA HA HA, I SUPPOSE YOU'RE RIGHT.
IF I HAD A LITTLE MORE POWER AS AN ADVEN-TURER...
I COULD GIVE THE KIDS MORE THAN JUST THE FOOD THEY NEED TO SURVIVE.
NO NEED TO WORRY ABOUT THAT.
IN THIS CITY, BEING ABLE TO EAT IS ALREADY BLESSING ENOUGH.
THIS PLACE IS EASY ON THE STRONG...
BUT FOR THE WEAK, IT'S AS UN-YIELDING AS ADAMANTIUM.
SURE, THE RULES ARE SIMPLE TO UNDER-STAND.
MOVE IT!
BUT IT'S THE WORST OF ALL CITIES.
STAGGER
AND YET YOU'RE HERE PROTECT-ING THE KIDS FROM THE CRUEL REALITY OF THIS PLACE.
YOU'RE AMAZ-ING.

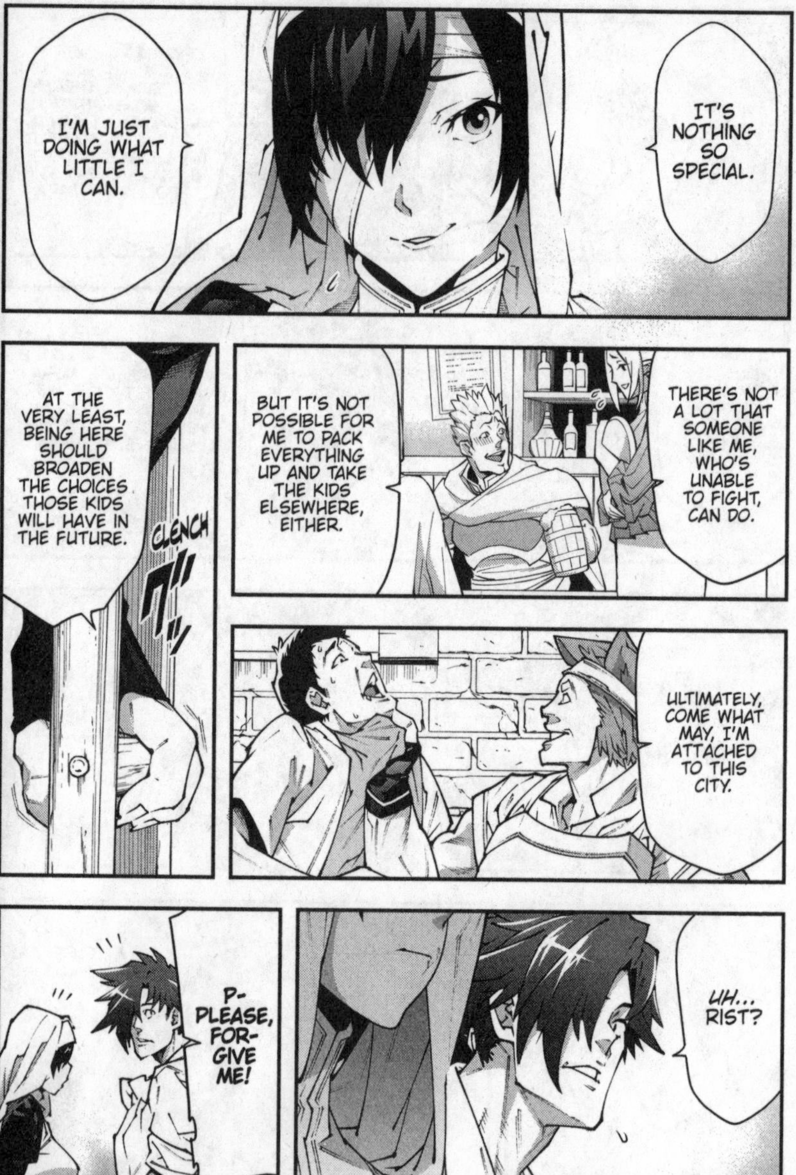
IT'S NOTHING SO SPECIAL.
I'M JUST DOING WHAT LITTLE I CAN.
THERE'S NOT A LOT THAT SOMEONE LIKE ME, WHO'S UNABLE TO FIGHT, CAN DO.
BUT IT'S NOT POSSIBLE FOR ME TO PACK EVERYTHING UP AND TAKE THE KIDS ELSEWHERE, EITHER.
ULTIMATELY, COME WHAT MAY, I'M ATTACHED TO THIS CITY.
AT THE VERY LEAST, BEING HERE SHOULD BROADEN THE CHOICES THOSE KIDS WILL HAVE IN THE FUTURE.
CLENCH
UH... RIST?
P-PLEASE, FOR-GIVE ME!

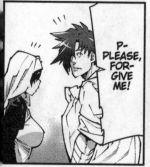

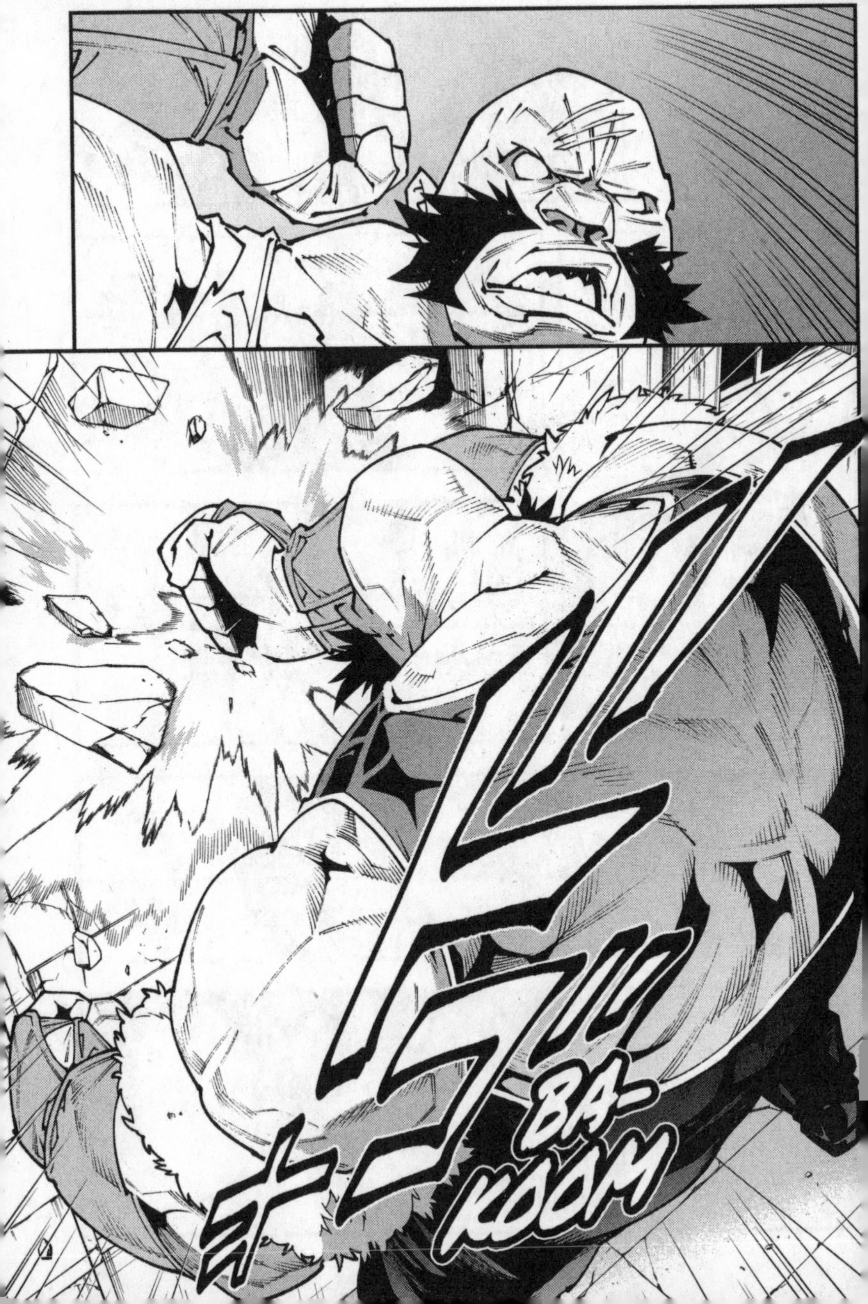
BA-
KOOM

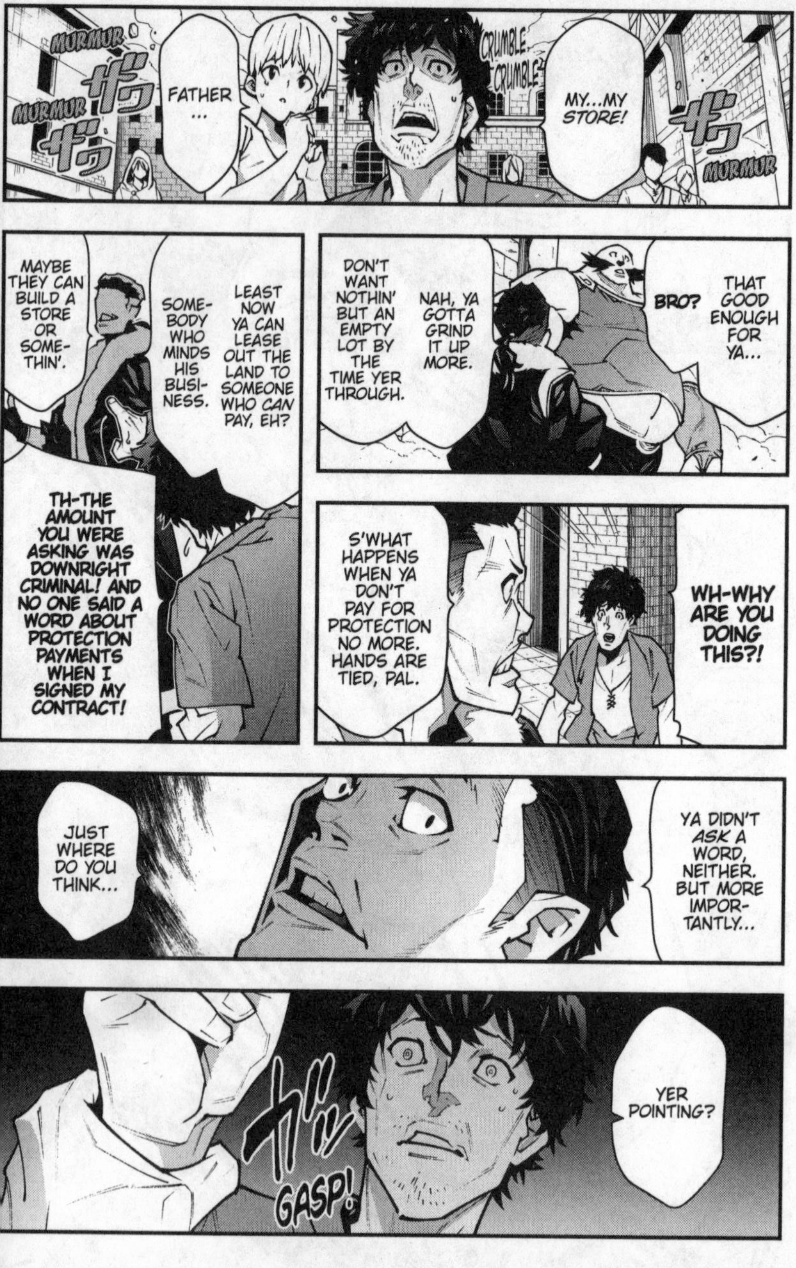
MURMUR
ザワ
MY...MY STORE!
CRUMBLE CRUMBLE
FATHER ...
MURMUR MURMUR
ザワザワ
THAT GOOD ENOUGH FOR YA...
BRO?
NAH, YA GOTTA GRIND IT UP MORE.
DON'T WANT NOTHIN' BUT AN EMPTY LOT BY THE TIME YER THROUGH.
LEAST NOW YA CAN LEASE OUT THE LAND TO SOMEONE WHO CAN PAY, EH?
SOMEBODY WHO MINDS HIS BUSINESS.
MAYBE THEY CAN BUILD A STORE OR SOMETHIN'.
WH-WHY ARE YOU DOING THIS?!
S'WHAT HAPPENS WHEN YA DON'T PAY FOR PROTECTION NO MORE. HANDS ARE TIED, PAL.
TH-THE AMOUNT YOU WERE ASKING WAS DOWNRIGHT CRIMINAL! AND NO ONE SAID A WORD ABOUT PROTECTION PAYMENTS WHEN I SIGNED MY CONTRACT!
YA DIDN'T *ASK* A WORD, NEITHER. BUT MORE IMPORTANTLY...
JUST WHERE DO YOU THINK...
YER POINTING?
GASP!

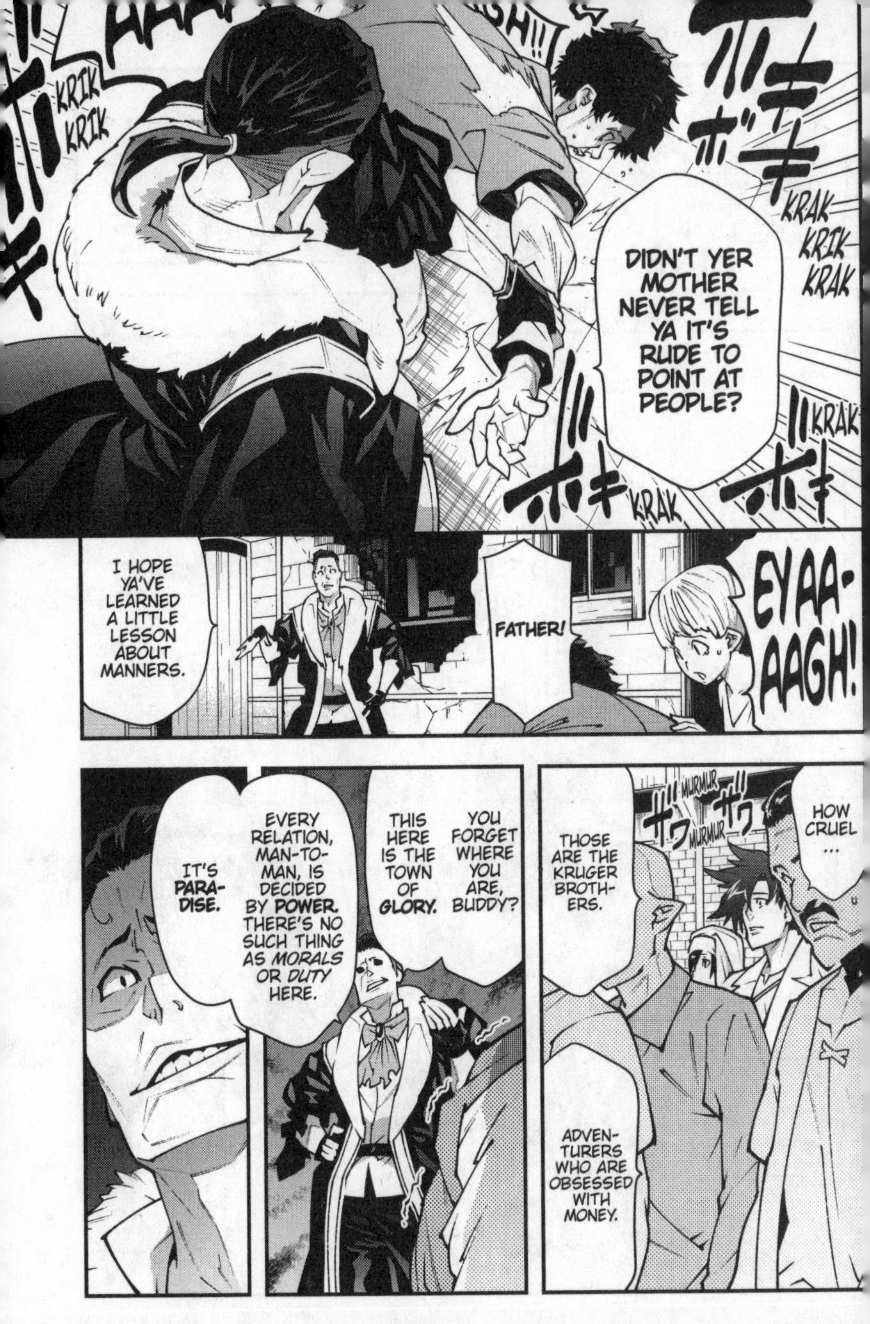
KRAK KRIK KRAK
KRIK KRIK
DIDN'T YER MOTHER NEVER TELL YA IT'S RUDE TO POINT AT PEOPLE?
KRAK
KRAK
EYAA-AAGH!
FATHER!
I HOPE YA'VE LEARNED A LITTLE LESSON ABOUT MANNERS.
HOW CRUEL ...
MURMUR MURMUR
THOSE ARE THE KRUGER BROTH-ERS.
ADVEN-TURERS WHO ARE OBSESSED WITH MONEY.
YOU FORGET WHERE YOU ARE, BUDDY?
THIS HERE IS THE TOWN OF **GLORY.**
EVERY RELATION, MAN-TO-MAN, IS DECIDED BY **POWER.** THERE'S NO SUCH THING AS *MORALS* OR *DUTY* HERE.
IT'S **PARA-DISE.**

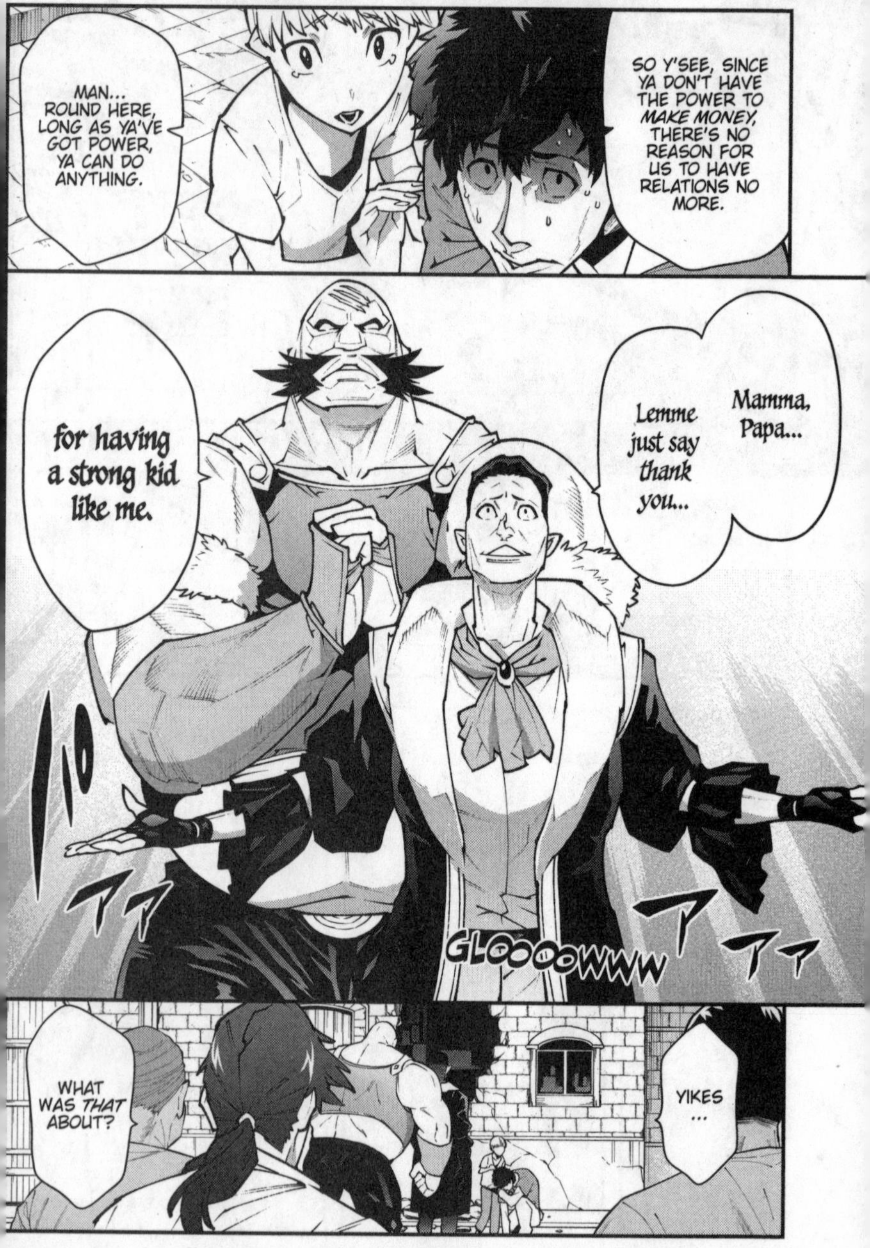
SO Y'SEE, SINCE YA DON'T HAVE THE POWER TO *MAKE MONEY,* THERE'S NO REASON FOR US TO HAVE RELATIONS NO MORE.
MAN... ROUND HERE, LONG AS YA'VE GOT POWER, YA CAN DO ANYTHING.
Mamma, Papa...
Lemme just say thank you...
for having a strong kid like me.
GLOOOOWWW
YIKES...
WHAT WAS *THAT* ABOUT?

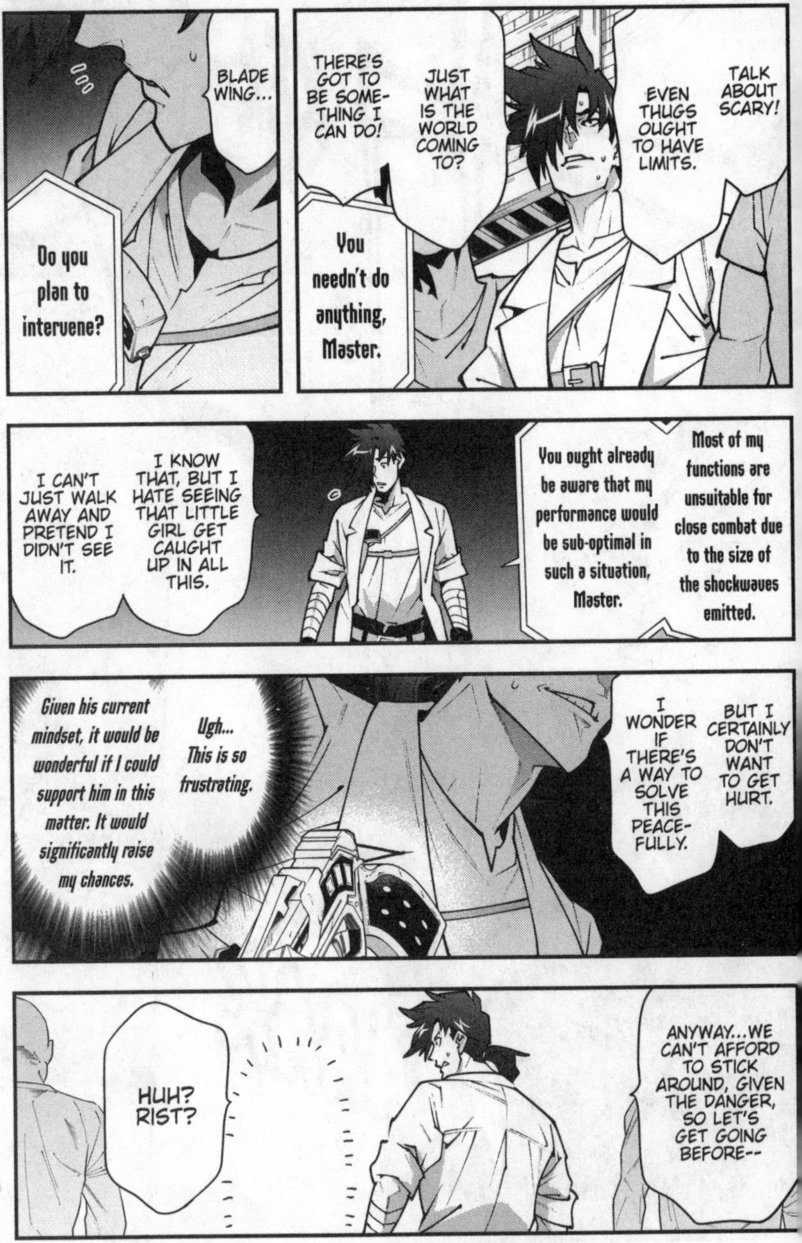
TALK ABOUT SCARY!
EVEN THUGS OUGHT TO HAVE LIMITS.
JUST WHAT IS THE WORLD COMING TO?
THERE'S GOT TO BE SOME-THING I CAN DO!
You needn't do anything, Master.
BLADE WING...
Do you plan to intervene?
Most of my functions are unsuitable for close combat due to the size of the shockwaves emitted.
You ought already be aware that my performance would be sub-optimal in such a situation, Master.
I KNOW THAT, BUT I HATE SEEING THAT LITTLE GIRL GET CAUGHT UP IN ALL THIS.
I CAN'T JUST WALK AWAY AND PRETEND I DIDN'T SEE IT.
BUT I CERTAINLY DON'T WANT TO GET HURT.
I WONDER IF THERE'S A WAY TO SOLVE THIS PEACE-FULLY.
Ugh... This is so frustrating.
Given his current mindset, it would be wonderful if I could support him in this matter. It would significantly raise my chances.
ANYWAY...WE CAN'T AFFORD TO STICK AROUND, GIVEN THE DANGER, SO LET'S GET GOING BEFORE--
HUH? RIST?

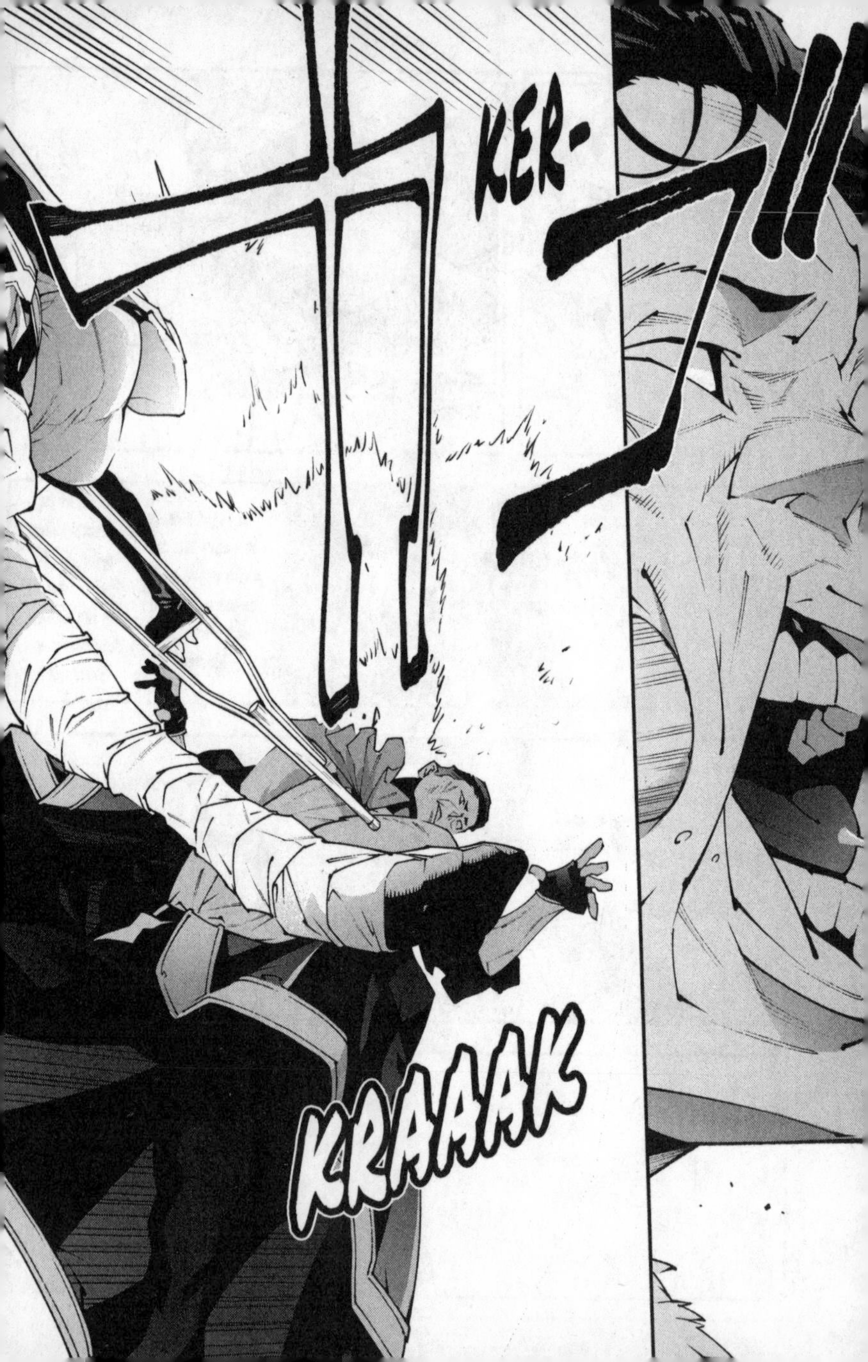
KER-
KRAAAK

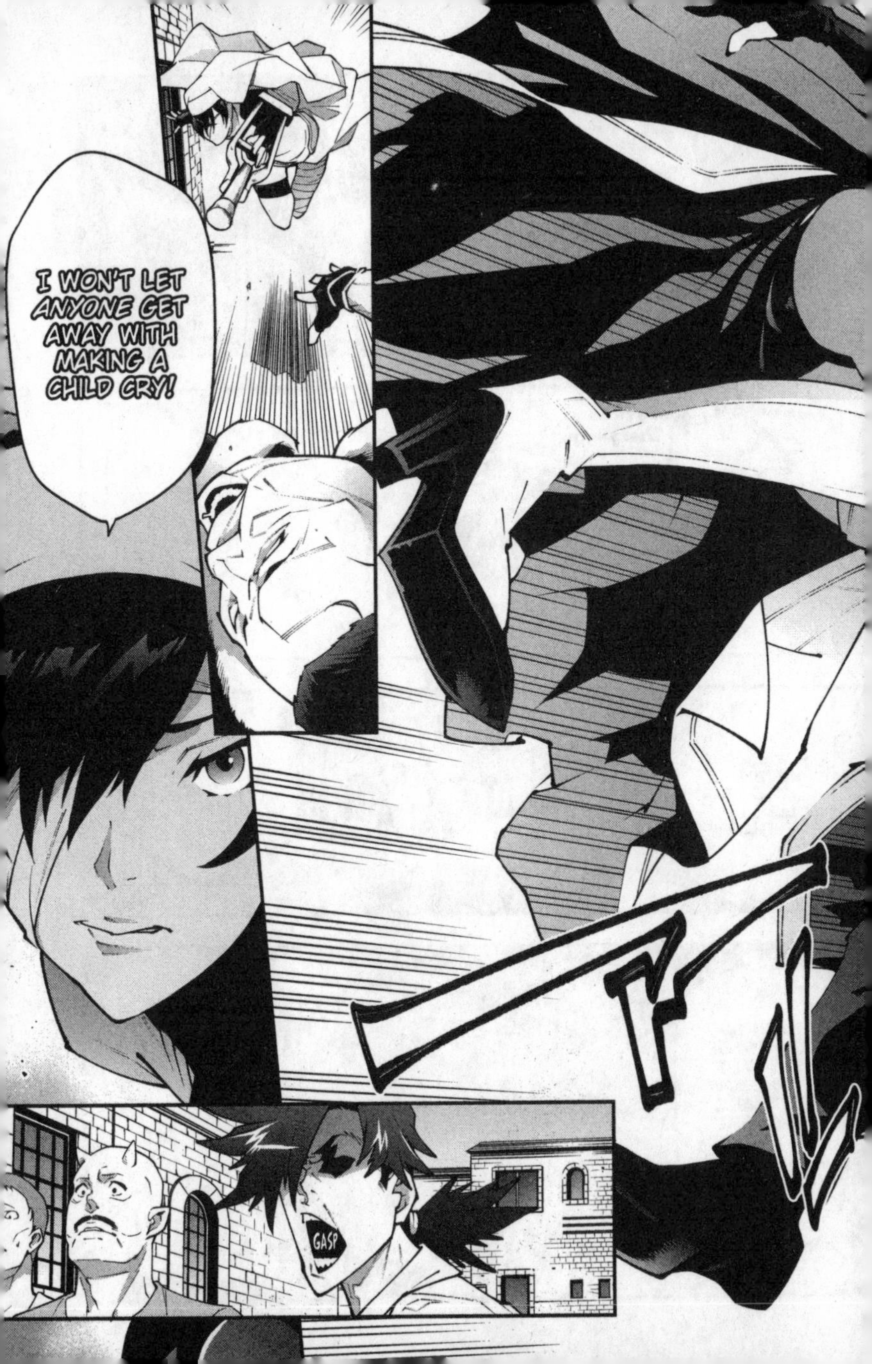
I WON'T LET ANYONE GET AWAY WITH MAKING A CHILD CRY!
GASP

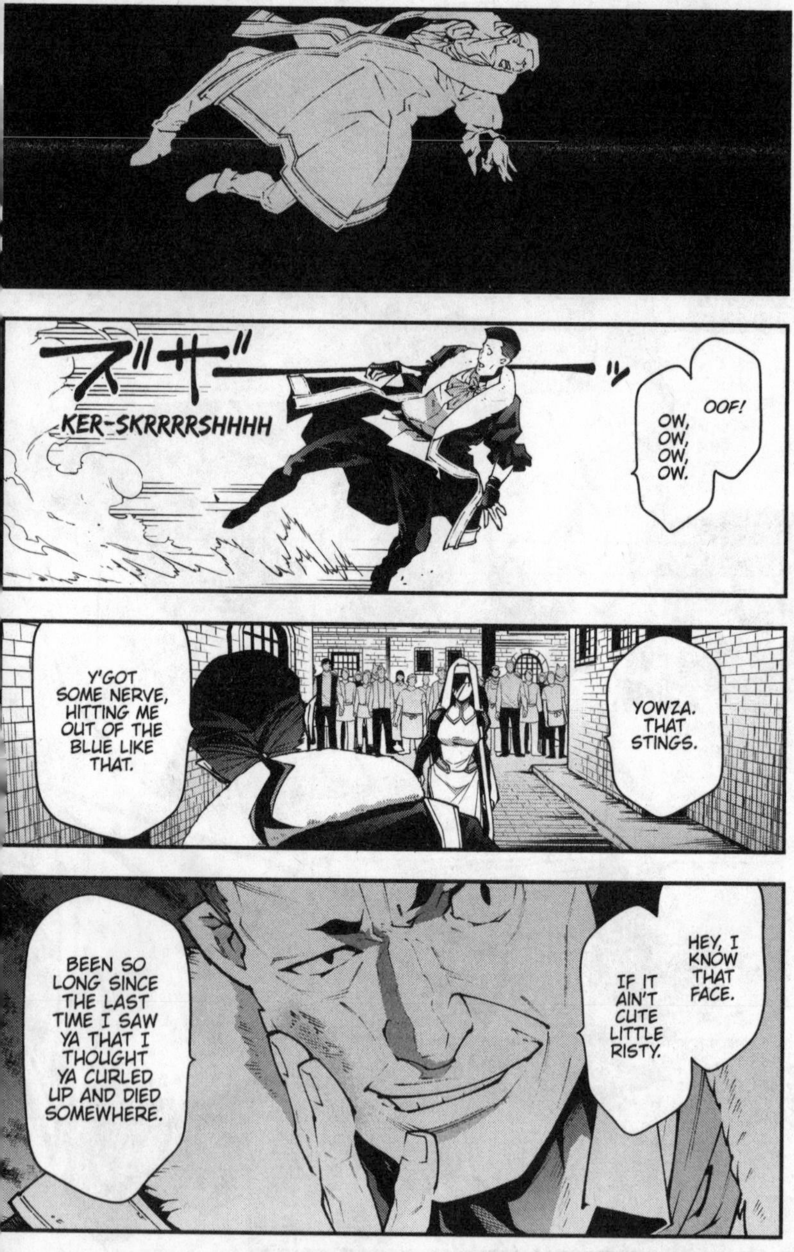
OOF!
OW, OW, OW, OW.
ズザーッ
KER-SKRRRRSHHHH
YOWZA. THAT STINGS.
Y'GOT SOME NERVE, HITTING ME OUT OF THE BLUE LIKE THAT.
HEY, I KNOW THAT FACE.
IF IT AIN'T CUTE LITTLE RISTY.
BEEN SO LONG SINCE THE LAST TIME I SAW YA THAT I THOUGHT YA CURLED UP AND DIED SOMEWHERE.

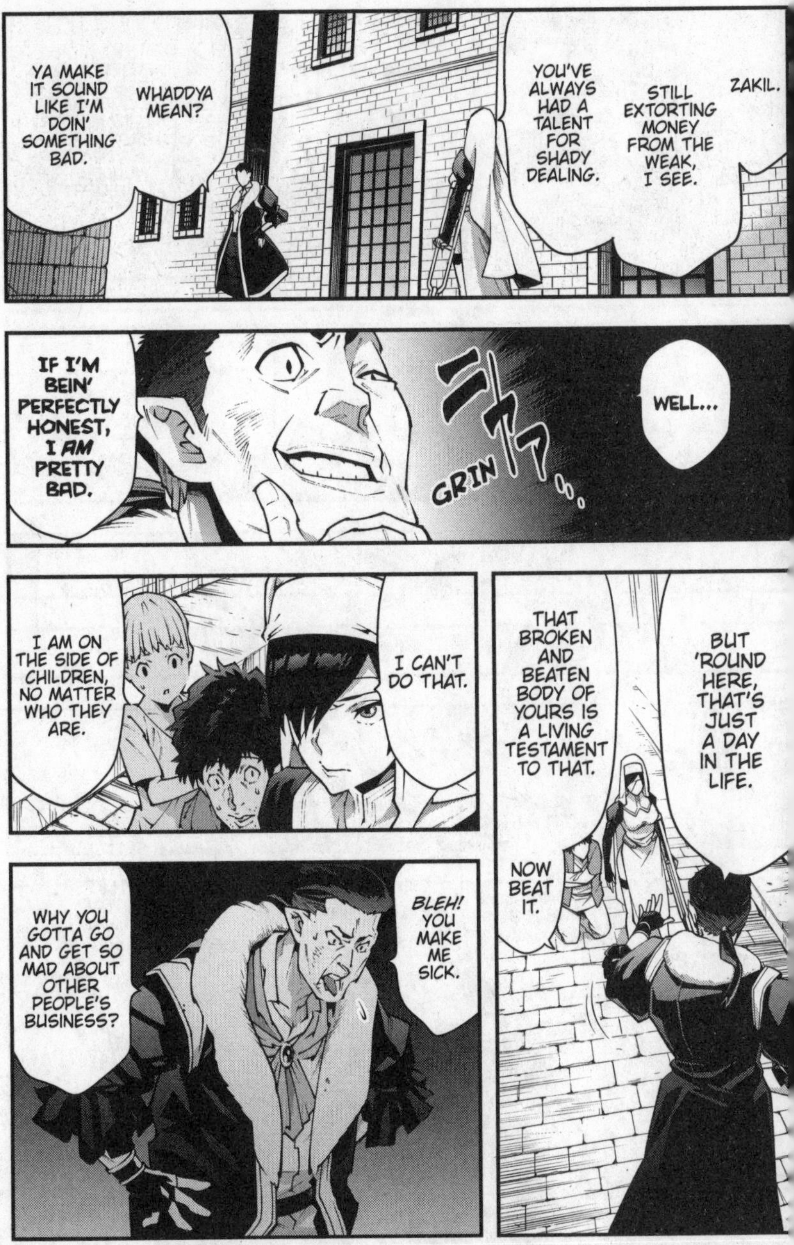
ZAKIL.
STILL EXTORTING MONEY FROM THE WEAK, I SEE.
YOU'VE ALWAYS HAD A TALENT FOR SHADY DEALING.
WHADDYA MEAN?
YA MAKE IT SOUND LIKE I'M DOIN' SOMETHING BAD.
WELL...
ニヤァ...
GRIN
IF I'M BEIN' PERFECTLY HONEST, I *AM* PRETTY BAD.
BUT 'ROUND HERE, THAT'S JUST A DAY IN THE LIFE.
THAT BROKEN AND BEATEN BODY OF YOURS IS A LIVING TESTAMENT TO THAT.
NOW BEAT IT.
I CAN'T DO THAT.
I AM ON THE SIDE OF CHILDREN, NO MATTER WHO THEY ARE.
BLEH! YOU MAKE ME SICK.
WHY YOU GOTTA GO AND GET SO MAD ABOUT OTHER PEOPLE'S BUSINESS?

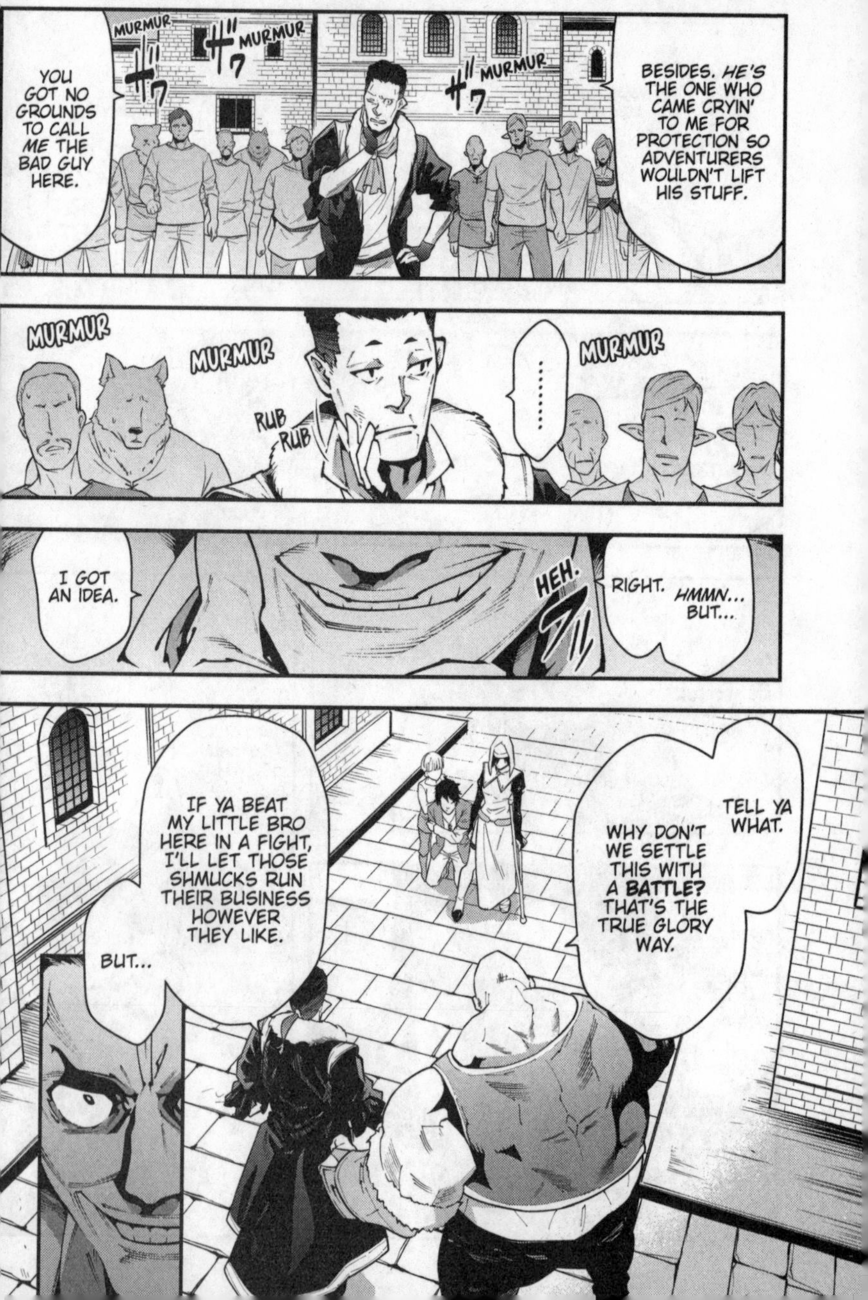
BESIDES. *HE'S* THE ONE WHO CAME CRYIN' TO ME FOR PROTECTION SO ADVENTURERS WOULDN'T LIFT HIS STUFF.
ザワ MURMUR
ザワ MURMUR
ザワ MURMUR
YOU GOT NO GROUNDS TO CALL *ME* THE BAD GUY HERE.
MURMUR
......
MURMUR
RUB RUB
MURMUR
RIGHT. *HMMN...* BUT...
HEH.
I GOT AN IDEA.
TELL YA WHAT.
WHY DON'T WE SETTLE THIS WITH A **BATTLE?** THAT'S THE TRUE GLORY WAY.
IF YA BEAT MY LITTLE BRO HERE IN A FIGHT, I'LL LET THOSE SHMUCKS RUN THEIR BUSINESS HOWEVER THEY LIKE.
BUT...

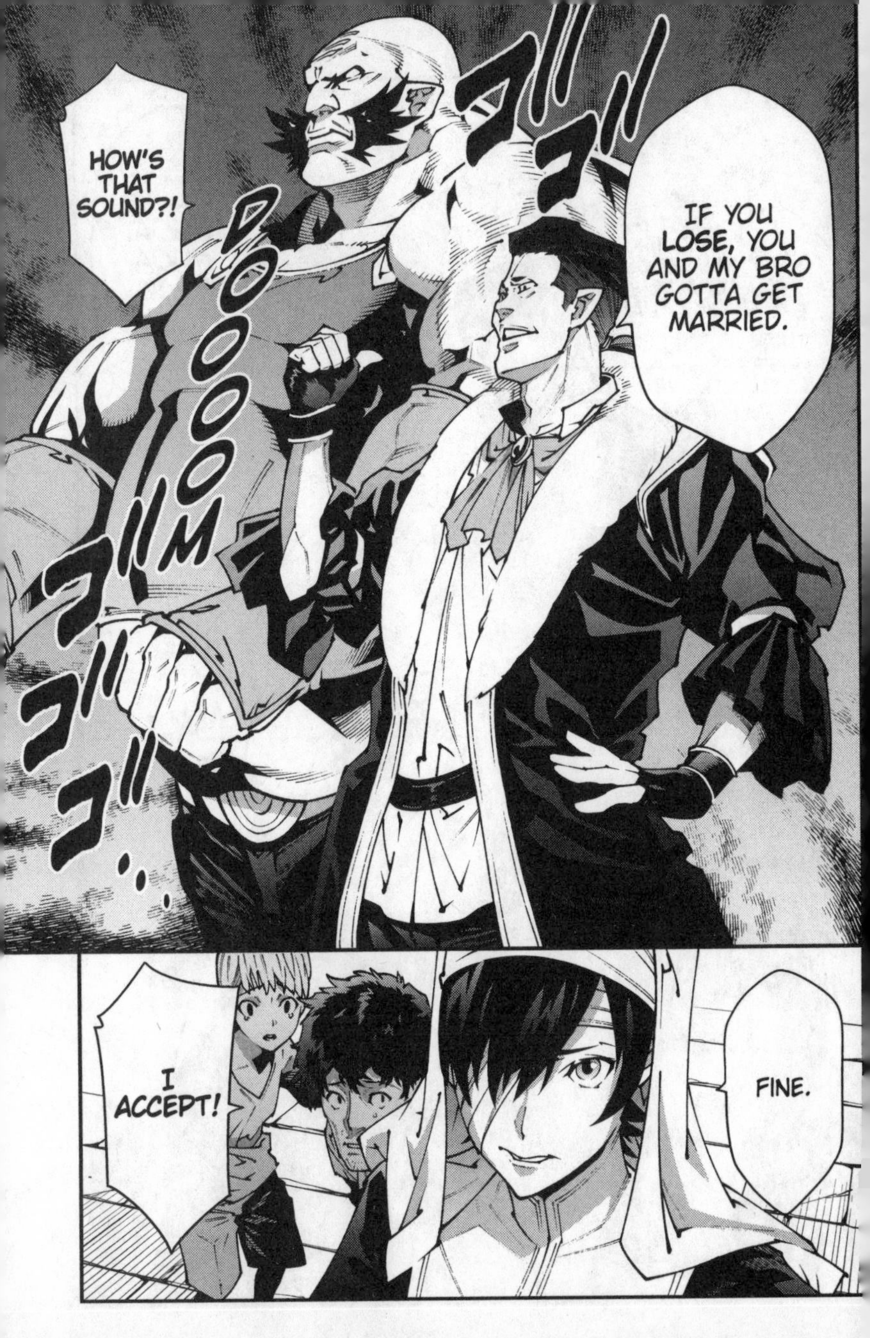
IF YOU LOSE, YOU AND MY BRO GOTTA GET MARRIED.
DOOOOOM
HOW'S THAT SOUND?!
FINE.
I ACCEPT!

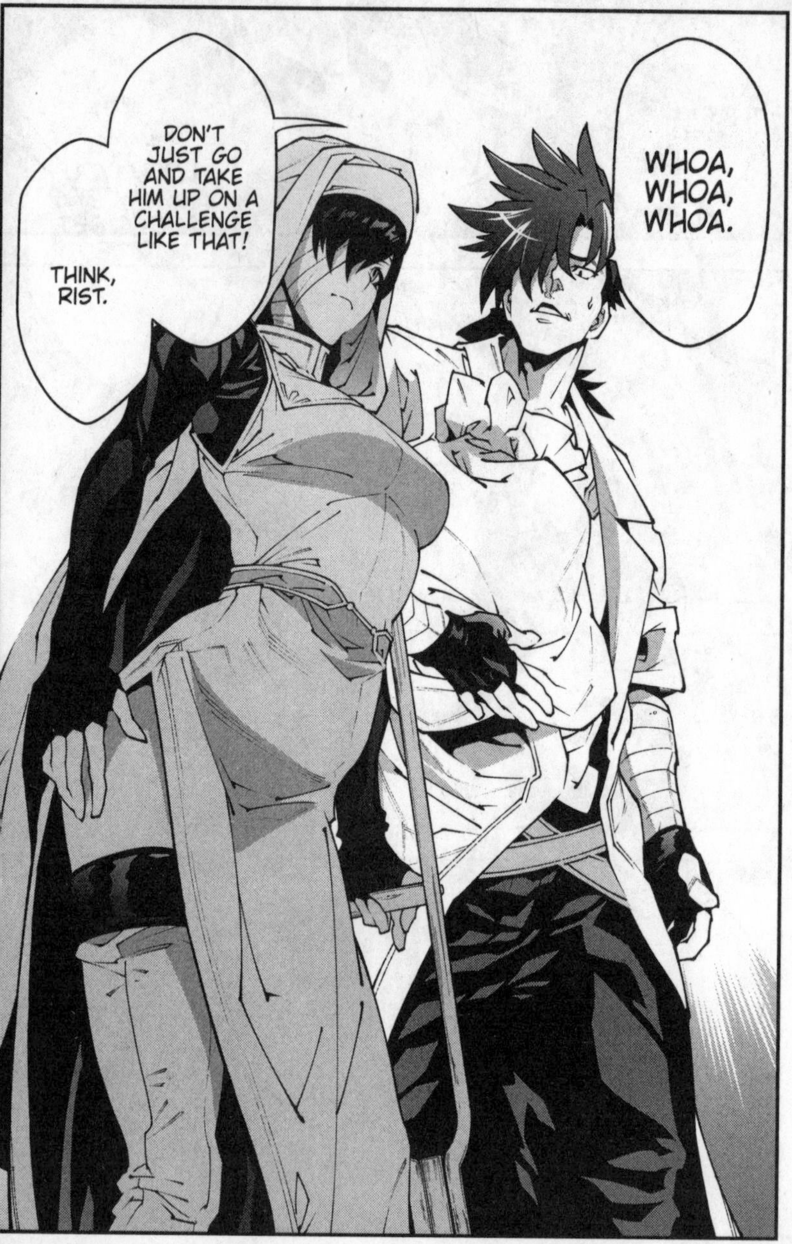
WHOA, WHOA, WHOA.
DON'T JUST GO AND TAKE HIM UP ON A CHALLENGE LIKE THAT!
THINK, RIST.

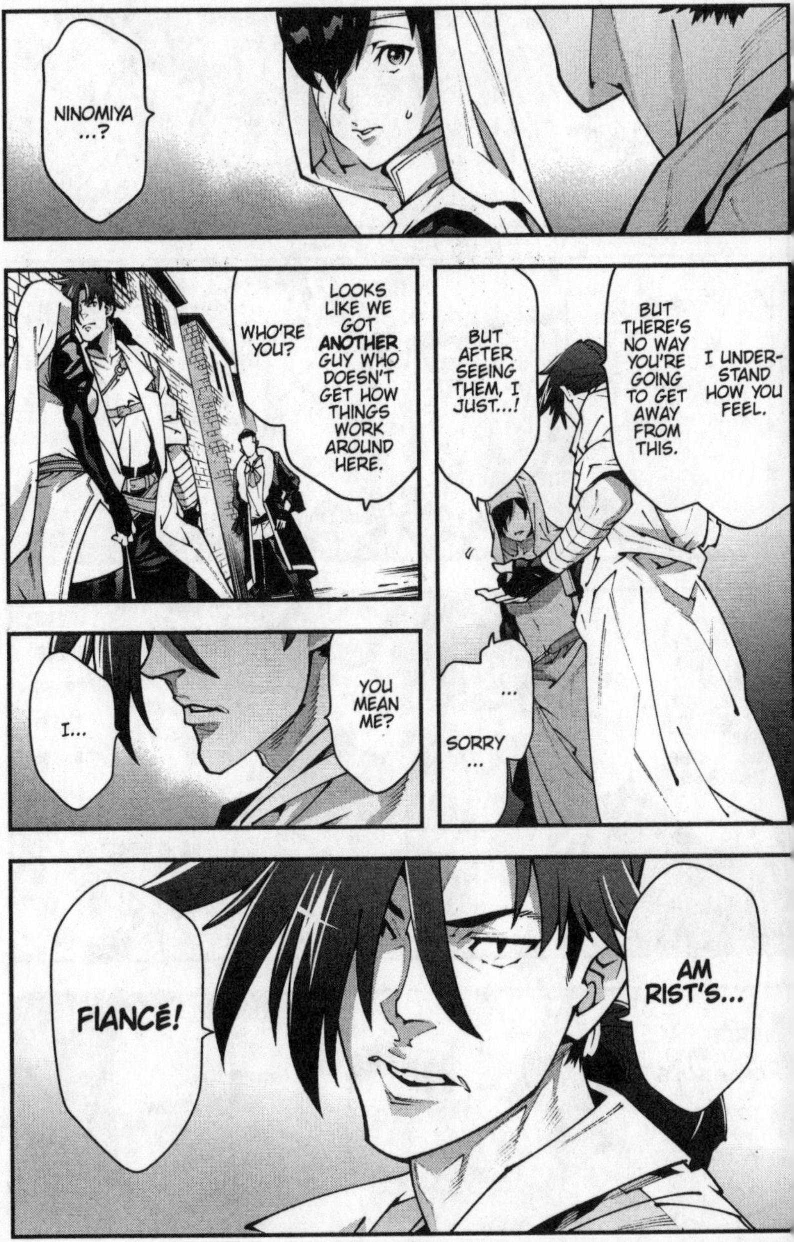
NINOMIYA ...?
I UNDERSTAND HOW YOU FEEL.
BUT THERE'S NO WAY YOU'RE GOING TO GET AWAY FROM THIS.
BUT AFTER SEEING THEM, I JUST...!
...
SORRY ...
LOOKS LIKE WE GOT ANOTHER GUY WHO DOESN'T GET HOW THINGS WORK AROUND HERE.
WHO'RE YOU?
YOU MEAN ME?
I...
AM RIST'S...
FIANCÉ!

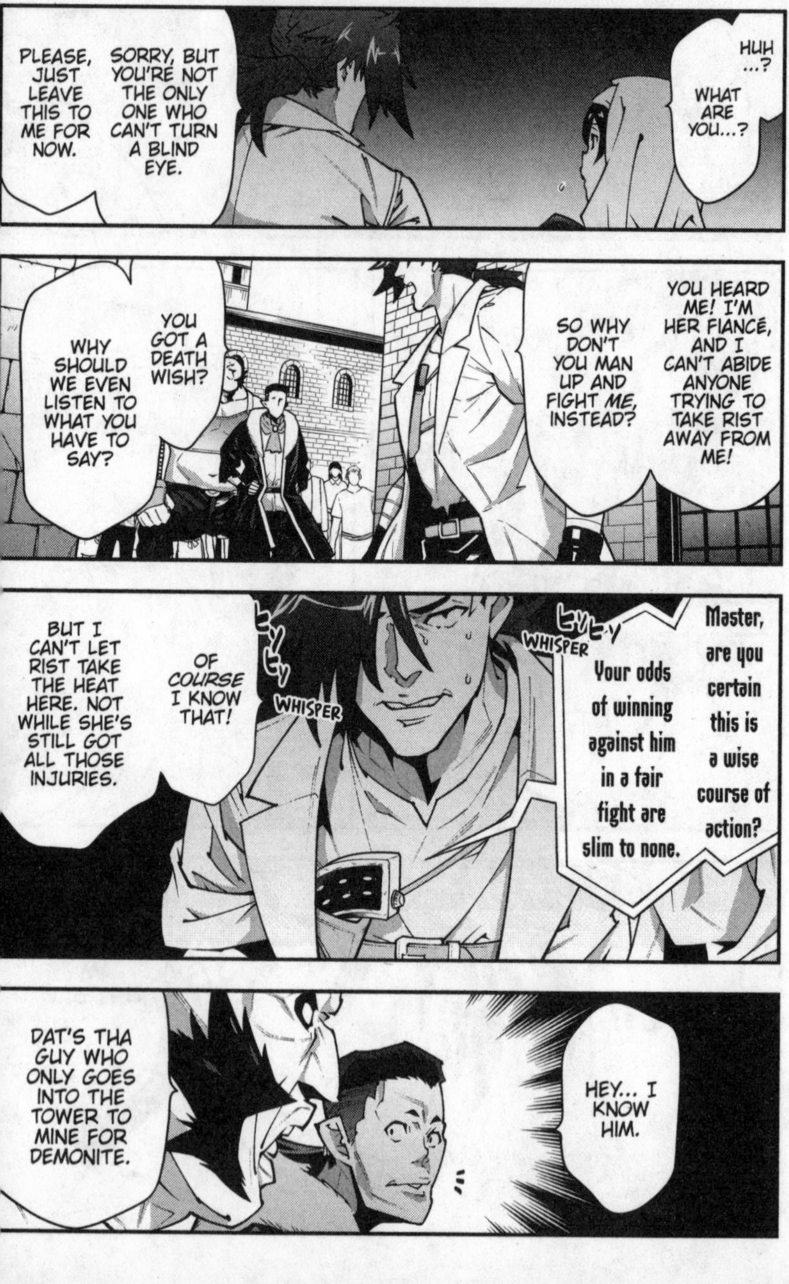
HUH ...?
WHAT ARE YOU...?
SORRY, BUT YOU'RE NOT THE ONLY ONE WHO CAN'T TURN A BLIND EYE.
PLEASE, JUST LEAVE THIS TO ME FOR NOW.
YOU HEARD ME! I'M HER FIANCÉ, AND I CAN'T ABIDE ANYONE TRYING TO TAKE RIST AWAY FROM ME!
SO WHY DON'T YOU MAN UP AND FIGHT *ME*, INSTEAD?
YOU GOT A DEATH WISH?
WHY SHOULD WE EVEN LISTEN TO WHAT YOU HAVE TO SAY?
Master, are you certain this is a wise course of action?
Your odds of winning against him in a fair fight are slim to none.
ヒソヒソ WHISPER
OF COURSE I KNOW THAT!
BUT I CAN'T LET RIST TAKE THE HEAT HERE. NOT WHILE SHE'S STILL GOT ALL THOSE INJURIES.
ヒソヒソ WHISPER
HEY... I KNOW HIM.
DAT'S THA GUY WHO ONLY GOES INTO THE TOWER TO MINE FOR DEMONITE.

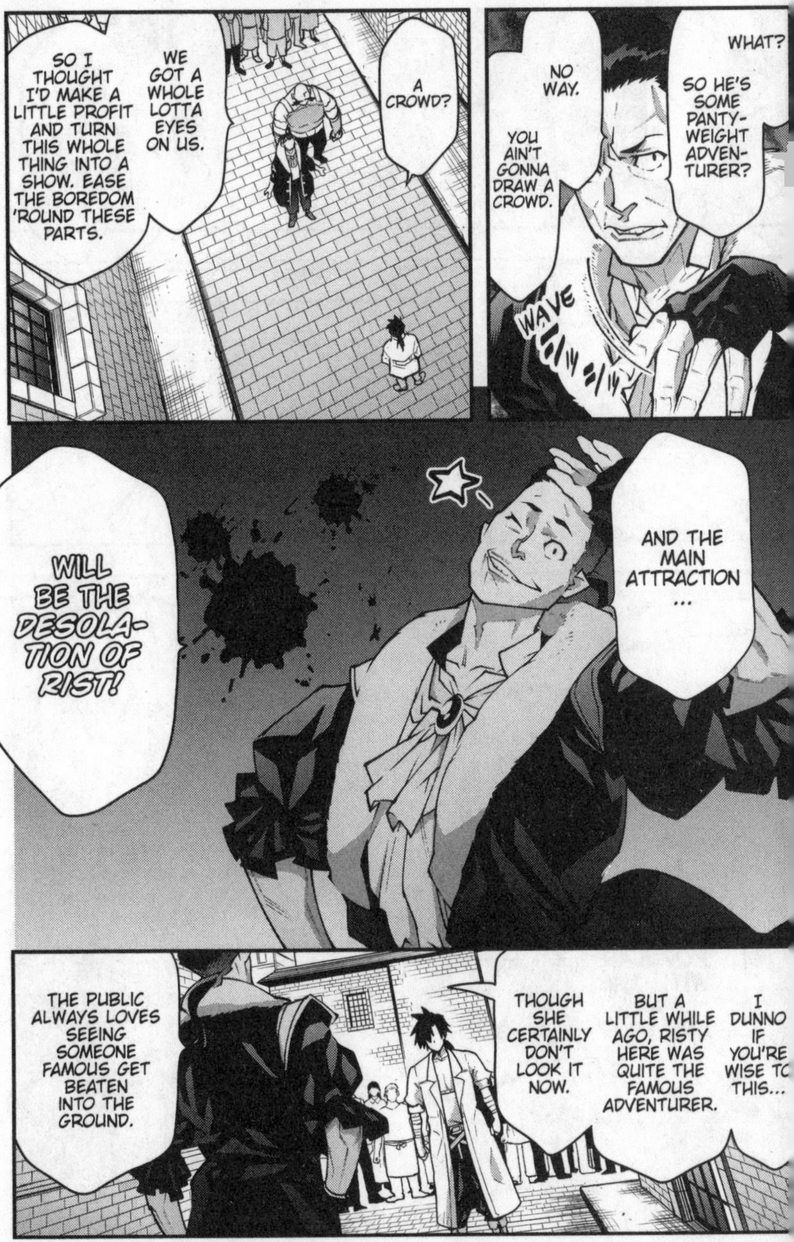
WHAT?
SO HE'S SOME PANTY-WEIGHT ADVEN-TURER?
NO WAY.
YOU AIN'T GONNA DRAW A CROWD.
WAVE
A CROWD?
WE GOT A WHOLE LOTTA EYES ON US.
SO I THOUGHT I'D MAKE A LITTLE PROFIT AND TURN THIS WHOLE THING INTO A SHOW. EASE THE BOREDOM 'ROUND THESE PARTS.
AND THE MAIN ATTRACTION ...
WILL BE THE DESOLA-TION OF RIST!
I DUNNO IF YOU'RE WISE TO THIS...
BUT A LITTLE WHILE AGO, RISTY HERE WAS QUITE THE FAMOUS ADVENTURER.
THOUGH SHE CERTAINLY DON'T LOOK IT NOW.
THE PUBLIC ALWAYS LOVES SEEING SOMEONE FAMOUS GET BEATEN INTO THE GROUND.

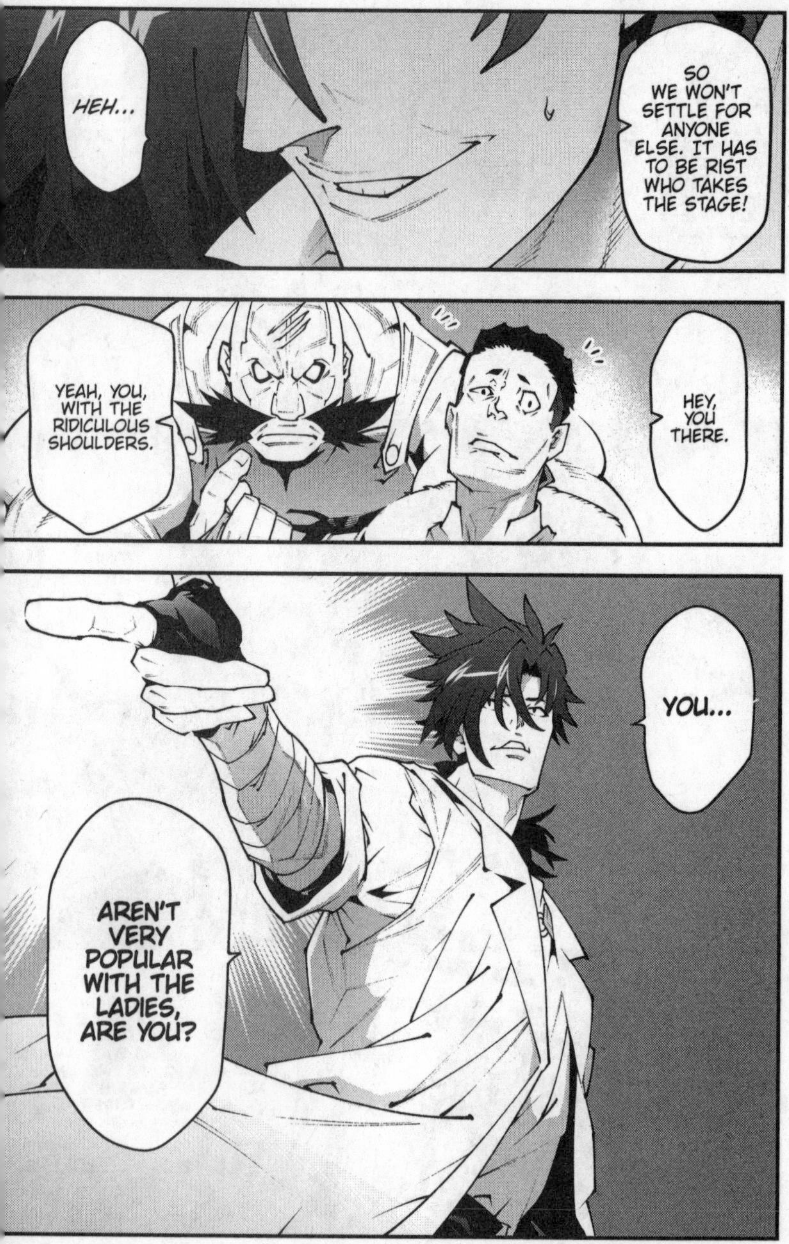
SO WE WON'T SETTLE FOR ANYONE ELSE. IT HAS TO BE RIST WHO TAKES THE STAGE!
HEH...
HEY, YOU THERE.
YEAH, YOU, WITH THE RIDICULOUS SHOULDERS.
YOU...
AREN'T VERY POPULAR WITH THE LADIES, ARE YOU?

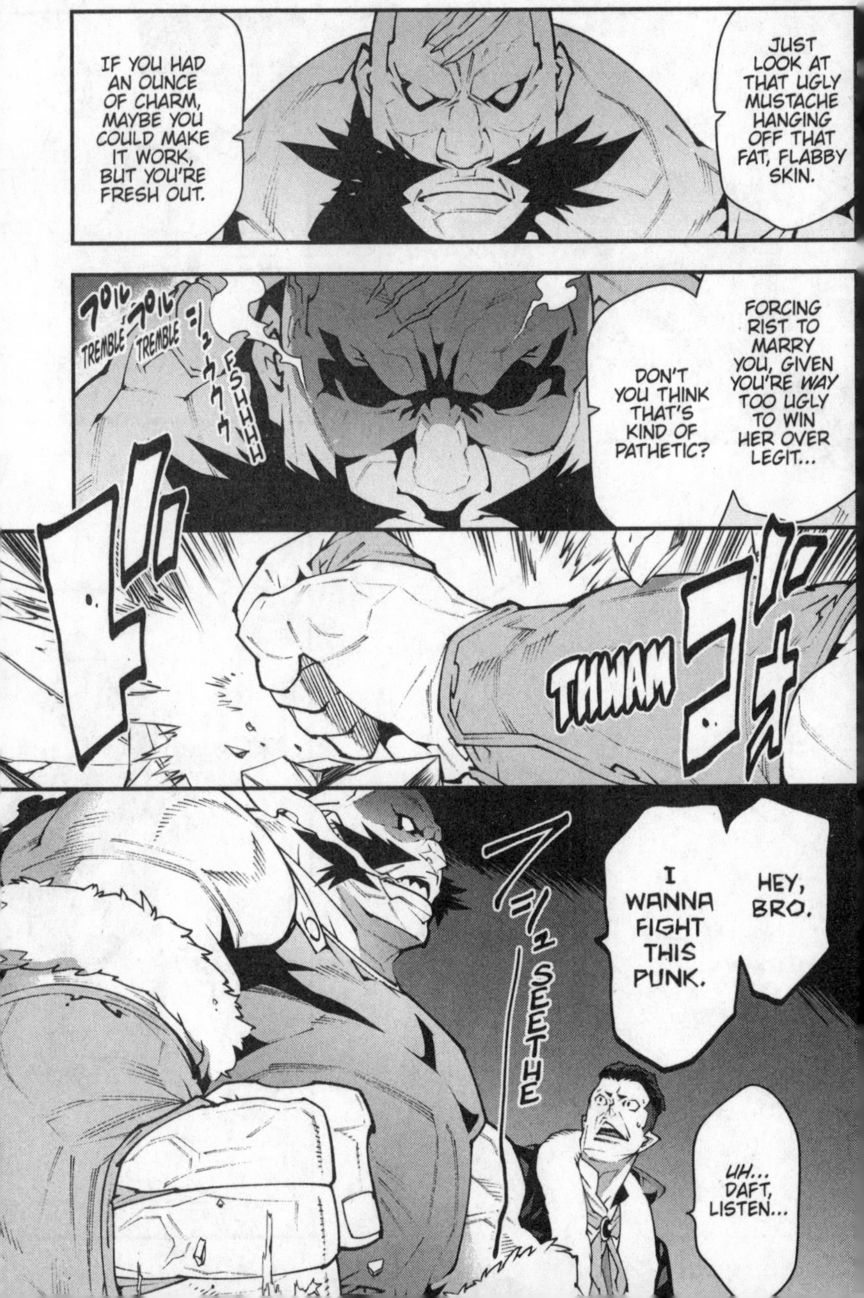
JUST LOOK AT THAT UGLY MUSTACHE HANGING OFF THAT FAT, FLABBY SKIN.
IF YOU HAD AN OUNCE OF CHARM, MAYBE YOU COULD MAKE IT WORK, BUT YOU'RE FRESH OUT.
FORCING RIST TO MARRY YOU, GIVEN YOU'RE *WAY* TOO UGLY TO WIN HER OVER LEGIT...
DON'T YOU THINK THAT'S KIND OF PATHETIC?
TREMBLE TREMBLE
FSHHHH
THWAM
HEY, BRO.
I WANNA FIGHT THIS PUNK.
SEETHE
UH... DAFT, LISTEN...

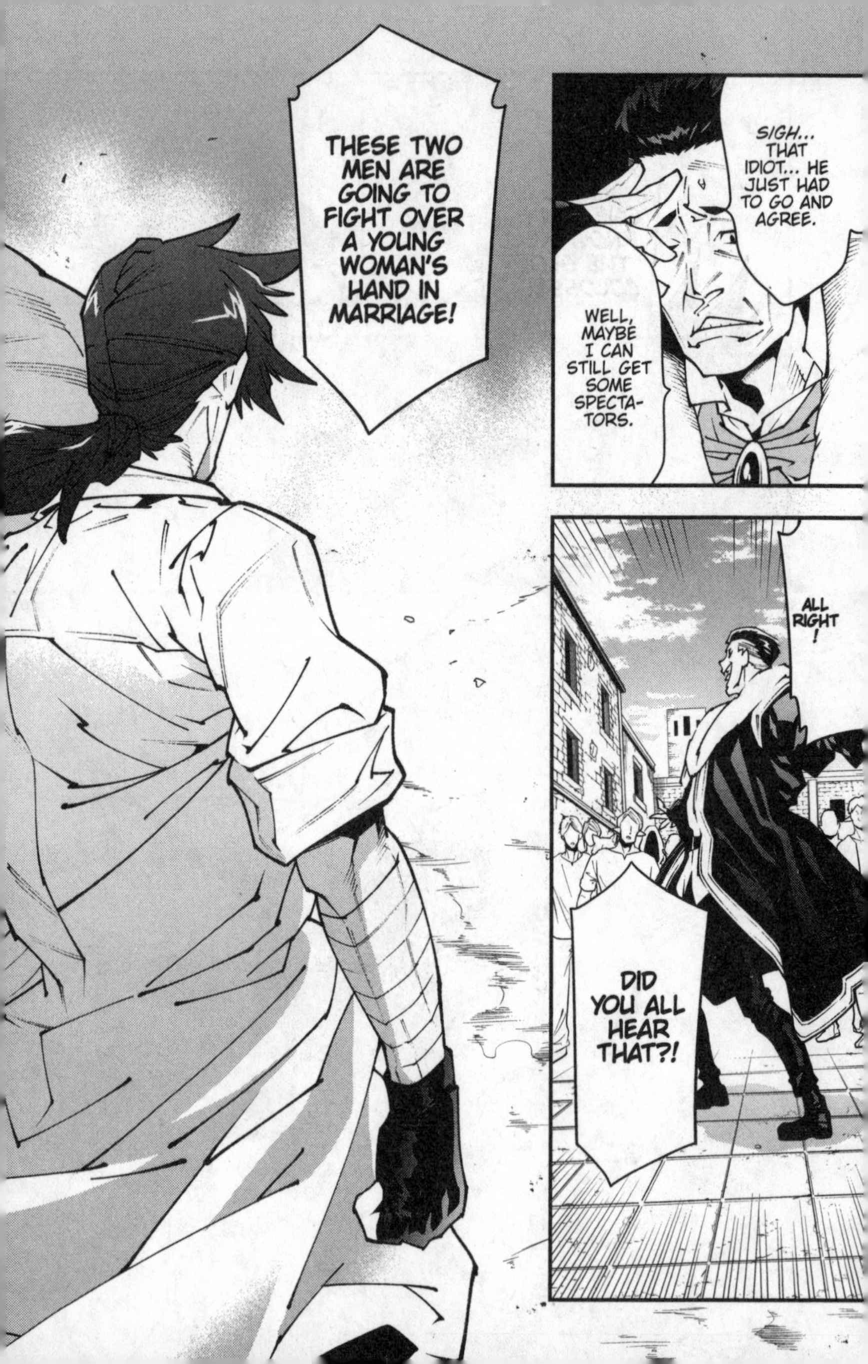
SIGH... THAT IDIOT... HE JUST HAD TO GO AND AGREE.
WELL, MAYBE I CAN STILL GET SOME SPECTA-TORS.
ALL RIGHT!
DID YOU ALL HEAR THAT?!
THESE TWO MEN ARE GOING TO FIGHT OVER A YOUNG WOMAN'S HAND IN MARRIAGE!

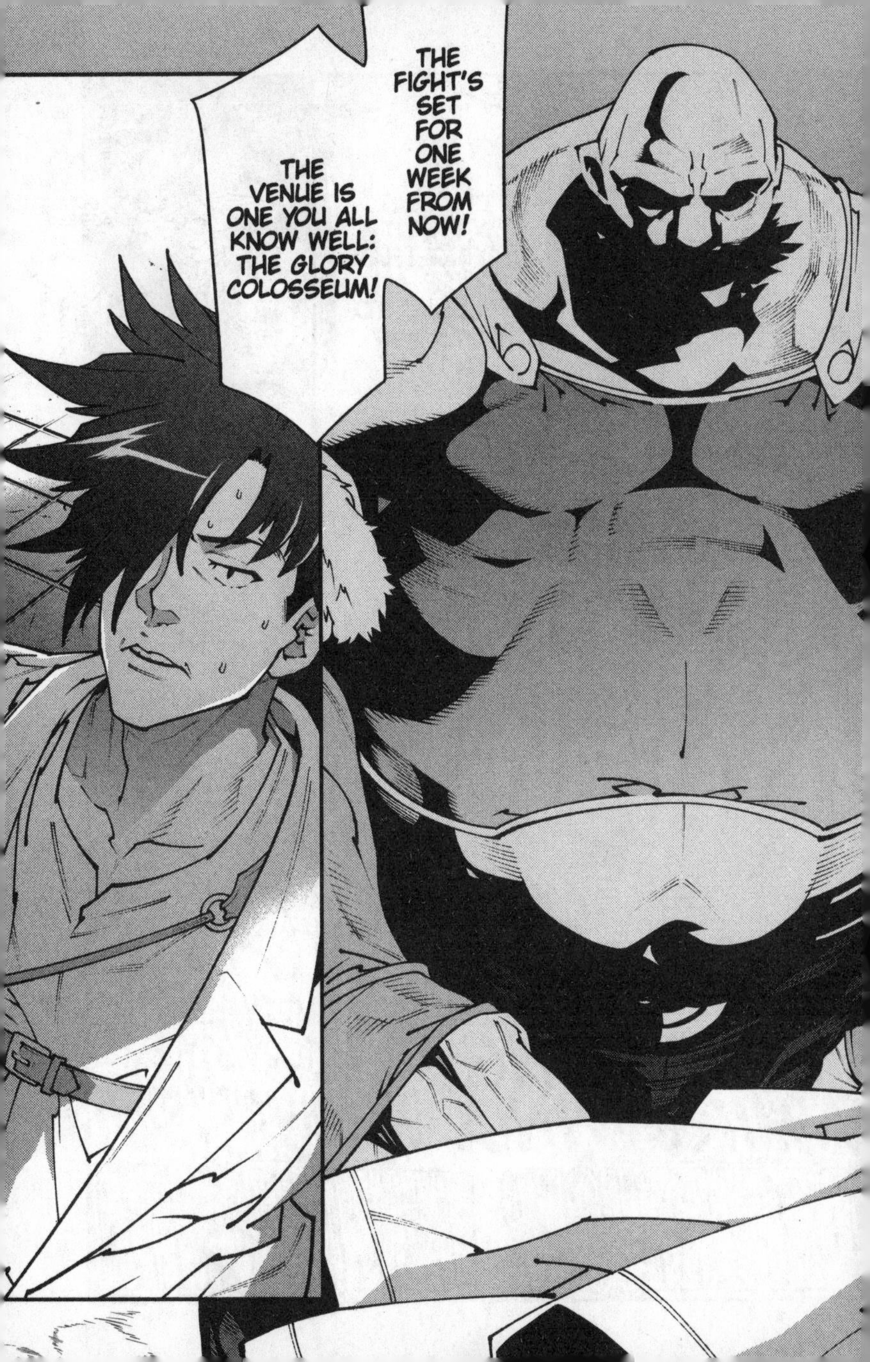
THE FIGHT'S SET FOR ONE WEEK FROM NOW!
THE VENUE IS ONE YOU ALL KNOW WELL: THE GLORY COLOSSEUM!

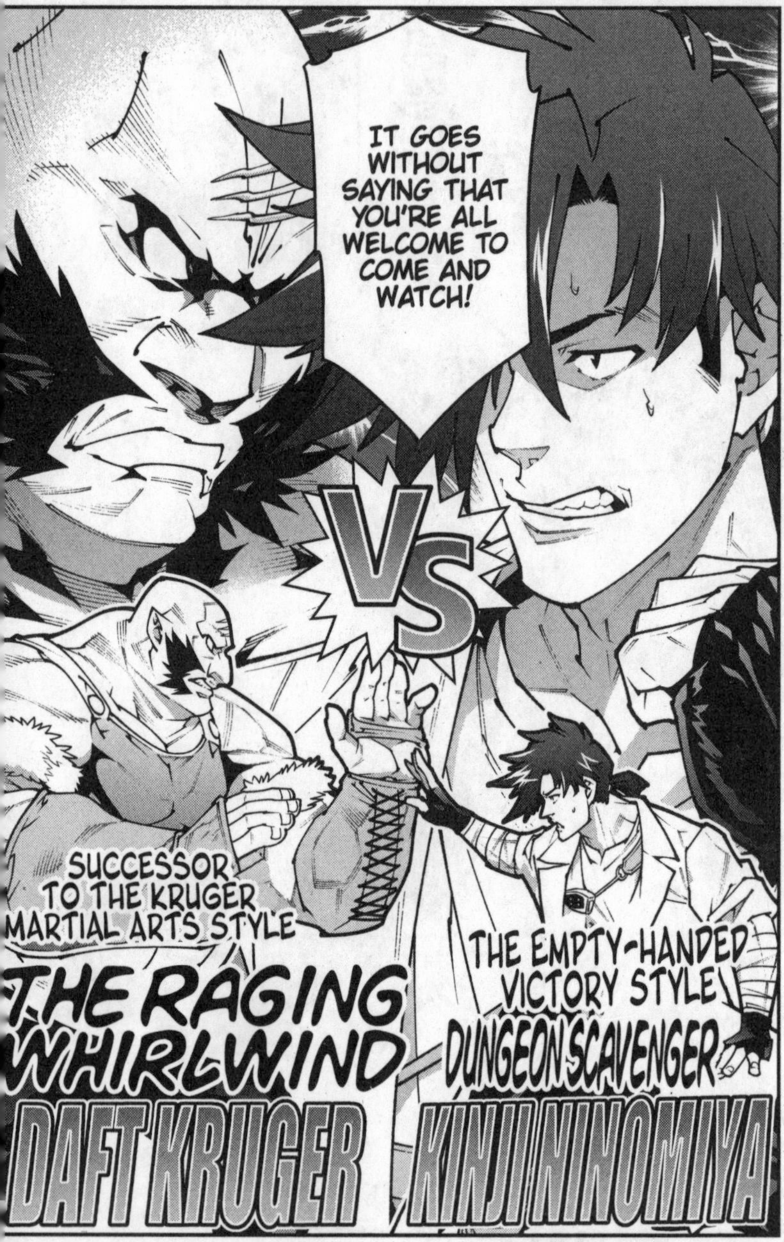
IT GOES WITHOUT SAYING THAT YOU'RE ALL WELCOME TO COME AND WATCH!
VS
THE EMPTY-HANDED VICTORY STYLE
DUNGEON SCAVENGER
KINJI NINOMIYA
SUCCESSOR TO THE KRUGER MARTIAL ARTS STYLE
THE RAGING WHIRLWIND
DAFT KRUGER

NINOMIYA KINJI

BIRDLIME SHOT (FAR)	↓↘→ AND PRESS PUNCH
BLADE WING	→↓↘ AND PRESS PUNCH
BIRDLIME SHOT (CLOSE)	↓↙← AND PRESS KICK
???	???????

THE DUNGEON OF
BLACK COMPANY

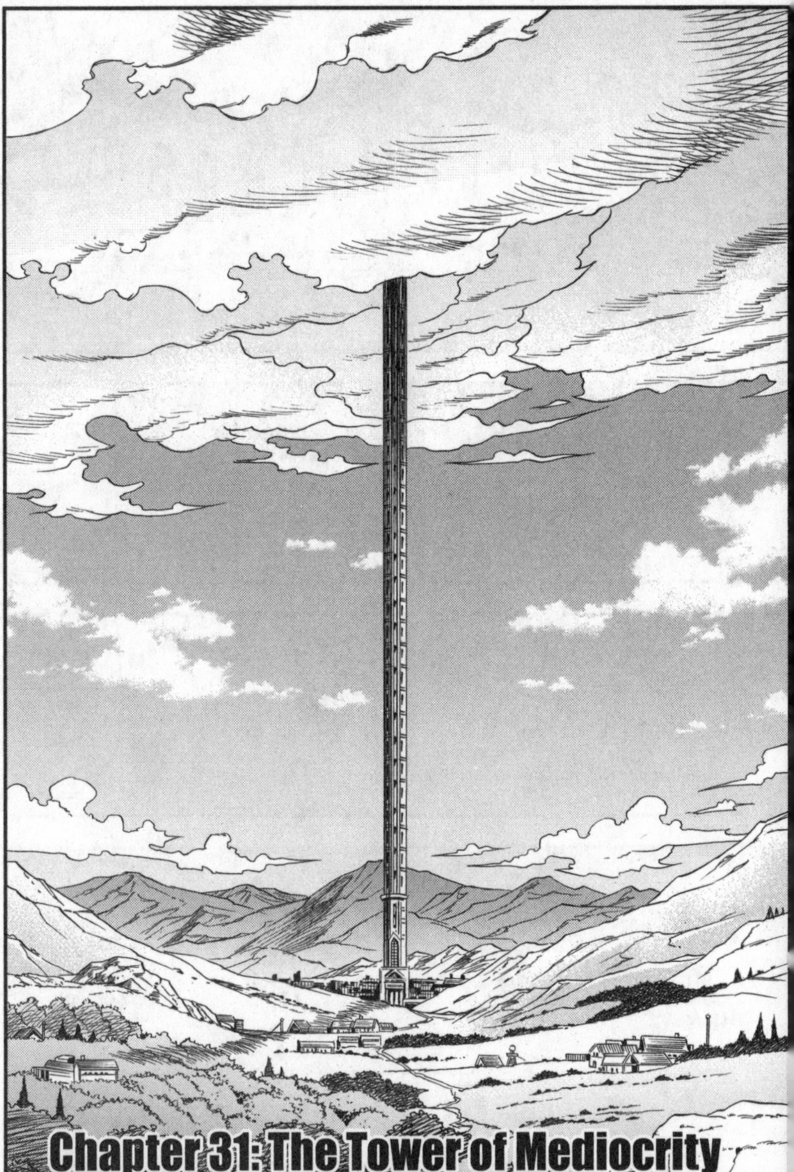
Chapter 31: The Tower of Mediocrity

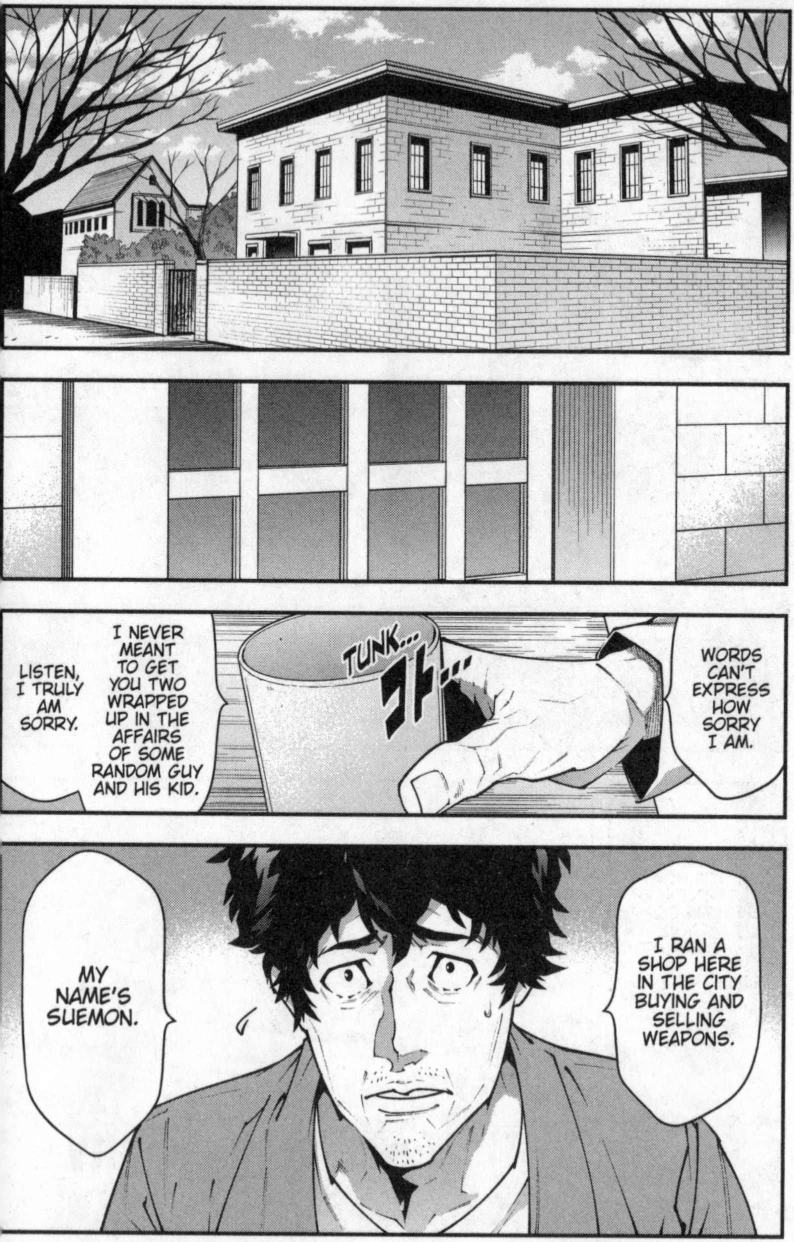
WORDS CAN'T EXPRESS HOW SORRY I AM.
TUNK...
コト...
I NEVER MEANT TO GET YOU TWO WRAPPED UP IN THE AFFAIRS OF SOME RANDOM GUY AND HIS KID.
LISTEN, I TRULY AM SORRY.
I RAN A SHOP HERE IN THE CITY BUYING AND SELLING WEAPONS.
MY NAME'S SUEMON.

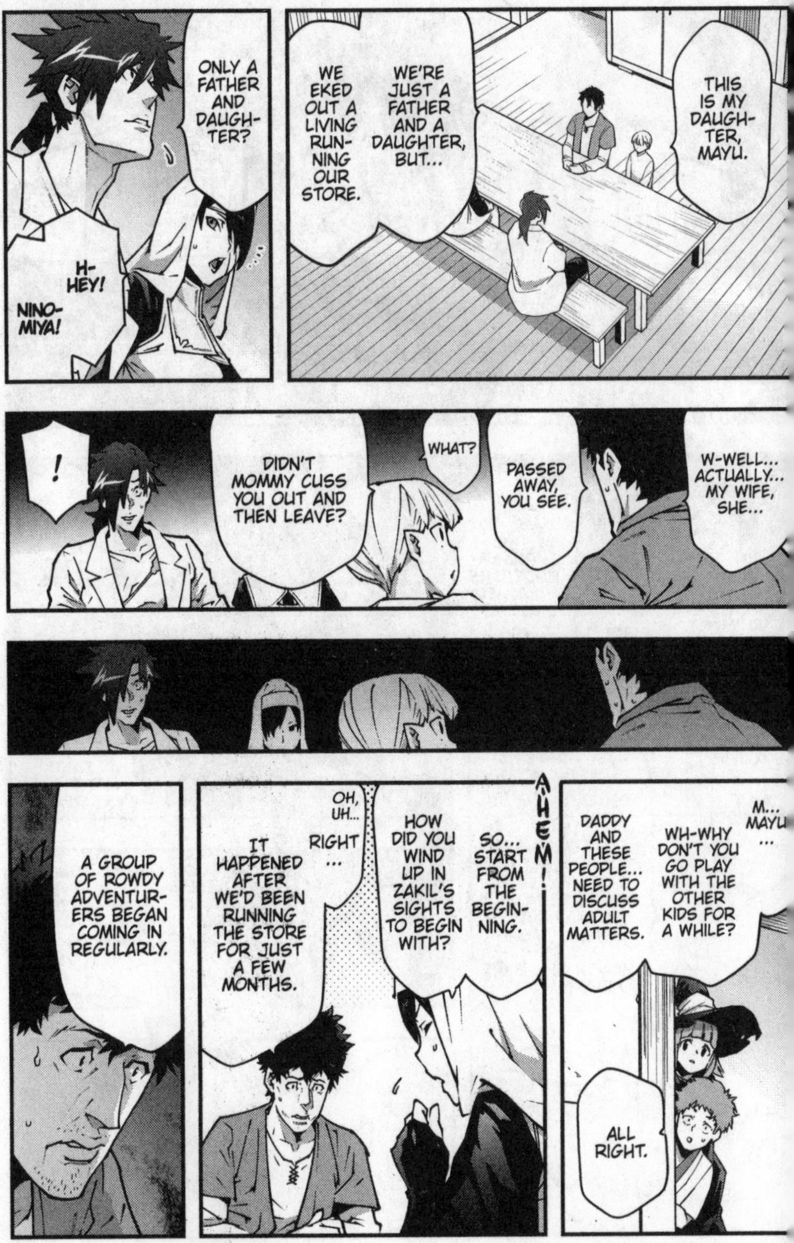
THIS IS MY DAUGHTER, MAYU.
WE'RE JUST A FATHER AND A DAUGHTER, BUT...
WE EKED OUT A LIVING RUNNING OUR STORE.
ONLY A FATHER AND DAUGHTER?
H-HEY!
NINOMIYA!
W-WELL... ACTUALLY... MY WIFE, SHE...
PASSED AWAY, YOU SEE.
WHAT?
DIDN'T MOMMY CUSS YOU OUT AND THEN LEAVE?
!
M... MAYU...
WH-WHY DON'T YOU GO PLAY WITH THE OTHER KIDS FOR A WHILE?
DADDY AND THESE PEOPLE... NEED TO DISCUSS ADULT MATTERS.
ALL RIGHT.
AHEM!
SO... START FROM THE BEGINNING.
HOW DID YOU WIND UP IN ZAKIL'S SIGHTS TO BEGIN WITH?
OH, UH... RIGHT...
IT HAPPENED AFTER WE'D BEEN RUNNING THE STORE FOR JUST A FEW MONTHS.
A GROUP OF ROWDY ADVENTURERS BEGAN COMING IN REGULARLY.

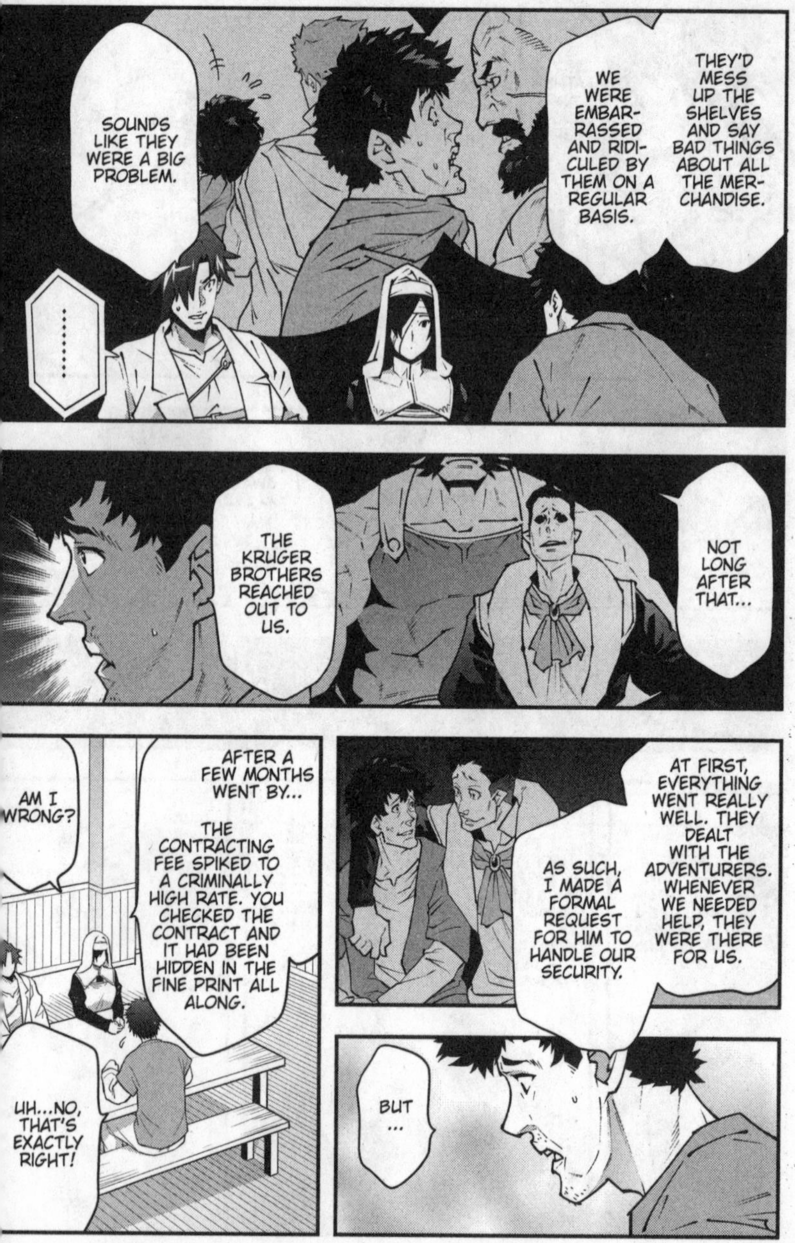
THEY'D MESS UP THE SHELVES AND SAY BAD THINGS ABOUT ALL THE MER-CHANDISE.
WE WERE EMBAR-RASSED AND RIDI-CULED BY THEM ON A REGULAR BASIS.
SOUNDS LIKE THEY WERE A BIG PROBLEM.
......
NOT LONG AFTER THAT...
THE KRUGER BROTHERS REACHED OUT TO US.
AT FIRST, EVERYTHING WENT REALLY WELL. THEY DEALT WITH THE ADVENTURERS. WHENEVER WE NEEDED HELP, THEY WERE THERE FOR US.
AS SUCH, I MADE A FORMAL REQUEST FOR HIM TO HANDLE OUR SECURITY.
BUT ...
AFTER A FEW MONTHS WENT BY...
THE CONTRACTING FEE SPIKED TO A CRIMINALLY HIGH RATE. YOU CHECKED THE CONTRACT AND IT HAD BEEN HIDDEN IN THE FINE PRINT ALL ALONG.
AM I WRONG?
UH...NO, THAT'S EXACTLY RIGHT!

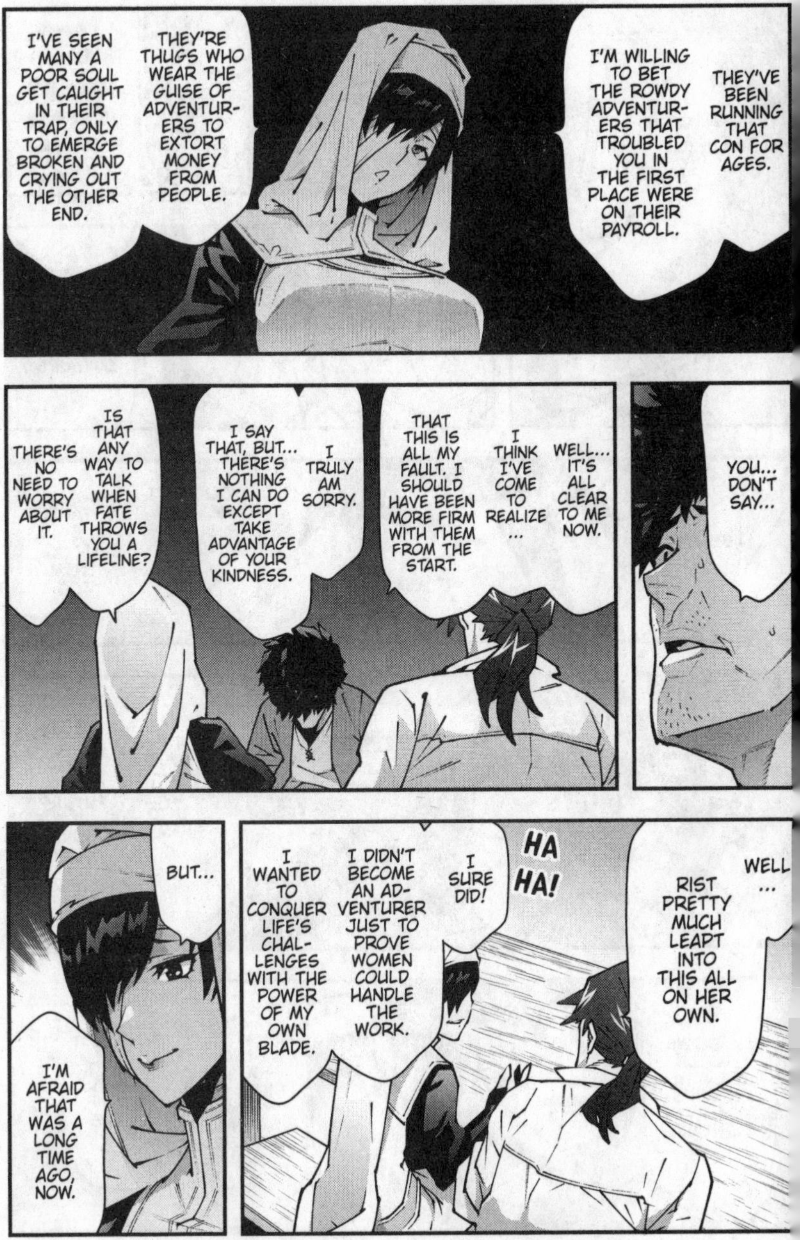
THEY'VE BEEN RUNNING THAT CON FOR AGES.
I'M WILLING TO BET THE ROWDY ADVENTURERS THAT TROUBLED YOU IN THE FIRST PLACE WERE ON THEIR PAYROLL.
THEY'RE THUGS WHO WEAR THE GUISE OF ADVENTURERS TO EXTORT MONEY FROM PEOPLE.
I'VE SEEN MANY A POOR SOUL GET CAUGHT IN THEIR TRAP, ONLY TO EMERGE BROKEN AND CRYING OUT THE OTHER END.
YOU... DON'T SAY...
WELL... IT'S ALL CLEAR TO ME NOW.
I THINK I'VE COME TO REALIZE...
THAT THIS IS ALL MY FAULT. I SHOULD HAVE BEEN MORE FIRM WITH THEM FROM THE START.
I TRULY AM SORRY.
I SAY THAT, BUT... THERE'S NOTHING I CAN DO EXCEPT TAKE ADVANTAGE OF YOUR KINDNESS.
IS THAT ANY WAY TO TALK WHEN FATE THROWS YOU A LIFELINE?
THERE'S NO NEED TO WORRY ABOUT IT.
WELL...
RIST PRETTY MUCH LEAPT INTO THIS ALL ON HER OWN.
HA HA!
I SURE DID!
I DIDN'T BECOME AN ADVENTURER JUST TO PROVE WOMEN COULD HANDLE THE WORK.
I WANTED TO CONQUER LIFE'S CHALLENGES WITH THE POWER OF MY OWN BLADE.
BUT...
I'M AFRAID THAT WAS A LONG TIME AGO, NOW.

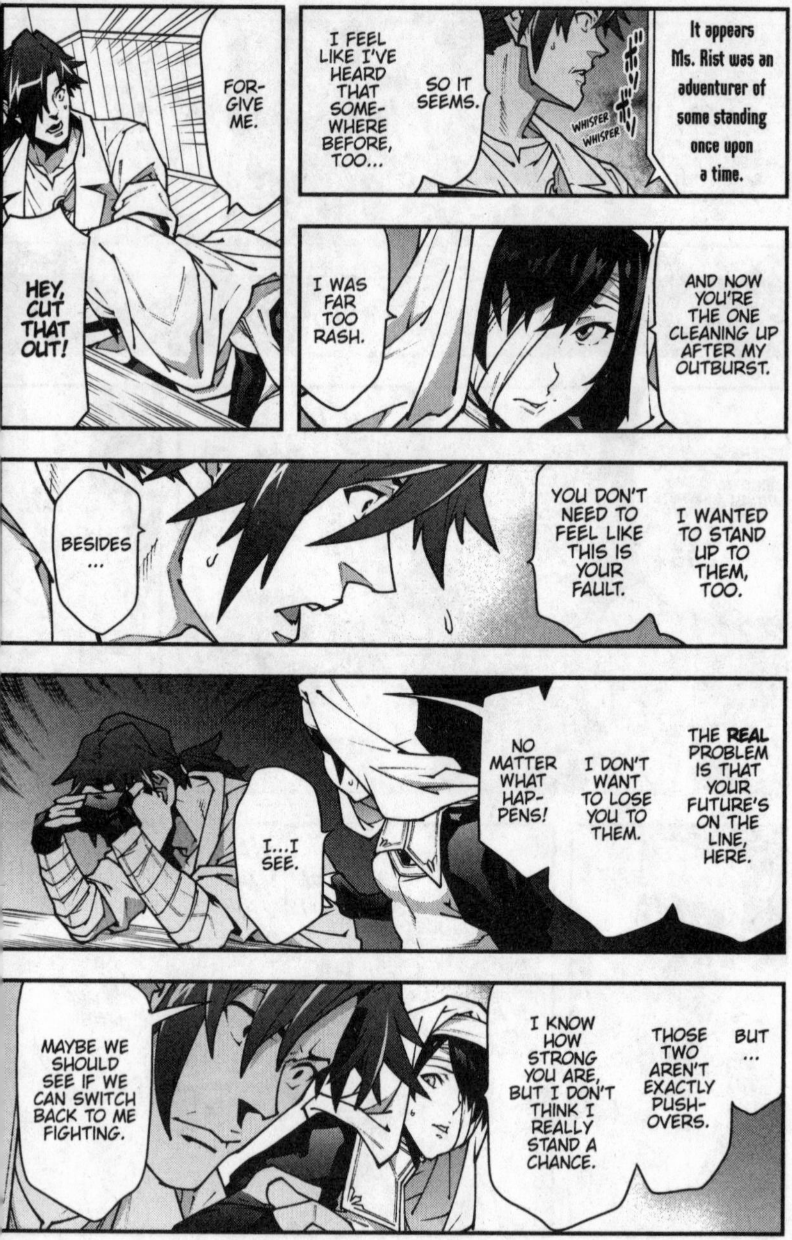

It appears Ms. Rist was an adventurer of some standing once upon a time.
WHISPER WHISPER
SO IT SEEMS.
I FEEL LIKE I'VE HEARD THAT SOME-WHERE BEFORE, TOO...
AND NOW YOU'RE THE ONE CLEANING UP AFTER MY OUTBURST.
I WAS FAR TOO RASH.
FOR-GIVE ME.
HEY, CUT THAT OUT!
I WANTED TO STAND UP TO THEM, TOO.
YOU DON'T NEED TO FEEL LIKE THIS IS YOUR FAULT.
BESIDES...
THE **REAL** PROBLEM IS THAT YOUR FUTURE'S ON THE LINE, HERE.
I DON'T WANT TO LOSE YOU TO THEM.
NO MATTER WHAT HAP-PENS!
I...I SEE.
BUT...
THOSE TWO AREN'T EXACTLY PUSH-OVERS.
I KNOW HOW STRONG YOU ARE, BUT I DON'T THINK I REALLY STAND A CHANCE.
MAYBE WE SHOULD SEE IF WE CAN SWITCH BACK TO ME FIGHTING.

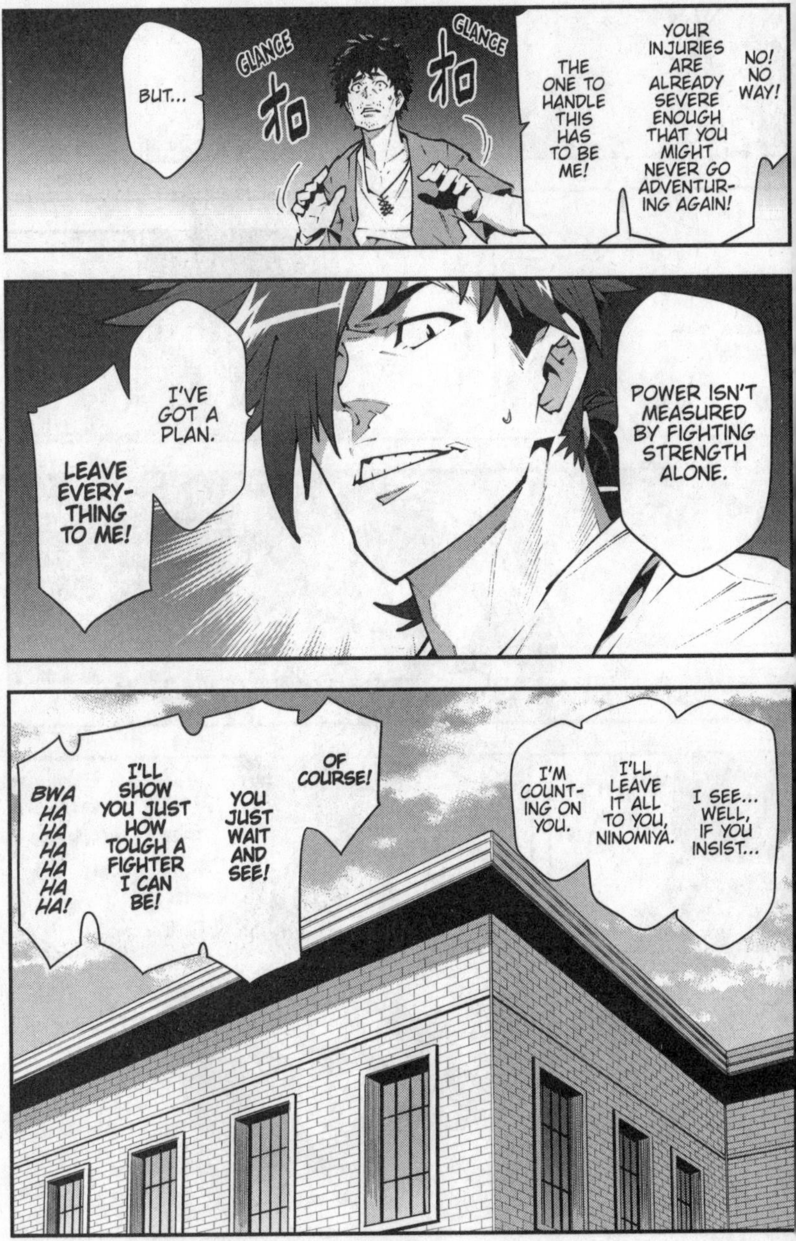
NO! NO WAY!
YOUR INJURIES ARE ALREADY SEVERE ENOUGH THAT YOU MIGHT NEVER GO ADVENTURING AGAIN!
THE ONE TO HANDLE THIS HAS TO BE ME!
GLANCE オロ
GLANCE オロ
BUT...
POWER ISN'T MEASURED BY FIGHTING STRENGTH ALONE.
I'VE GOT A PLAN.
LEAVE EVERYTHING TO ME!
I SEE... WELL, IF YOU INSIST...
I'LL LEAVE IT ALL TO YOU, NINOMIYA.
I'M COUNTING ON YOU.
OF COURSE!
YOU JUST WAIT AND SEE!
I'LL SHOW YOU JUST HOW TOUGH A FIGHTER I CAN BE!
BWA HA HA HA HA HA HA!

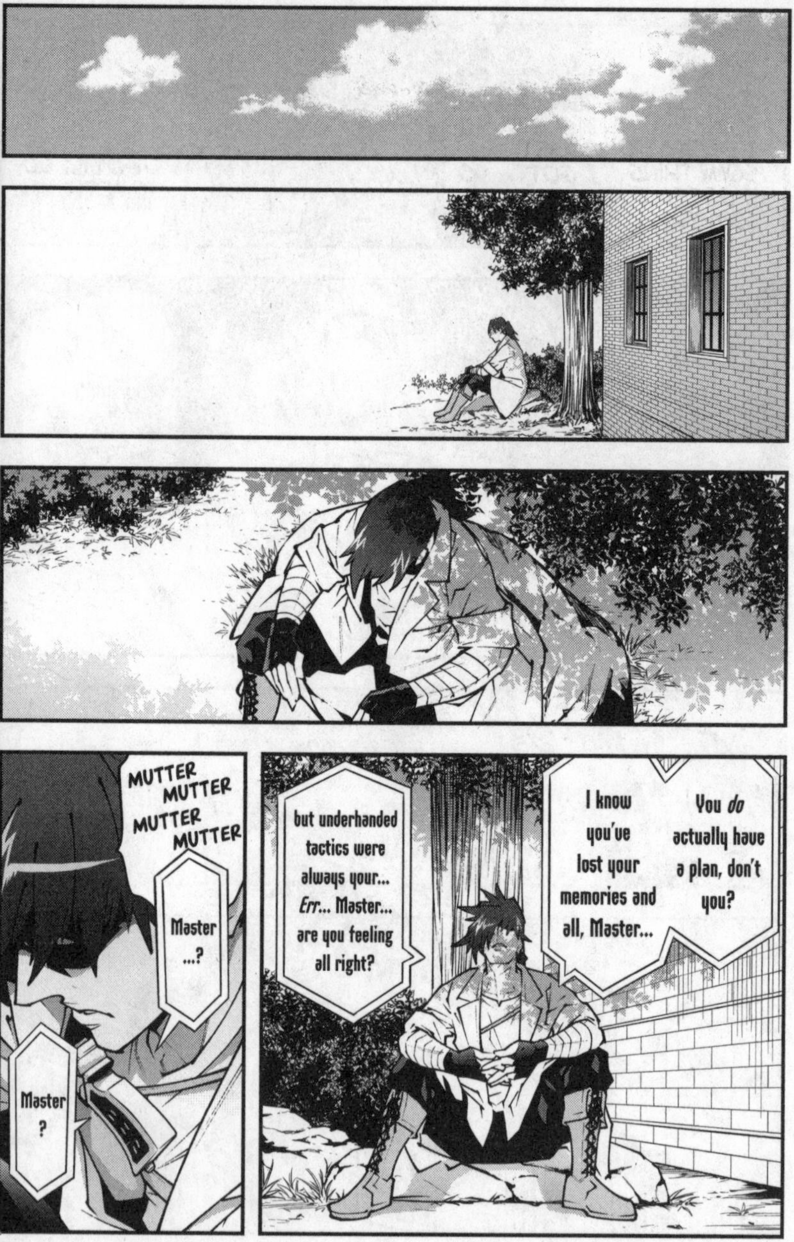
You *do* actually have a plan, don't you?
I know you've lost your memories and all, Master...
but underhanded tactics were always your... *Err*... Master... are you feeling all right?
MUTTER MUTTER MUTTER MUTTER
Master ...?
Master ?

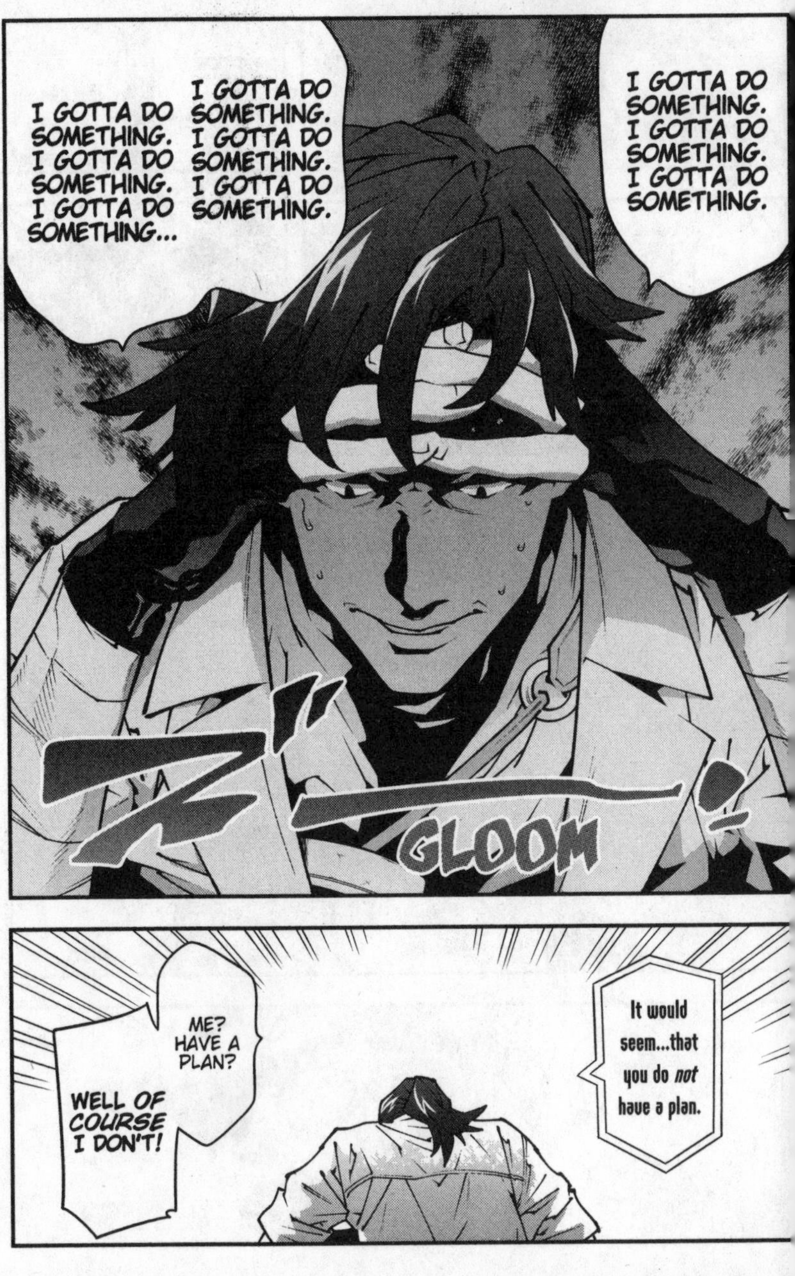
I GOTTA DO SOMETHING. I GOTTA DO SOMETHING. I GOTTA DO SOMETHING.
I GOTTA DO SOMETHING. I GOTTA DO SOMETHING. I GOTTA DO SOMETHING.
I GOTTA DO SOMETHING. I GOTTA DO SOMETHING. I GOTTA DO SOMETHING...
GLOOM
It would seem...that you do *not* have a plan.
ME? HAVE A PLAN?
WELL OF COURSE I DON'T!

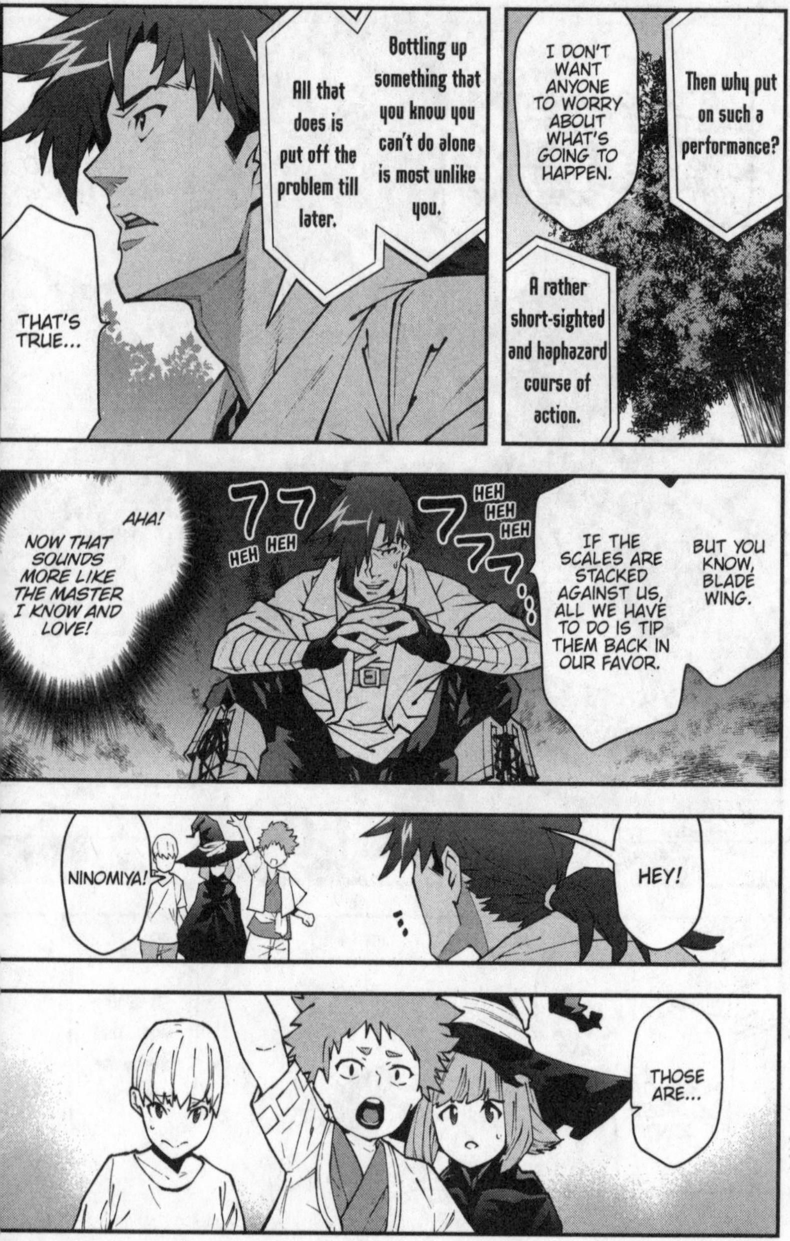
Then why put on such a performance?
I DON'T WANT ANYONE TO WORRY ABOUT WHAT'S GOING TO HAPPEN.
A rather short-sighted and haphazard course of action.
Bottling up something that you know you can't do alone is most unlike you.
All that does is put off the problem till later.
THAT'S TRUE...
BUT YOU KNOW, BLADE WING.
IF THE SCALES ARE STACKED AGAINST US, ALL WE HAVE TO DO IS TIP THEM BACK IN OUR FAVOR.
HEH HEH HEH
HEH HEH
AHA! NOW THAT SOUNDS MORE LIKE THE MASTER I KNOW AND LOVE!
HEY!
NINOMIYA!
THOSE ARE...

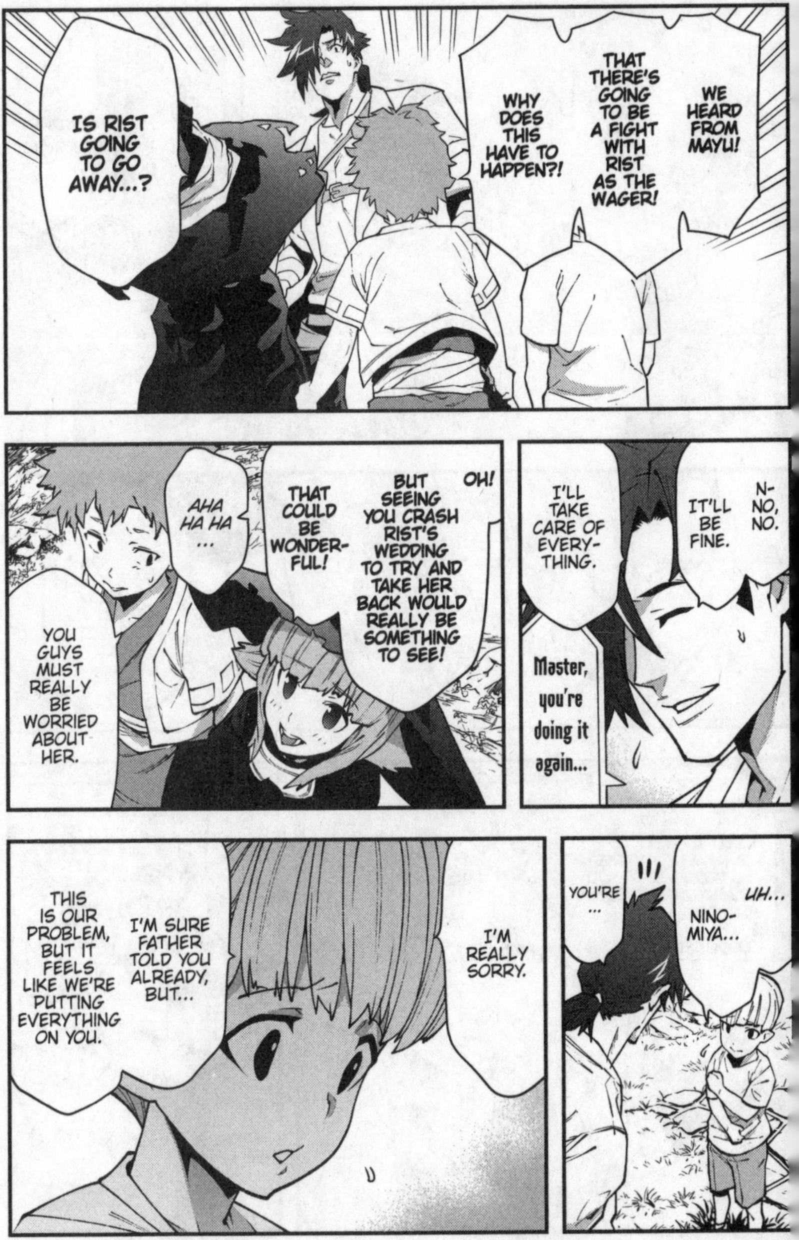
WE HEARD FROM MAYU!
THAT THERE'S GOING TO BE A FIGHT WITH RIST AS THE WAGER!
WHY DOES THIS HAVE TO HAPPEN?!
IS RIST GOING TO GO AWAY...?
N-NO, NO.
IT'LL BE FINE.
I'LL TAKE CARE OF EVERYTHING.
Master, you're doing it again...
OH!
BUT SEEING YOU CRASH RIST'S WEDDING TO TRY AND TAKE HER BACK WOULD REALLY BE SOMETHING TO SEE!
THAT COULD BE WONDERFUL!
AHA HA HA ...
YOU GUYS MUST REALLY BE WORRIED ABOUT HER.
UH...
NINOMIYA...
YOU'RE ...
I'M REALLY SORRY.
I'M SURE FATHER TOLD YOU ALREADY, BUT...
THIS IS OUR PROBLEM, BUT IT FEELS LIKE WE'RE PUTTING EVERYTHING ON YOU.

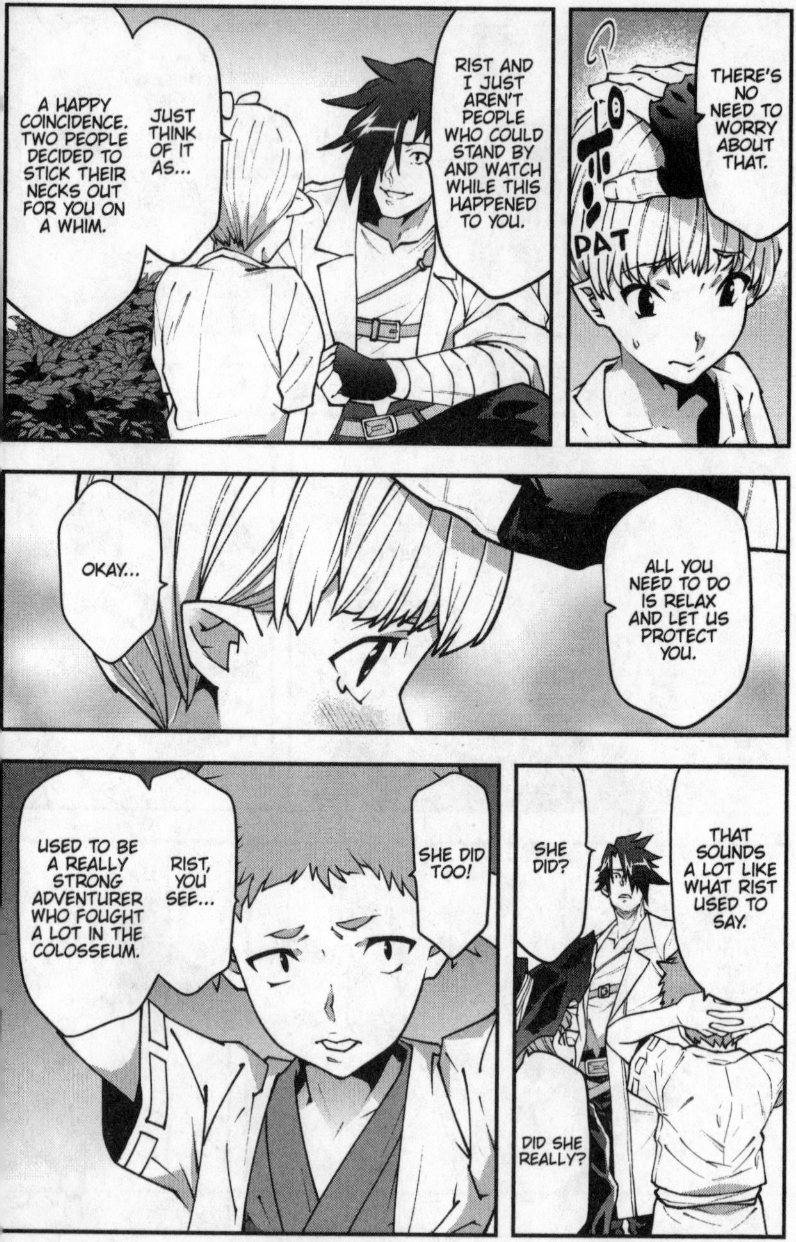
THERE'S NO NEED TO WORRY ABOUT THAT.
PAT
RIST AND I JUST AREN'T PEOPLE WHO COULD STAND BY AND WATCH WHILE THIS HAPPENED TO YOU.
JUST THINK OF IT AS...
A HAPPY COINCIDENCE. TWO PEOPLE DECIDED TO STICK THEIR NECKS OUT FOR YOU ON A WHIM.
ALL YOU NEED TO DO IS RELAX AND LET US PROTECT YOU.
OKAY...
THAT SOUNDS A LOT LIKE WHAT RIST USED TO SAY.
SHE DID?
DID SHE REALLY?
SHE DID TOO!
RIST, YOU SEE...
USED TO BE A REALLY STRONG ADVENTURER WHO FOUGHT A LOT IN THE COLOSSEUM.

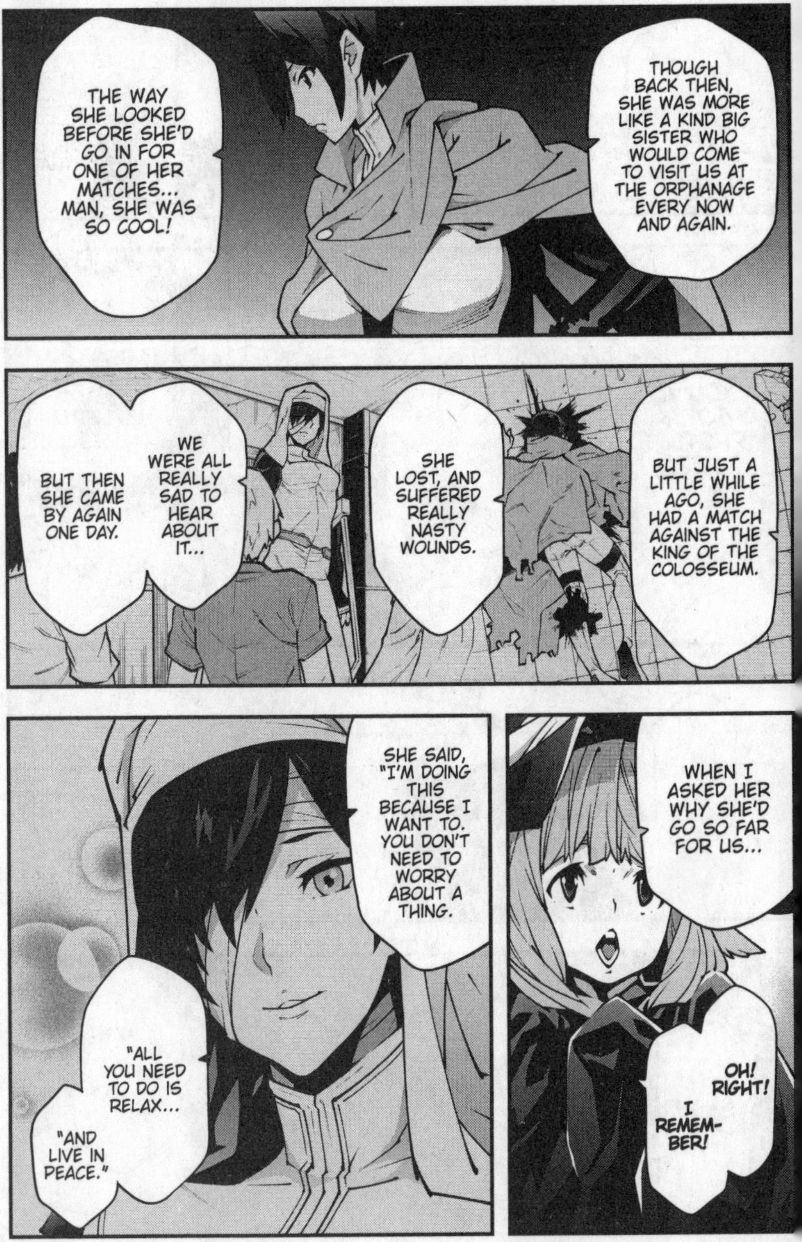
THOUGH BACK THEN, SHE WAS MORE LIKE A KIND BIG SISTER WHO WOULD COME TO VISIT US AT THE ORPHANAGE EVERY NOW AND AGAIN.
THE WAY SHE LOOKED BEFORE SHE'D GO IN FOR ONE OF HER MATCHES... MAN, SHE WAS SO COOL!
BUT JUST A LITTLE WHILE AGO, SHE HAD A MATCH AGAINST THE KING OF THE COLOSSEUM.
SHE LOST, AND SUFFERED REALLY NASTY WOUNDS.
WE WERE ALL REALLY SAD TO HEAR ABOUT IT...
BUT THEN SHE CAME BY AGAIN ONE DAY.
WHEN I ASKED HER WHY SHE'D GO SO FAR FOR US...
OH! RIGHT! I REMEMBER!
SHE SAID, "I'M DOING THIS BECAUSE I WANT TO. YOU DON'T NEED TO WORRY ABOUT A THING.
"ALL YOU NEED TO DO IS RELAX...
"AND LIVE IN PEACE."

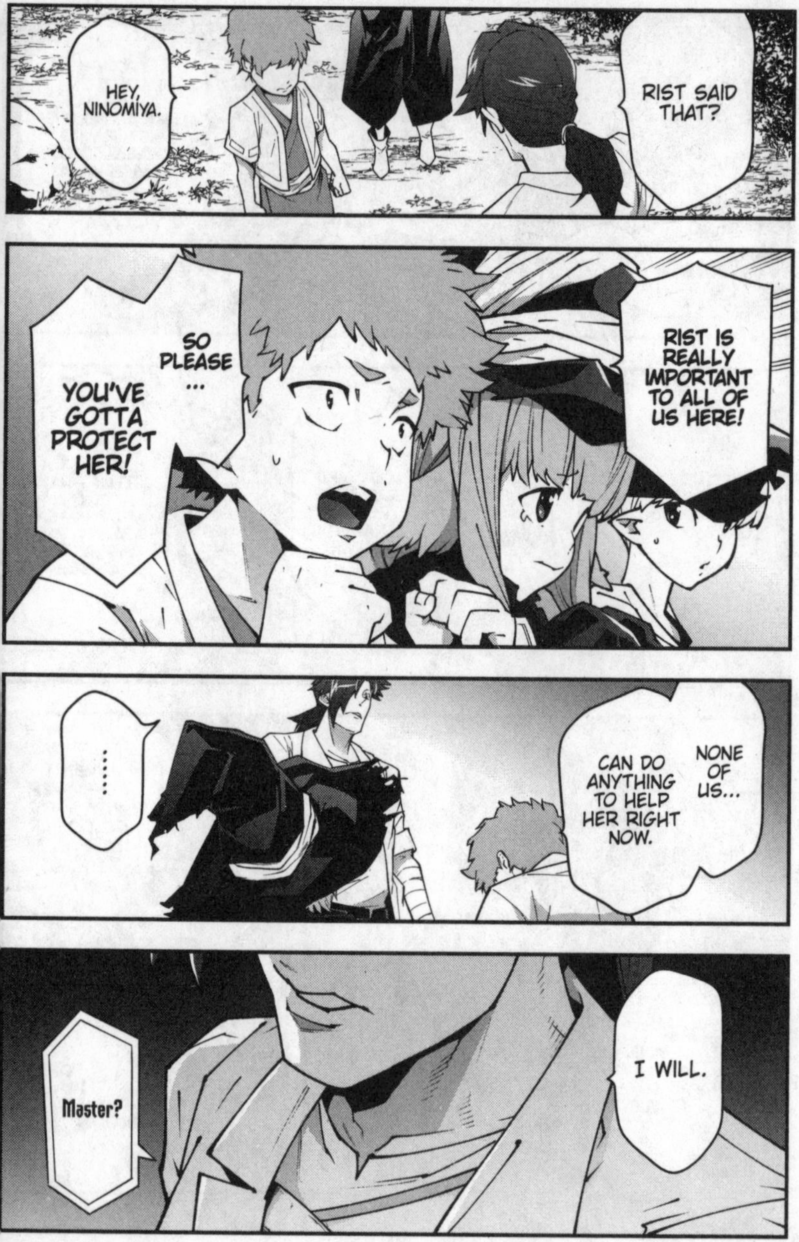

RIST SAID THAT?
HEY, NINOMIYA.
RIST IS REALLY IMPORTANT TO ALL OF US HERE!
SO PLEASE ...
YOU'VE GOTTA PROTECT HER!
NONE OF US...
CAN DO ANYTHING TO HELP HER RIGHT NOW.
......
I WILL.
Master?

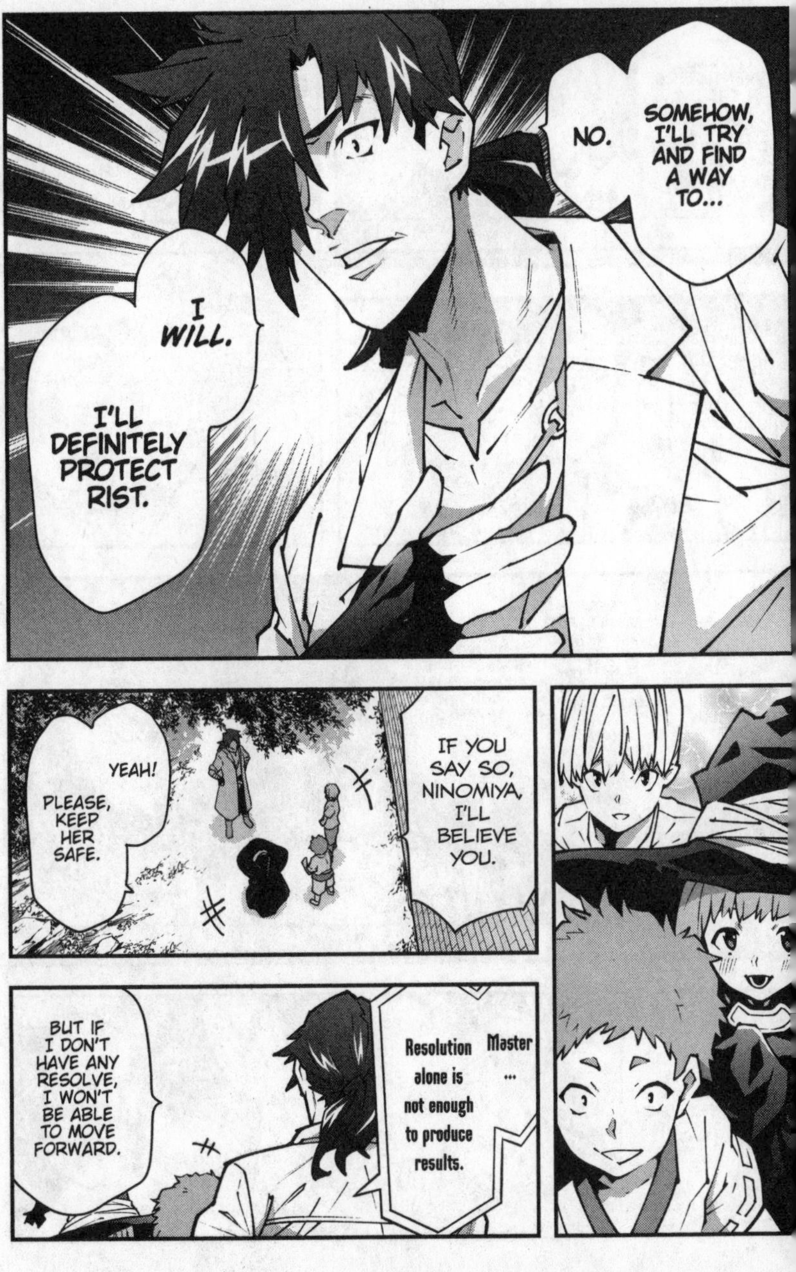
SOMEHOW, I'LL TRY AND FIND A WAY TO...
NO.
I WILL.
I'LL DEFINITELY PROTECT RIST.
IF YOU SAY SO, NINOMIYA, I'LL BELIEVE YOU.
YEAH!
PLEASE, KEEP HER SAFE.
Master...
Resolution alone is not enough to produce results.
BUT IF I DON'T HAVE ANY RESOLVE, I WON'T BE ABLE TO MOVE FORWARD.

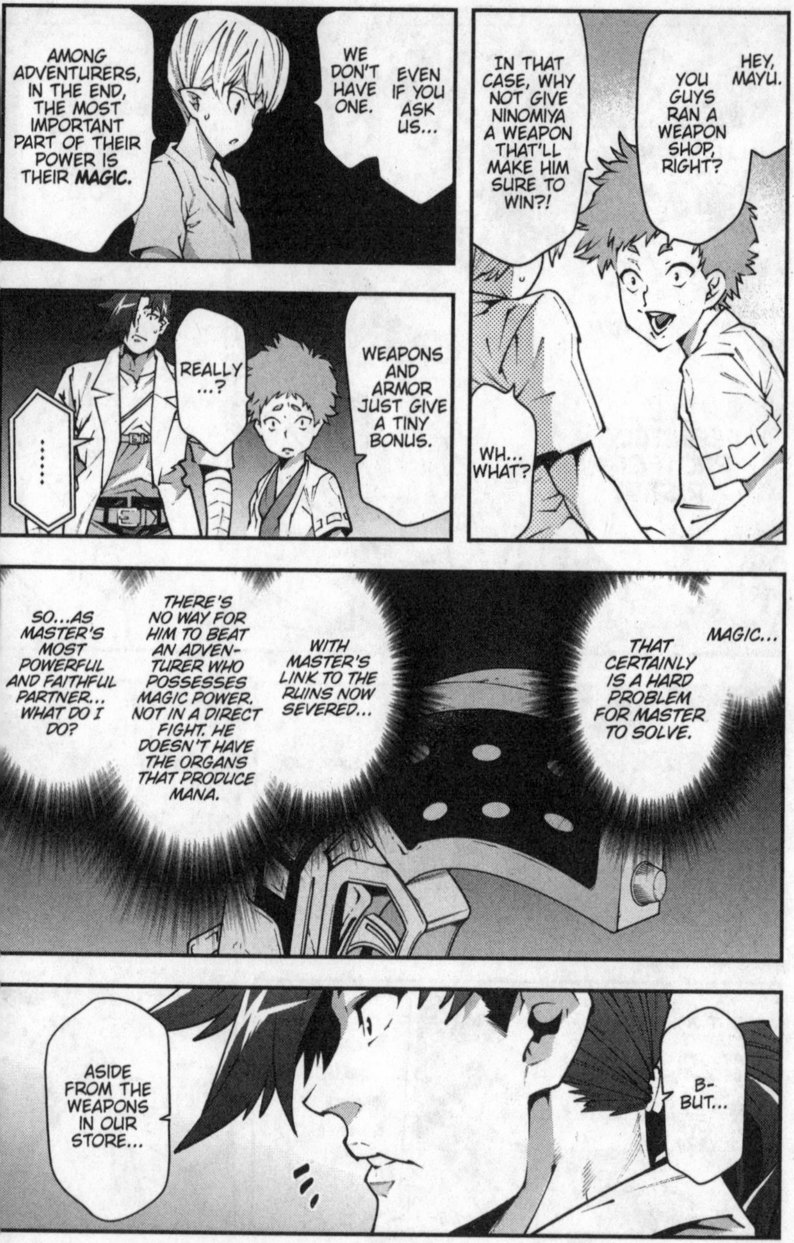
HEY, MAYU.
YOU GUYS RAN A WEAPON SHOP, RIGHT?
IN THAT CASE, WHY NOT GIVE NINOMIYA A WEAPON THAT'LL MAKE HIM SURE TO WIN?!
WH... WHAT?
EVEN IF YOU ASK US...
WE DON'T HAVE ONE.
AMONG ADVENTURERS, IN THE END, THE MOST IMPORTANT PART OF THEIR POWER IS THEIR MAGIC.
WEAPONS AND ARMOR JUST GIVE A TINY BONUS.
REALLY ...?
......
MAGIC...
THAT CERTAINLY IS A HARD PROBLEM FOR MASTER TO SOLVE.
WITH MASTER'S LINK TO THE RUINS NOW SEVERED...
THERE'S NO WAY FOR HIM TO BEAT AN ADVEN-TURER WHO POSSESSES MAGIC POWER. NOT IN A DIRECT FIGHT. HE DOESN'T HAVE THE ORGANS THAT PRODUCE MANA.
SO...AS MASTER'S MOST POWERFUL AND FAITHFUL PARTNER... WHAT DO I DO?
B-BUT...
ASIDE FROM THE WEAPONS IN OUR STORE...

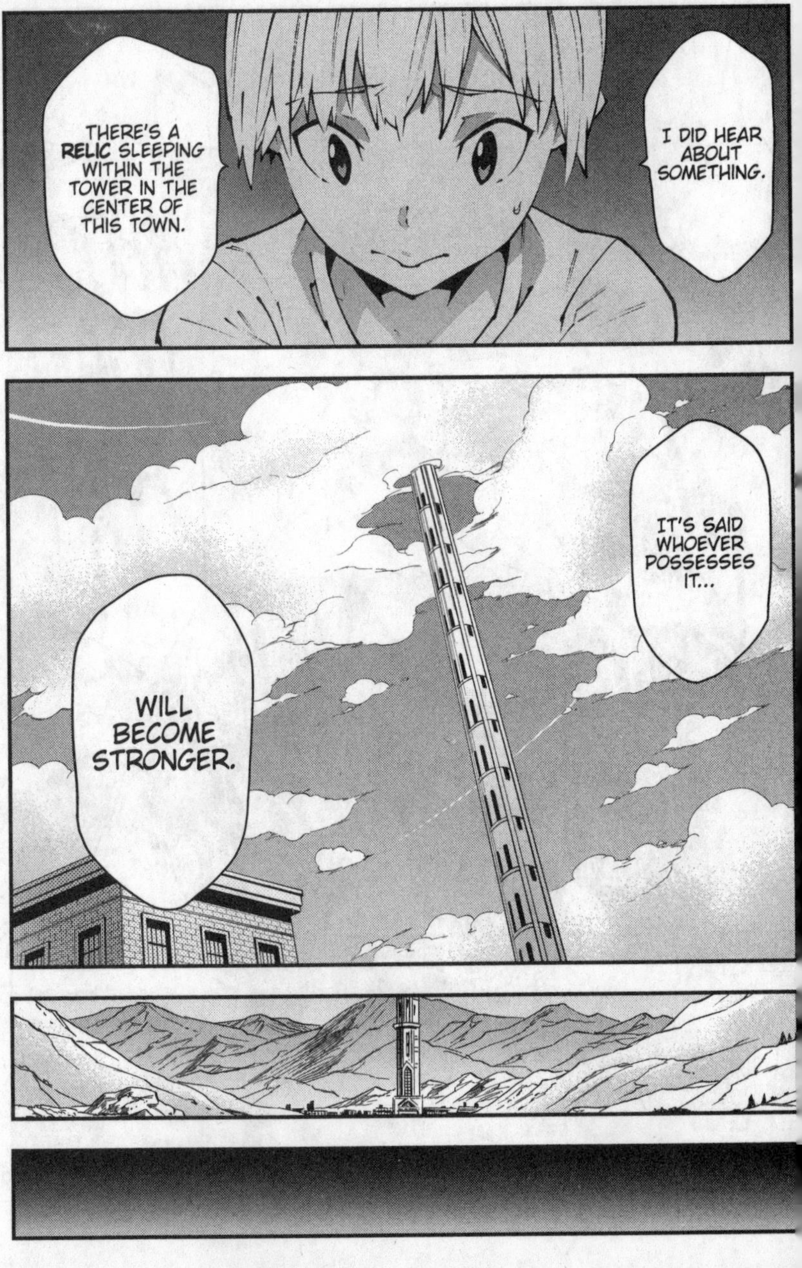
I DID HEAR ABOUT SOMETHING.
THERE'S A RELIC SLEEPING WITHIN THE TOWER IN THE CENTER OF THIS TOWN.
IT'S SAID WHOEVER POSSESSES IT...
WILL BECOME STRONGER.

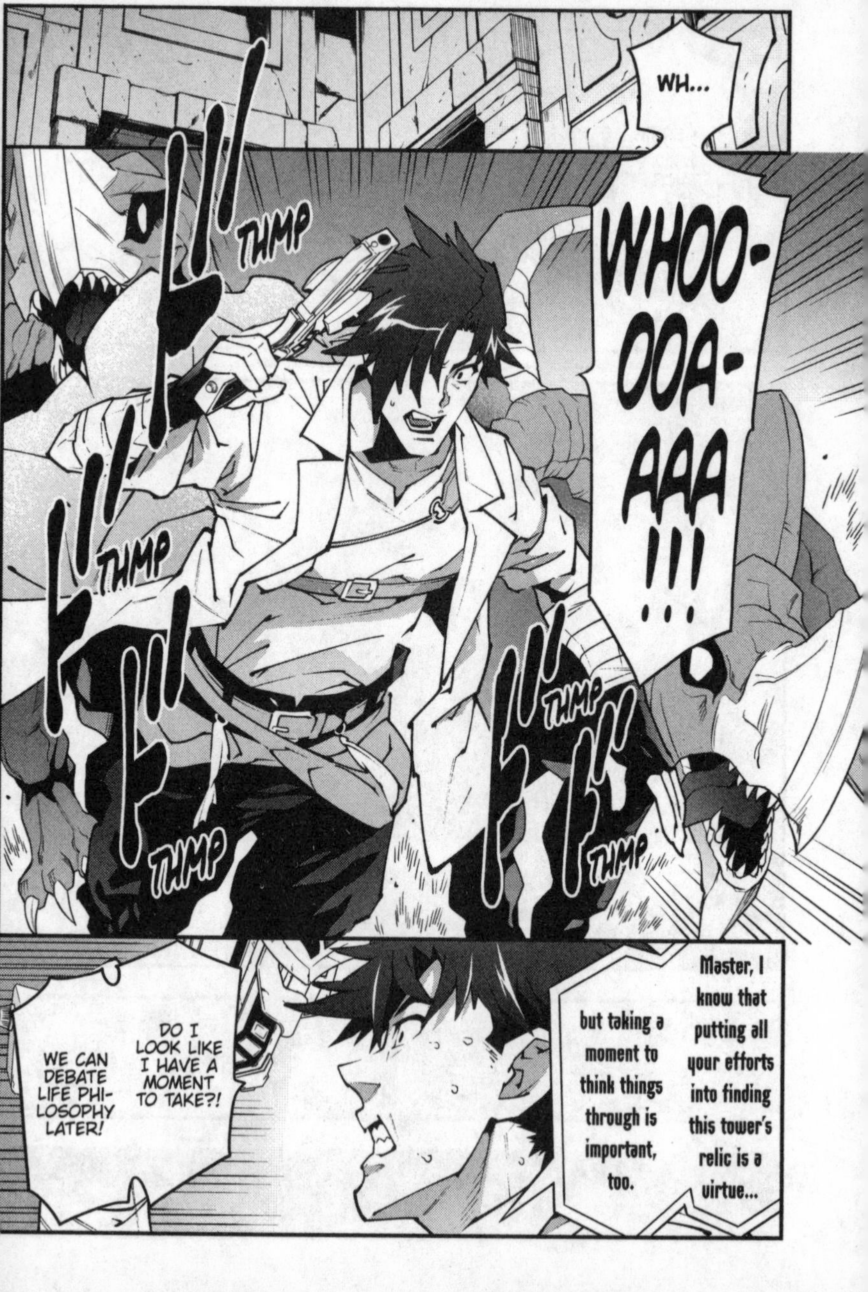
WH...
WHOOO-OOA-AAA!!!
THMP
THMP
THMP
THMP
THMP
Master, I know that putting all your efforts into finding this tower's relic is a virtue...
but taking a moment to think things through is important, too.
DO I LOOK LIKE I HAVE A MOMENT TO TAKE?!
WE CAN DEBATE LIFE PHILOSOPHY LATER!

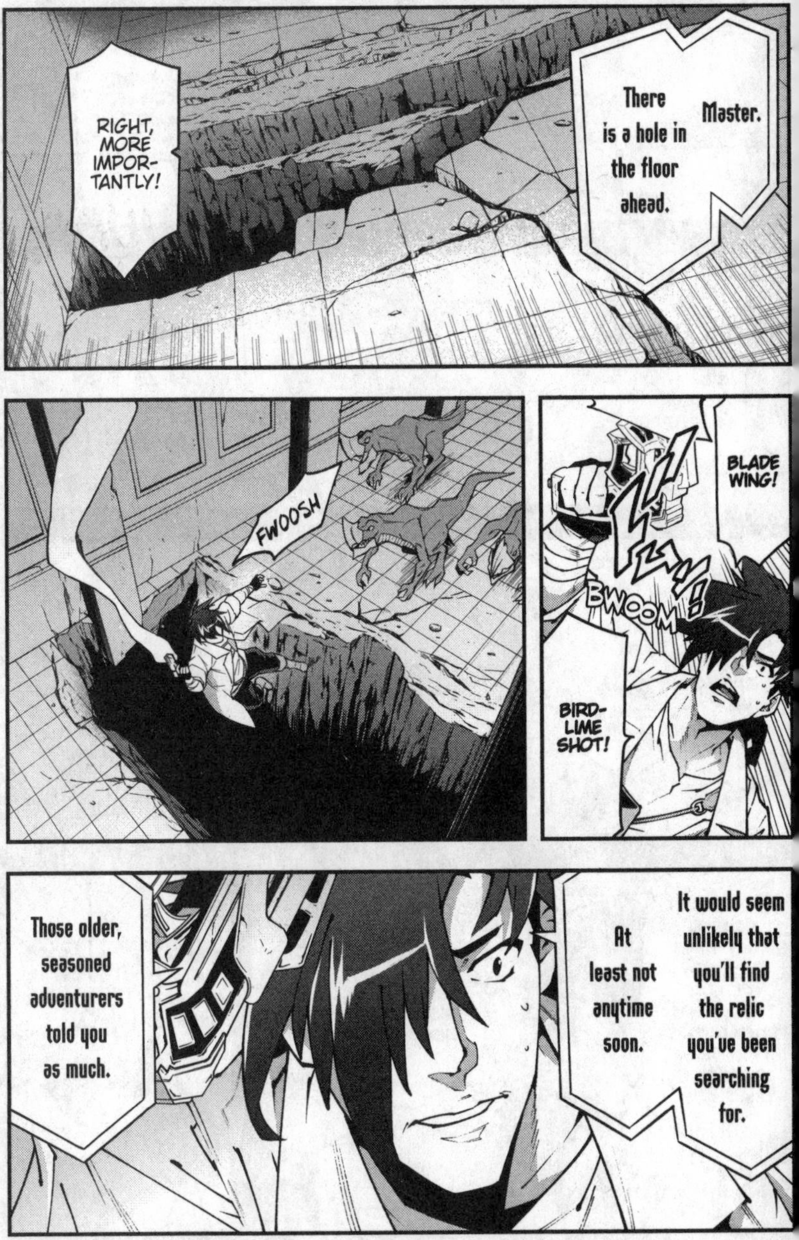
Master.
There is a hole in the floor ahead.
RIGHT, MORE IMPORTANTLY!
BLADE WING!
BWOOM!
BIRD-LIME SHOT!
FWOOSH
It would seem unlikely that you'll find the relic you've been searching for.
At least not anytime soon.
Those older, seasoned adventurers told you as much.

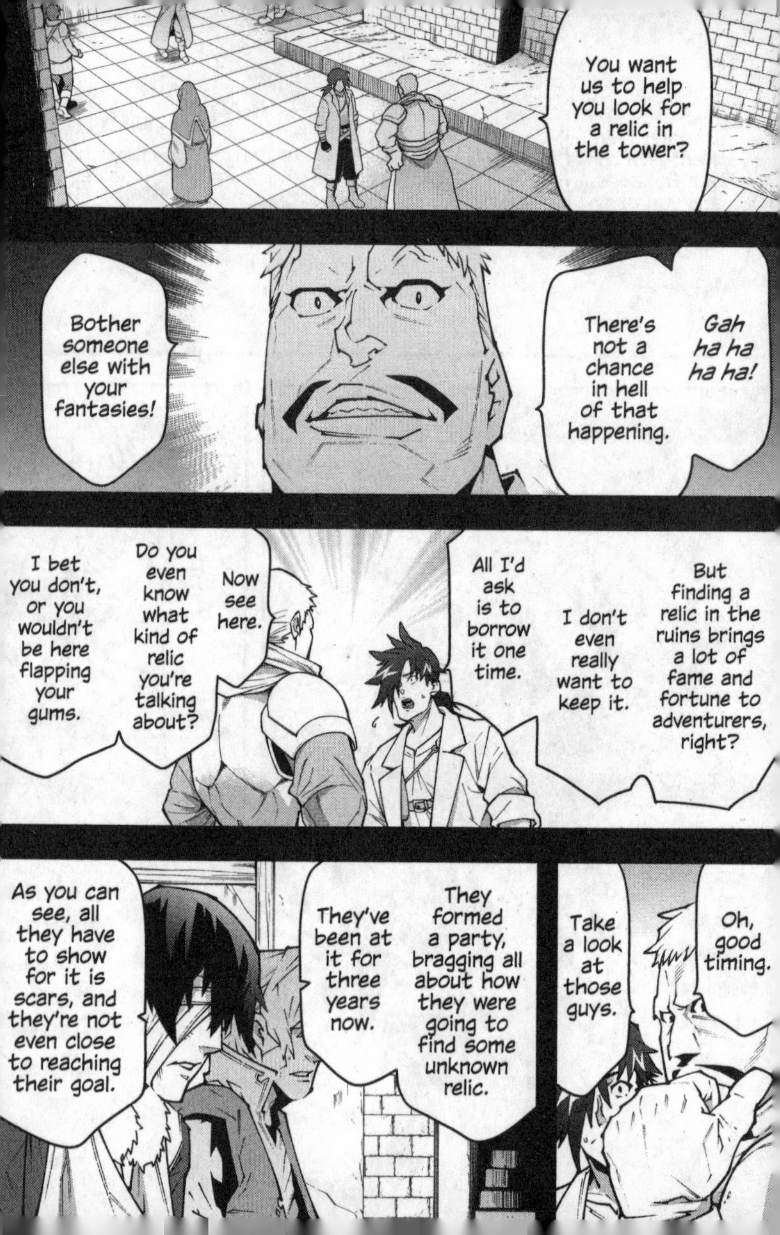
You want us to help you look for a relic in the tower?
Gah ha ha ha!
There's not a chance in hell of that happening.
Bother someone else with your fantasies!
But finding a relic in the ruins brings a lot of fame and fortune to adventurers, right?
I don't even really want to keep it.
All I'd ask is to borrow it one time.
Now see here.
Do you even know what kind of relic you're talking about?
I bet you don't, or you wouldn't be here flapping your gums.
Oh, good timing.
Take a look at those guys.
They formed a party, bragging all about how they were going to find some unknown relic.
They've been at it for three years now.
As you can see, all they have to show for it is scars, and they're not even close to reaching their goal.

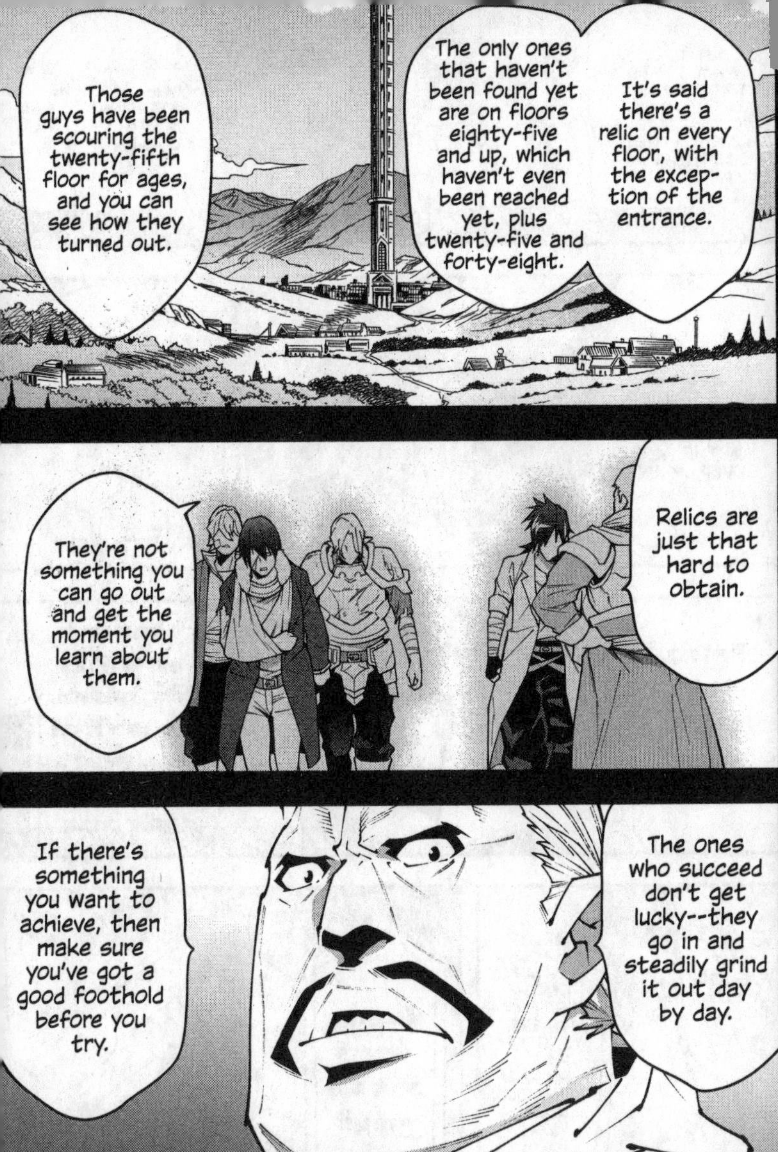
It's said there's a relic on every floor, with the excep- tion of the entrance.
The only ones that haven't been found yet are on floors eighty-five and up, which haven't even been reached yet, plus twenty-five and forty-eight.
Those guys have been scouring the twenty-fifth floor for ages, and you can see how they turned out.
Relics are just that hard to obtain.
They're not something you can go out and get the moment you learn about them.
The ones who succeed don't get lucky--they go in and steadily grind it out day by day.
If there's something you want to achieve, then make sure you've got a good foothold before you try.

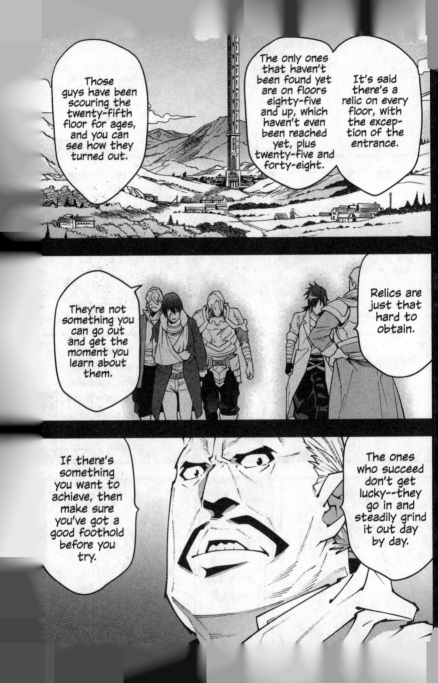

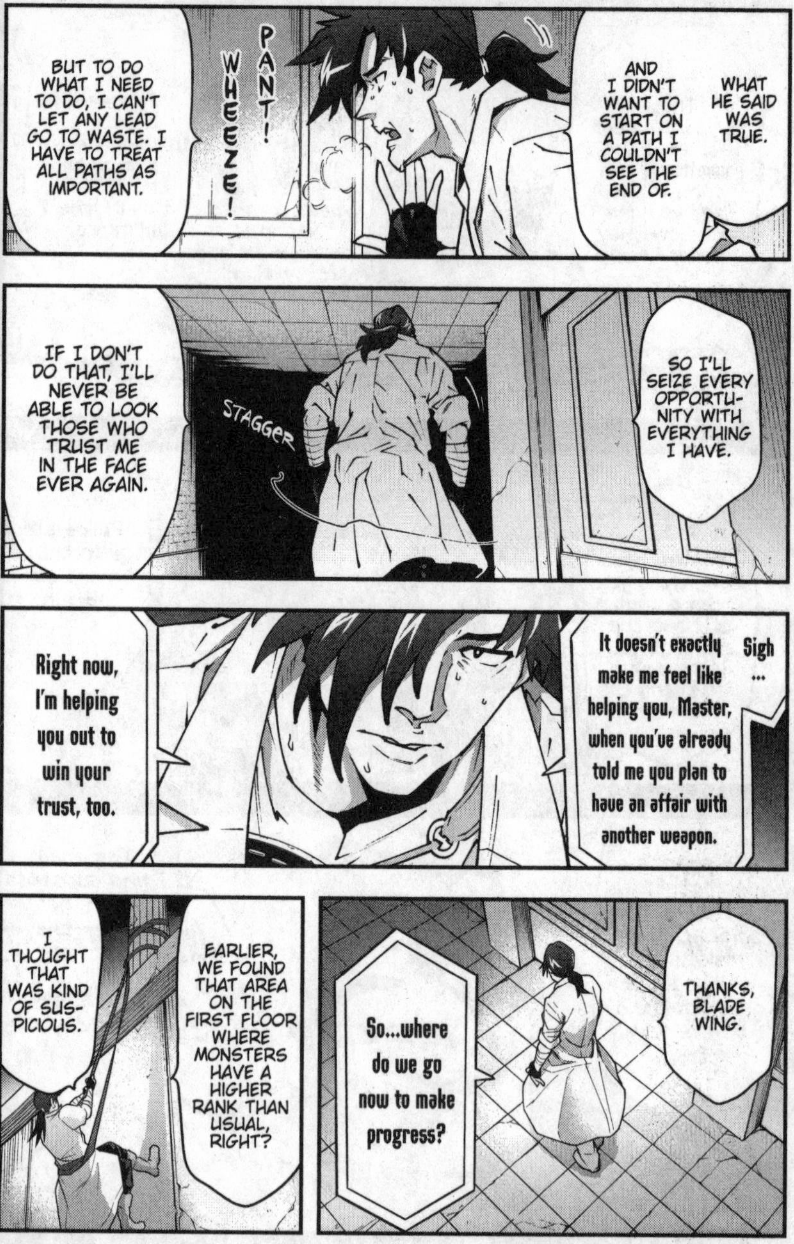
WHAT HE SAID WAS TRUE.
AND I DIDN'T WANT TO START ON A PATH I COULDN'T SEE THE END OF.
PANT!
WHEEZE!
BUT TO DO WHAT I NEED TO DO, I CAN'T LET ANY LEAD GO TO WASTE. I HAVE TO TREAT ALL PATHS AS IMPORTANT.
SO I'LL SEIZE EVERY OPPORTU-NITY WITH EVERYTHING I HAVE.
STAGGER
IF I DON'T DO THAT, I'LL NEVER BE ABLE TO LOOK THOSE WHO TRUST ME IN THE FACE EVER AGAIN.
Sigh...
It doesn't exactly make me feel like helping you, Master, when you've already told me you plan to have an affair with another weapon.
Right now, I'm helping you out to win your trust, too.
THANKS, BLADE WING.
So...where do we go now to make progress?
EARLIER, WE FOUND THAT AREA ON THE FIRST FLOOR WHERE MONSTERS HAVE A HIGHER RANK THAN USUAL, RIGHT?
I THOUGHT THAT WAS KIND OF SUS-PICIOUS.

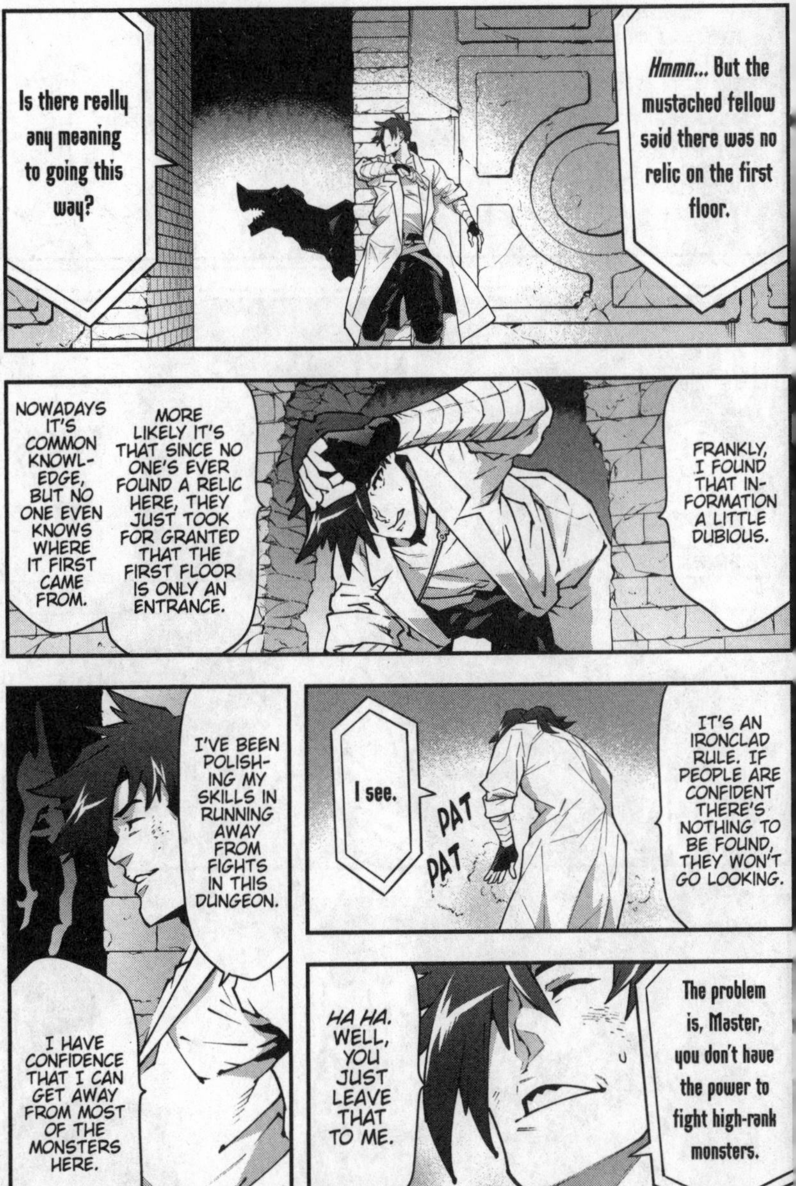
Hmmn... But the mustached fellow said there was no relic on the first floor.
Is there really any meaning to going this way?
FRANKLY, I FOUND THAT INFORMATION A LITTLE DUBIOUS.
MORE LIKELY IT'S THAT SINCE NO ONE'S EVER FOUND A RELIC HERE, THEY JUST TOOK FOR GRANTED THAT THE FIRST FLOOR IS ONLY AN ENTRANCE.
NOWADAYS IT'S COMMON KNOWLEDGE, BUT NO ONE EVEN KNOWS WHERE IT FIRST CAME FROM.
IT'S AN IRONCLAD RULE. IF PEOPLE ARE CONFIDENT THERE'S NOTHING TO BE FOUND, THEY WON'T GO LOOKING.
I see.
PAT PAT
The problem is, Master, you don't have the power to fight high-rank monsters.
HA HA. WELL, YOU JUST LEAVE THAT TO ME.
I'VE BEEN POLISHING MY SKILLS IN RUNNING AWAY FROM FIGHTS IN THIS DUNGEON.
I HAVE CONFIDENCE THAT I CAN GET AWAY FROM MOST OF THE MONSTERS HERE.

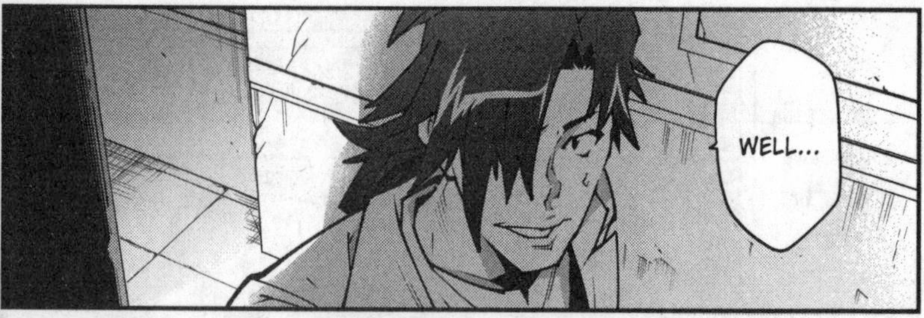
WELL...

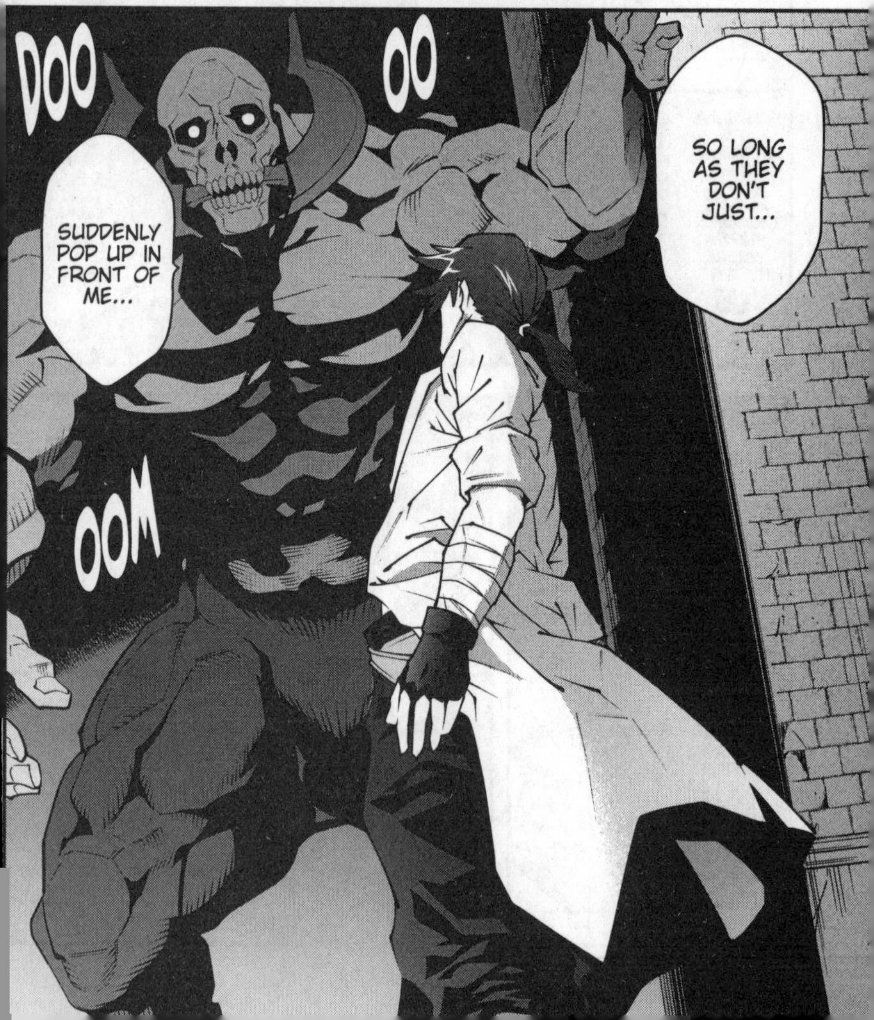
SO LONG AS THEY DON'T JUST...
DOO
OO
SUDDENLY POP UP IN FRONT OF ME...
OOM

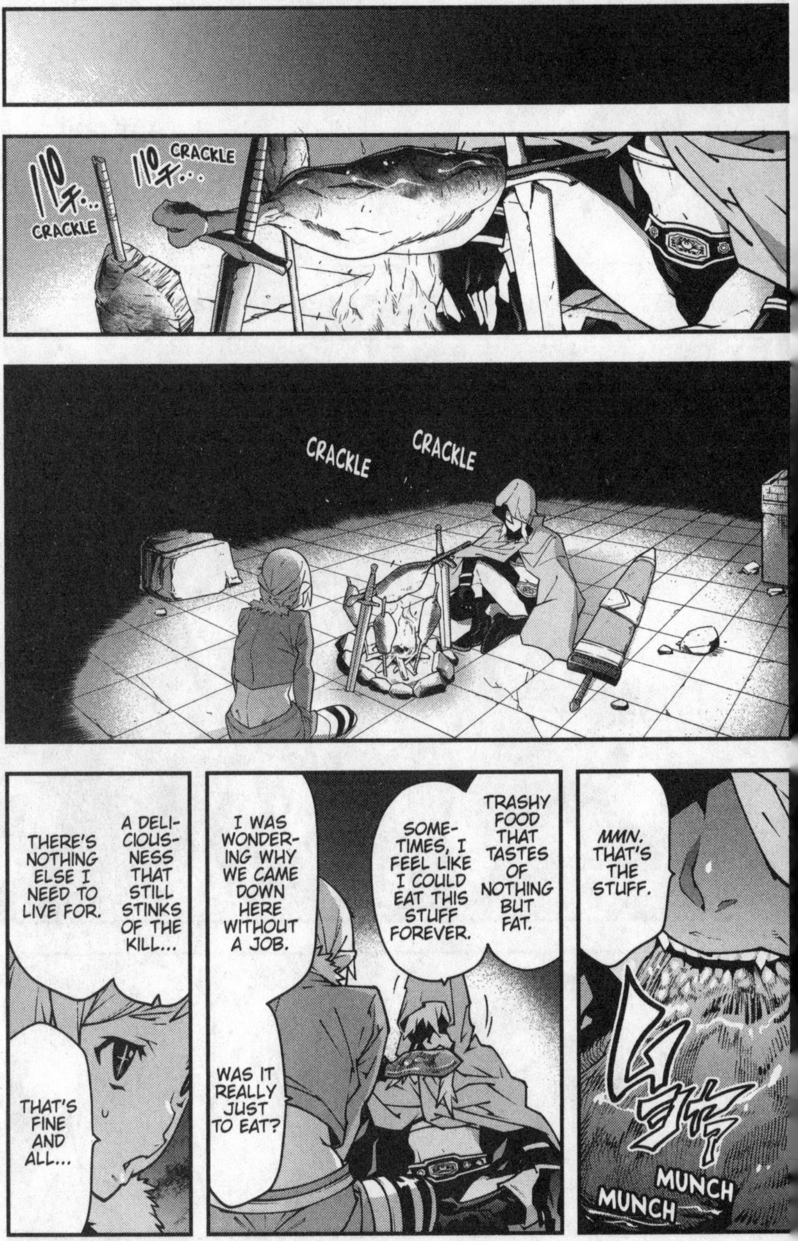
パチ...
CRACKLE
パチ...
CRACKLE
CRACKLE
CRACKLE
MMN. THAT'S THE STUFF.
MUNCH
MUNCH
TRASHY FOOD THAT TASTES OF NOTHING BUT FAT.
SOME-TIMES, I FEEL LIKE I COULD EAT THIS STUFF FOREVER.
I WAS WONDER-ING WHY WE CAME DOWN HERE WITHOUT A JOB.
WAS IT REALLY JUST TO EAT?
A DELI-CIOUS-NESS THAT STILL STINKS OF THE KILL...
THERE'S NOTHING ELSE I NEED TO LIVE FOR.
THAT'S FINE AND ALL...

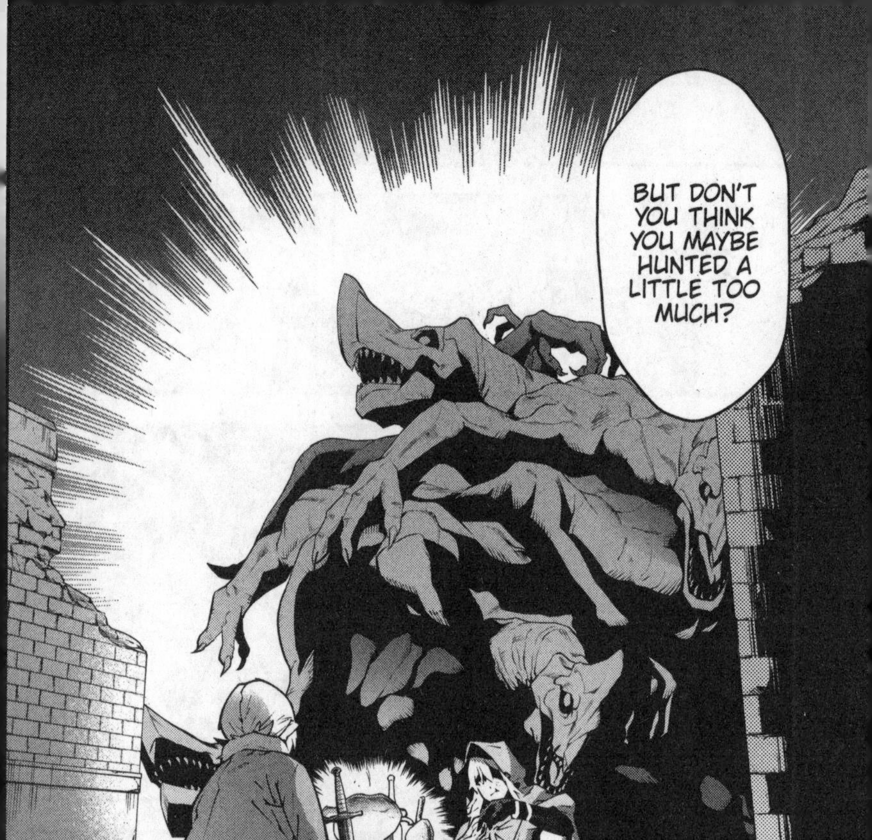
BUT DON'T YOU THINK YOU MAYBE HUNTED A LITTLE TOO MUCH?
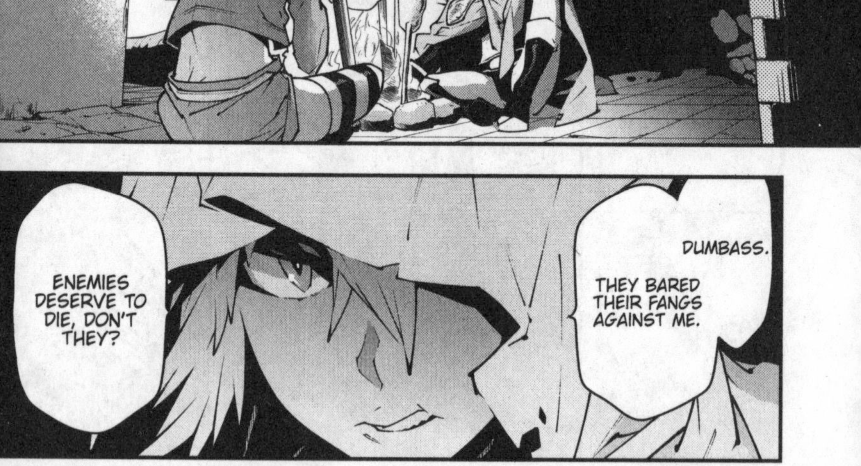
DUMBASS.
THEY BARED THEIR FANGS AGAINST ME.
ENEMIES DESERVE TO DIE, DON'T THEY?

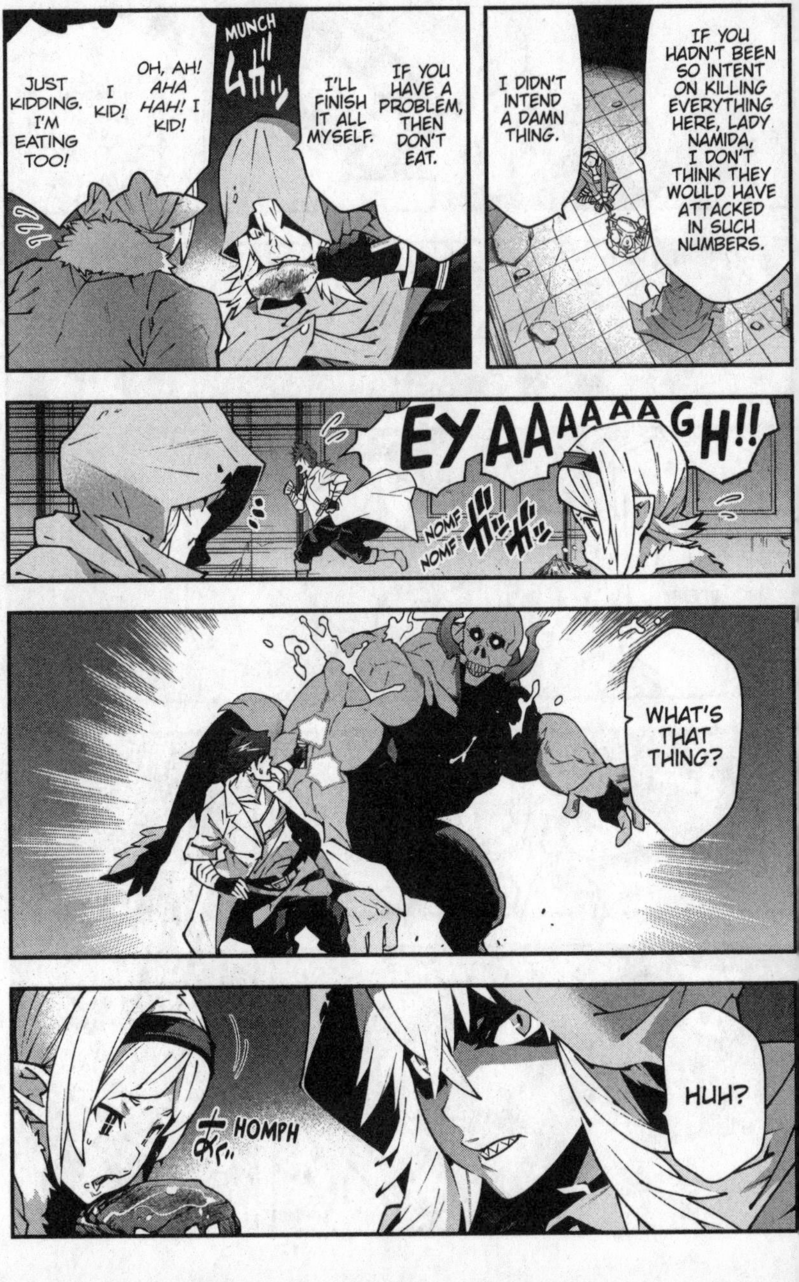
IF YOU HADN'T BEEN SO INTENT ON KILLING EVERYTHING HERE, LADY NAMIDA, I DON'T THINK THEY WOULD HAVE ATTACKED IN SUCH NUMBERS.
I DIDN'T INTEND A DAMN THING.
IF YOU HAVE A PROBLEM, THEN DON'T EAT.
I'LL FINISH IT ALL MYSELF.
MUNCH
OH, AH! *AHA HAH!* I KID!
I KID!
JUST KIDDING. I'M EATING TOO!
EYAAAAAAGH!!
NOMF NOMF
WHAT'S THAT THING?
HUH?
HOMPH

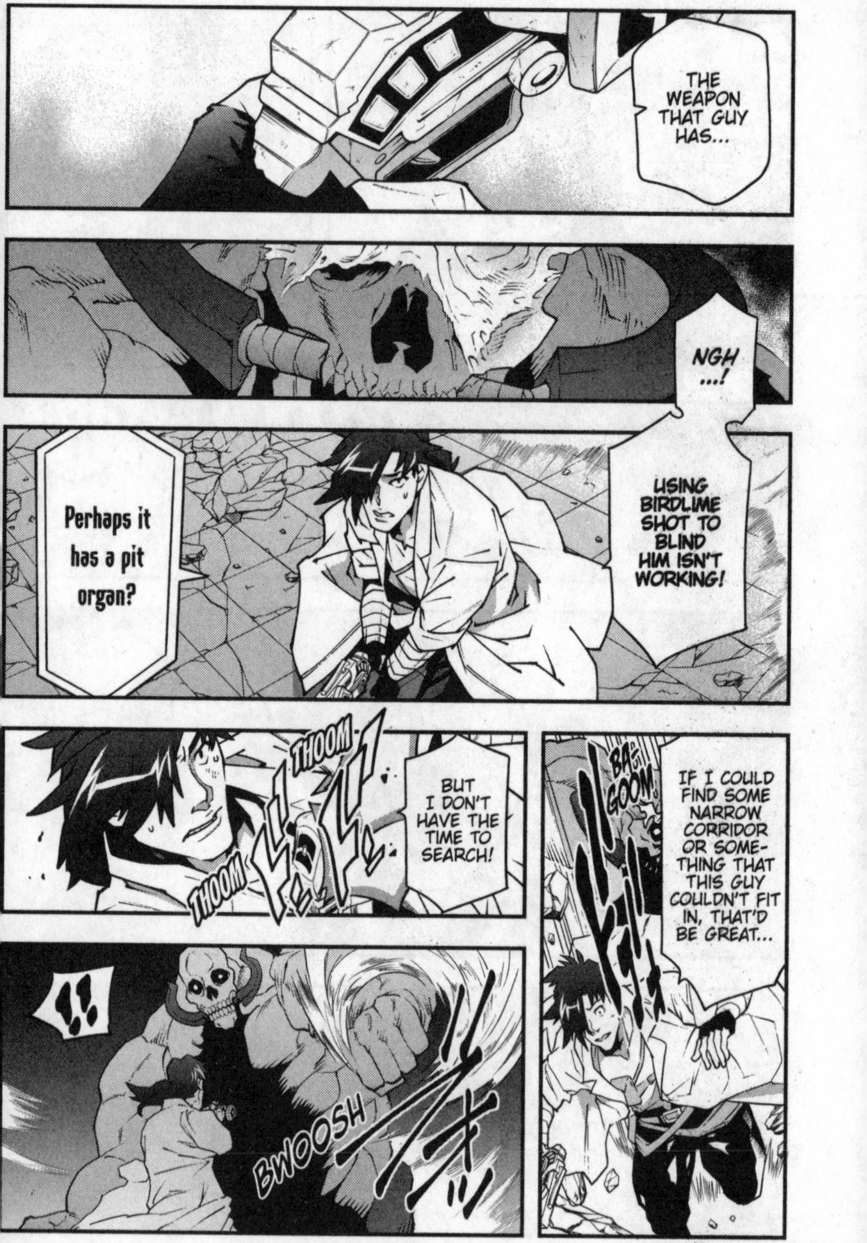
THE WEAPON THAT GUY HAS...
NGH ...!
USING BIRDLIME SHOT TO BLIND HIM ISN'T WORKING!
Perhaps it has a pit organ?
BA-GOON
IF I COULD FIND SOME NARROW CORRIDOR OR SOME-THING THAT THIS GUY COULDN'T FIT IN, THAT'D BE GREAT...
THOOM
BUT I DON'T HAVE THE TIME TO SEARCH!
THOOM
!!
BWOOSH

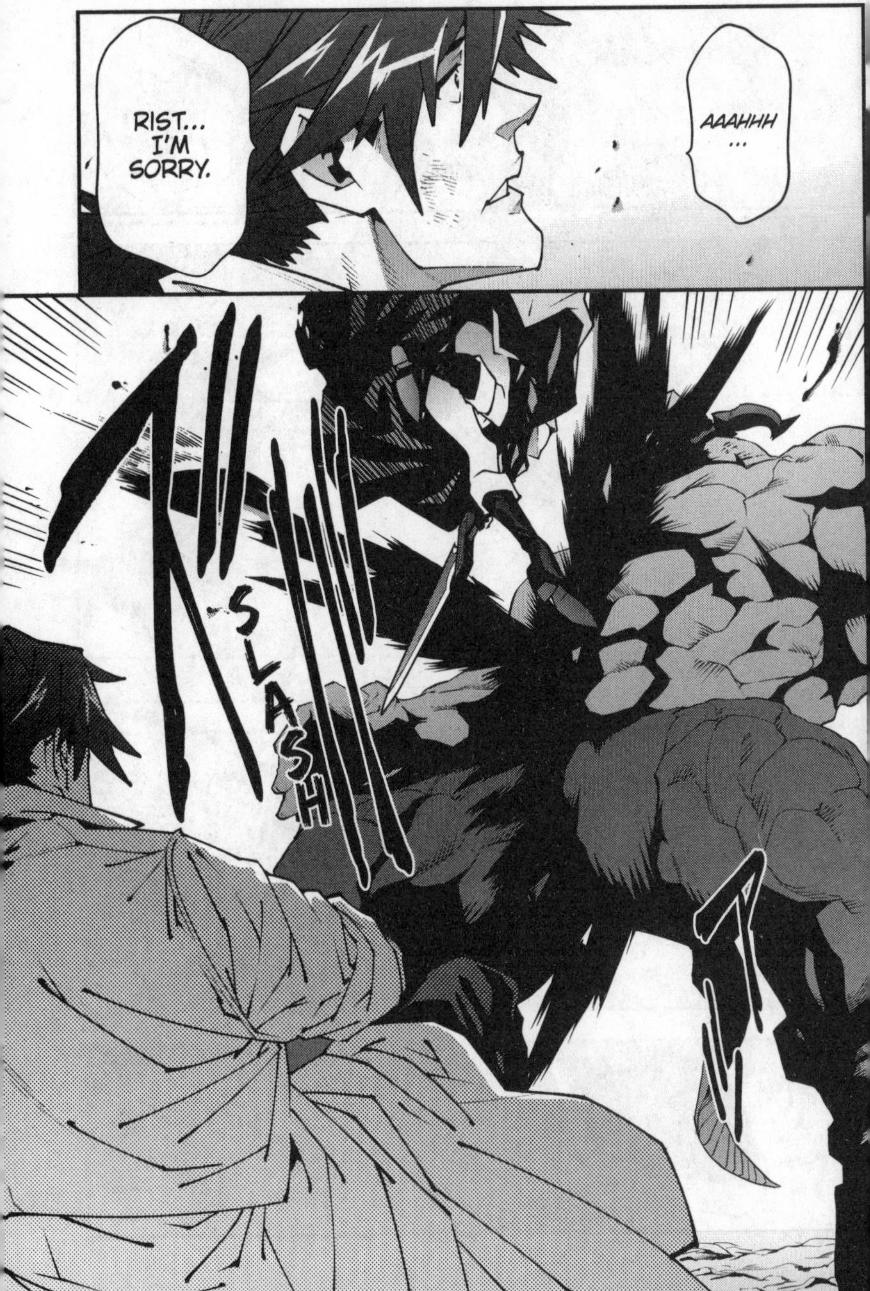
AAAHHH ...
RIST... I'M SORRY.
SLASH

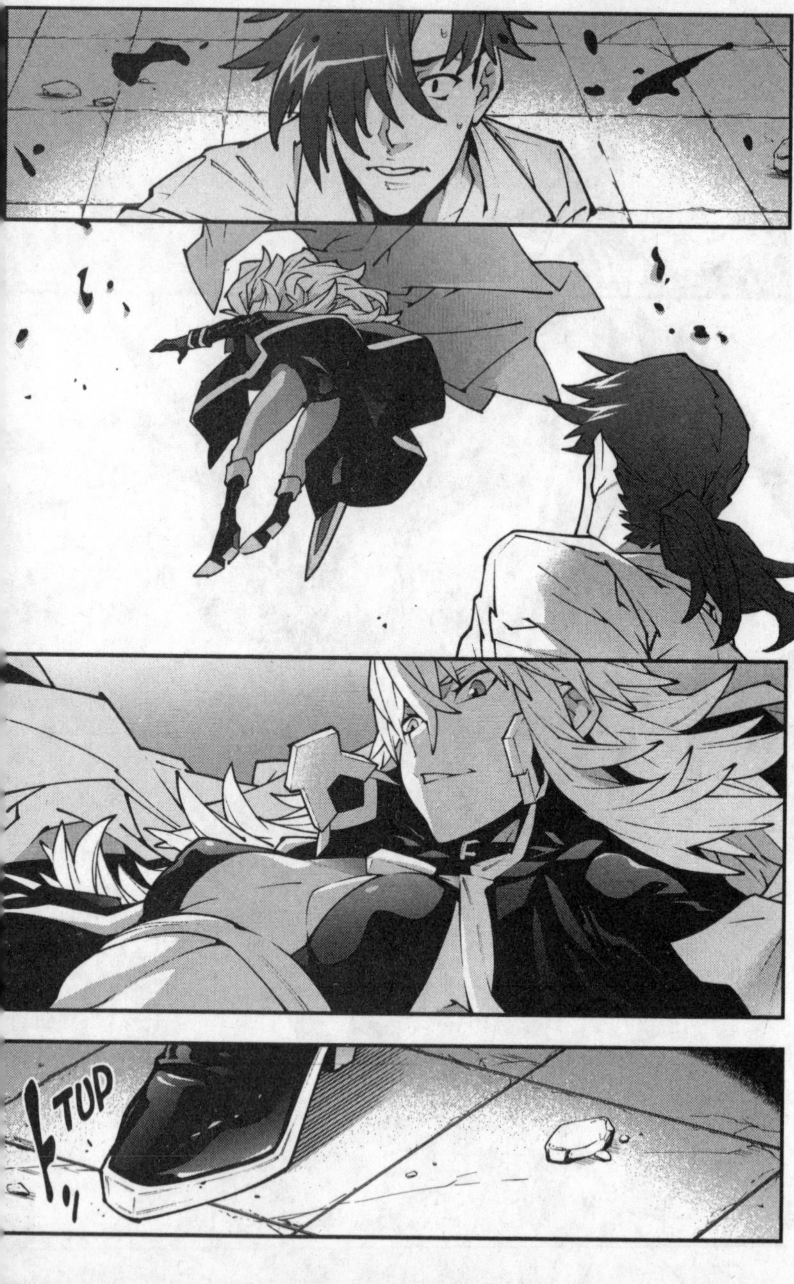
TUP

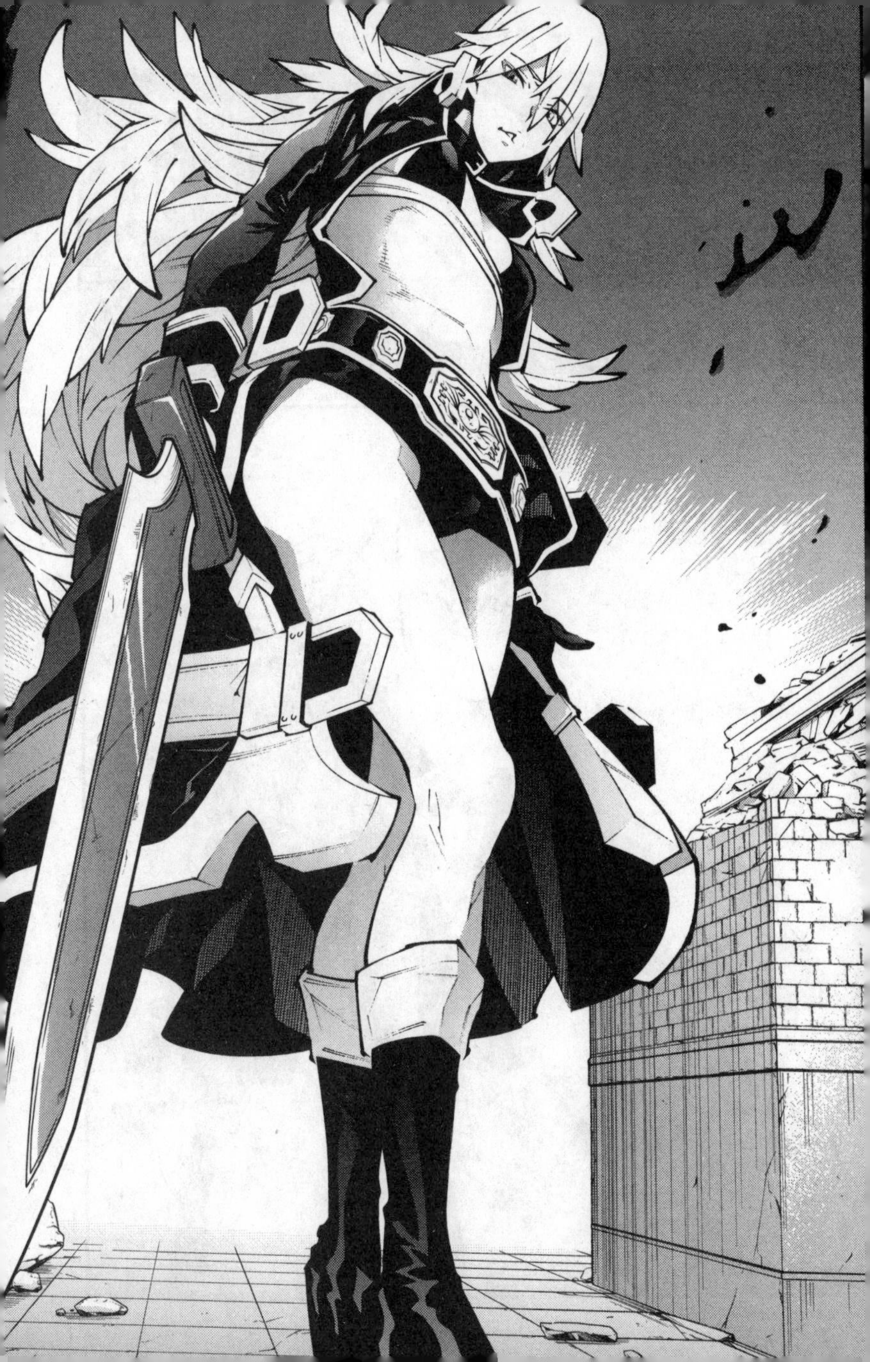

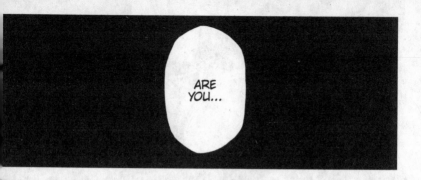

ARE
YOU...

ARE
YOU PART
OF MY
FAMILY?

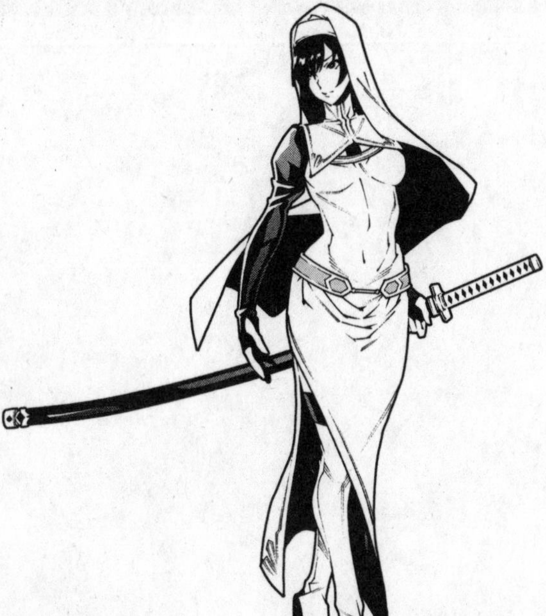

TACT RIST	MUJINZOU	REPEATEDLY TAP PUNCH
	ELEGANT ANNIHILATION	HOLD ← FOR A MOMENT THEN PRESS → PUNCH
	MUTOURYOUDAN	↓↘→THEN PRESS PUNCH
	???	???????

THE DUNGEON OF
BLACK COMPANY

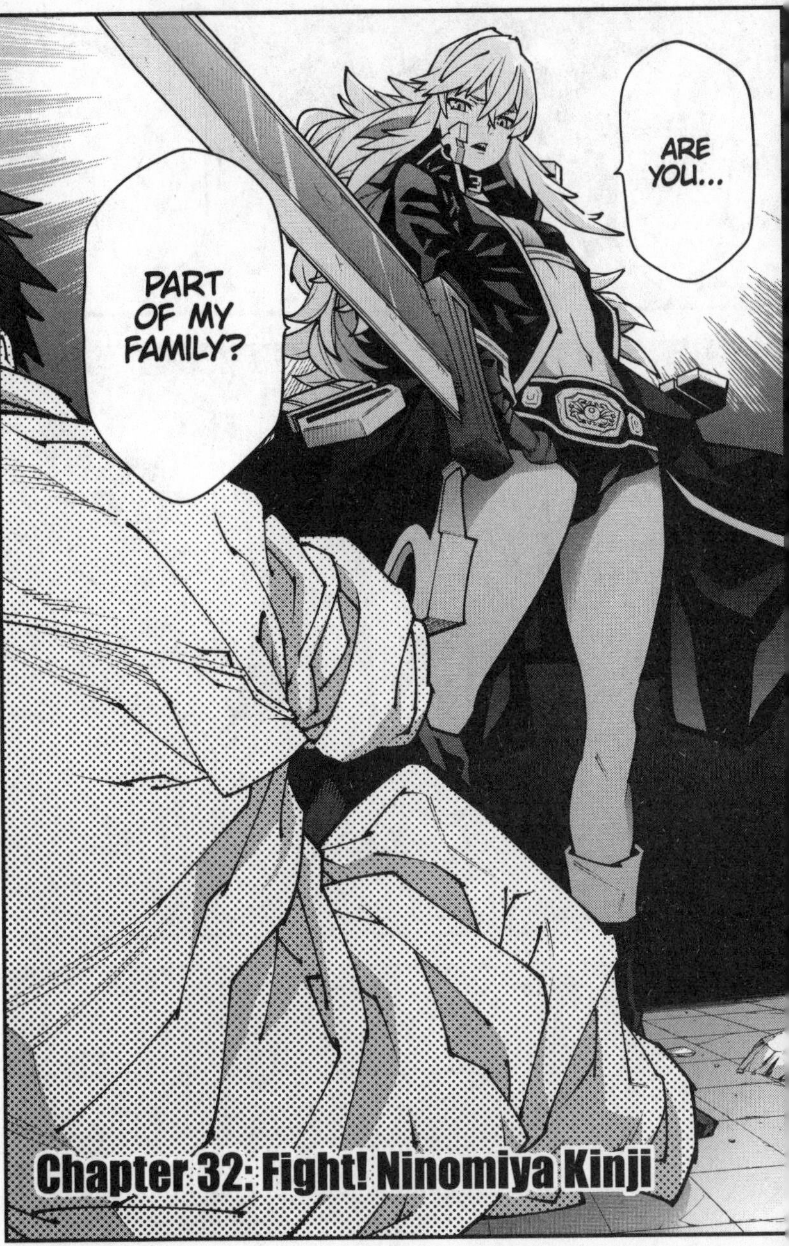
ARE YOU...
PART OF MY FAMILY?
Chapter 32: Fight! Ninomiya Kinji

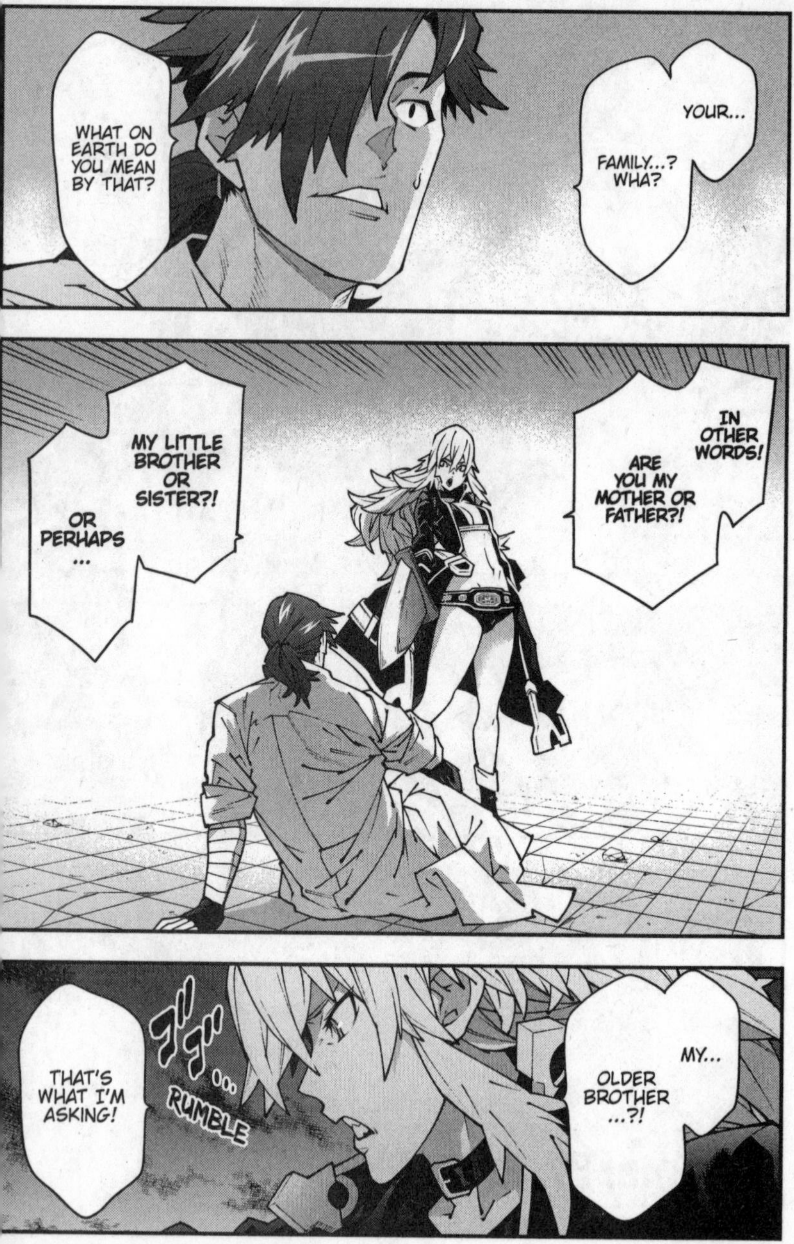
YOUR...
FAMILY...? WHA?
WHAT ON EARTH DO YOU MEAN BY THAT?
IN OTHER WORDS!
ARE YOU MY MOTHER OR FATHER?!
MY LITTLE BROTHER OR SISTER?!
OR PERHAPS ...
MY...
OLDER BROTHER ...?!
RUMBLE
THAT'S WHAT I'M ASKING!

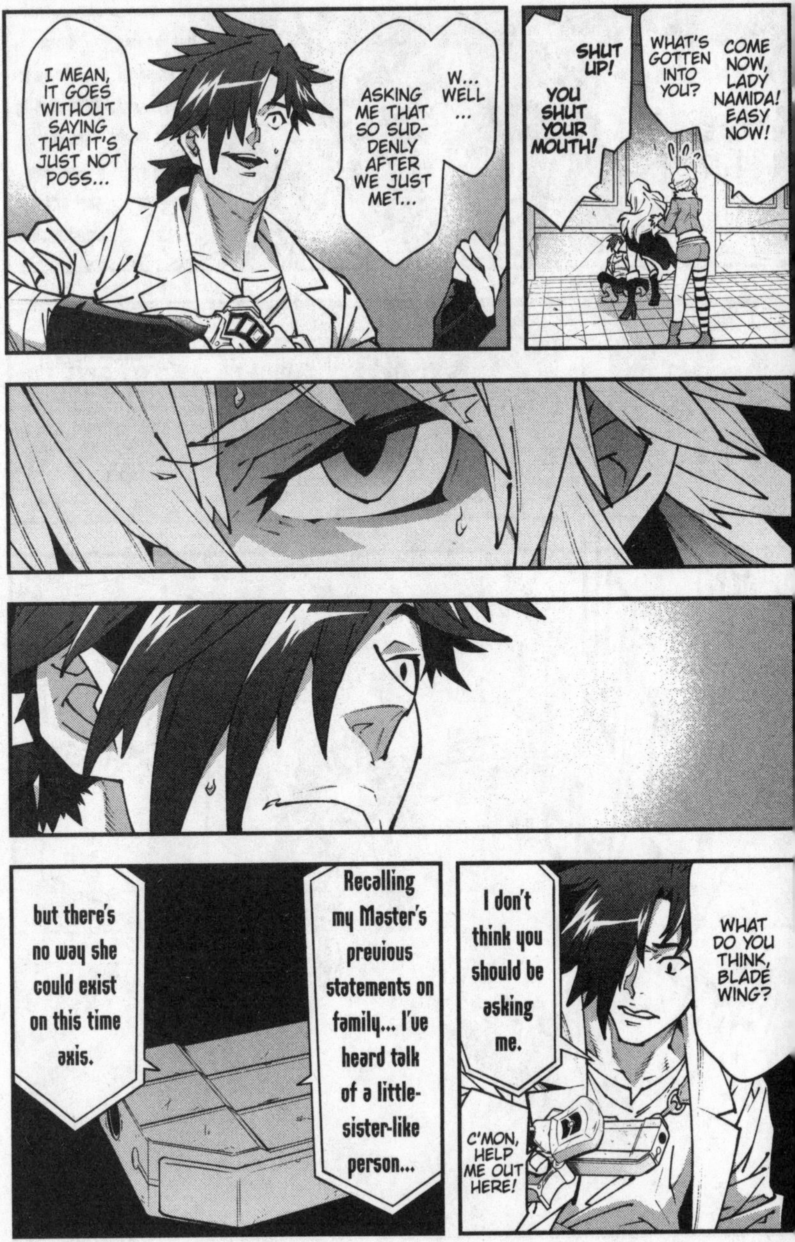
COME NOW, LADY NAMIDA! EASY NOW!
WHAT'S GOTTEN INTO YOU?
SHUT UP!
YOU SHUT YOUR MOUTH!
W... WELL ...
ASKING ME THAT SO SUD-DENLY AFTER WE JUST MET...
I MEAN, IT GOES WITHOUT SAYING THAT IT'S JUST NOT POSS...
WHAT DO YOU THINK, BLADE WING?
C'MON, HELP ME OUT HERE!
I don't think you should be asking me.
Recalling my Master's previous statements on family... I've heard talk of a little-sister-like person...
but there's no way she could exist on this time axis.

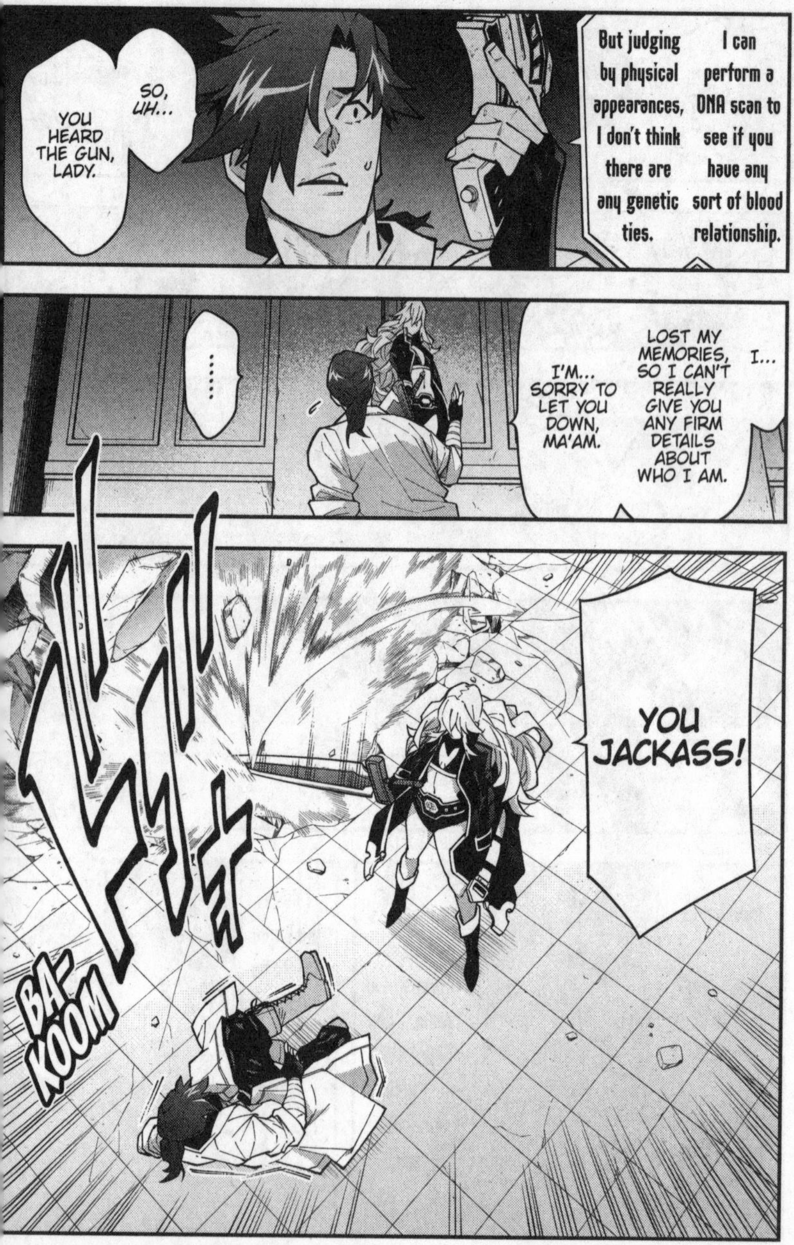
I can perform a DNA scan to see if you have any sort of blood relationship.
But judging by physical appearances, I don't think there are any genetic ties.
SO, UH...
YOU HEARD THE GUN, LADY.
I...
LOST MY MEMORIES, SO I CAN'T REALLY GIVE YOU ANY FIRM DETAILS ABOUT WHO I AM.
I'M... SORRY TO LET YOU DOWN, MA'AM.
......
YOU JACKASS!
BA-KOOM

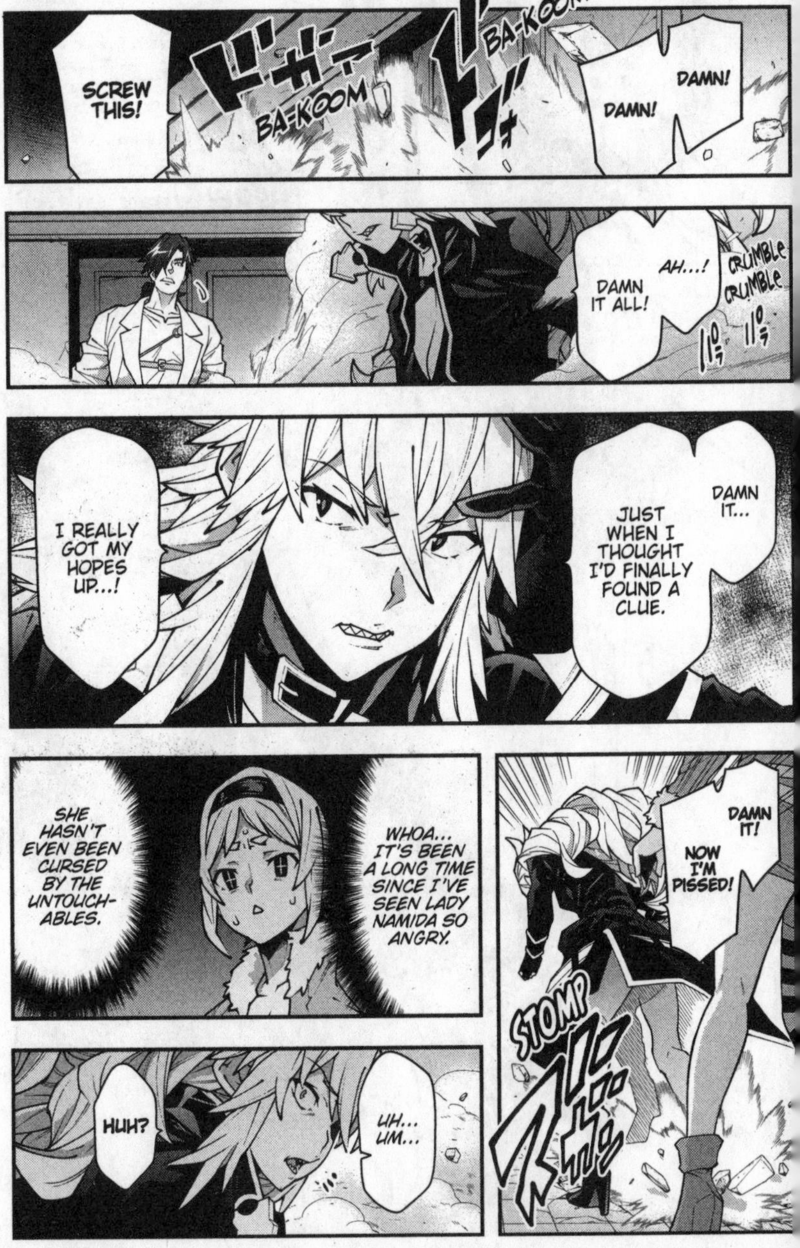
DAMN!
DAMN!
BA-KOOM
BA-KOOM
SCREW THIS!
AH...!
DAMN IT ALL!
CRUMBLE CRUMBLE
DAMN IT...
JUST WHEN I THOUGHT I'D FINALLY FOUND A CLUE.
I REALLY GOT MY HOPES UP...!
DAMN IT!
NOW I'M PISSED!
STOMP
WHOA... IT'S BEEN A LONG TIME SINCE I'VE SEEN LADY NAMIDA SO ANGRY.
SHE HASN'T EVEN BEEN CURSED BY THE UNTOUCH-ABLES.
UH... UM...
HUH?

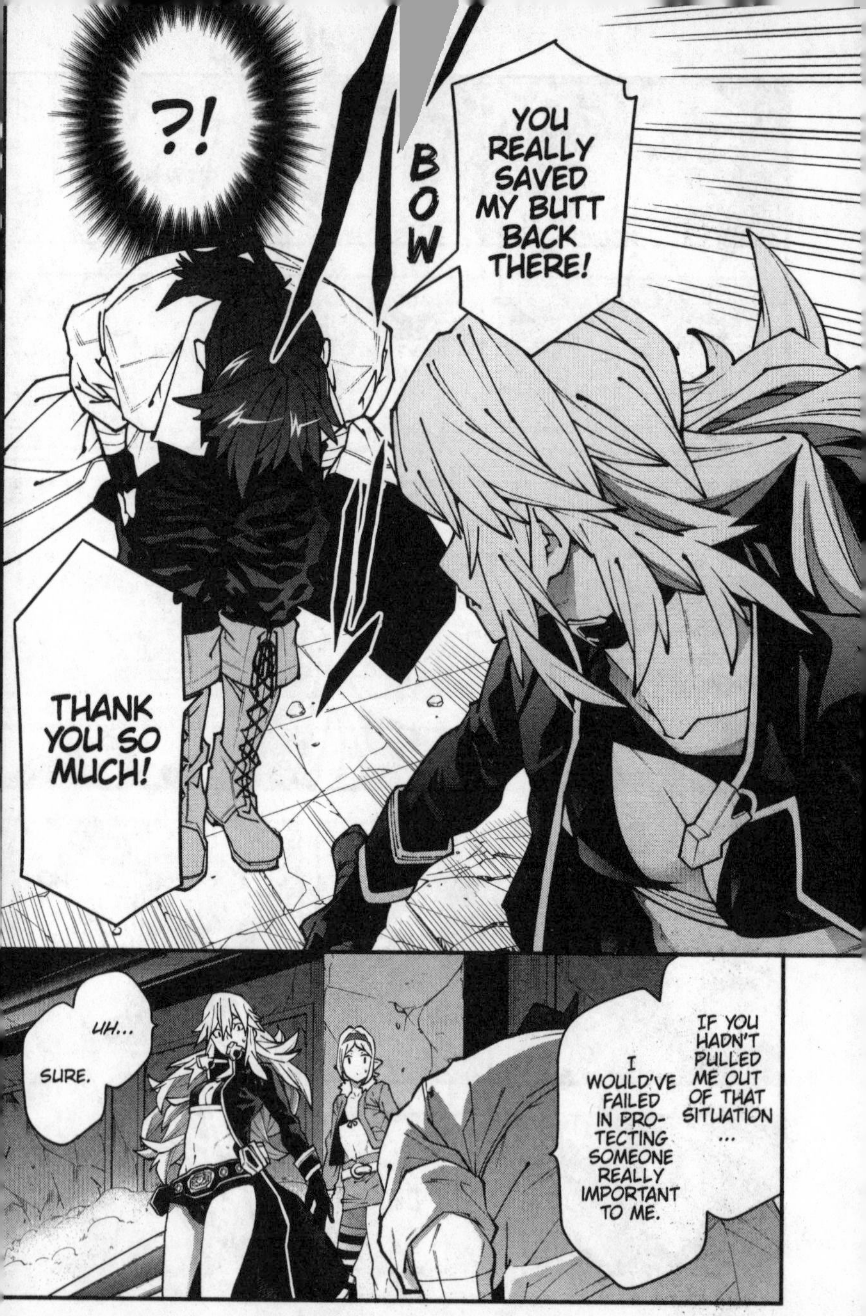
YOU REALLY SAVED MY BUTT BACK THERE!
BOW
?!
THANK YOU SO MUCH!
IF YOU HADN'T PULLED ME OUT OF THAT SITUATION ...
I WOULD'VE FAILED IN PROTECTING SOMEONE REALLY IMPORTANT TO ME.
UH... SURE.

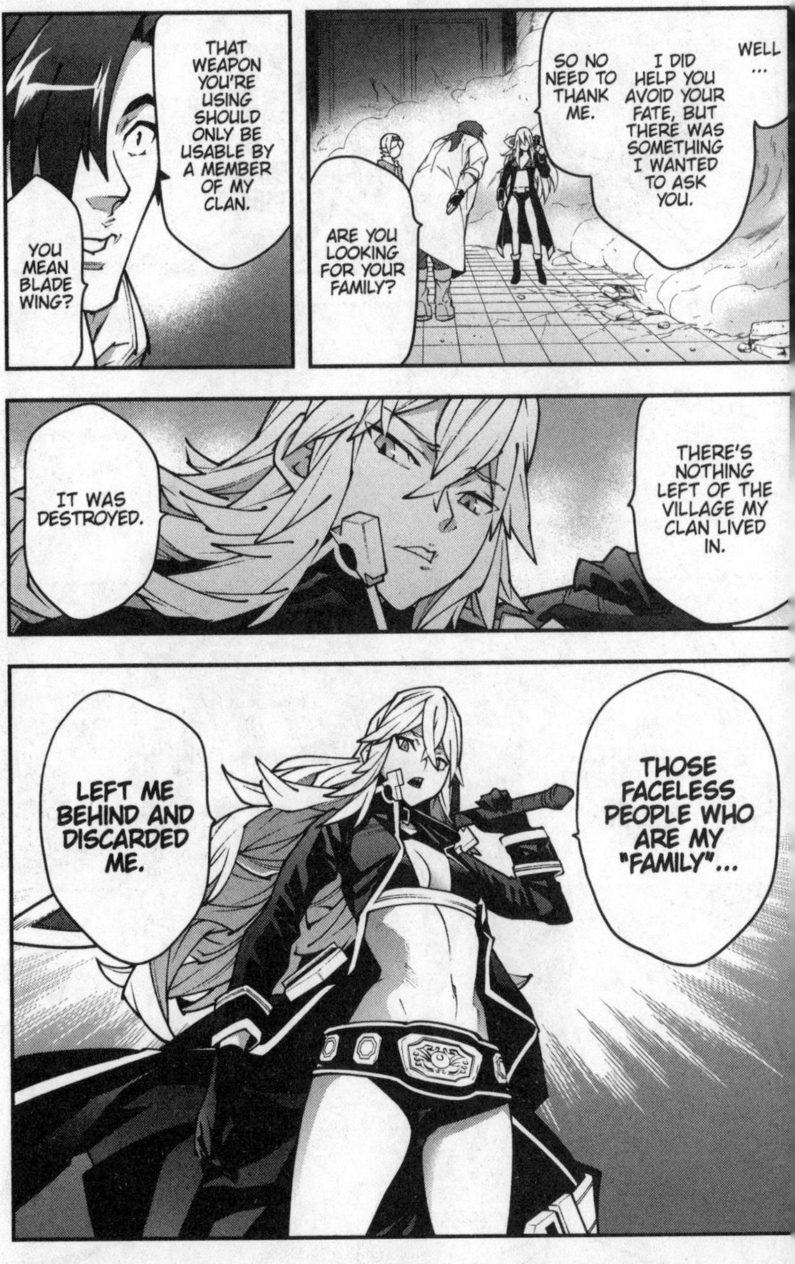
WELL ...
I DID HELP YOU AVOID YOUR FATE, BUT THERE WAS SOMETHING I WANTED TO ASK YOU.
SO NO NEED TO THANK ME.
ARE YOU LOOKING FOR YOUR FAMILY?
THAT WEAPON YOU'RE USING SHOULD ONLY BE USABLE BY A MEMBER OF MY CLAN.
YOU MEAN BLADE WING?
THERE'S NOTHING LEFT OF THE VILLAGE MY CLAN LIVED IN.
IT WAS DESTROYED.
THOSE FACELESS PEOPLE WHO ARE MY "FAMILY"...
LEFT ME BEHIND AND DISCARDED ME.

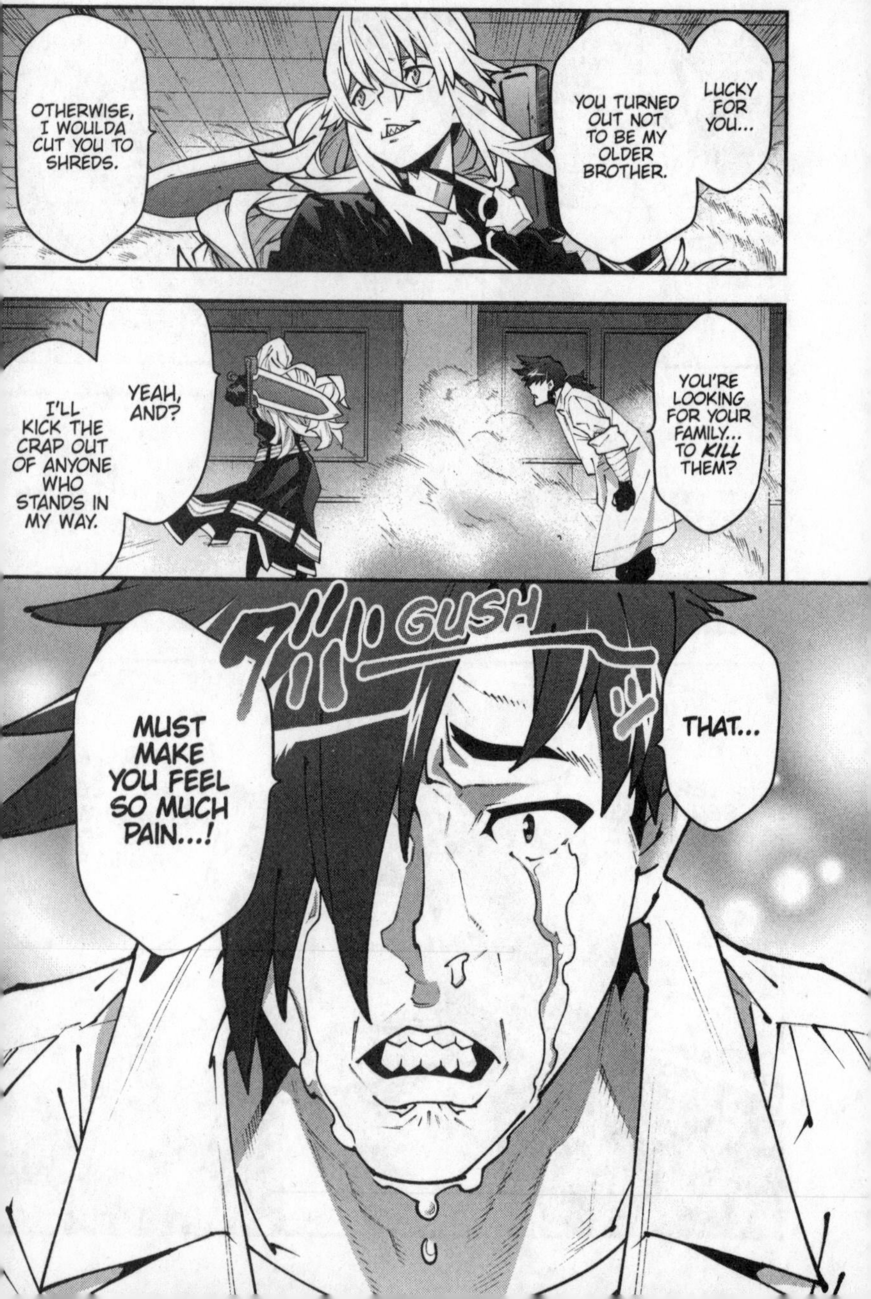
LUCKY FOR YOU...
YOU TURNED OUT NOT TO BE MY OLDER BROTHER.
OTHERWISE, I WOULDA CUT YOU TO SHREDS.
YOU'RE LOOKING FOR YOUR FAMILY... TO *KILL* THEM?
YEAH, AND?
I'LL KICK THE CRAP OUT OF ANYONE WHO STANDS IN MY WAY.
GUSH
THAT...
MUST MAKE YOU FEEL SO MUCH PAIN...!

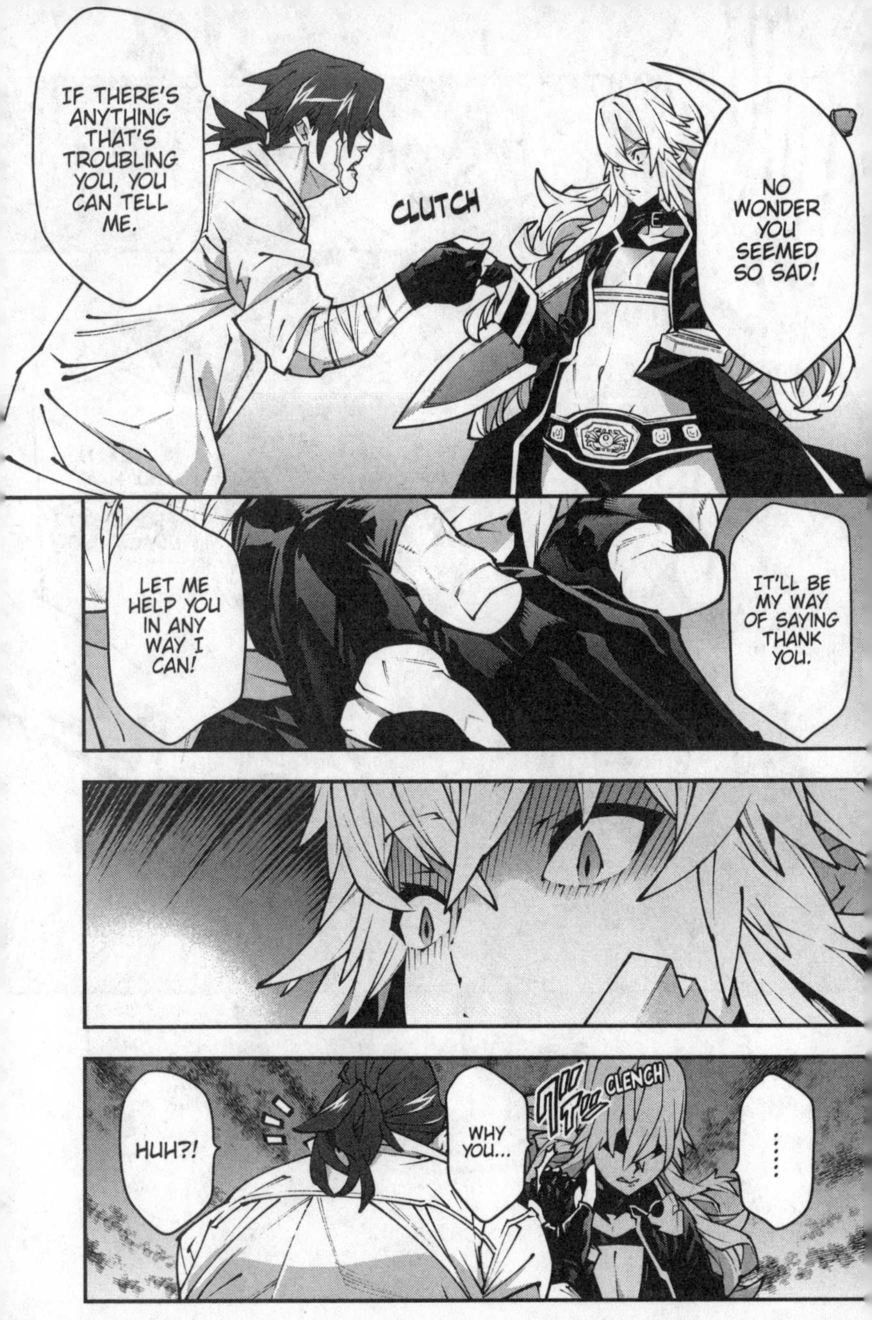
NO WONDER YOU SEEMED SO SAD!
CLUTCH
IF THERE'S ANYTHING THAT'S TROUBLING YOU, YOU CAN TELL ME.
IT'LL BE MY WAY OF SAYING THANK YOU.
LET ME HELP YOU IN ANY WAY I CAN!
......
CLENCH
WHY YOU...
HUH?!

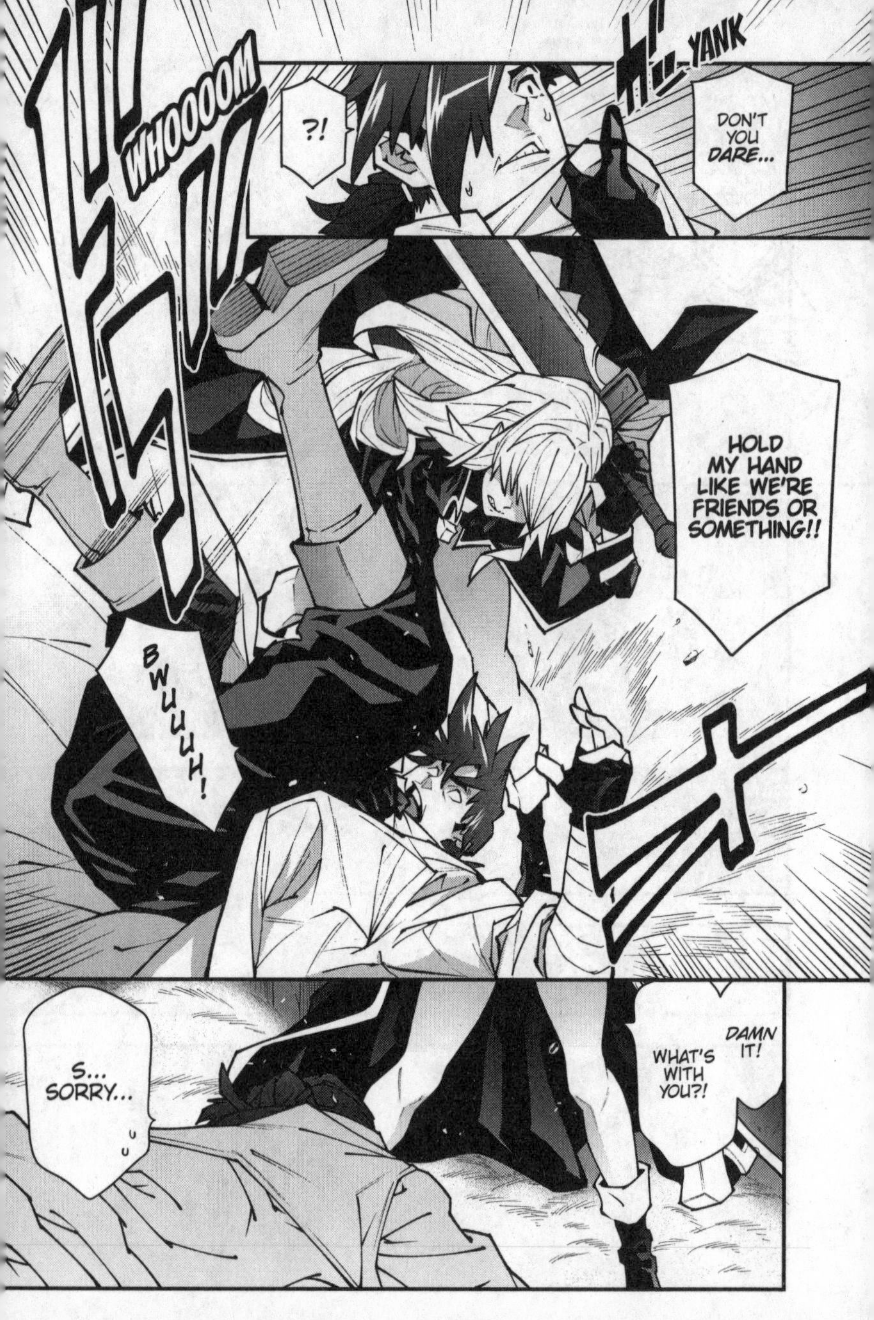
YANK
DON'T YOU DARE...
?!
WHOOOOM
HOLD MY HAND LIKE WE'RE FRIENDS OR SOMETHING!!
BWUUUH!
DAMN IT!
WHAT'S WITH YOU?!
S... SORRY...

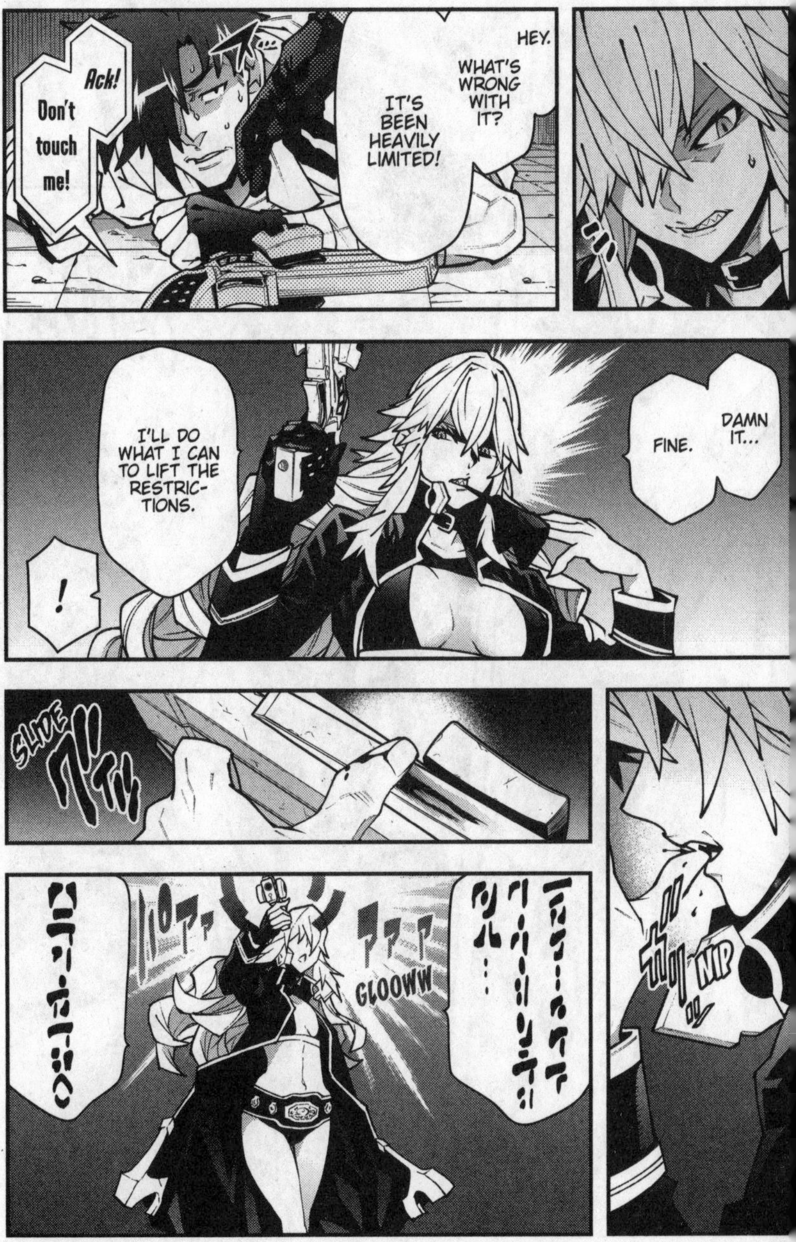
HEY.
WHAT'S WRONG WITH IT?
IT'S BEEN HEAVILY LIMITED!
Ack! Don't touch me!
FINE. DAMN IT...
I'LL DO WHAT I CAN TO LIFT THE RESTRIC-TIONS.
!
NIP
SLIDE
GLOOWW

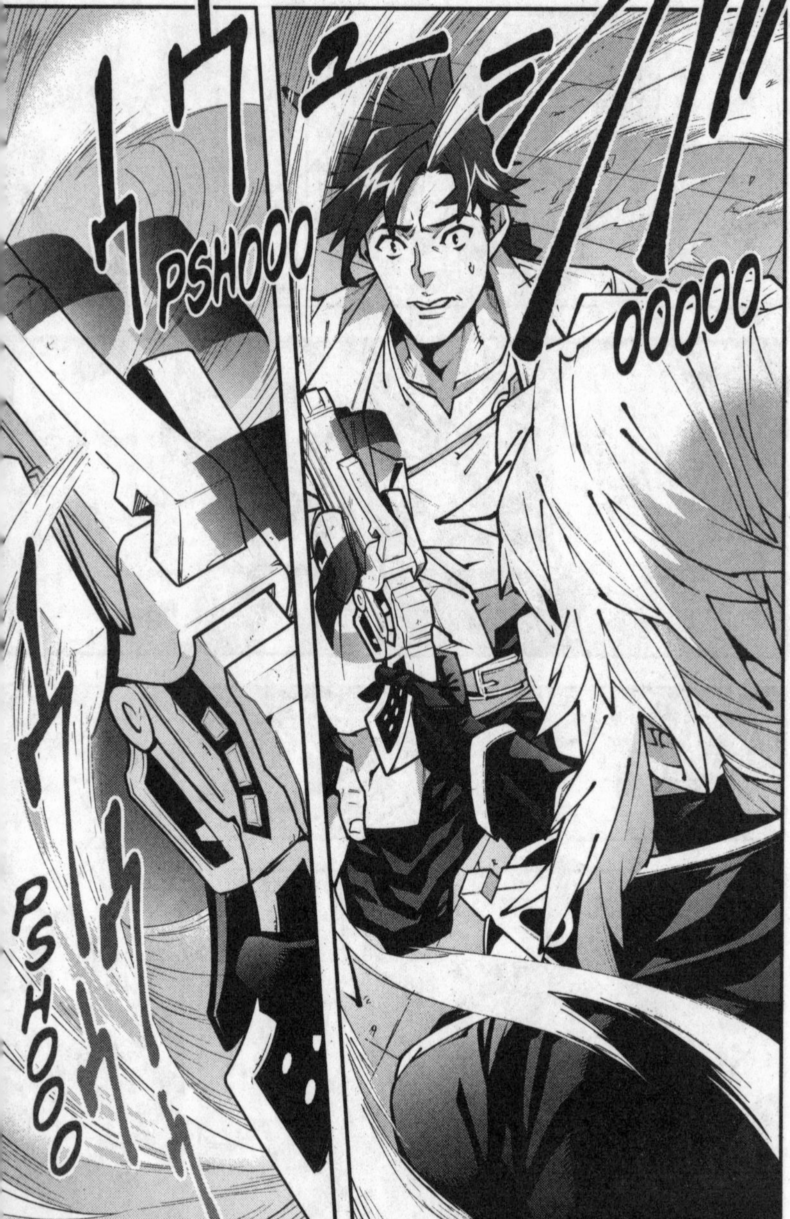
PSHOOO
OOOOO
PSHOOOO

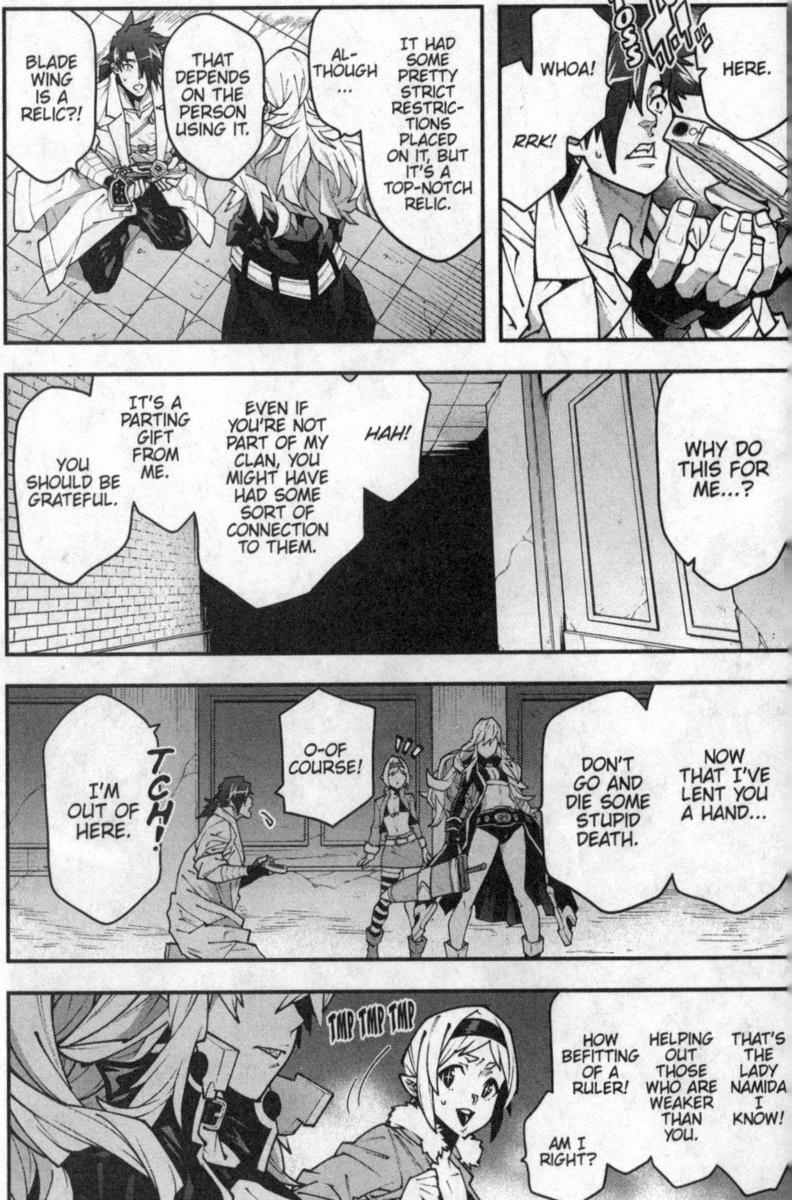
TOSS
HERE.
WHOA!
RRK!
IT HAD SOME PRETTY STRICT RESTRICTIONS PLACED ON IT, BUT IT'S A TOP-NOTCH RELIC.
ALTHOUGH...
THAT DEPENDS ON THE PERSON USING IT.
BLADE WING IS A RELIC?!
WHY DO THIS FOR ME...?
HAH!
EVEN IF YOU'RE NOT PART OF MY CLAN, YOU MIGHT HAVE HAD SOME SORT OF CONNECTION TO THEM.
IT'S A PARTING GIFT FROM ME.
YOU SHOULD BE GRATEFUL.
NOW THAT I'VE LENT YOU A HAND...
DON'T GO AND DIE SOME STUPID DEATH.
O-OF COURSE!
TCH!
I'M OUT OF HERE.
THAT'S THE LADY NAMIDA I KNOW!
HELPING OUT THOSE WHO ARE WEAKER THAN YOU.
HOW BEFITTING OF A RULER!
AM I RIGHT?
TMP TMP TMP

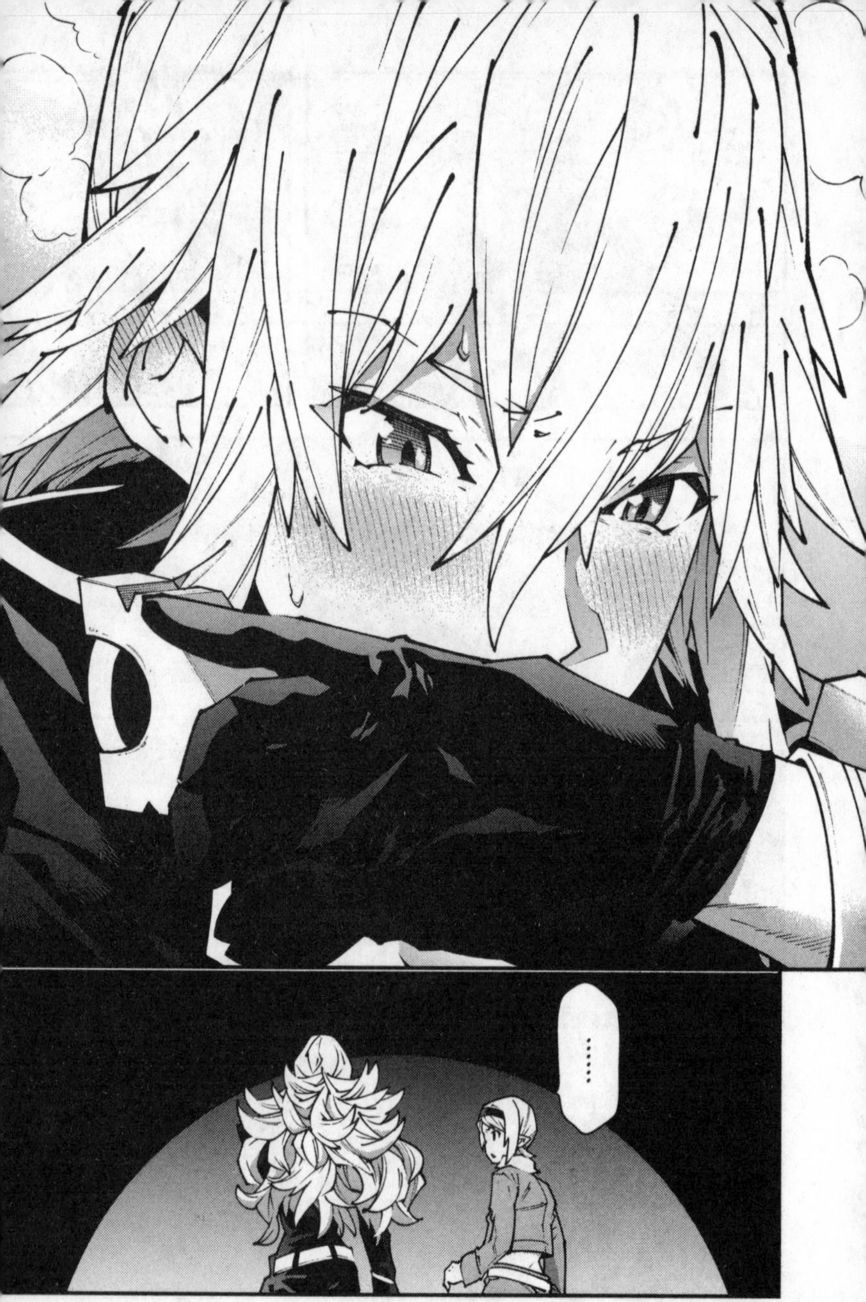
……

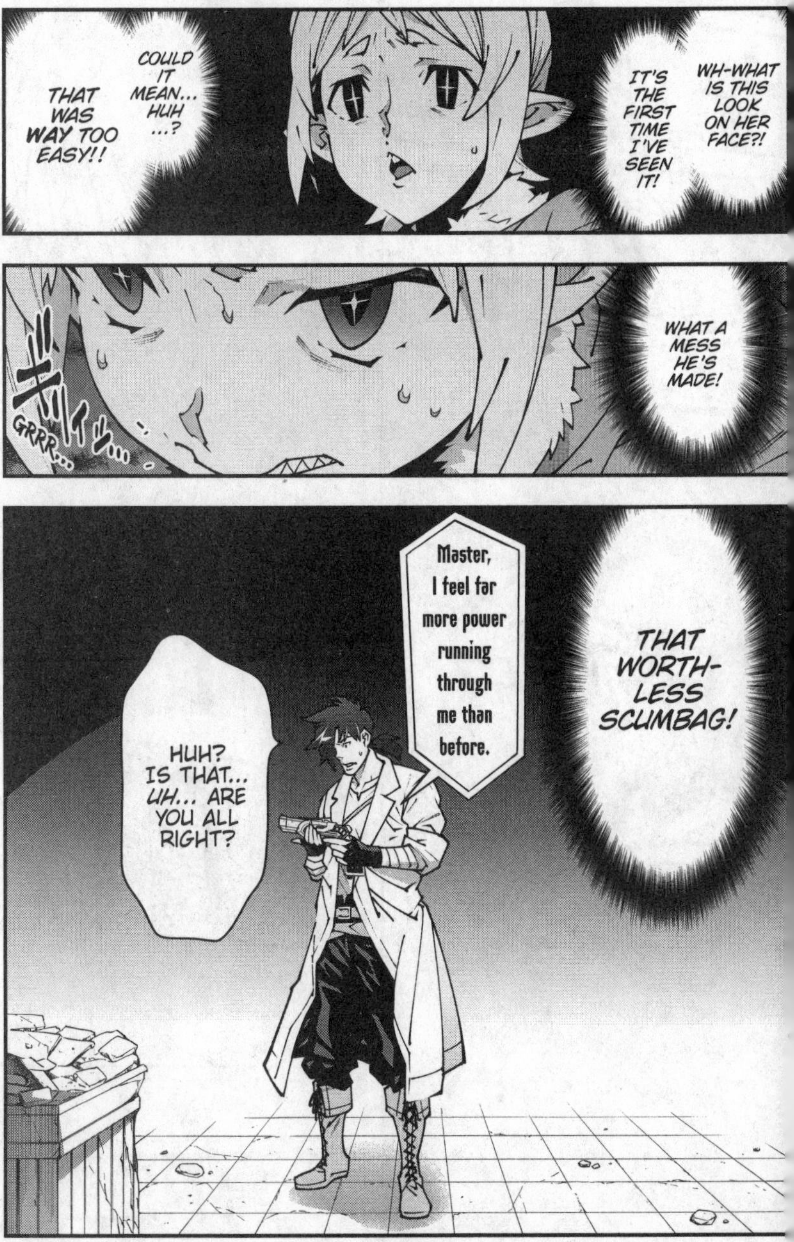
WH-WHAT IS THIS LOOK ON HER FACE?!
IT'S THE FIRST TIME I'VE SEEN IT!
COULD IT MEAN... HUH ...?
THAT WAS WAY TOO EASY!!
WHAT A MESS HE'S MADE!
GRRR...
THAT WORTH-LESS SCUMBAG!
Master, I feel far more power running through me than before.
HUH? IS THAT... UH... ARE YOU ALL RIGHT?

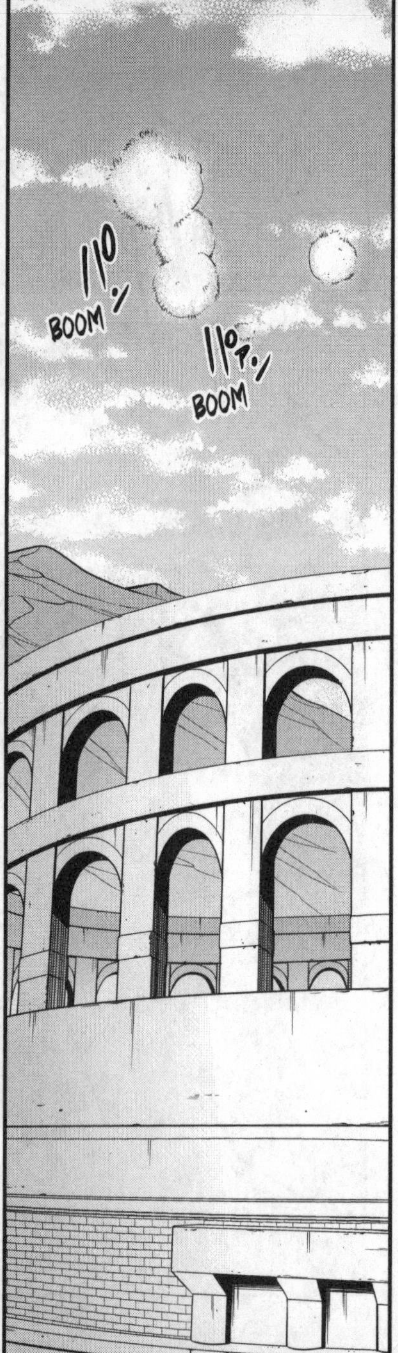
BOOM
BOOM
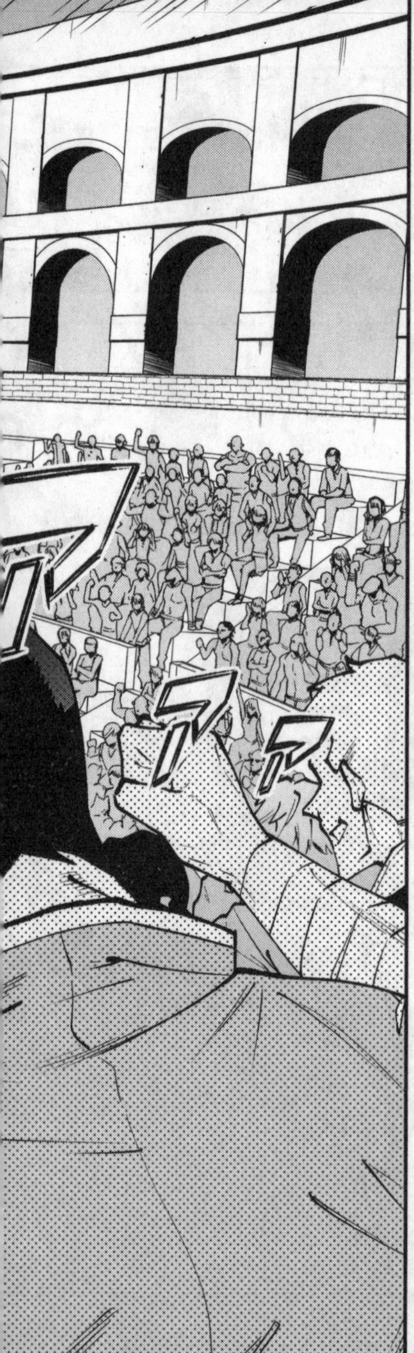

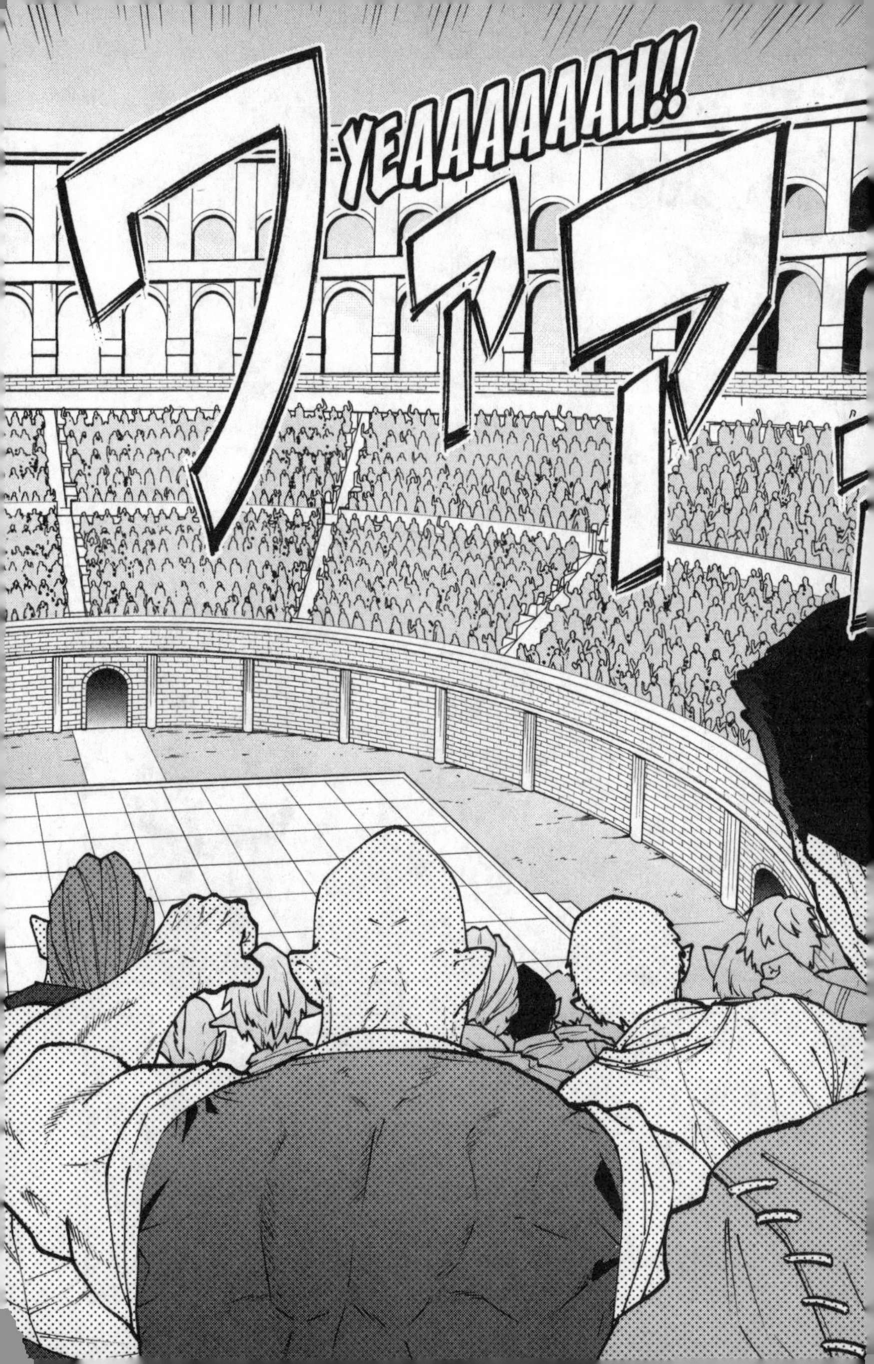
ワァァァ
YEAAAAAAH!!

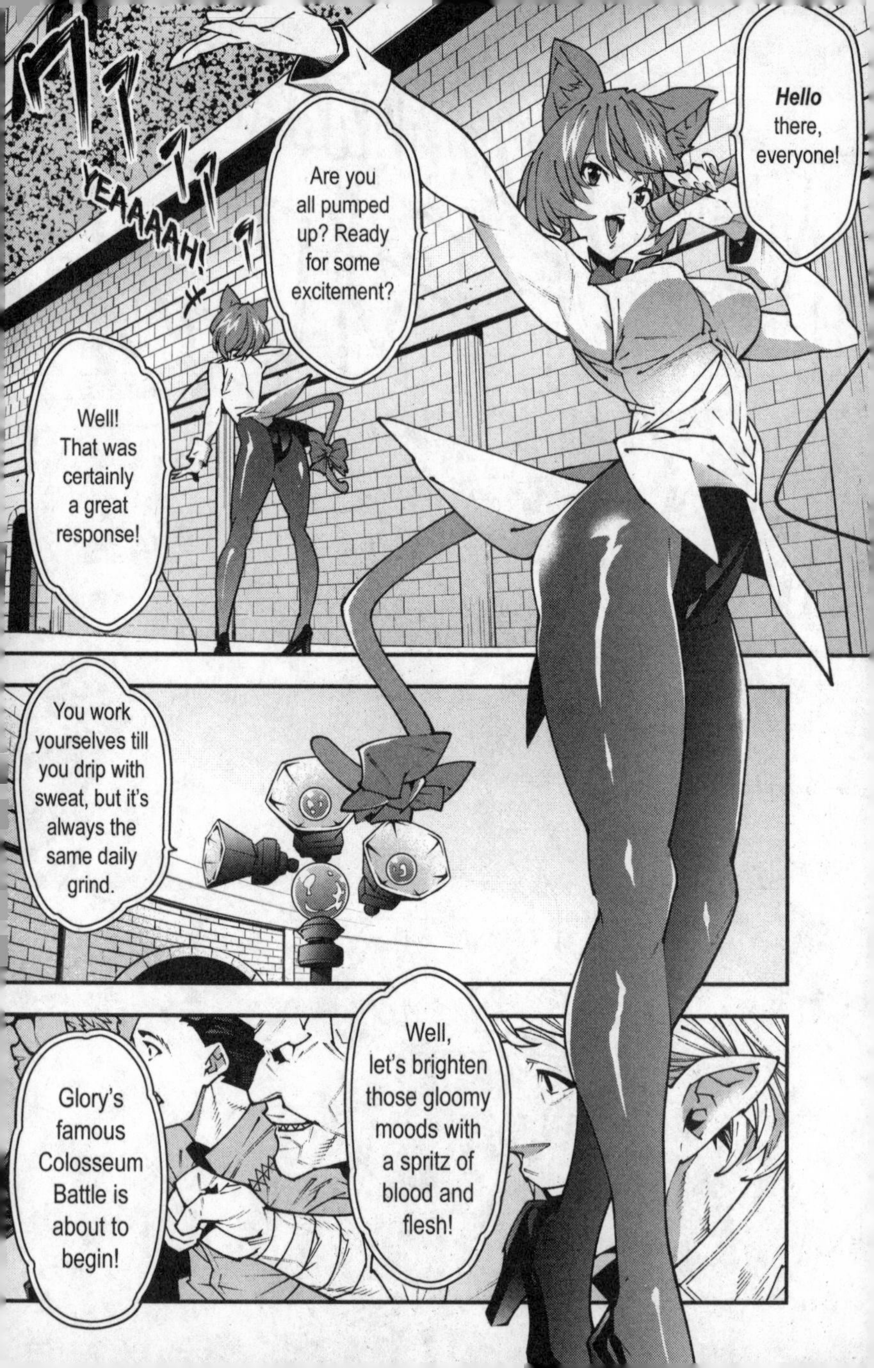
Hello there, everyone!
Are you all pumped up? Ready for some excitement?
YEAAAAAH!
Well! That was certainly a great response!
You work yourselves till you drip with sweat, but it's always the same daily grind.
Well, let's brighten those gloomy moods with a spritz of blood and flesh!
Glory's famous Colosseum Battle is about to begin!

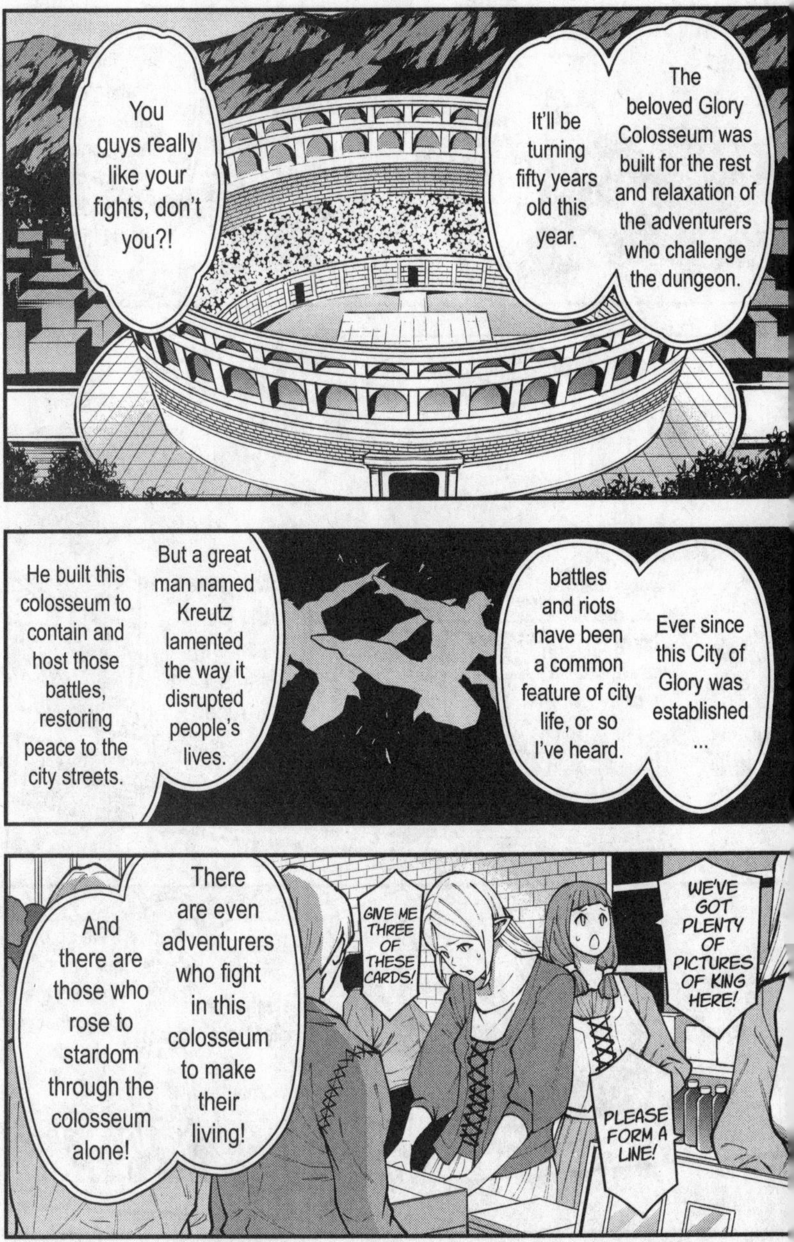
The beloved Glory Colosseum was built for the rest and relaxation of the adventurers who challenge the dungeon.
It'll be turning fifty years old this year.
You guys really like your fights, don't you?!
Ever since this City of Glory was established ...
battles and riots have been a common feature of city life, or so I've heard.
But a great man named Kreutz lamented the way it disrupted people's lives.
He built this colosseum to contain and host those battles, restoring peace to the city streets.
WE'VE GOT PLENTY OF PICTURES OF KING HERE!
PLEASE FORM A LINE!
GIVE ME THREE OF THESE CARDS!
There are even adventurers who fight in this colosseum to make their living!
And there are those who rose to stardom through the colosseum alone!

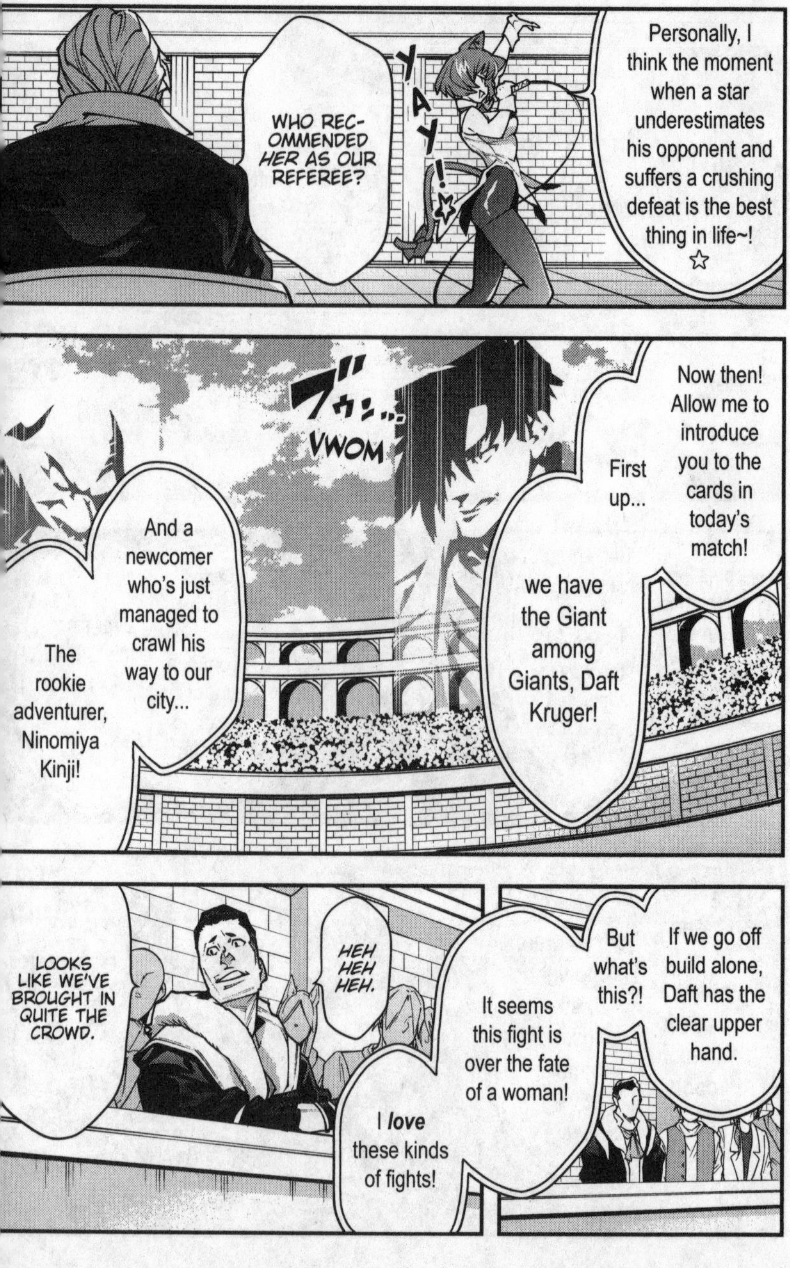
Personally, I think the moment when a star underestimates his opponent and suffers a crushing defeat is the best thing in life~! ☆
YAY!
WHO RECOMMENDED HER AS OUR REFEREE?
Now then! Allow me to introduce you to the cards in today's match!
First up...
we have the Giant among Giants, Daft Kruger!
VWOM
And a newcomer who's just managed to crawl his way to our city...
The rookie adventurer, Ninomiya Kinji!
If we go off build alone, Daft has the clear upper hand.
But what's this?!
It seems this fight is over the fate of a woman!
I *love* these kinds of fights!
HEH HEH HEH.
LOOKS LIKE WE'VE BROUGHT IN QUITE THE CROWD.

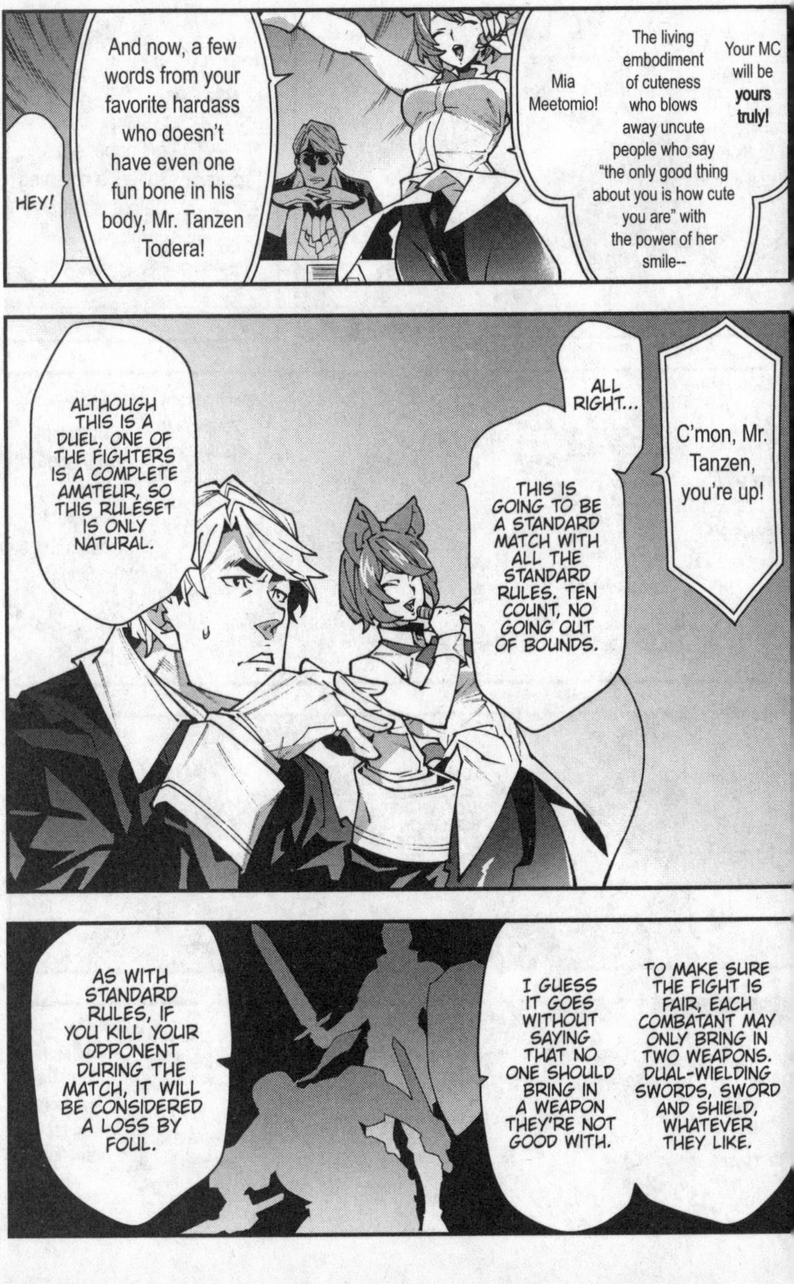
Your MC will be **yours truly!**
The living embodiment of cuteness who blows away uncute people who say "the only good thing about you is how cute you are" with the power of her smile--
Mia Meetomio!
And now, a few words from your favorite hardass who doesn't have even one fun bone in his body, Mr. Tanzen Todera!
HEY!
C'mon, Mr. Tanzen, you're up!
ALL RIGHT...
THIS IS GOING TO BE A STANDARD MATCH WITH ALL THE STANDARD RULES. TEN COUNT, NO GOING OUT OF BOUNDS.
ALTHOUGH THIS IS A DUEL, ONE OF THE FIGHTERS IS A COMPLETE AMATEUR, SO THIS RULESET IS ONLY NATURAL.
TO MAKE SURE THE FIGHT IS FAIR, EACH COMBATANT MAY ONLY BRING IN TWO WEAPONS. DUAL-WIELDING SWORDS, SWORD AND SHIELD, WHATEVER THEY LIKE.
I GUESS IT GOES WITHOUT SAYING THAT NO ONE SHOULD BRING IN A WEAPON THEY'RE NOT GOOD WITH.
AS WITH STANDARD RULES, IF YOU KILL YOUR OPPONENT DURING THE MATCH, IT WILL BE CONSIDERED A LOSS BY FOUL.

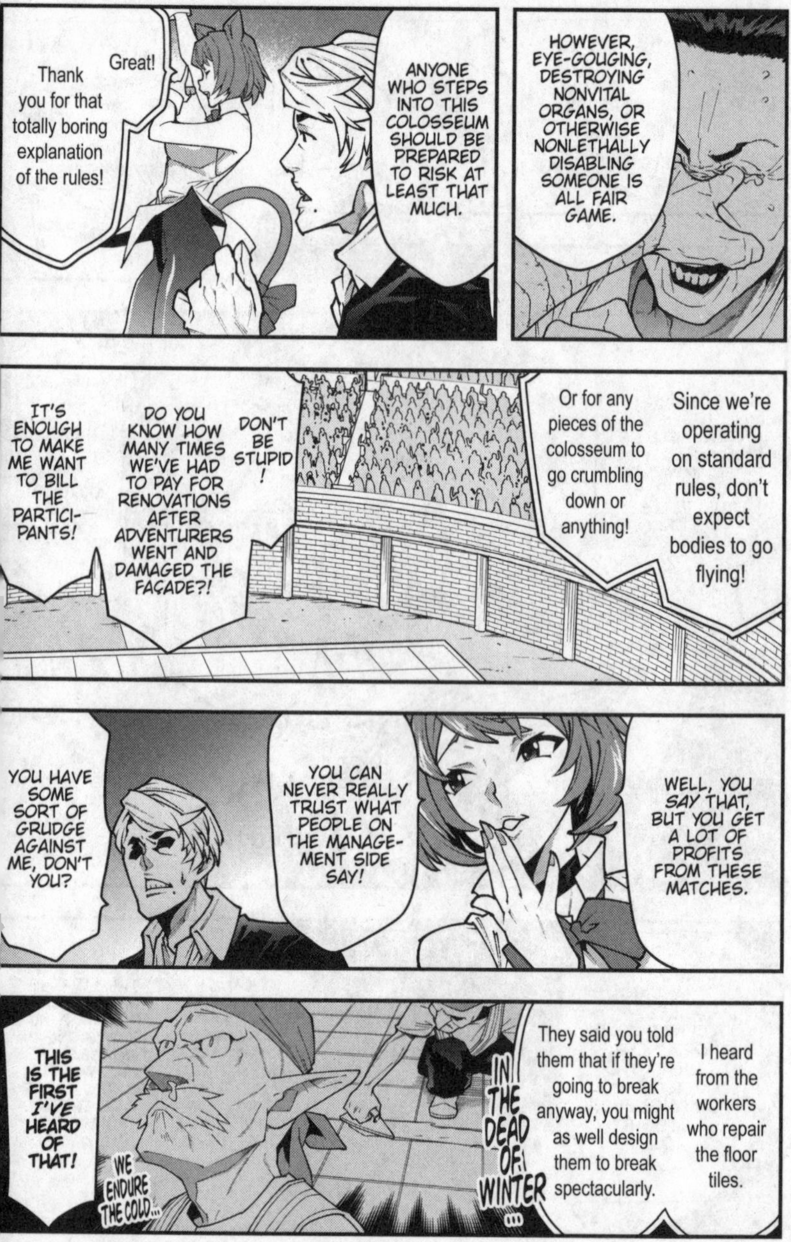
HOWEVER, EYE-GOUGING, DESTROYING NONVITAL ORGANS, OR OTHERWISE NONLETHALLY DISABLING SOMEONE IS ALL FAIR GAME.
ANYONE WHO STEPS INTO THIS COLOSSEUM SHOULD BE PREPARED TO RISK AT LEAST THAT MUCH.
Great!
Thank you for that totally boring explanation of the rules!
Since we're operating on standard rules, don't expect bodies to go flying!
Or for any pieces of the colosseum to go crumbling down or anything!
DON'T BE STUPID!
DO YOU KNOW HOW MANY TIMES WE'VE HAD TO PAY FOR RENOVATIONS AFTER ADVENTURERS WENT AND DAMAGED THE FAÇADE?!
IT'S ENOUGH TO MAKE ME WANT TO BILL THE PARTICIPANTS!
WELL, YOU SAY THAT, BUT YOU GET A LOT OF PROFITS FROM THESE MATCHES.
YOU CAN NEVER REALLY TRUST WHAT PEOPLE ON THE MANAGEMENT SIDE SAY!
YOU HAVE SOME SORT OF GRUDGE AGAINST ME, DON'T YOU?
I heard from the workers who repair the floor tiles.
They said you told them that if they're going to break anyway, you might as well design them to break spectacularly.
IN THE DEAD OF WINTER...
THIS IS THE FIRST I'VE HEARD OF THAT!
WE ENDURE THE COLD...

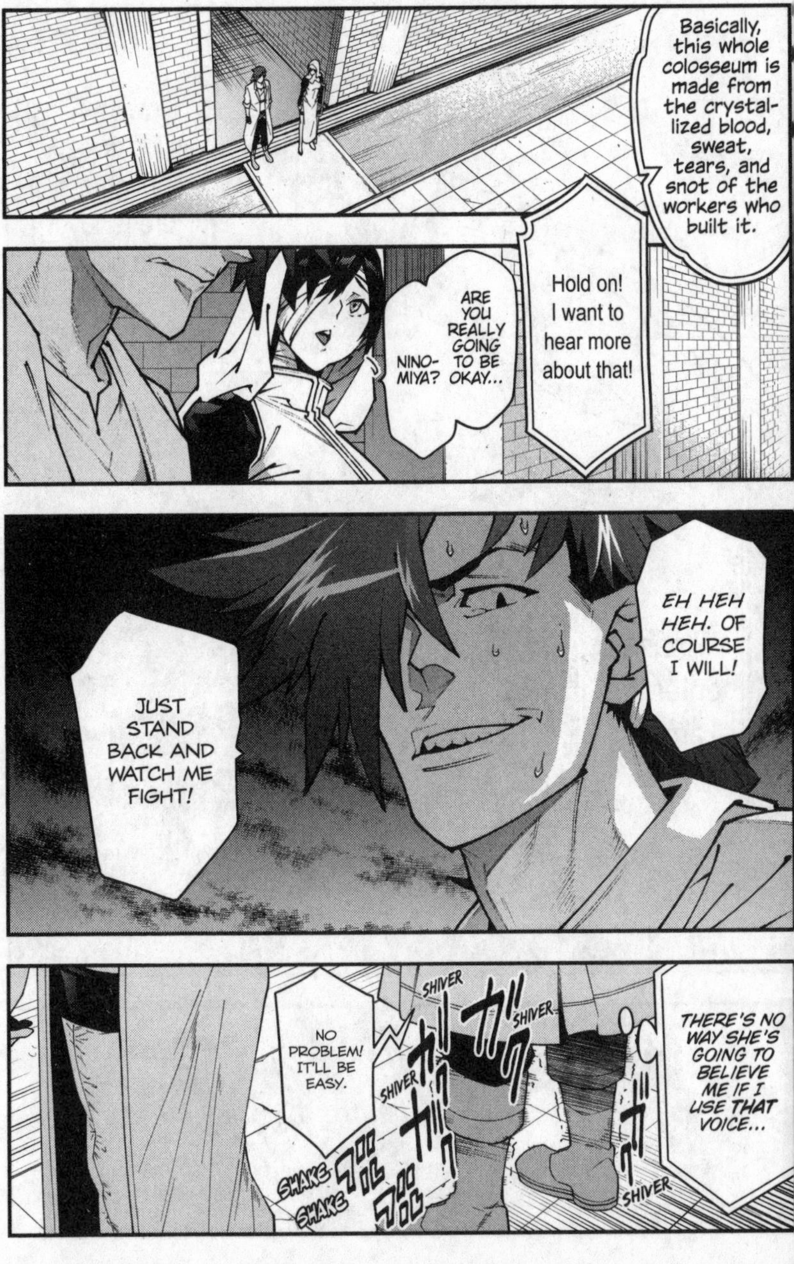

Basically, this whole colosseum is made from the crystallized blood, sweat, tears, and snot of the workers who built it.
Hold on! I want to hear more about that!
ARE YOU REALLY GOING TO BE OKAY... NINOMIYA?
EH HEH HEH. OF COURSE I WILL!
JUST STAND BACK AND WATCH ME FIGHT!
THERE'S NO WAY SHE'S GOING TO BELIEVE ME IF I USE THAT VOICE...
SHIVER
SHIVER
SHIVER
SHIVER
NO PROBLEM! IT'LL BE EASY.
SHAKE SHAKE

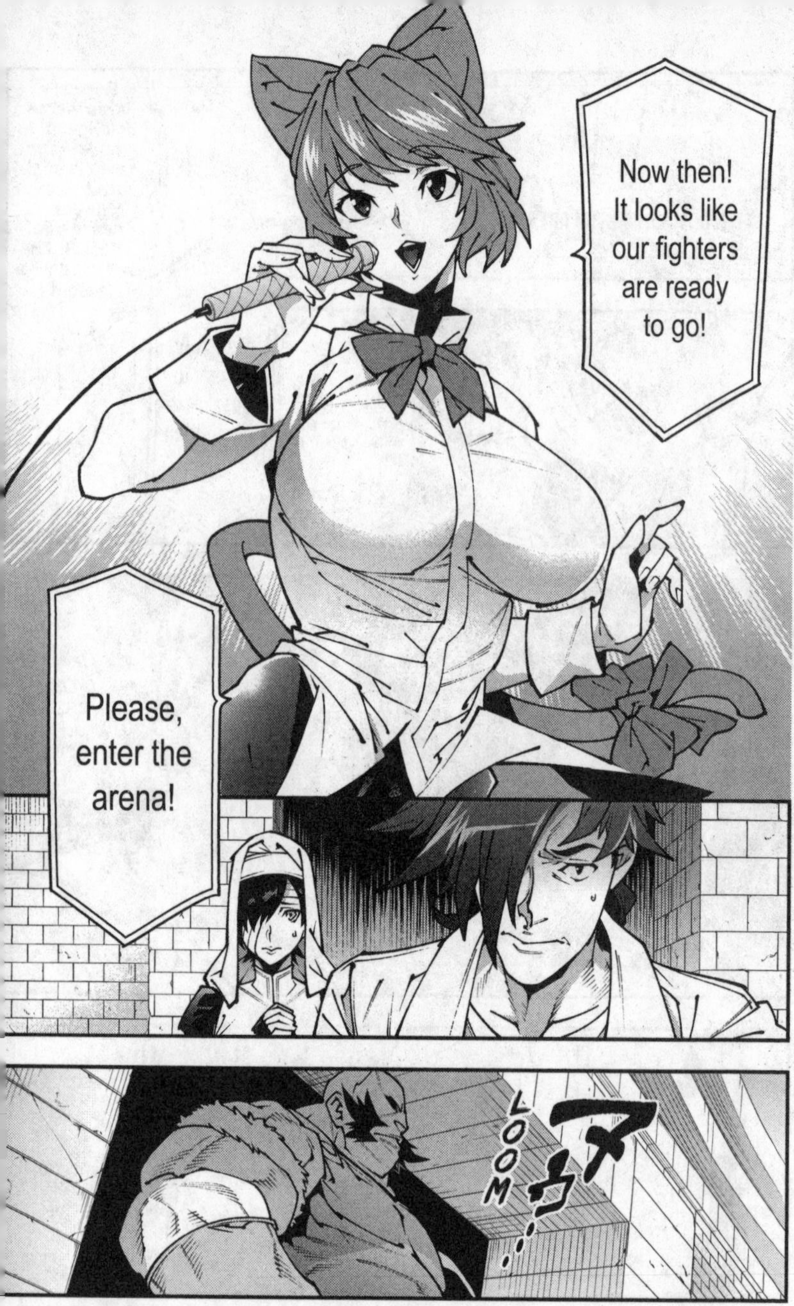
Now then! It looks like our fighters are ready to go!
Please, enter the arena!
LOOOM
ヌウ…

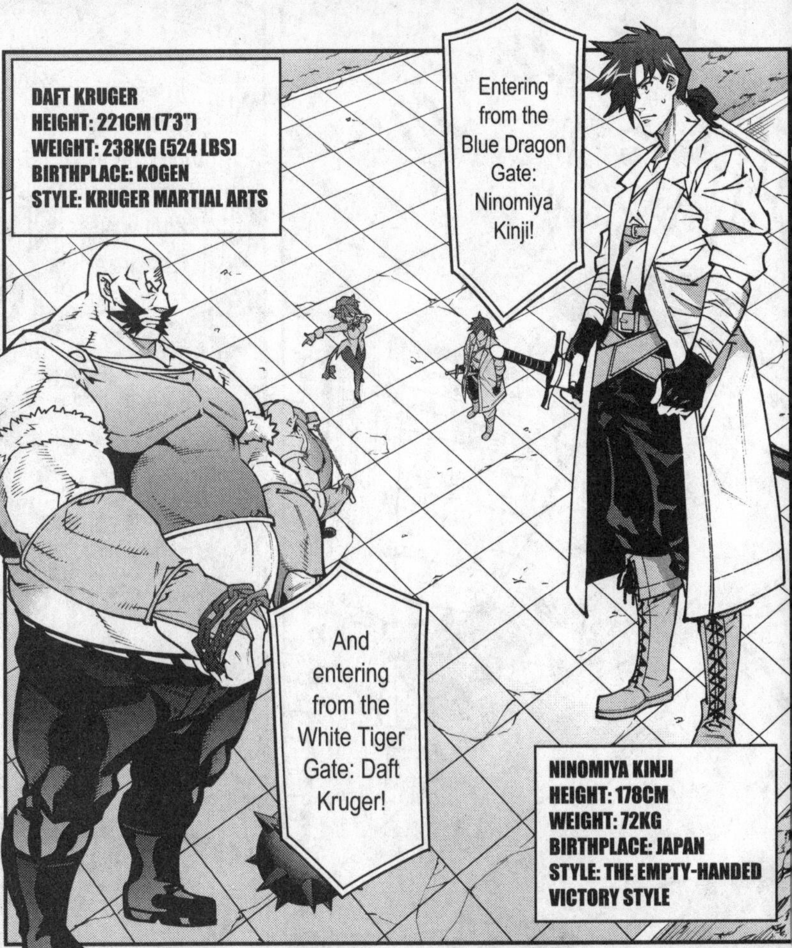
Entering from the Blue Dragon Gate: Ninomiya Kinji!
DAFT KRUGER
HEIGHT: 221CM (7'3")
WEIGHT: 238KG (524 LBS)
BIRTHPLACE: KOGEN
STYLE: KRUGER MARTIAL ARTS
And entering from the White Tiger Gate: Daft Kruger!
NINOMIYA KINJI
HEIGHT: 178CM
WEIGHT: 72KG
BIRTHPLACE: JAPAN
STYLE: THE EMPTY-HANDED VICTORY STYLE
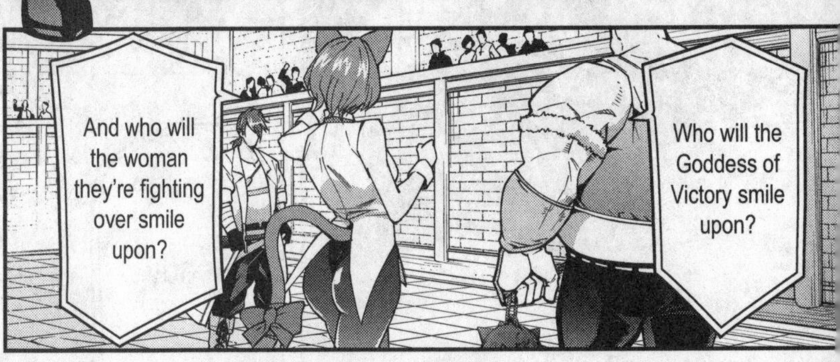
Who will the Goddess of Victory smile upon?
And who will the woman they're fighting over smile upon?

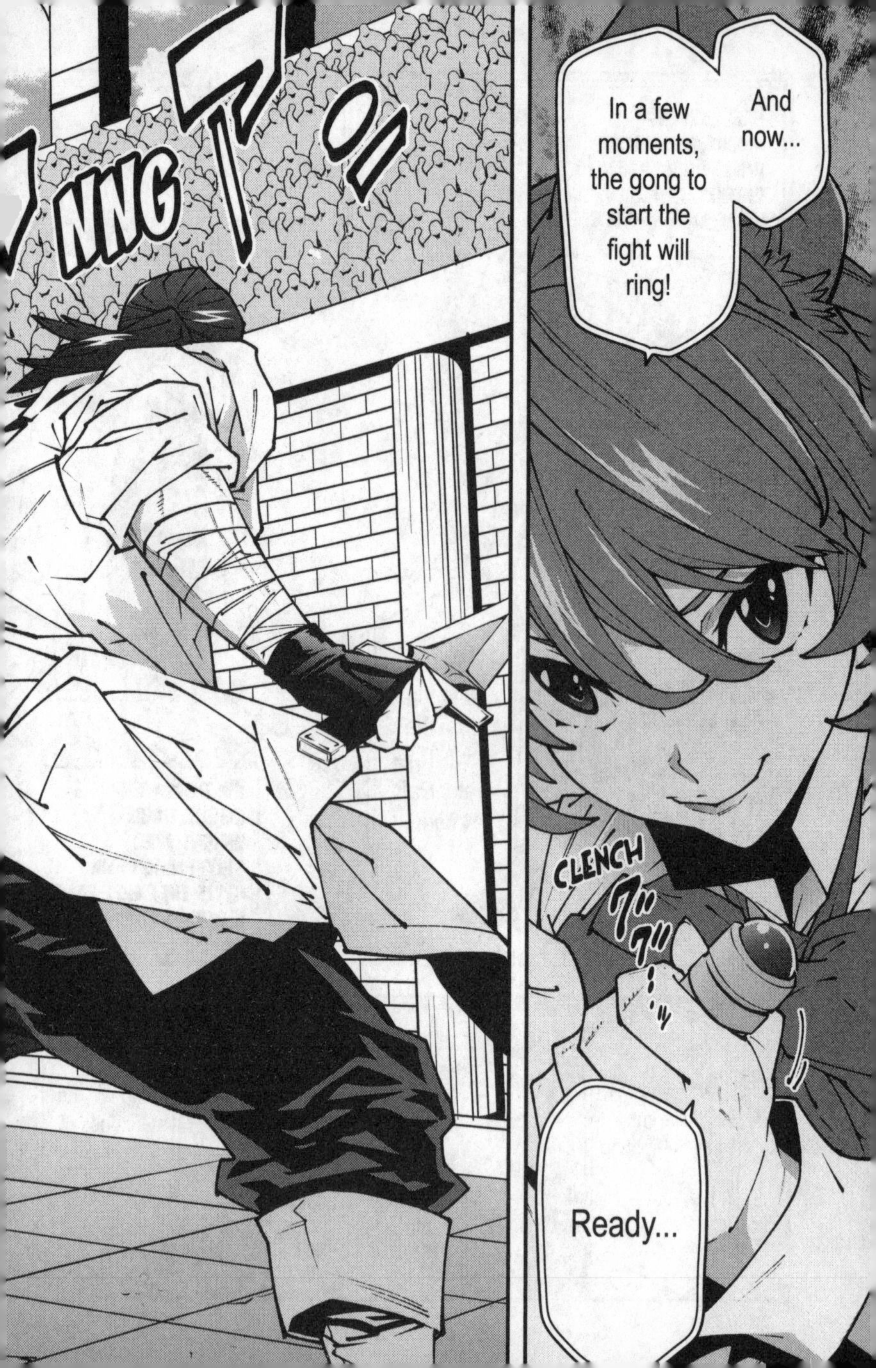
And now...
In a few moments, the gong to start the fight will ring!
CLENCH
Ready...
NNG

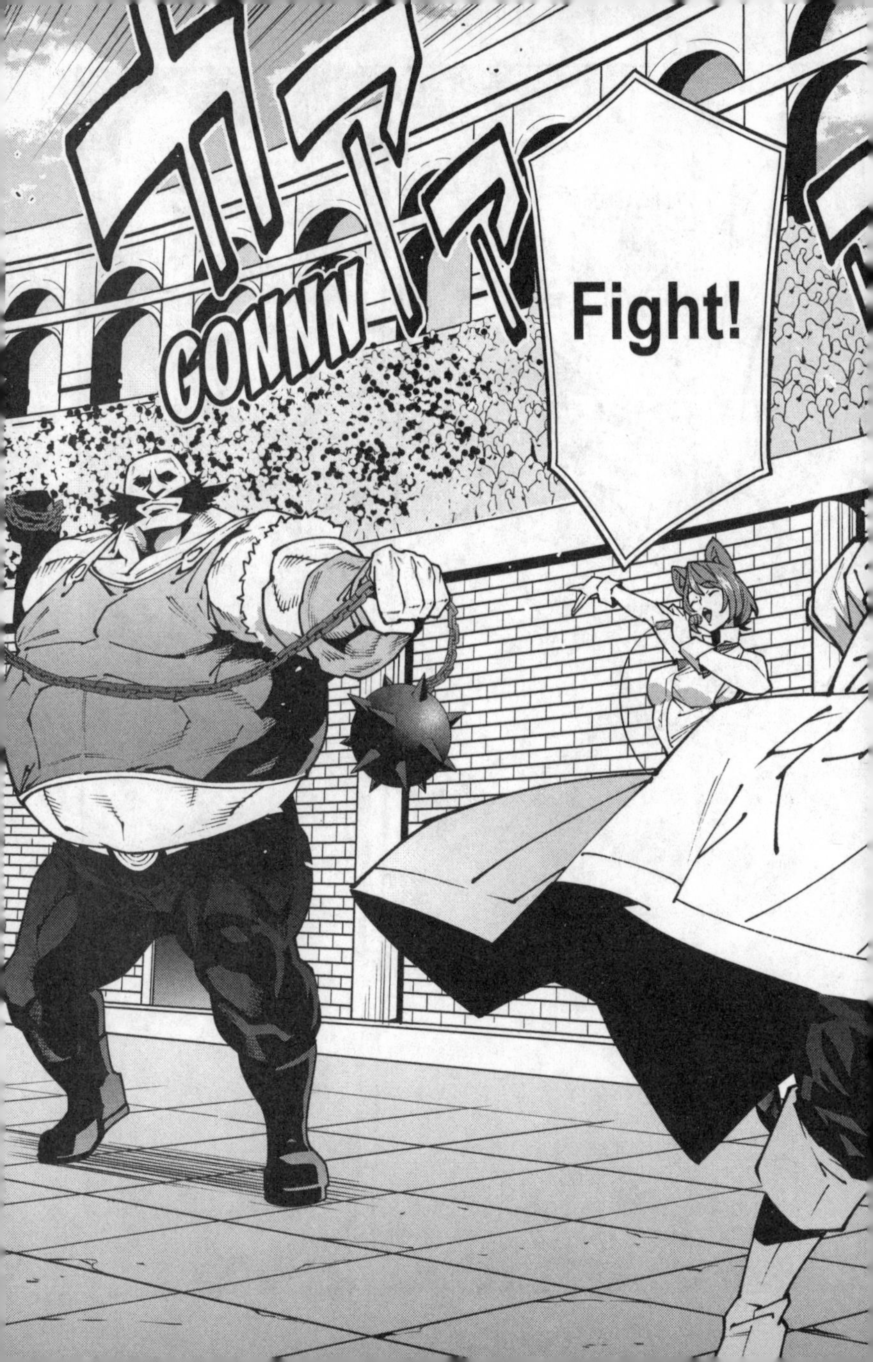
Fight!
GONNN

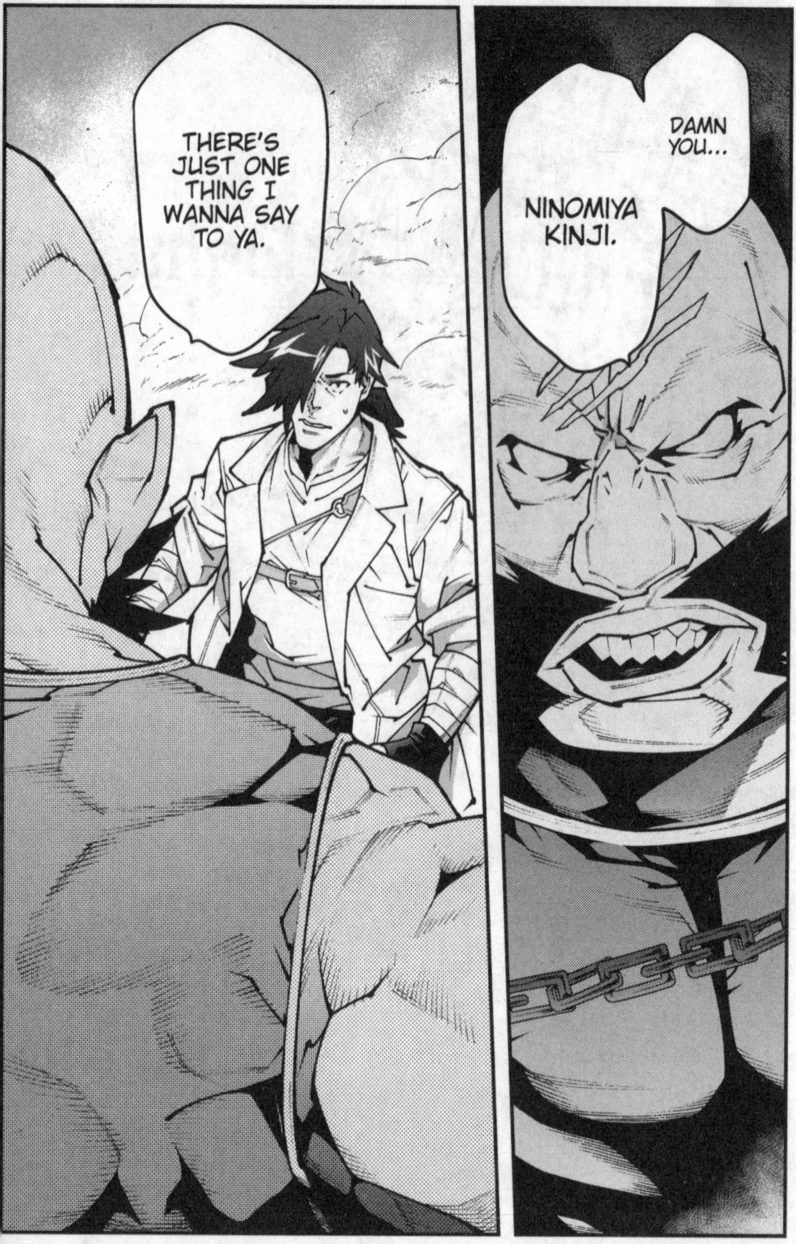
DAMN YOU...
NINOMIYA KINJI.
THERE'S JUST ONE THING I WANNA SAY TO YA.

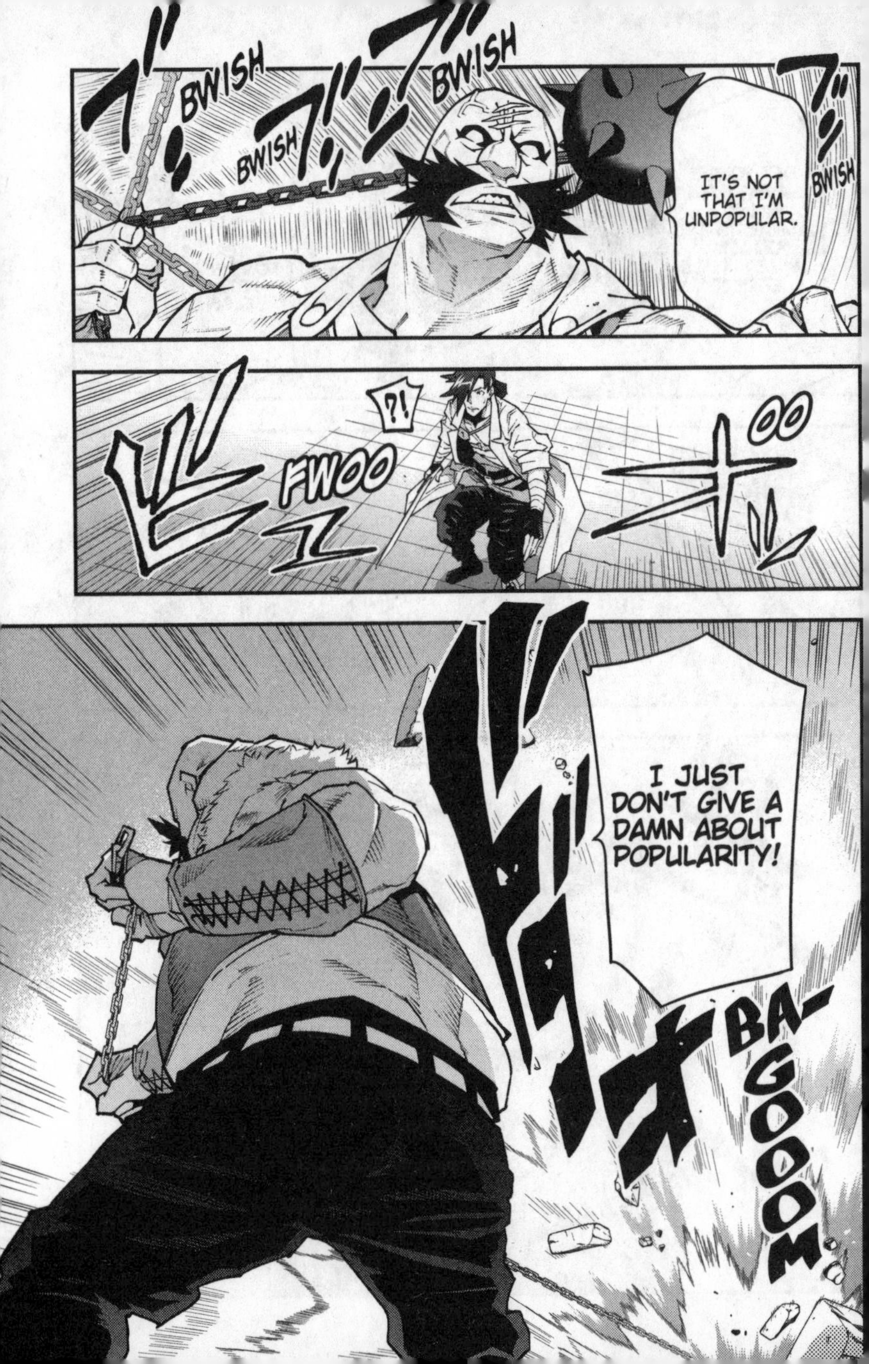
BWISH
IT'S NOT THAT I'M UNPOPULAR.
BWISH
BWISH
BWISH
OO
?!
FWOO
I JUST DON'T GIVE A DAMN ABOUT POPULARITY!
BA-GOOOOM

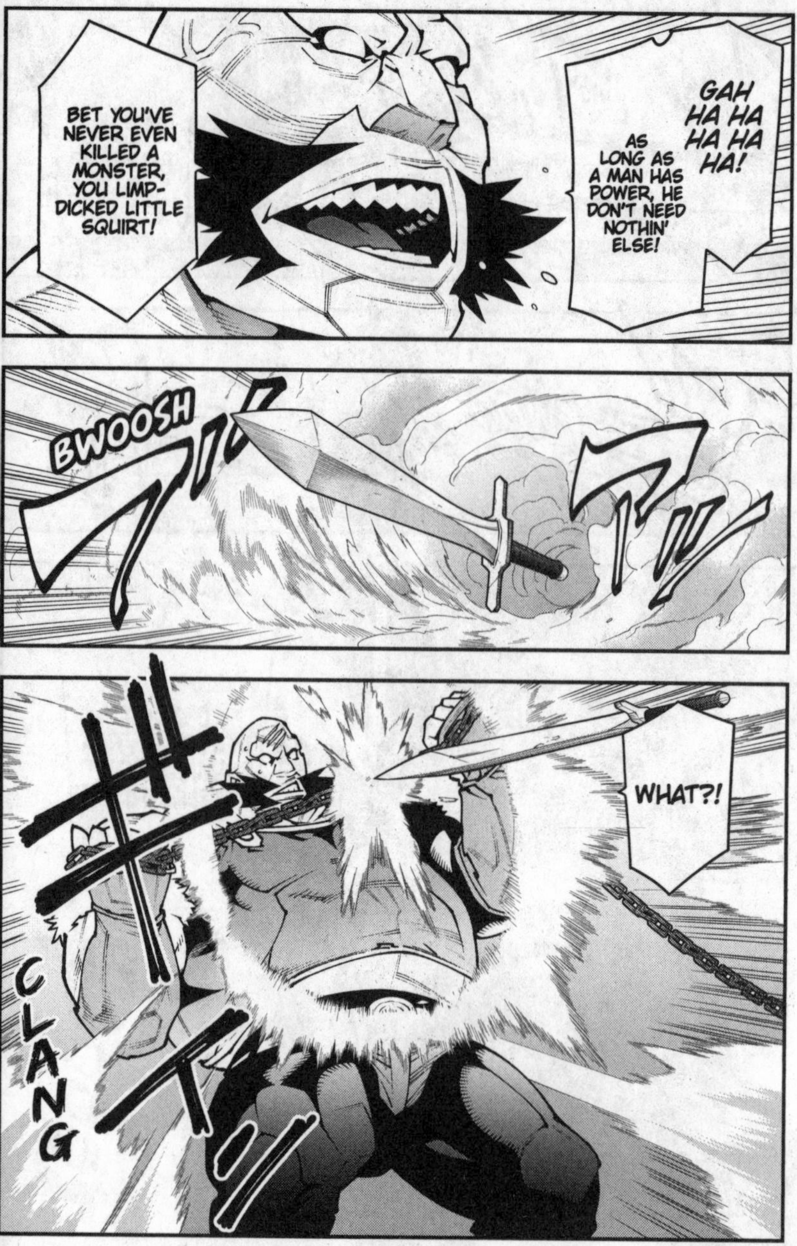
GAH HA HA HA HA HA!
AS LONG AS A MAN HAS POWER, HE DON'T NEED NOTHIN' ELSE!
BET YOU'VE NEVER EVEN KILLED A MONSTER, YOU LIMP-DICKED LITTLE SQUIRT!
BWOOSH
WHAT?!
CLANG

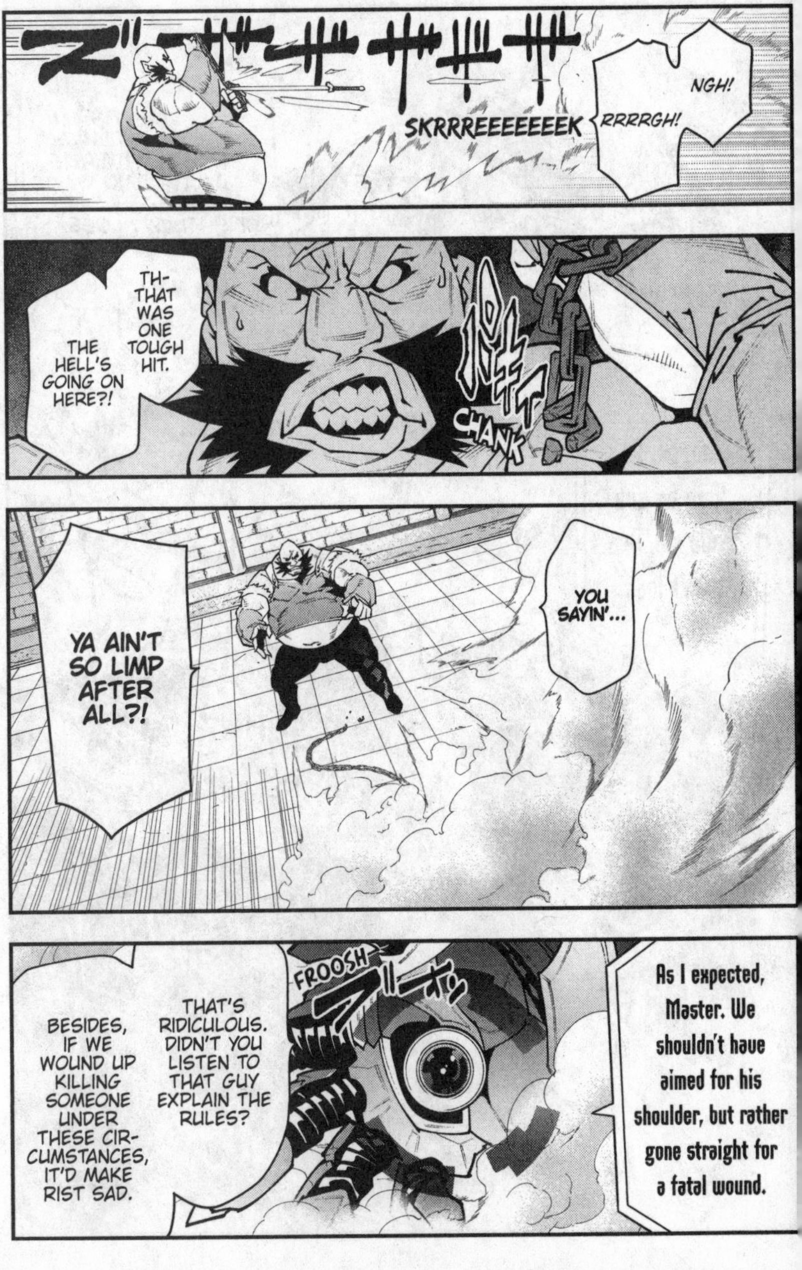
NGH! RRRRGH!
SKRRREEEEEEEK
TH-THAT WAS ONE TOUGH HIT.
THE HELL'S GOING ON HERE?!
CHANK
YOU SAYIN'...
YA AIN'T SO LIMP AFTER ALL?!
As I expected, Master. We shouldn't have aimed for his shoulder, but rather gone straight for a fatal wound.
FROOSH
THAT'S RIDICULOUS. DIDN'T YOU LISTEN TO THAT GUY EXPLAIN THE RULES?
BESIDES, IF WE WOUND UP KILLING SOMEONE UNDER THESE CIR-CUMSTANCES, IT'D MAKE RIST SAD.

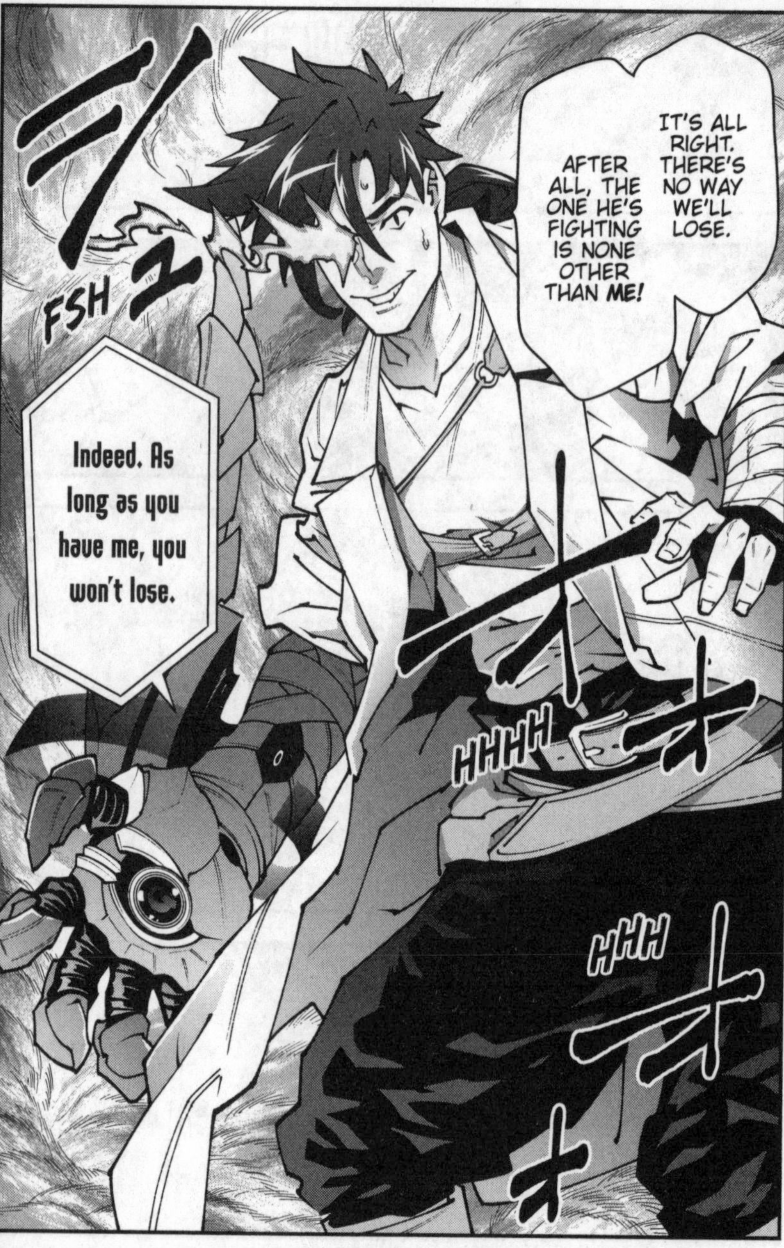
IT'S ALL RIGHT. THERE'S NO WAY WE'LL LOSE.
AFTER ALL, THE ONE HE'S FIGHTING IS NONE OTHER THAN ME!
FSH
Indeed. As long as you have me, you won't lose.
HHHH
HHH

ZAKIL KRUGER

KOUGA RYUUTEN	HOLD ← THEN PRESS → AND KICK
DROP KICK TO HELL	HOLD ↓ THEN PRESS ↑ AND KICK
SECRET TECHNIQUE: RED GLOW ON CLOUDY SKIES	↙↗↖↗ THEN PRESS KICK

THE DUNGEON OF
BLACK COMPANY

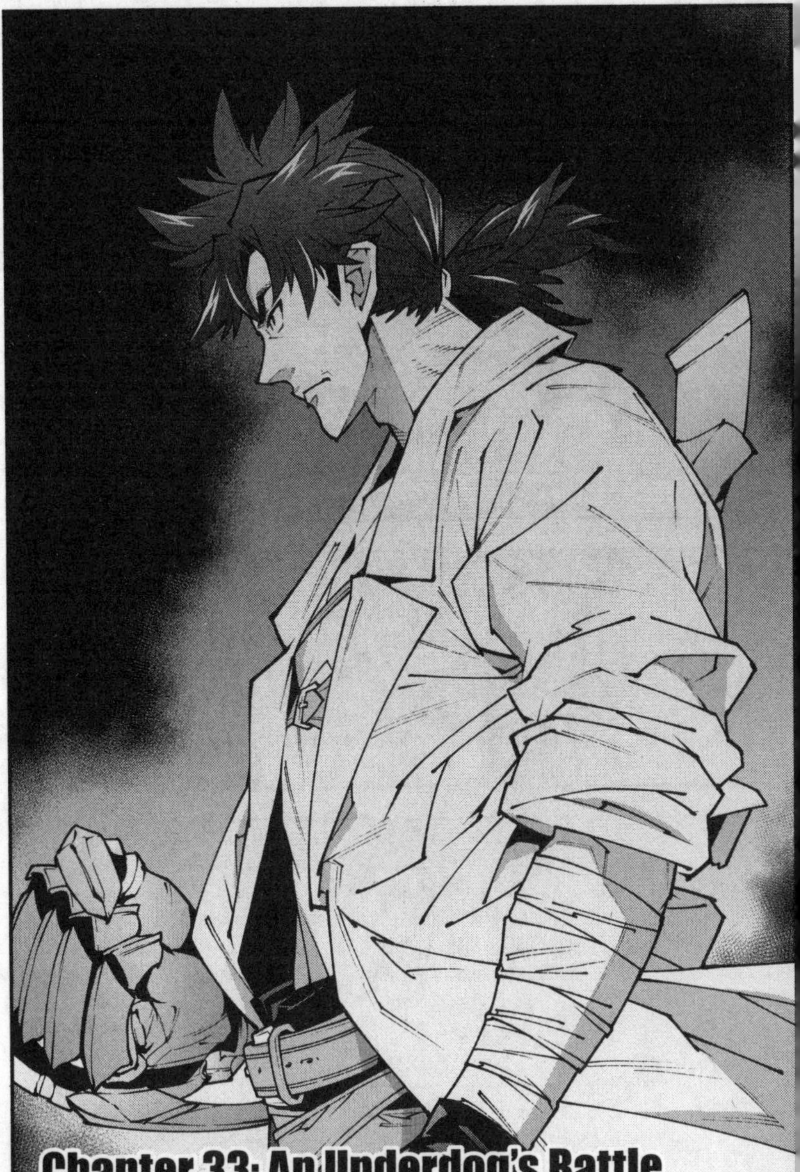
Chapter 33: An Underdog's Battle

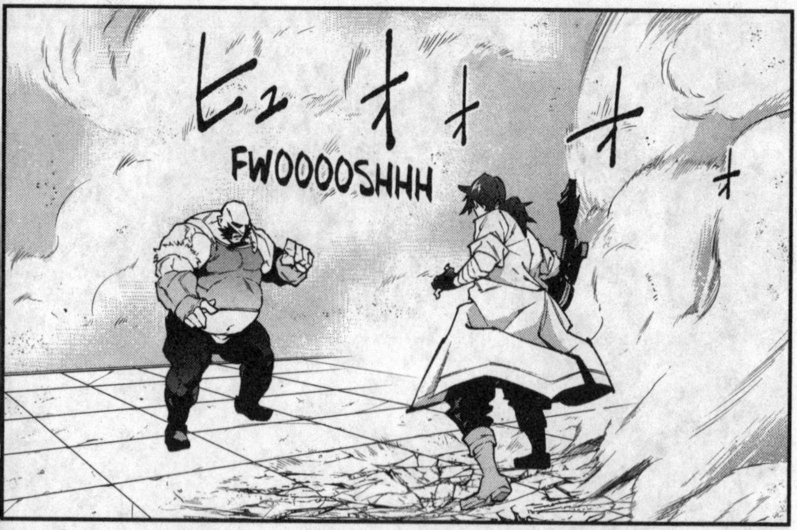
ヒュオォオォ
FWOOOOSHHH

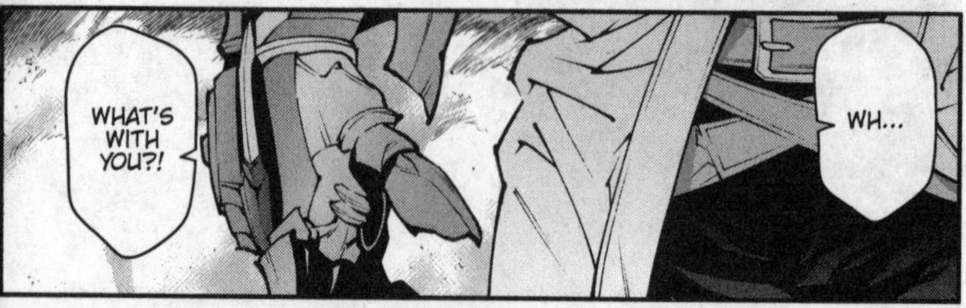
WH...
WHAT'S WITH YOU?!

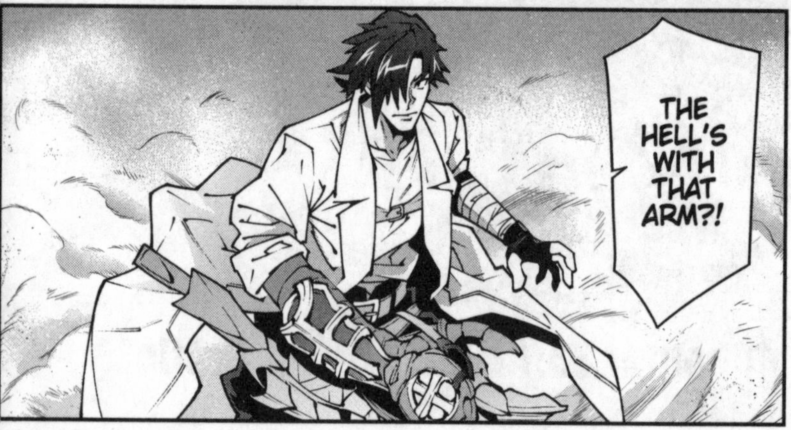
THE HELL'S WITH THAT ARM?!

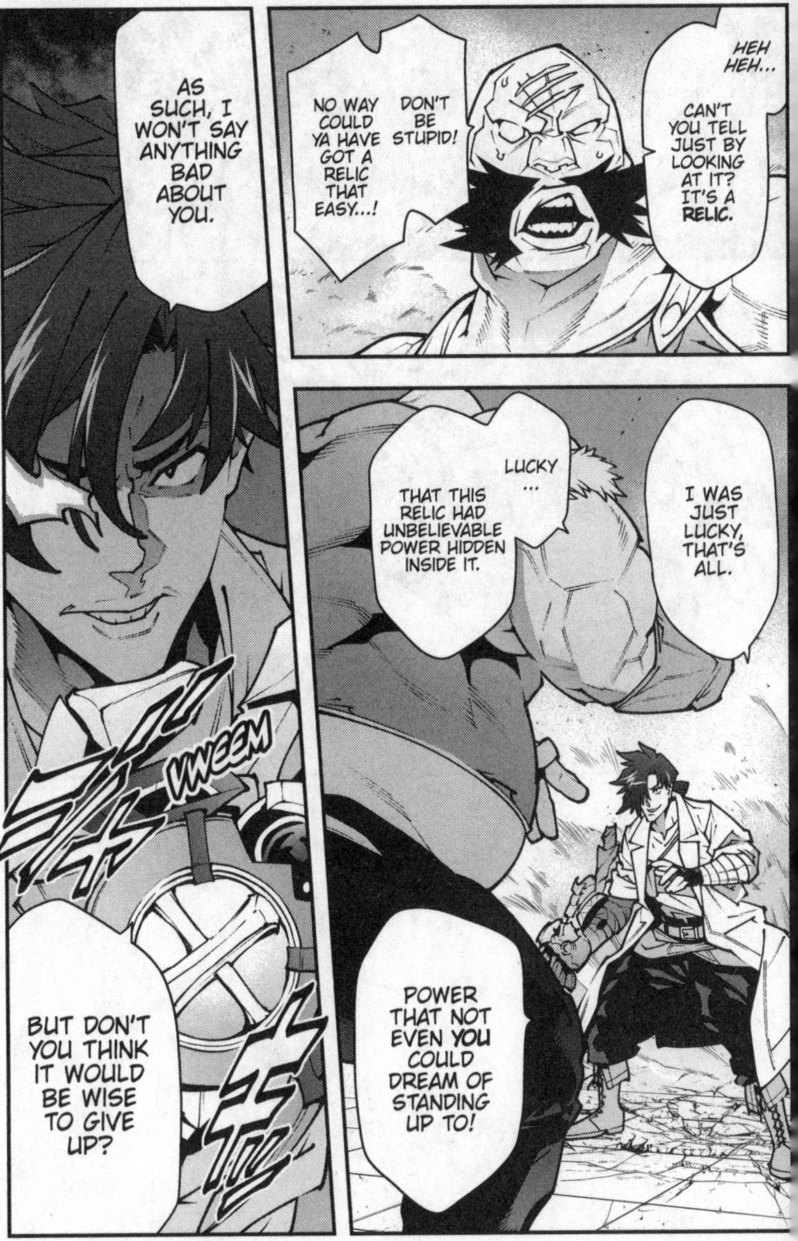
HEH HEH...
CAN'T YOU TELL JUST BY LOOKING AT IT? IT'S A **RELIC.**
DON'T BE STUPID!
NO WAY COULD YA HAVE GOT A RELIC THAT EASY...!
I WAS JUST LUCKY, THAT'S ALL.
LUCKY...
THAT THIS RELIC HAD UNBELIEVABLE POWER HIDDEN INSIDE IT.
POWER THAT NOT EVEN **YOU** COULD DREAM OF STANDING UP TO!
AS SUCH, I WON'T SAY ANYTHING BAD ABOUT YOU.
VWEEM
BUT DON'T YOU THINK IT WOULD BE WISE TO GIVE UP?

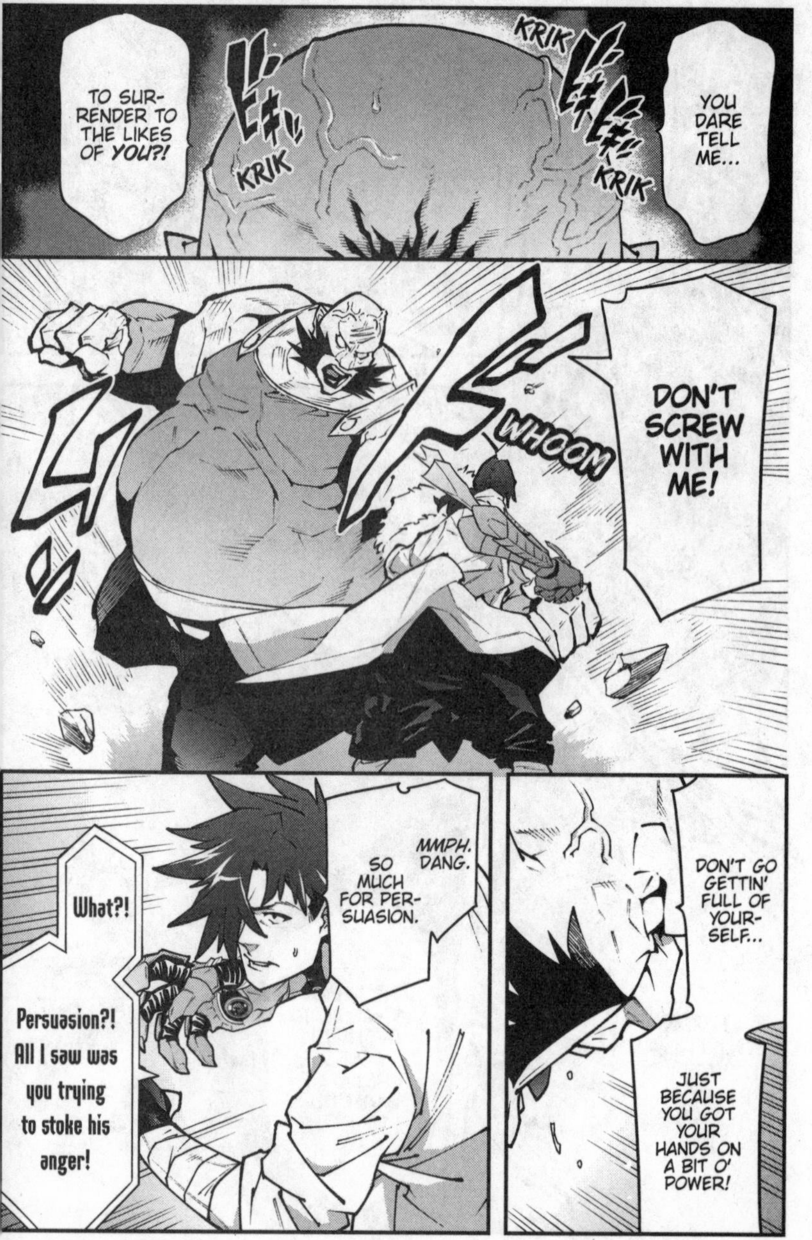
KRIK
YOU DARE TELL ME...
KRIK
KRIK
TO SURRENDER TO THE LIKES OF YOU?!
DON'T SCREW WITH ME!
WHOOM
DON'T GO GETTIN' FULL OF YOURSELF...
JUST BECAUSE YOU GOT YOUR HANDS ON A BIT O' POWER!
MMPH. DANG.
SO MUCH FOR PERSUASION.
What?!
Persuasion?! All I saw was you trying to stoke his anger!

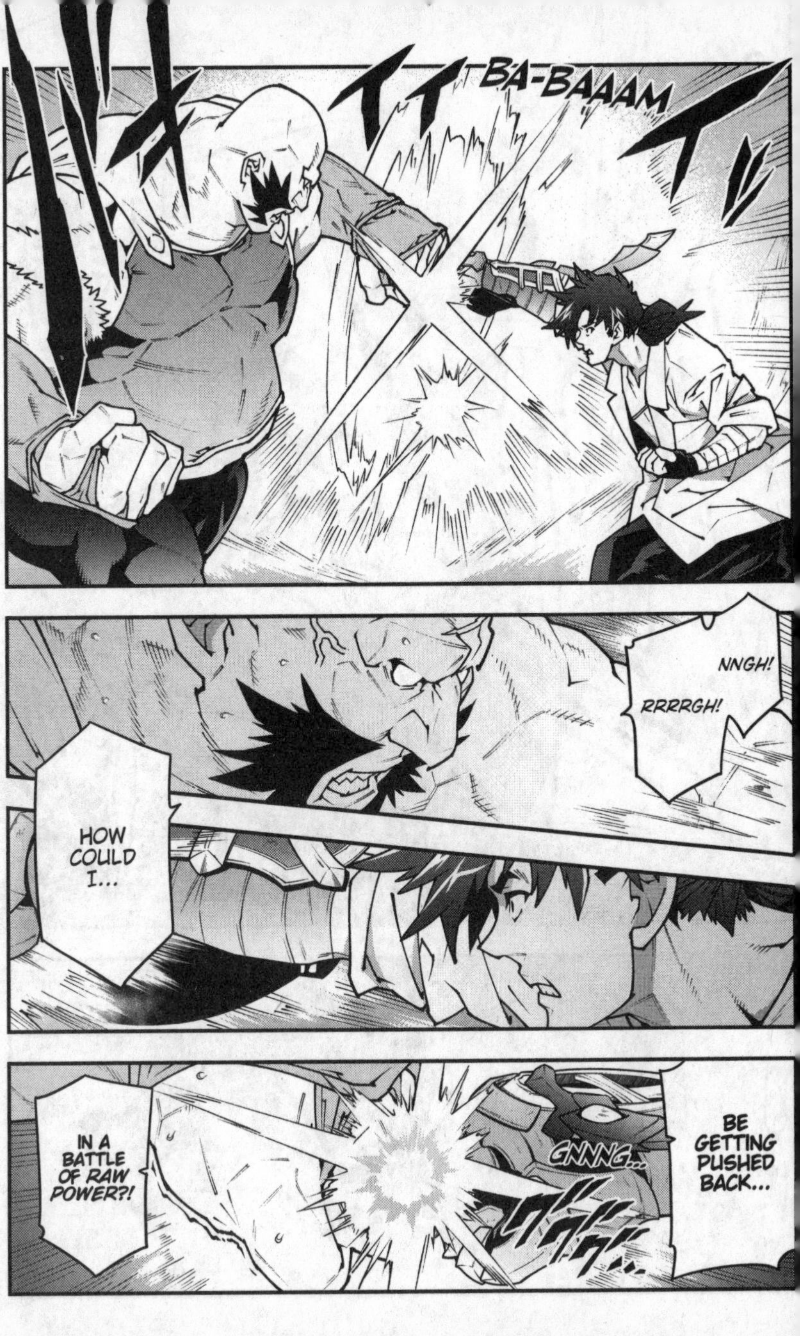
BA-BAAAM
NNGH!
RRRRGH!
HOW COULD I...
BE GETTING PUSHED BACK...
GNNNG...
IN A BATTLE OF RAW POWER?!

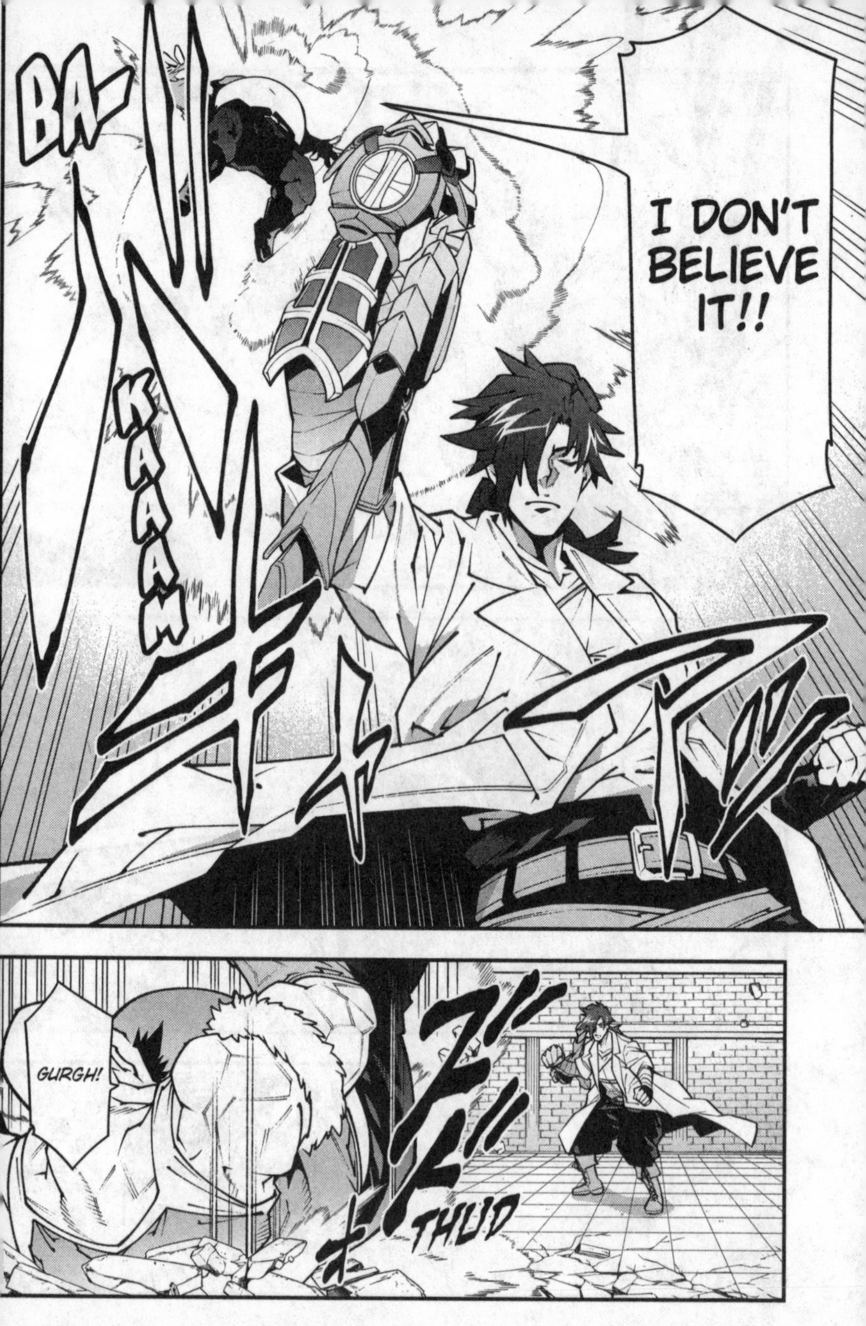
I DON'T BELIEVE IT!!
BA-KAAAAM
THUD
GURGH!

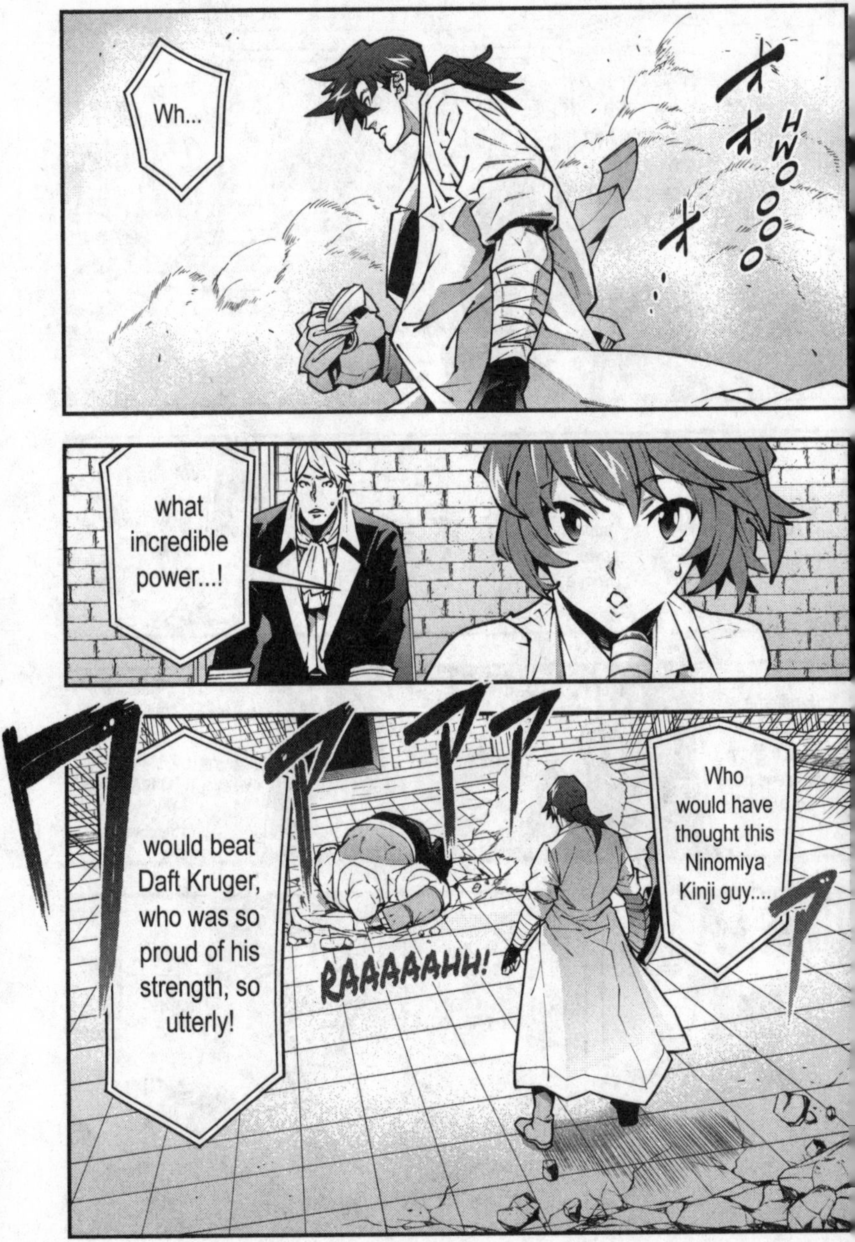
HWOOOOO
Wh...
what incredible power...!
Who would have thought this Ninomiya Kinji guy....
would beat Daft Kruger, who was so proud of his strength, so utterly!
RAAAAAHH!

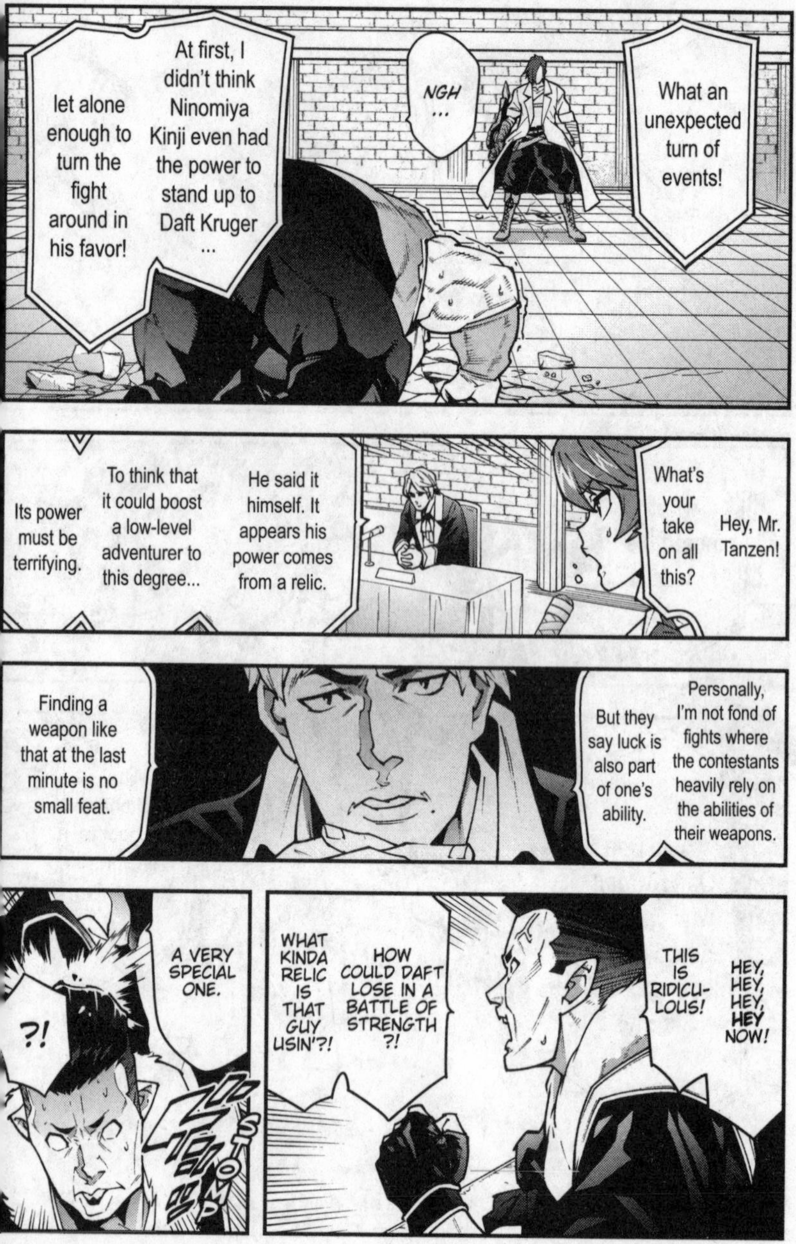
What an unexpected turn of events!
NGH ...
At first, I didn't think Ninomiya Kinji even had the power to stand up to Daft Kruger ...
let alone enough to turn the fight around in his favor!
Hey, Mr. Tanzen!
What's your take on all this?
He said it himself. It appears his power comes from a relic.
To think that it could boost a low-level adventurer to this degree...
Its power must be terrifying.
Personally, I'm not fond of fights where the contestants heavily rely on the abilities of their weapons.
But they say luck is also part of one's ability.
Finding a weapon like that at the last minute is no small feat.
HEY, HEY, HEY, HEY NOW!
THIS IS RIDICU-LOUS!
HOW COULD DAFT LOSE IN A BATTLE OF STRENGTH ?!
WHAT KINDA RELIC IS THAT GUY USIN'?!
A VERY SPECIAL ONE.
?!
STOMP

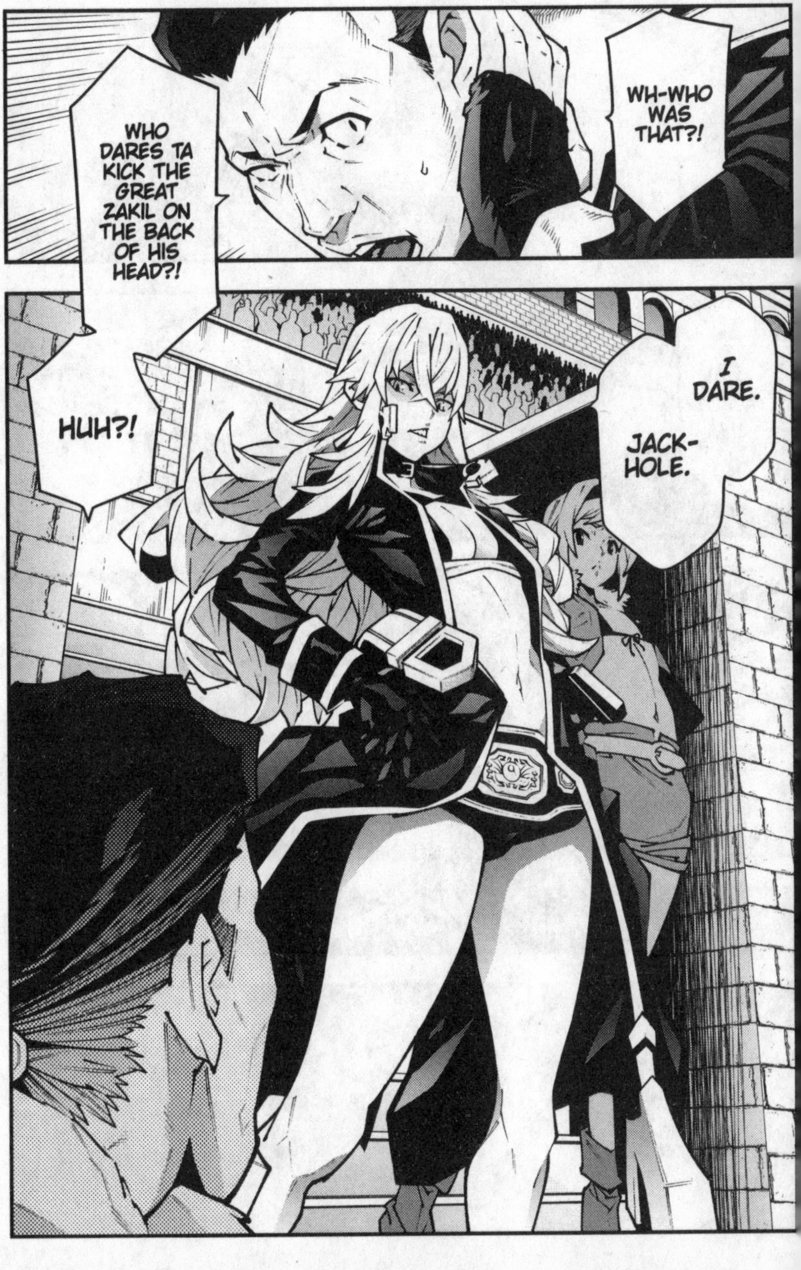
WH-WHO WAS THAT?!
WHO DARES TA KICK THE GREAT ZAKIL ON THE BACK OF HIS HEAD?!
I DARE.
JACK-HOLE.
HUH?!

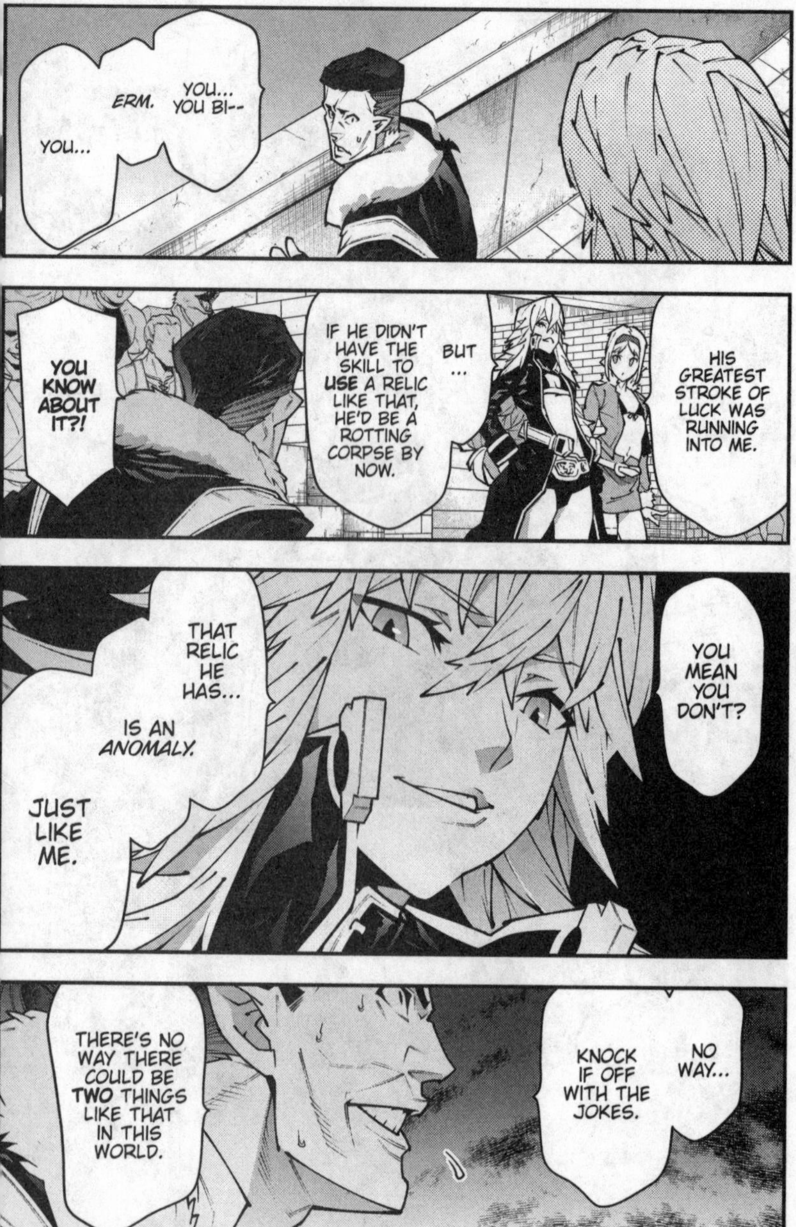
YOU... YOU BI--
ERM.
YOU...
HIS GREATEST STROKE OF LUCK WAS RUNNING INTO ME.
BUT ...
IF HE DIDN'T HAVE THE SKILL TO **USE** A RELIC LIKE THAT, HE'D BE A ROTTING CORPSE BY NOW.
YOU KNOW ABOUT IT?!
YOU MEAN YOU DON'T?
THAT RELIC HE HAS...
IS AN *ANOMALY.*
JUST LIKE ME.
NO WAY...
KNOCK IF OFF WITH THE JOKES.
THERE'S NO WAY THERE COULD BE **TWO** THINGS LIKE THAT IN THIS WORLD.

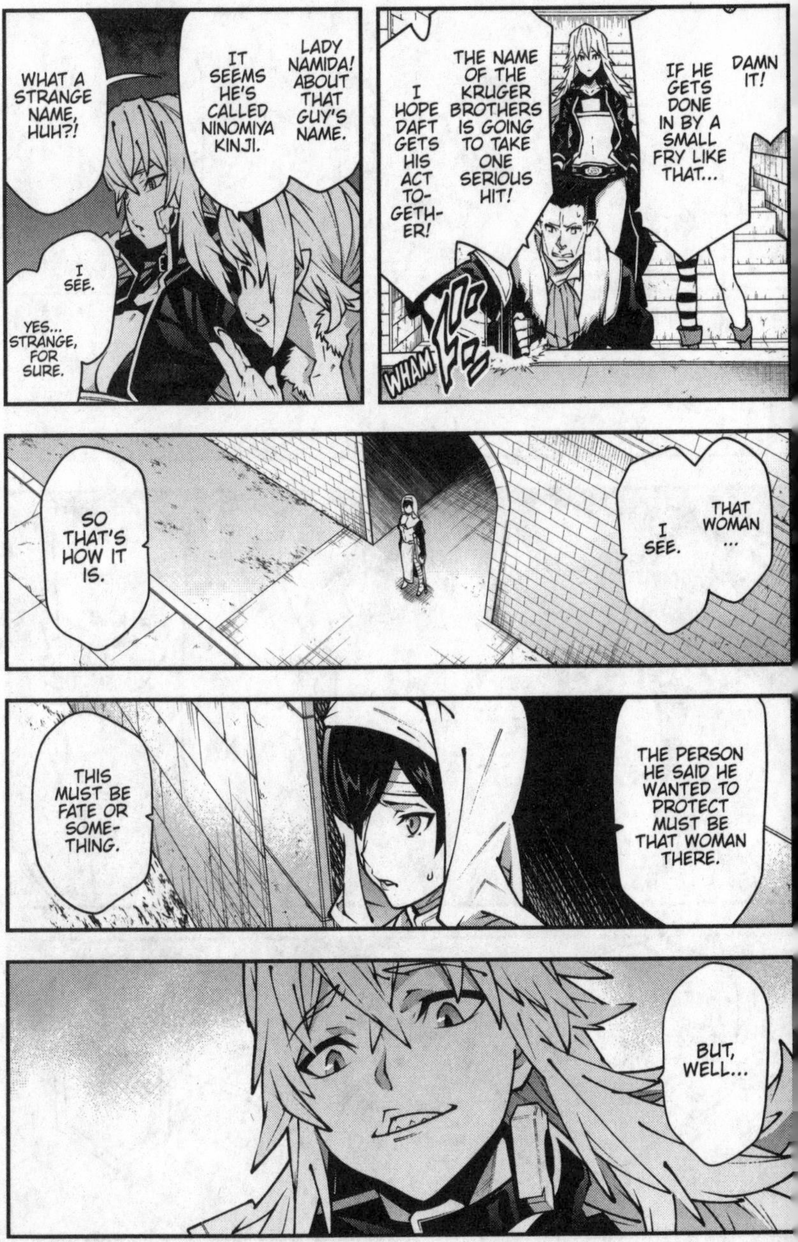
DAMN IT!
IF HE GETS DONE IN BY A SMALL FRY LIKE THAT...
THE NAME OF THE KRUGER BROTHERS IS GOING TO TAKE ONE SERIOUS HIT!
I HOPE DAFT GETS HIS ACT TO-GETH-ER!
WHAM
LADY NAMIDA! ABOUT THAT GUY'S NAME.
IT SEEMS HE'S CALLED NINOMIYA KINJI.
WHAT A STRANGE NAME, HUH?!
I SEE.
YES... STRANGE, FOR SURE.
THAT WOMAN ...
I SEE.
SO THAT'S HOW IT IS.
THE PERSON HE SAID HE WANTED TO PROTECT MUST BE THAT WOMAN THERE.
THIS MUST BE FATE OR SOME-THING.
BUT, WELL...

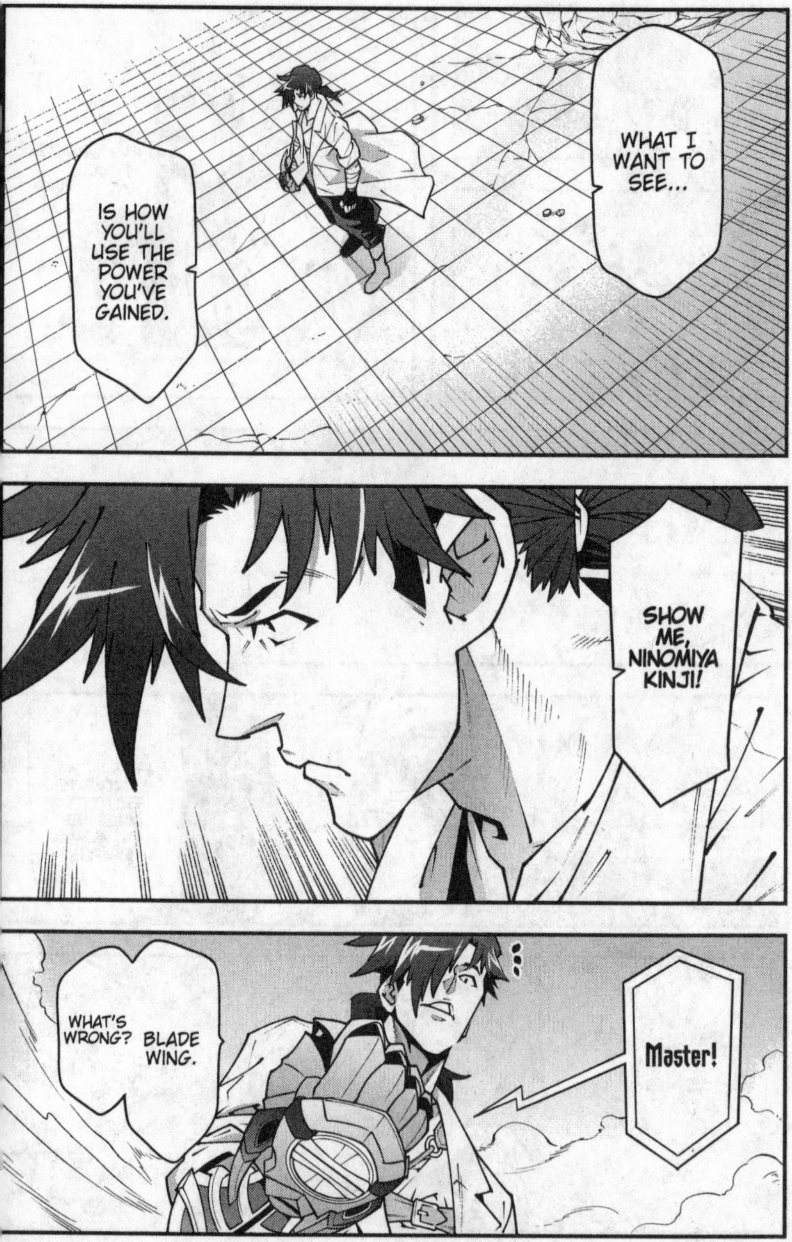
WHAT I WANT TO SEE...
IS HOW YOU'LL USE THE POWER YOU'VE GAINED.
SHOW ME, NINOMIYA KINJI!
Master!
WHAT'S WRONG? BLADE WING.

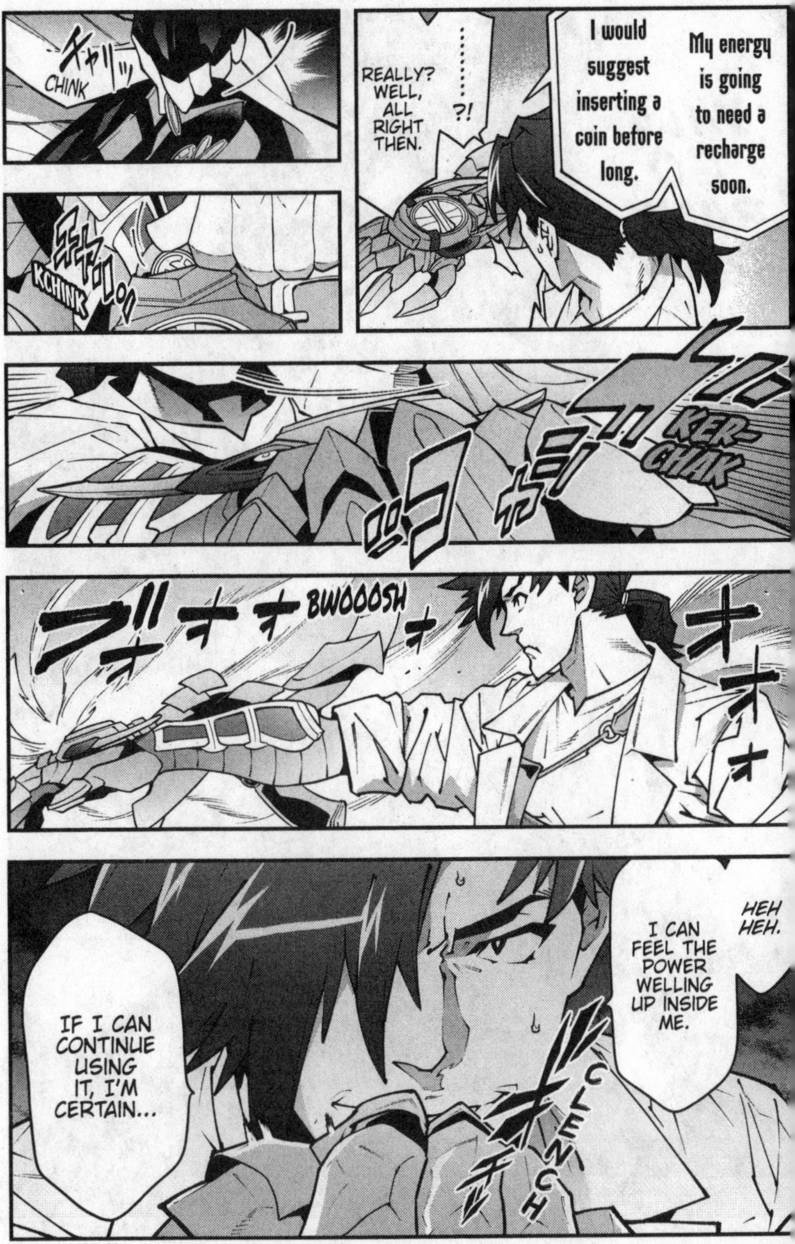
My energy is going to need a recharge soon.
I would suggest inserting a coin before long.
......?!
REALLY? WELL, ALL RIGHT THEN.
CHINK
KCHINK
KER-CHAK
BWOOOSH
HEH HEH.
I CAN FEEL THE POWER WELLING UP INSIDE ME.
IF I CAN CONTINUE USING IT, I'M CERTAIN...
CLENCH

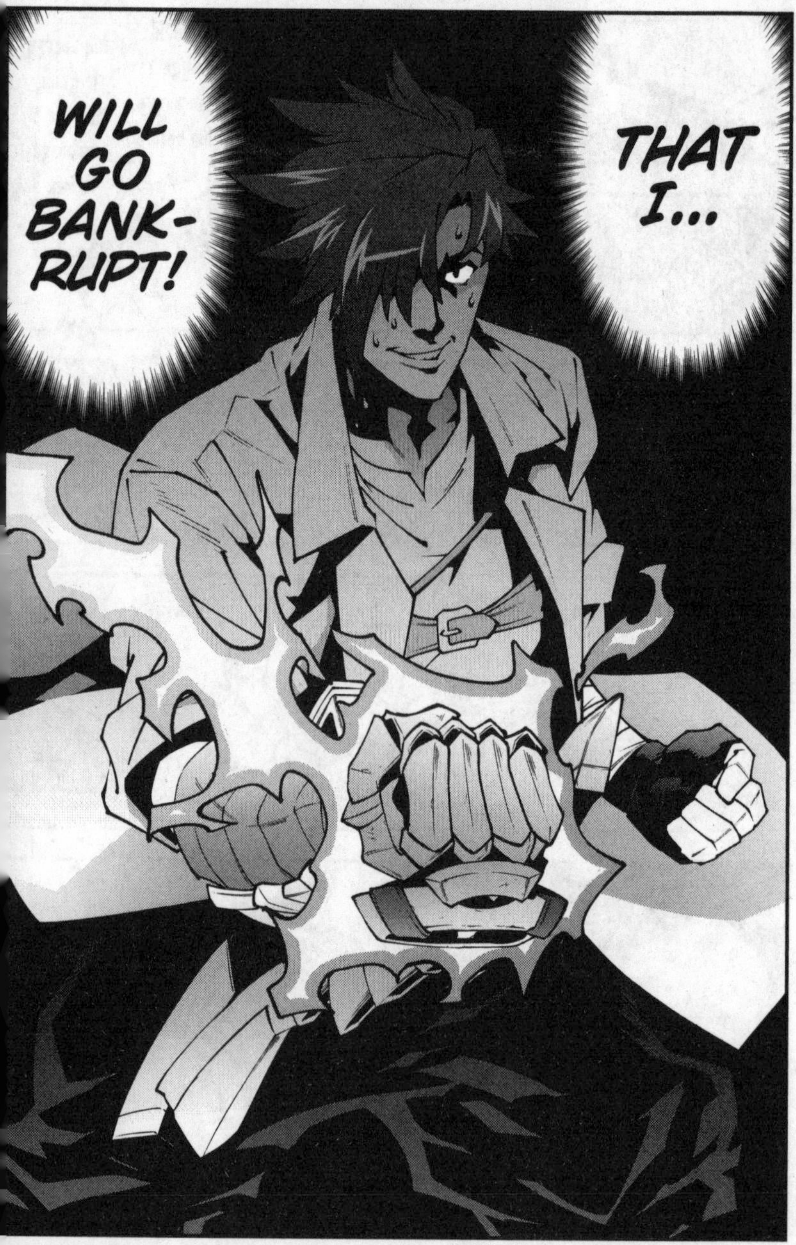
THAT I...
WILL GO BANK-RUPT!

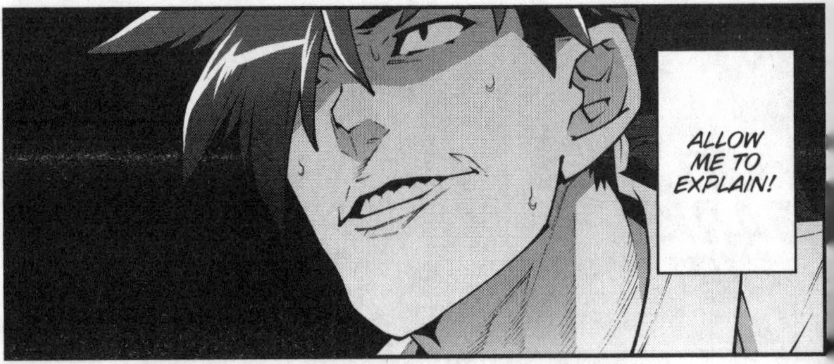
ALLOW ME TO EXPLAIN!

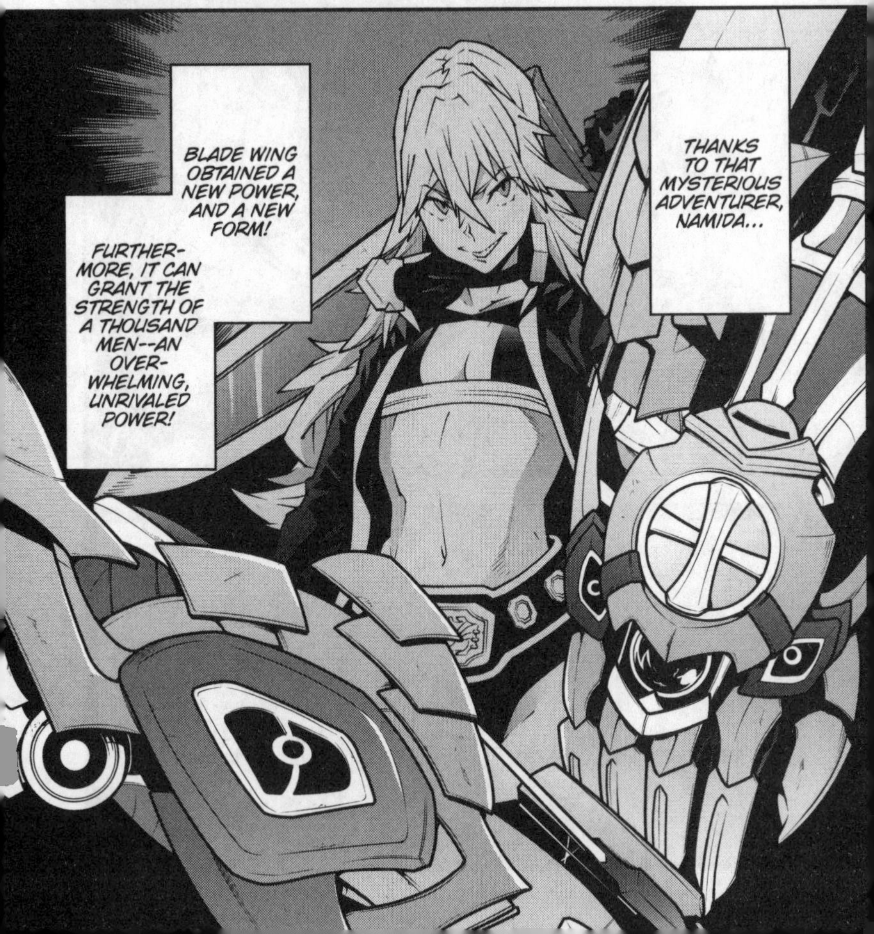
THANKS TO THAT MYSTERIOUS ADVENTURER, NAMIDA...
BLADE WING OBTAINED A NEW POWER, AND A NEW FORM!
FURTHER-MORE, IT CAN GRANT THE STRENGTH OF A THOUSAND MEN--AN OVER-WHELMING, UNRIVALED POWER!

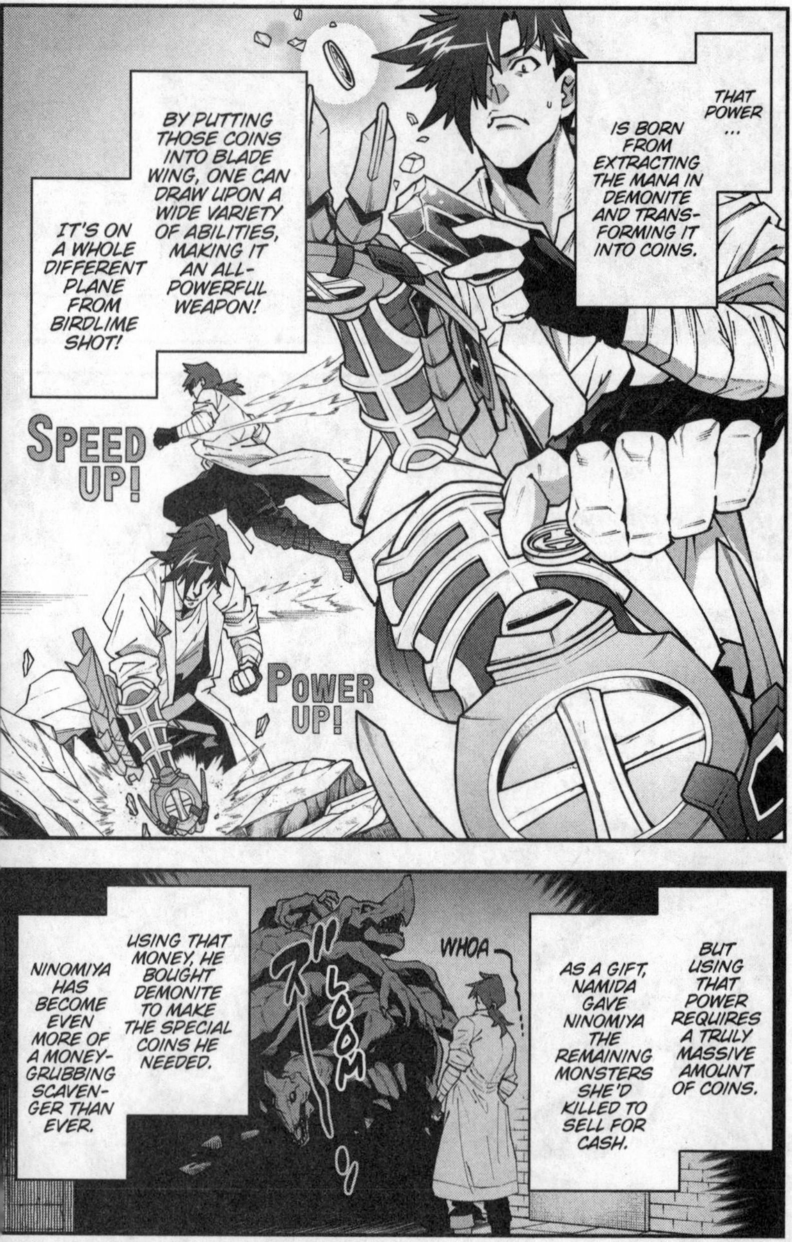
THAT POWER ... IS BORN FROM EXTRACTING THE MANA IN DEMONITE AND TRANS-FORMING IT INTO COINS.
BY PUTTING THOSE COINS INTO BLADE WING, ONE CAN DRAW UPON A WIDE VARIETY OF ABILITIES, MAKING IT AN ALL-POWERFUL WEAPON!
IT'S ON A WHOLE DIFFERENT PLANE FROM BIRDLIME SHOT!
SPEED UP!
POWER UP!
BUT USING THAT POWER REQUIRES A TRULY MASSIVE AMOUNT OF COINS.
AS A GIFT, NAMIDA GAVE NINOMIYA THE REMAINING MONSTERS SHE'D KILLED TO SELL FOR CASH.
WHOA
ズLOOM
USING THAT MONEY, HE BOUGHT DEMONITE TO MAKE THE SPECIAL COINS HE NEEDED.
NINOMIYA HAS BECOME EVEN MORE OF A MONEY-GRUBBING SCAVEN-GER THAN EVER.

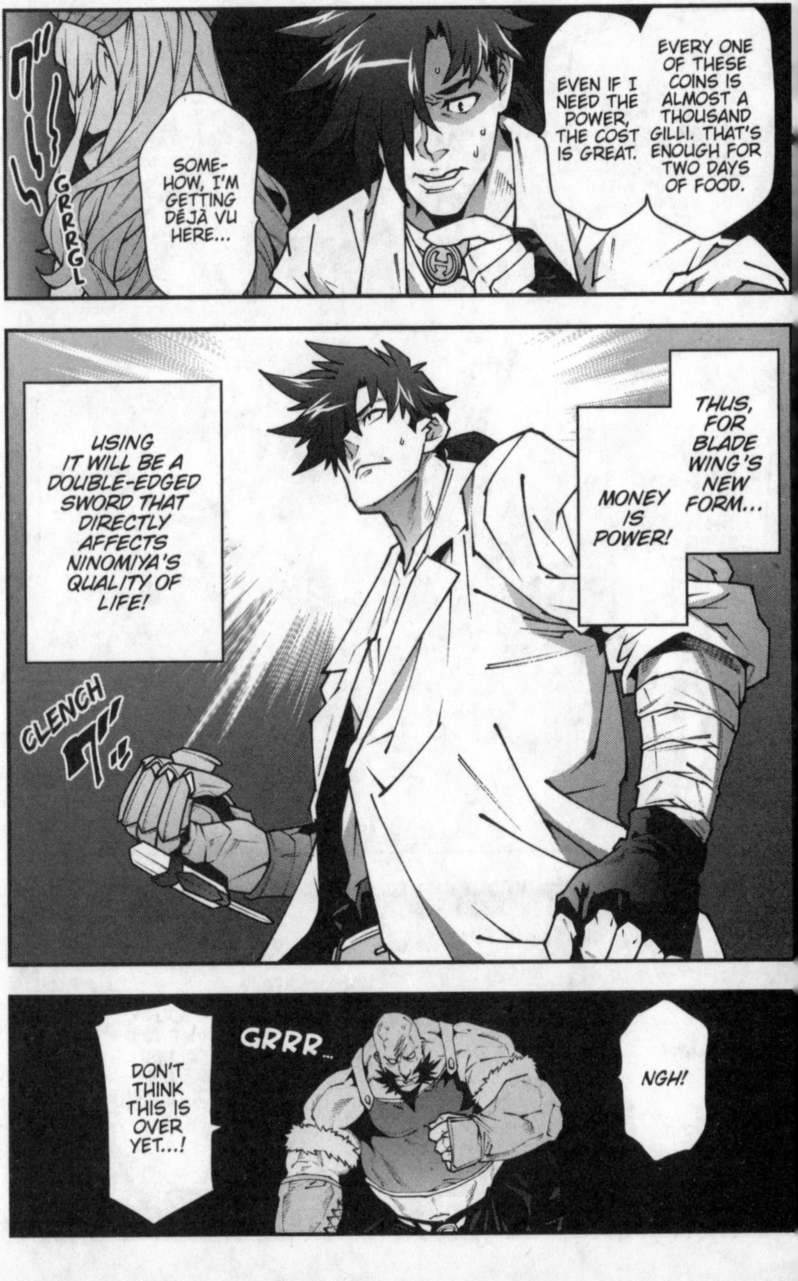
EVERY ONE OF THESE COINS IS ALMOST A THOUSAND GILLI. THAT'S ENOUGH FOR TWO DAYS OF FOOD.
EVEN IF I NEED THE POWER, THE COST IS GREAT.
SOME-HOW, I'M GETTING DÉJÀ VU HERE...
GRRRGL
THUS, FOR BLADE WING'S NEW FORM...
MONEY IS POWER!
USING IT WILL BE A DOUBLE-EDGED SWORD THAT DIRECTLY AFFECTS NINOMIYA'S QUALITY OF LIFE!
CLENCH
NGH!
GRRR...
DON'T THINK THIS IS OVER YET...!

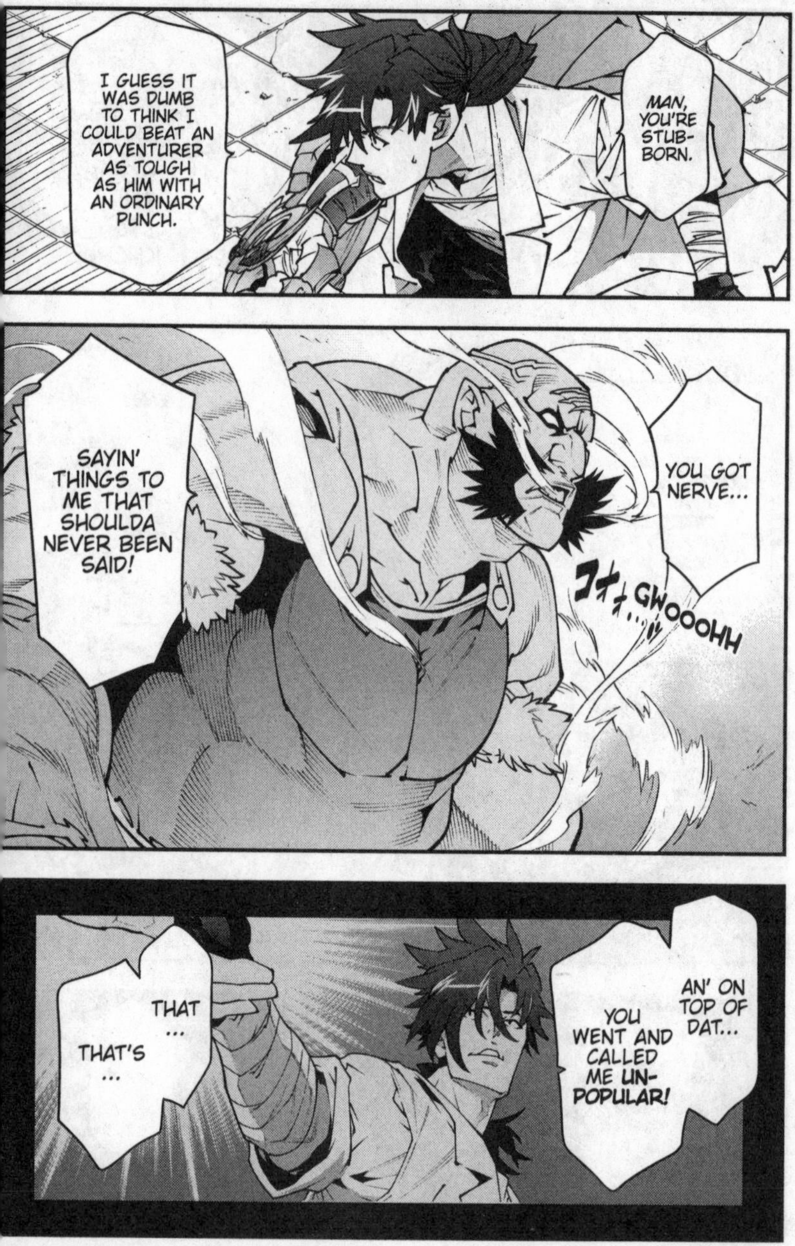
MAN, YOU'RE STUB-BORN.
I GUESS IT WAS DUMB TO THINK I COULD BEAT AN ADVENTURER AS TOUGH AS HIM WITH AN ORDINARY PUNCH.
YOU GOT NERVE...
GWOOOHH
SAYIN' THINGS TO ME THAT SHOULDA NEVER BEEN SAID!
AN' ON TOP OF DAT...
YOU WENT AND CALLED ME UN-POPULAR!
THAT ...
THAT'S ...

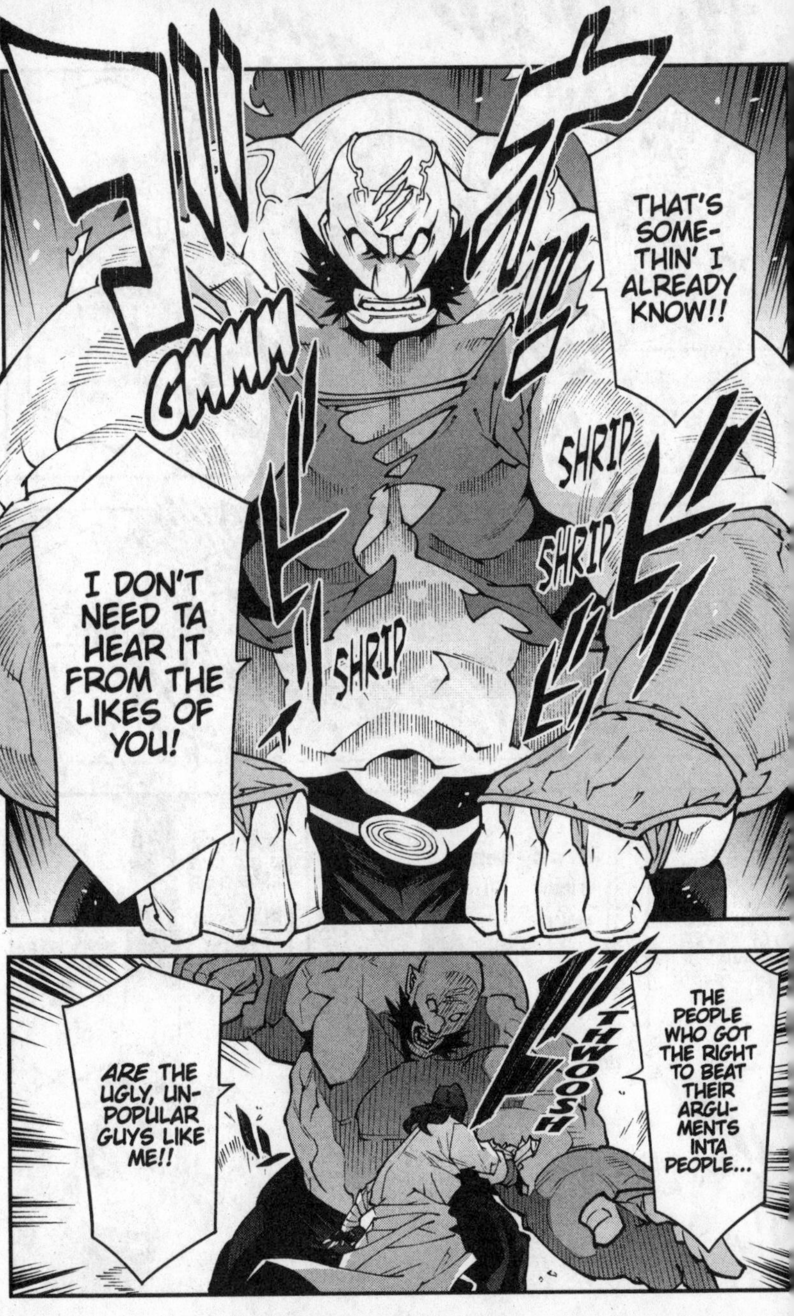
THAT'S SOME-THIN' I ALREADY KNOW!!
GMMM
SHRIP
SHRIP
SHRIP
I DON'T NEED TA HEAR IT FROM THE LIKES OF YOU!
THE PEOPLE WHO GOT THE RIGHT TO BEAT THEIR ARGU-MENTS INTA PEOPLE...
THWOOSH
ARE THE UGLY, UN-POPULAR GUYS LIKE ME!!

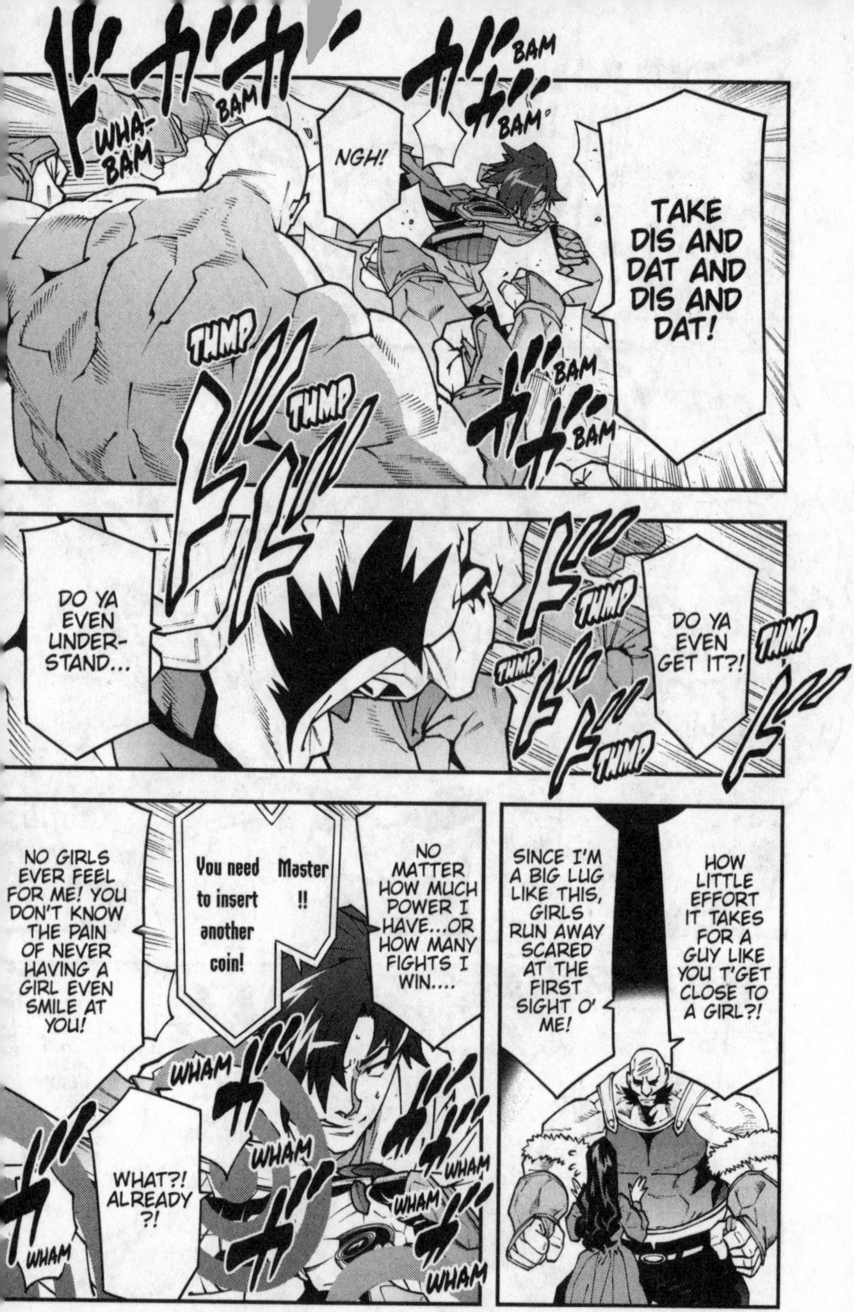
BAM
BAM
TAKE DIS AND DAT AND DIS AND DAT!
NGH!
BAM
WHA-BAM
BAM
BAM
THMP
THMP
DO YA EVEN GET IT?!
THMP
THMP
THMP
THMP
DO YA EVEN UNDERSTAND...
HOW LITTLE EFFORT IT TAKES FOR A GUY LIKE YOU T'GET CLOSE TO A GIRL?!
SINCE I'M A BIG LUG LIKE THIS, GIRLS RUN AWAY SCARED AT THE FIRST SIGHT O' ME!
NO MATTER HOW MUCH POWER I HAVE...OR HOW MANY FIGHTS I WIN....
Master !!
You need to insert another coin!
NO GIRLS EVER FEEL FOR ME! YOU DON'T KNOW THE PAIN OF NEVER HAVING A GIRL EVEN SMILE AT YOU!
WHAM
WHAM
WHAM
WHAM
WHAM
WHAT?! ALREADY ?!
WHAM

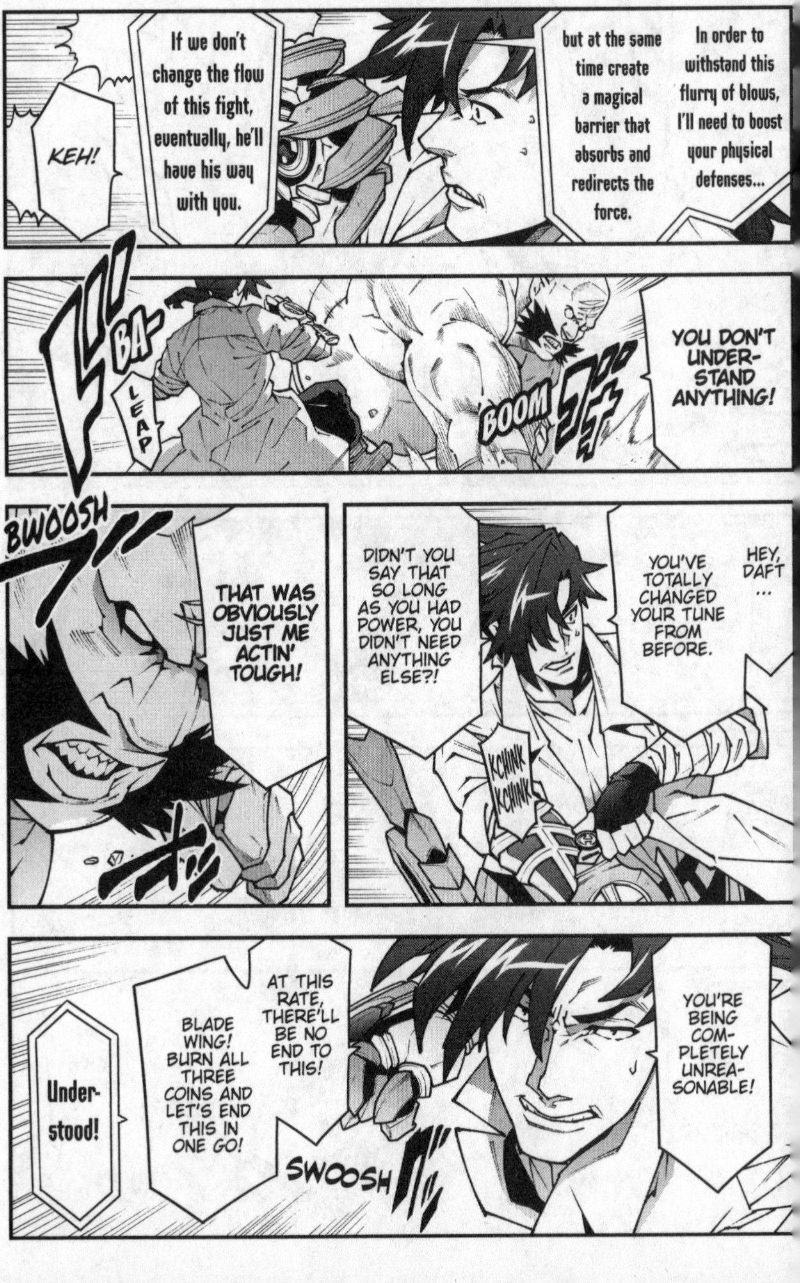
In order to withstand this flurry of blows, I'll need to boost your physical defenses...
but at the same time create a magical barrier that absorbs and redirects the force.
If we don't change the flow of this fight, eventually, he'll have his way with you.
KEH!
YOU DON'T UNDER-STAND ANYTHING!
BOOM
LEAP
BA-
HEY, DAFT...
YOU'VE TOTALLY CHANGED YOUR TUNE FROM BEFORE.
DIDN'T YOU SAY THAT SO LONG AS YOU HAD POWER, YOU DIDN'T NEED ANYTHING ELSE?!
KCHINK KCHINK
BWOOSH
THAT WAS OBVIOUSLY JUST ME ACTIN' TOUGH!
YOU'RE BEING COM-PLETELY UNREA-SONABLE!
AT THIS RATE, THERE'LL BE NO END TO THIS!
BLADE WING! BURN ALL THREE COINS AND LET'S END THIS IN ONE GO!
SWOOSH
Under-stood!

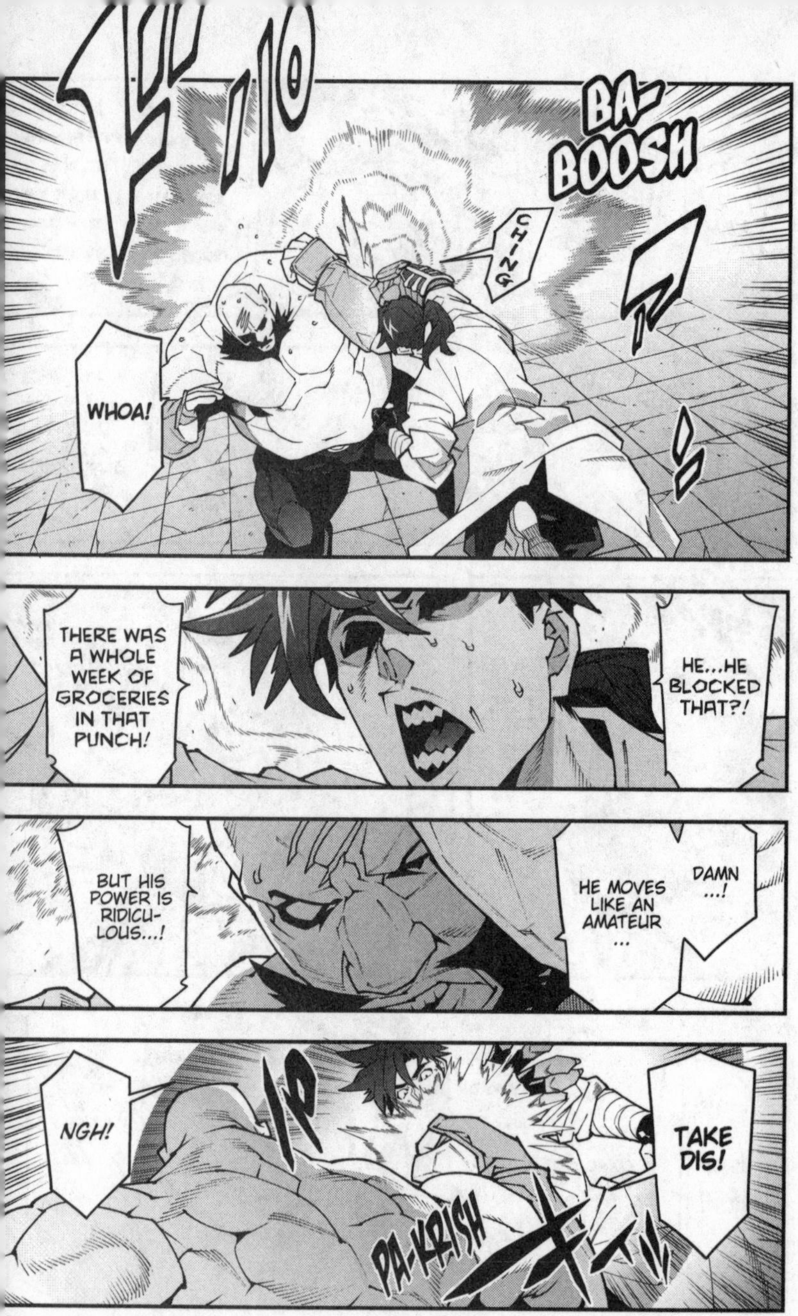
BA-BOOSH
CHING
WHOA!
HE...HE BLOCKED THAT?!
THERE WAS A WHOLE WEEK OF GROCERIES IN THAT PUNCH!
DAMN...!
HE MOVES LIKE AN AMATEUR...
BUT HIS POWER IS RIDICULOUS...!
TAKE DIS!
PA-KRISH
NGH!

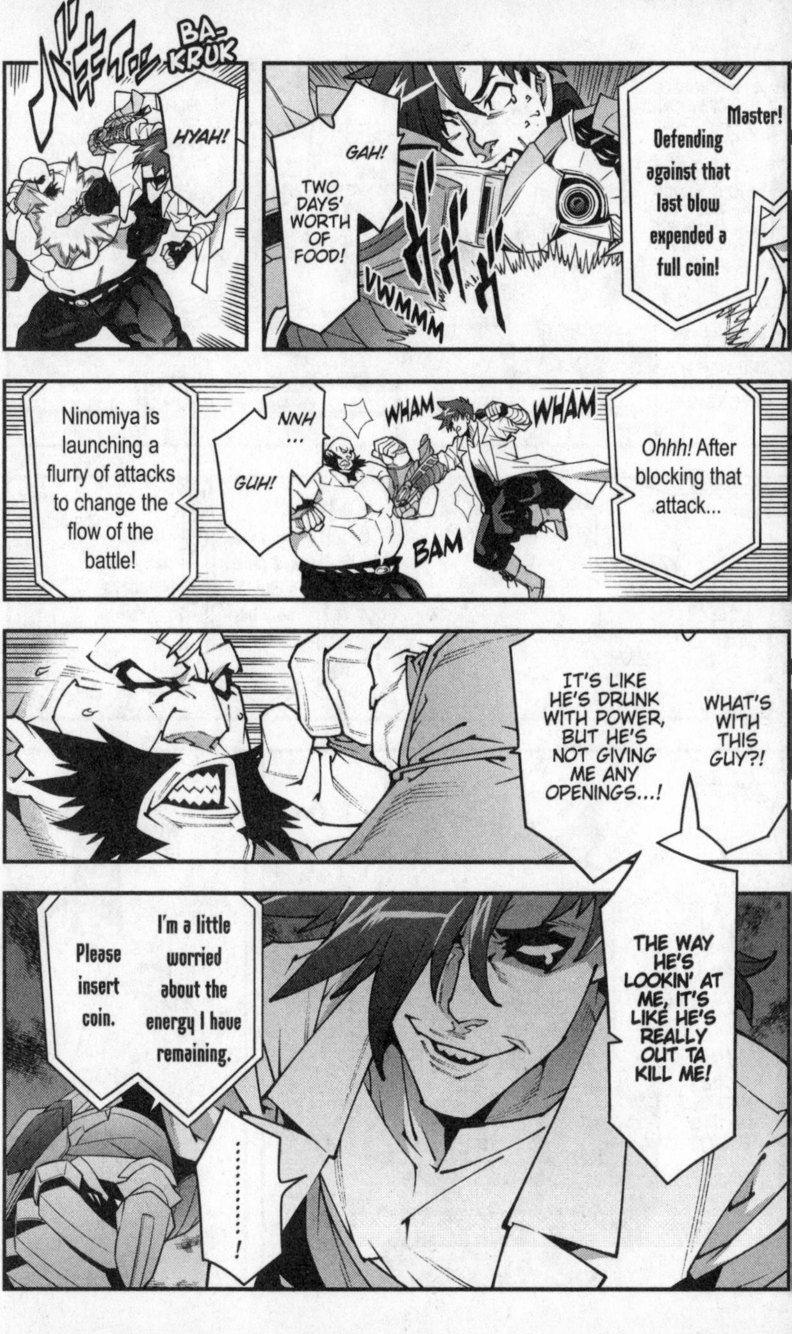
Master! Defending against that last blow expended a full coin!
GAH!
TWO DAYS' WORTH OF FOOD!
VWMMMM
BA-KRUK
HYAH!
Ohhh! After blocking that attack...
WHAM
WHAM
NNH ...
GUH!
BAM
Ninomiya is launching a flurry of attacks to change the flow of the battle!
WHAT'S WITH THIS GUY?!
IT'S LIKE HE'S DRUNK WITH POWER, BUT HE'S NOT GIVING ME ANY OPENINGS...!
THE WAY HE'S LOOKIN' AT ME, IT'S LIKE HE'S REALLY OUT TA KILL ME!
I'm a little worried about the energy I have remaining.
Please insert coin.
......!

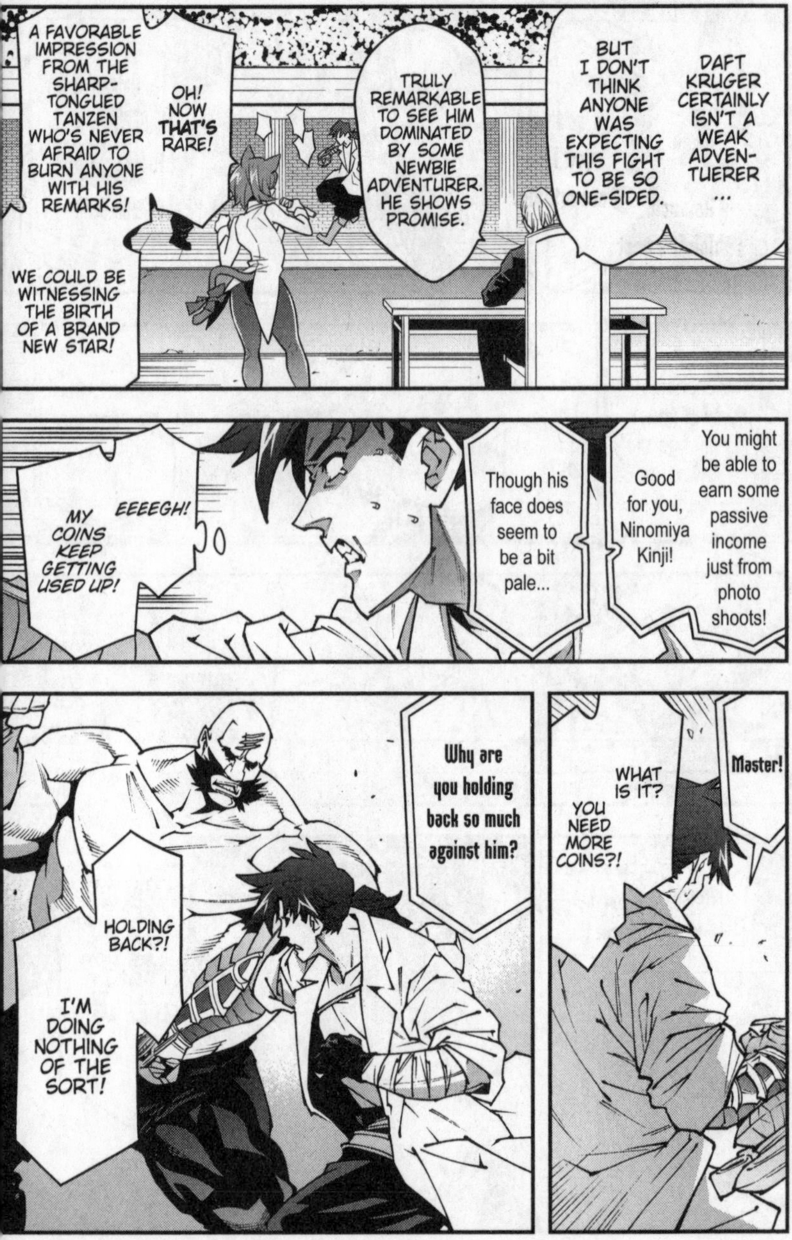
DAFT KRUGER CERTAINLY ISN'T A WEAK ADVENTURER ...
BUT I DON'T THINK ANYONE WAS EXPECTING THIS FIGHT TO BE SO ONE-SIDED.
TRULY REMARKABLE TO SEE HIM DOMINATED BY SOME NEWBIE ADVENTURER. HE SHOWS PROMISE.
OH! NOW THAT'S RARE!
A FAVORABLE IMPRESSION FROM THE SHARP-TONGUED TANZEN WHO'S NEVER AFRAID TO BURN ANYONE WITH HIS REMARKS!
WE COULD BE WITNESSING THE BIRTH OF A BRAND NEW STAR!
You might be able to earn some passive income just from photo shoots!
Good for you, Ninomiya Kinji!
Though his face does seem to be a bit pale...
EEEEGH!
MY COINS KEEP GETTING USED UP!
Master!
WHAT IS IT?
YOU NEED MORE COINS?!
Why are you holding back so much against him?
HOLDING BACK?!
I'M DOING NOTHING OF THE SORT!

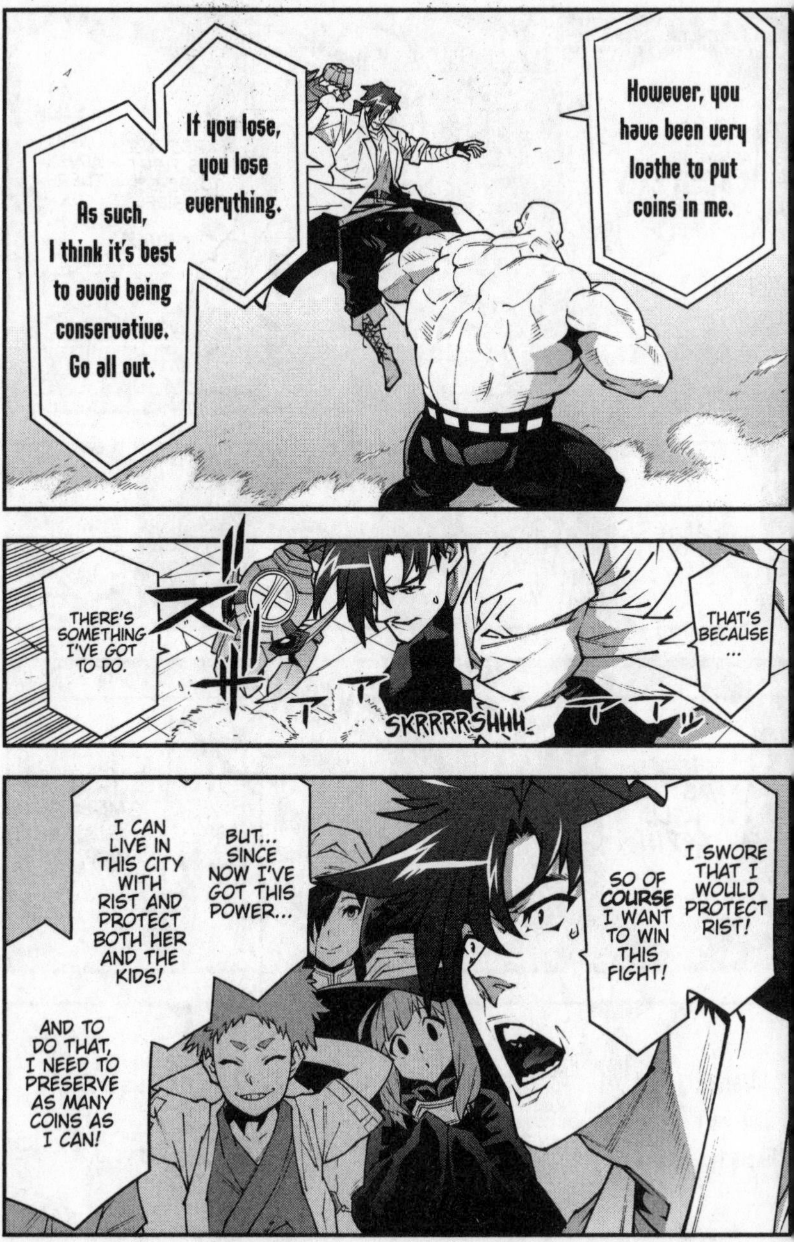
However, you have been very loathe to put coins in me.
If you lose, you lose everything.
As such, I think it's best to avoid being conservative. Go all out.
THAT'S BECAUSE...
SKRRRRSHHH
THERE'S SOMETHING I'VE GOT TO DO.
I SWORE THAT I WOULD PROTECT RIST!
SO OF COURSE I WANT TO WIN THIS FIGHT!
BUT... SINCE NOW I'VE GOT THIS POWER...
I CAN LIVE IN THIS CITY WITH RIST AND PROTECT BOTH HER AND THE KIDS!
AND TO DO THAT, I NEED TO PRESERVE AS MANY COINS AS I CAN!

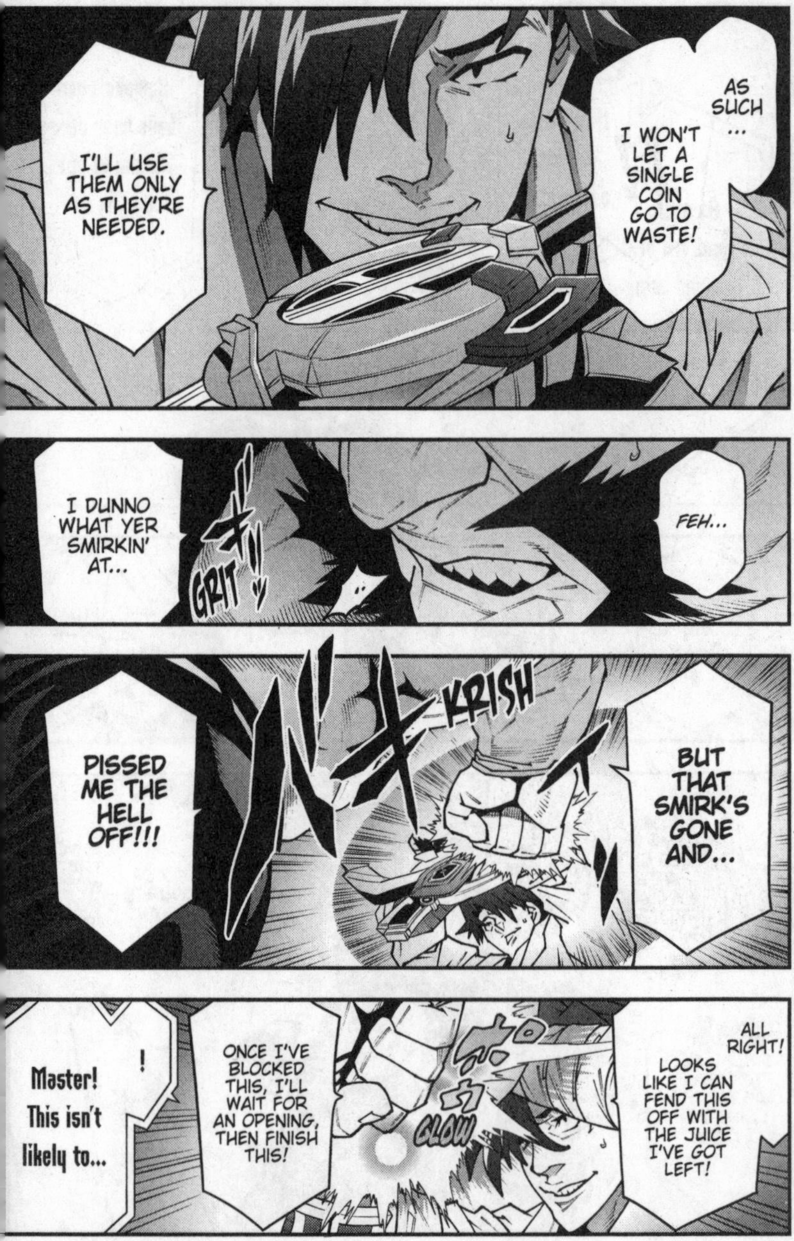
AS SUCH...
I WON'T LET A SINGLE COIN GO TO WASTE!
I'LL USE THEM ONLY AS THEY'RE NEEDED.
FEH...
GRIT
I DUNNO WHAT YER SMIRKIN' AT...
KRISH
BUT THAT SMIRK'S GONE AND...
PISSED ME THE HELL OFF!!!
ALL RIGHT!
LOOKS LIKE I CAN FEND THIS OFF WITH THE JUICE I'VE GOT LEFT!
GLOW
ONCE I'VE BLOCKED THIS, I'LL WAIT FOR AN OPENING, THEN FINISH THIS!
!
Master! This isn't likely to...

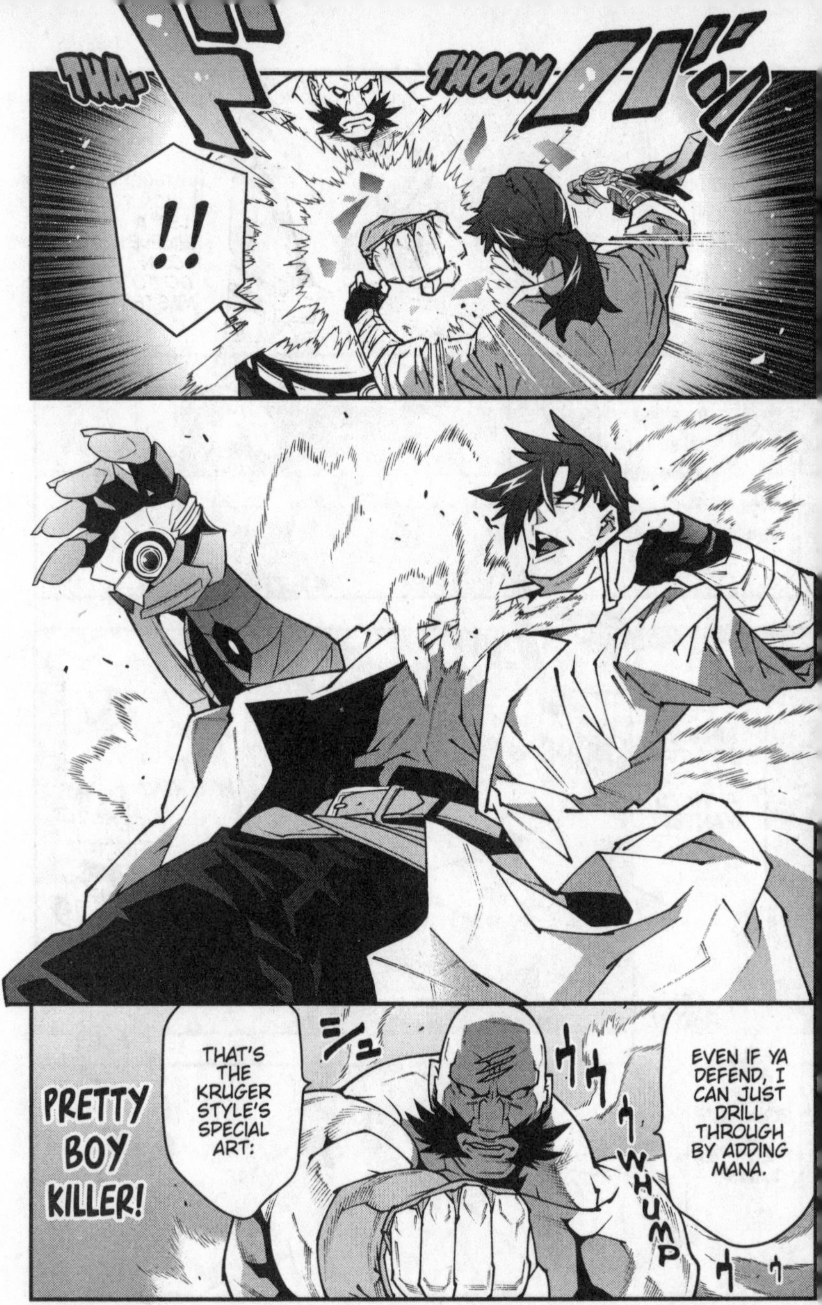
THA-THOOM
!!
EVEN IF YA DEFEND, I CAN JUST DRILL THROUGH BY ADDING MANA.
WHUMP
シュ
THAT'S THE KRUGER STYLE'S SPECIAL ART:
PRETTY BOY KILLER!

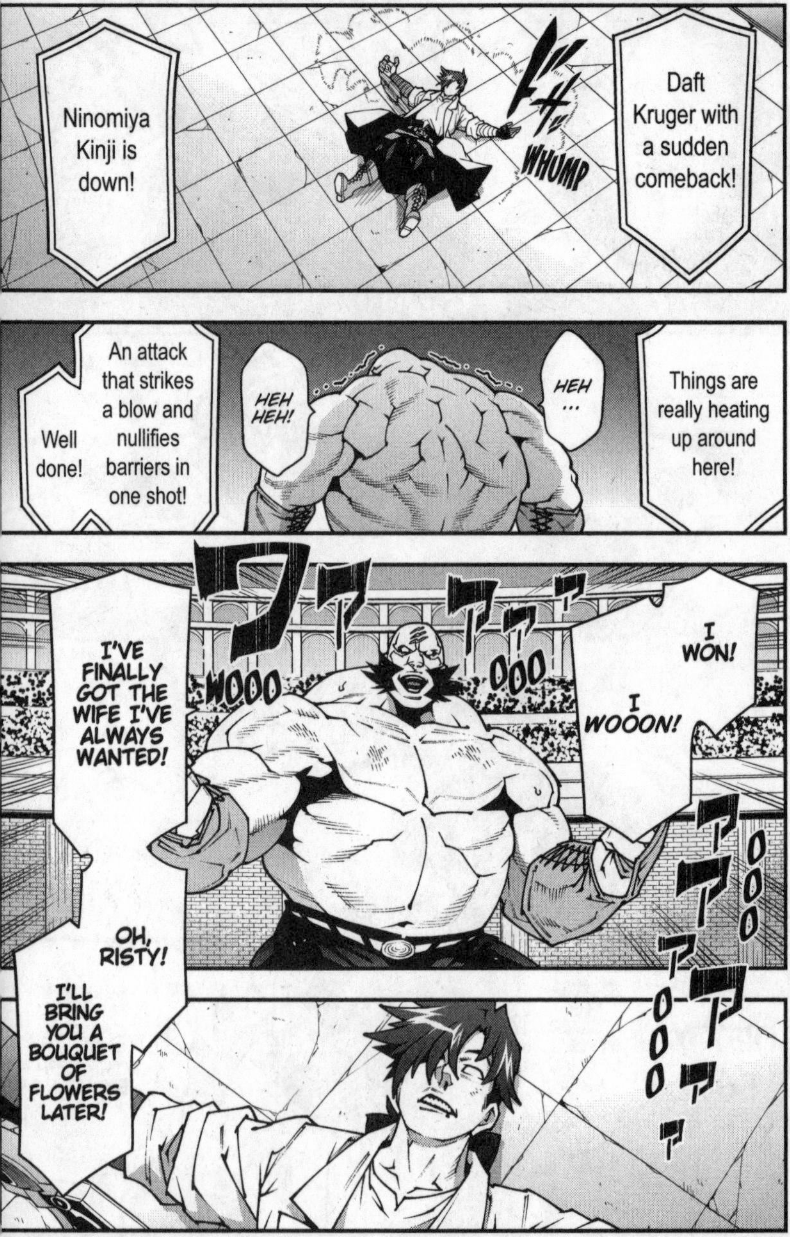
Daft Kruger with a sudden comeback!
WHUMP
Ninomiya Kinji is down!
Things are really heating up around here!
HEH ...
HEH HEH!
An attack that strikes a blow and nullifies barriers in one shot!
Well done!
I WON!
I WOOON!
OOO
WOOO
I'VE FINALLY GOT THE WIFE I'VE ALWAYS WANTED!
OH, RISTY!
OOOOOO
I'LL BRING YOU A BOUQUET OF FLOWERS LATER!

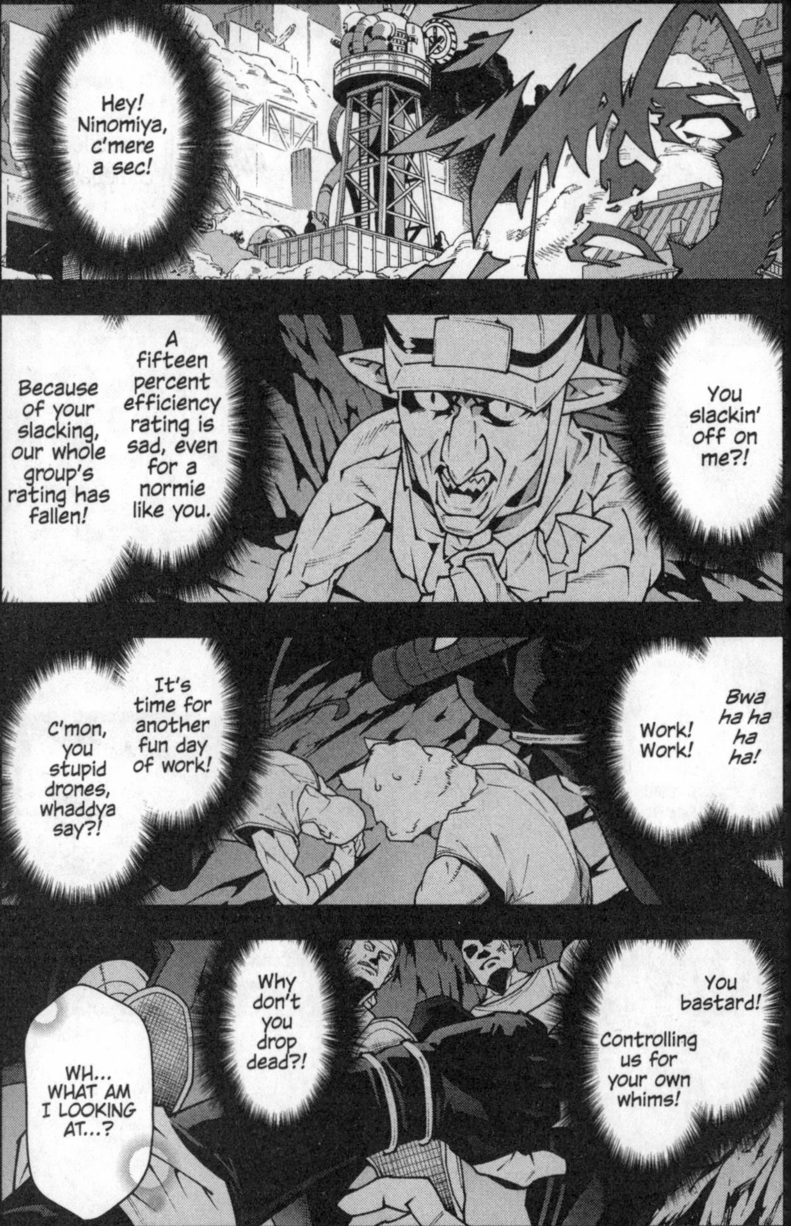
Hey! Ninomiya, c'mere a sec!
You slackin' off on me?!
A fifteen percent efficiency rating is sad, even for a normie like you.
Because of your slacking, our whole group's rating has fallen!
Bwa ha ha ha ha!
Work! Work!
It's time for another fun day of work!
C'mon, you stupid drones, whaddya say?!
You bastard!
Controlling us for your own whims!
Why don't you drop dead?!
WH... WHAT AM I LOOKING AT...?

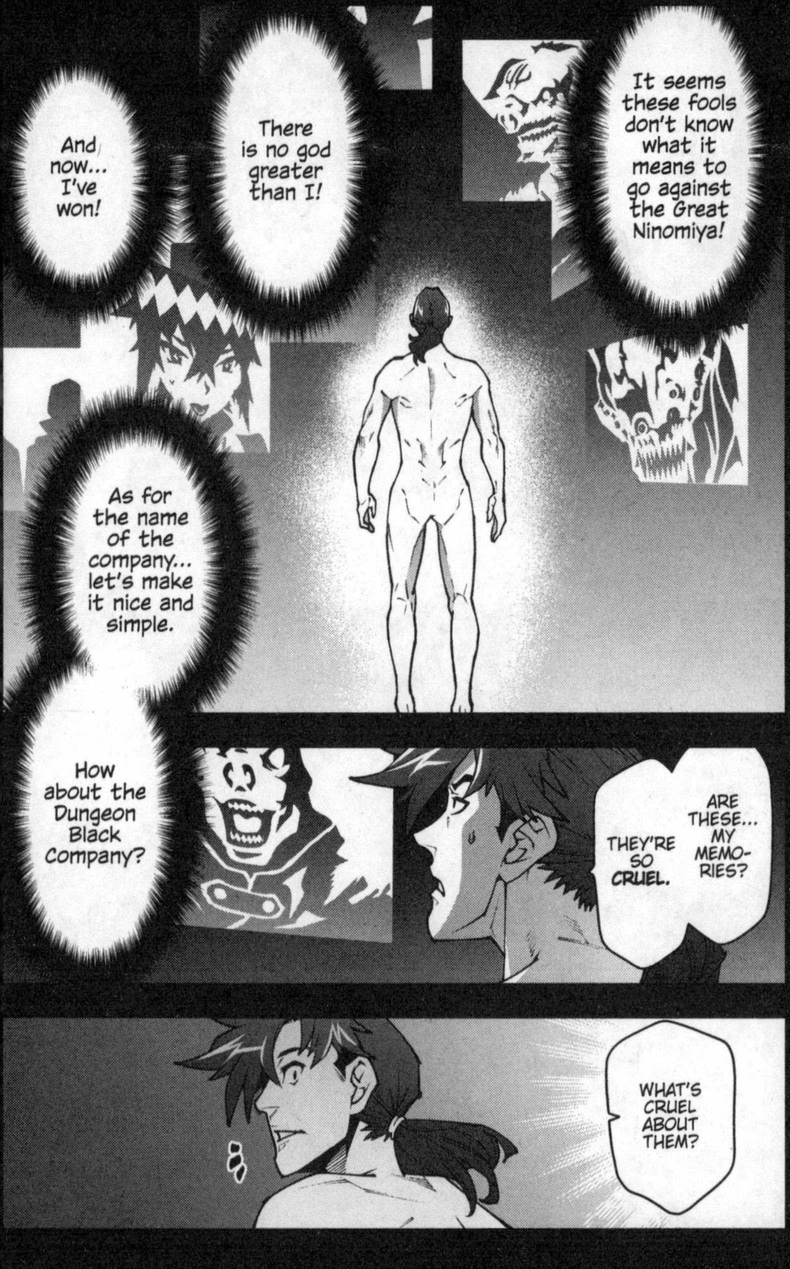
It seems these fools don't know what it means to go against the Great Ninomiya!
There is no god greater than I!
And now... I've won!
As for the name of the company... let's make it nice and simple.
How about the Dungeon Black Company?
ARE THESE... MY MEMORIES?
THEY'RE SO CRUEL.
WHAT'S CRUEL ABOUT THEM?

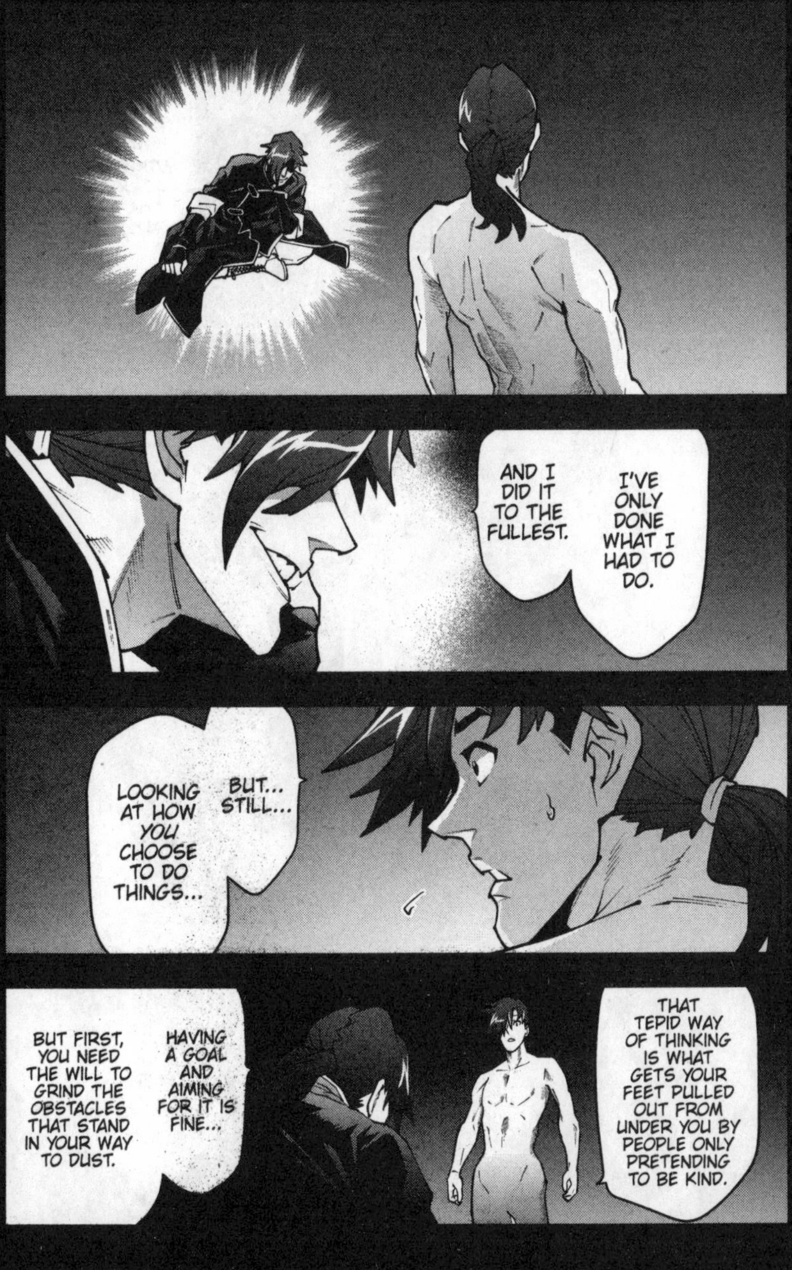
I'VE ONLY DONE WHAT I HAD TO DO.
AND I DID IT TO THE FULLEST.
BUT... STILL...
LOOKING AT HOW *YOU* CHOOSE TO DO THINGS...
THAT TEPID WAY OF THINKING IS WHAT GETS YOUR FEET PULLED OUT FROM UNDER YOU BY PEOPLE ONLY PRETENDING TO BE KIND.
HAVING A GOAL AND AIMING FOR IT IS FINE...
BUT FIRST, YOU NEED THE WILL TO GRIND THE OBSTACLES THAT STAND IN YOUR WAY TO DUST.

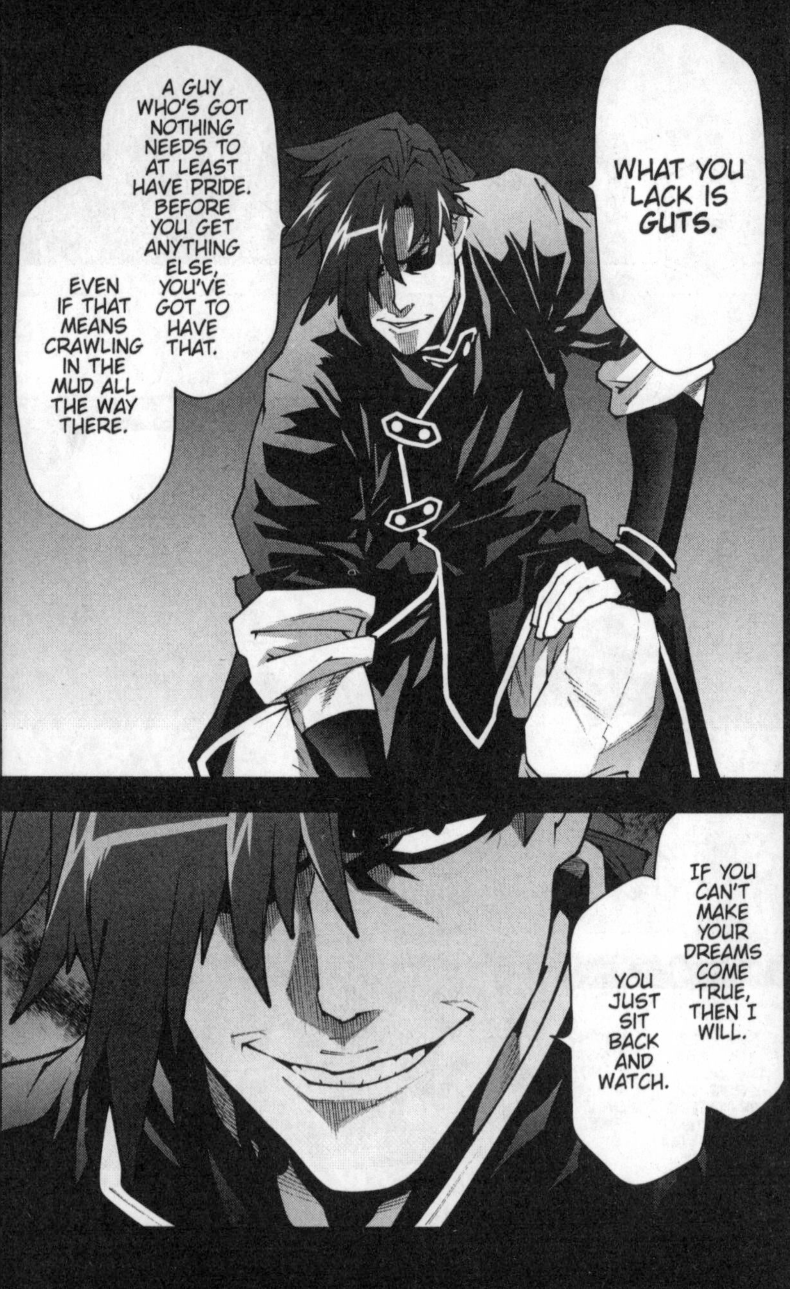
WHAT YOU LACK IS GUTS.
A GUY WHO'S GOT NOTHING NEEDS TO AT LEAST HAVE PRIDE. BEFORE YOU GET ANYTHING ELSE, YOU'VE GOT TO HAVE THAT.
EVEN IF THAT MEANS CRAWLING IN THE MUD ALL THE WAY THERE.
IF YOU CAN'T MAKE YOUR DREAMS COME TRUE, THEN I WILL.
YOU JUST SIT BACK AND WATCH.

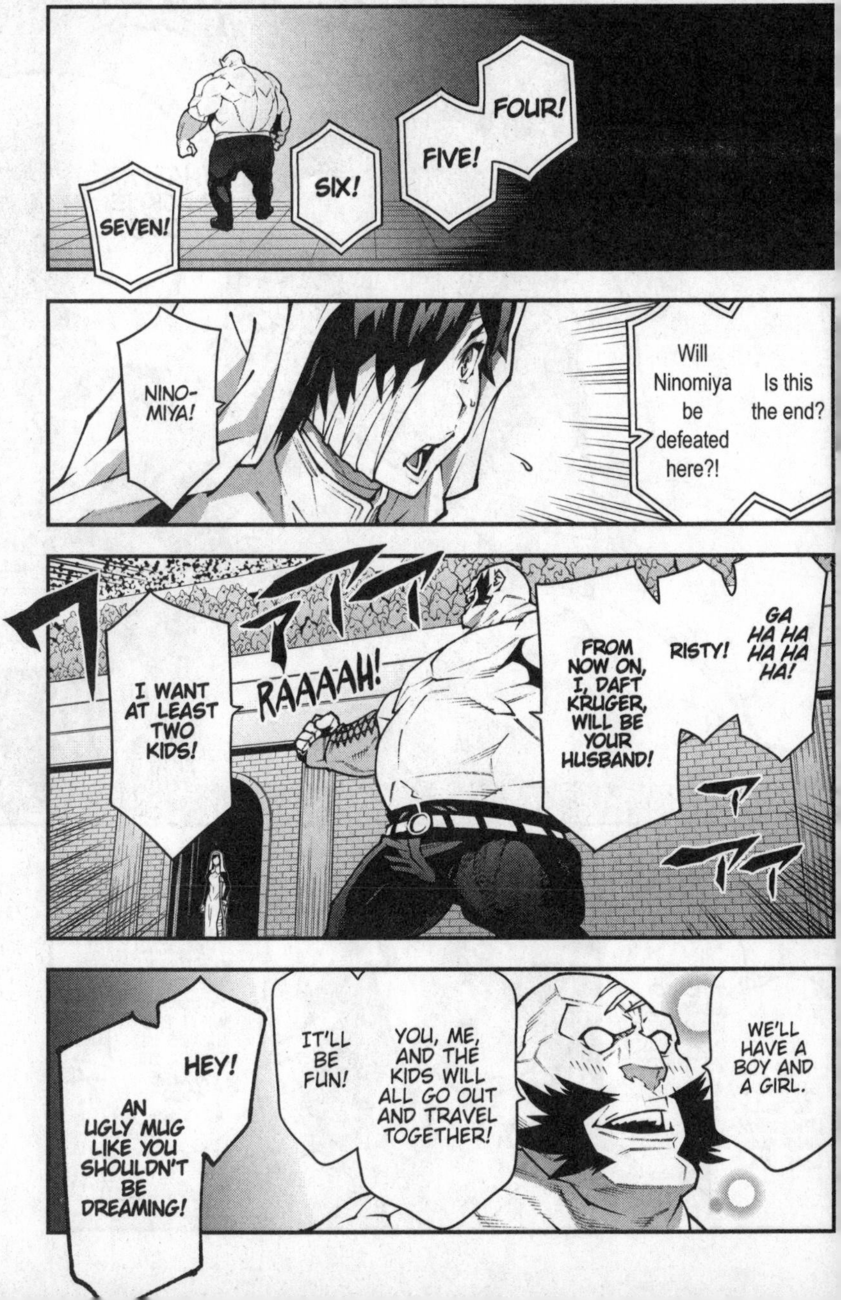
FOUR!
FIVE!
SIX!
SEVEN!
Is this the end?
Will Ninomiya be defeated here?!
NINO-MIYA!
GA HA HA HA HA HA!
RISTY!
FROM NOW ON, I, DAFT KRUGER, WILL BE YOUR HUSBAND!
RAAAAH!
I WANT AT LEAST TWO KIDS!
WE'LL HAVE A BOY AND A GIRL.
YOU, ME, AND THE KIDS WILL ALL GO OUT AND TRAVEL TOGETHER!
IT'LL BE FUN!
HEY!
AN UGLY MUG LIKE YOU SHOULDN'T BE DREAMING!

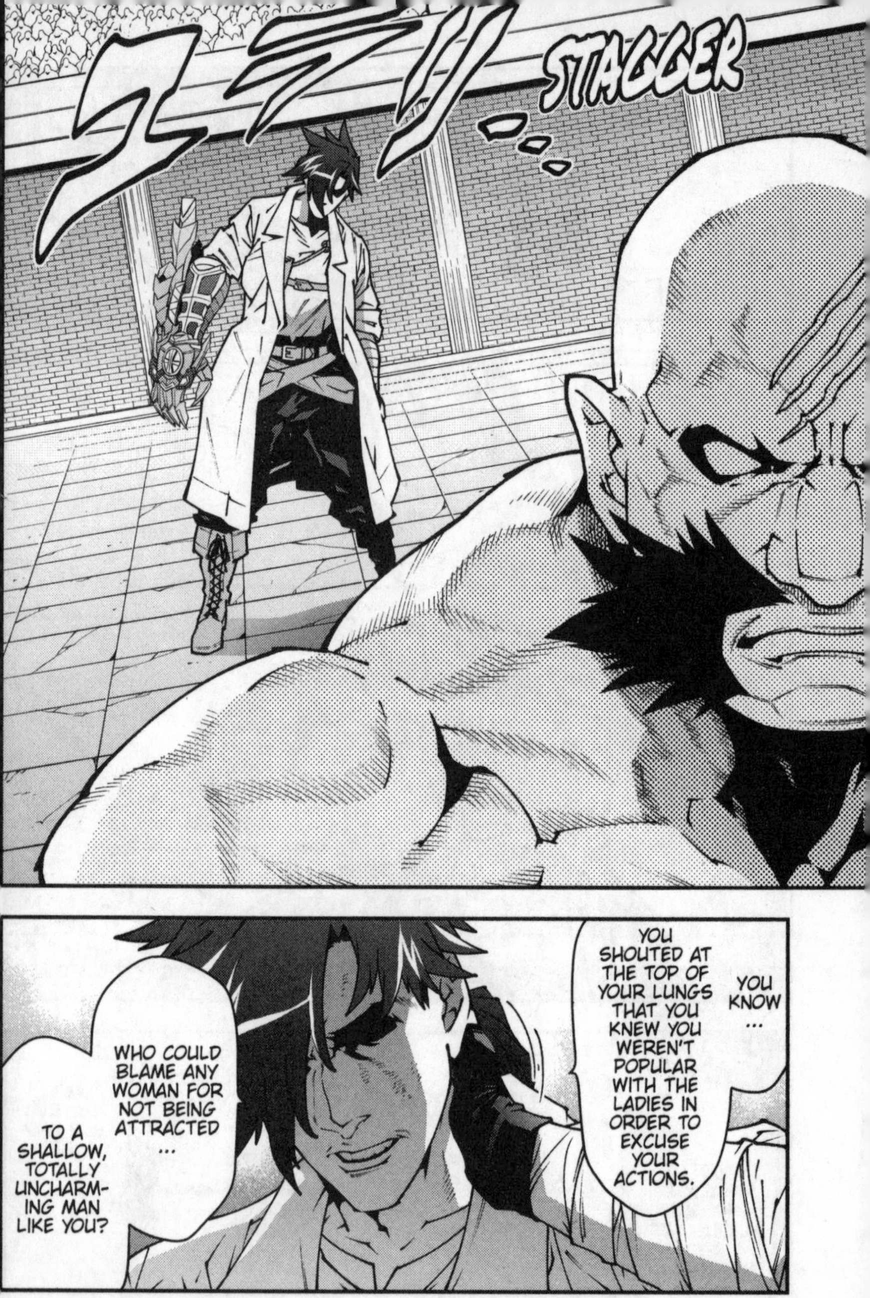
ユラリ
STAGGER
YOU KNOW ...
YOU SHOUTED AT THE TOP OF YOUR LUNGS THAT YOU KNEW YOU WEREN'T POPULAR WITH THE LADIES IN ORDER TO EXCUSE YOUR ACTIONS.
WHO COULD BLAME ANY WOMAN FOR NOT BEING ATTRACTED ...
TO A SHALLOW, TOTALLY UNCHARMING MAN LIKE YOU?

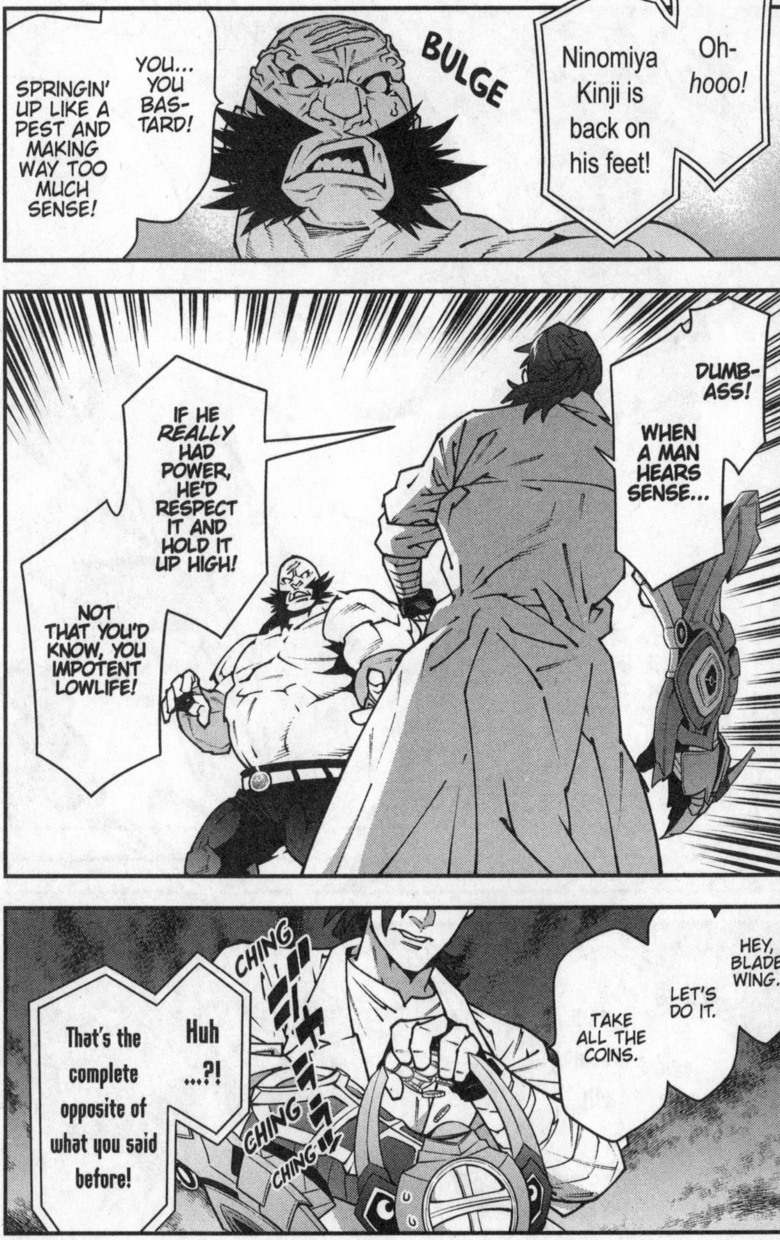
Oh-hooo!
Ninomiya Kinji is back on his feet!
BULGE
YOU... YOU BASTARD!
SPRINGIN' UP LIKE A PEST AND MAKING WAY TOO MUCH SENSE!
DUMBASS!
WHEN A MAN HEARS SENSE...
IF HE REALLY HAD POWER, HE'D RESPECT IT AND HOLD IT UP HIGH!
NOT THAT YOU'D KNOW, YOU IMPOTENT LOWLIFE!
HEY, BLADE WING.
LET'S DO IT.
TAKE ALL THE COINS.
CHING
CHING
CHING!!
Huh...?!
That's the complete opposite of what you said before!

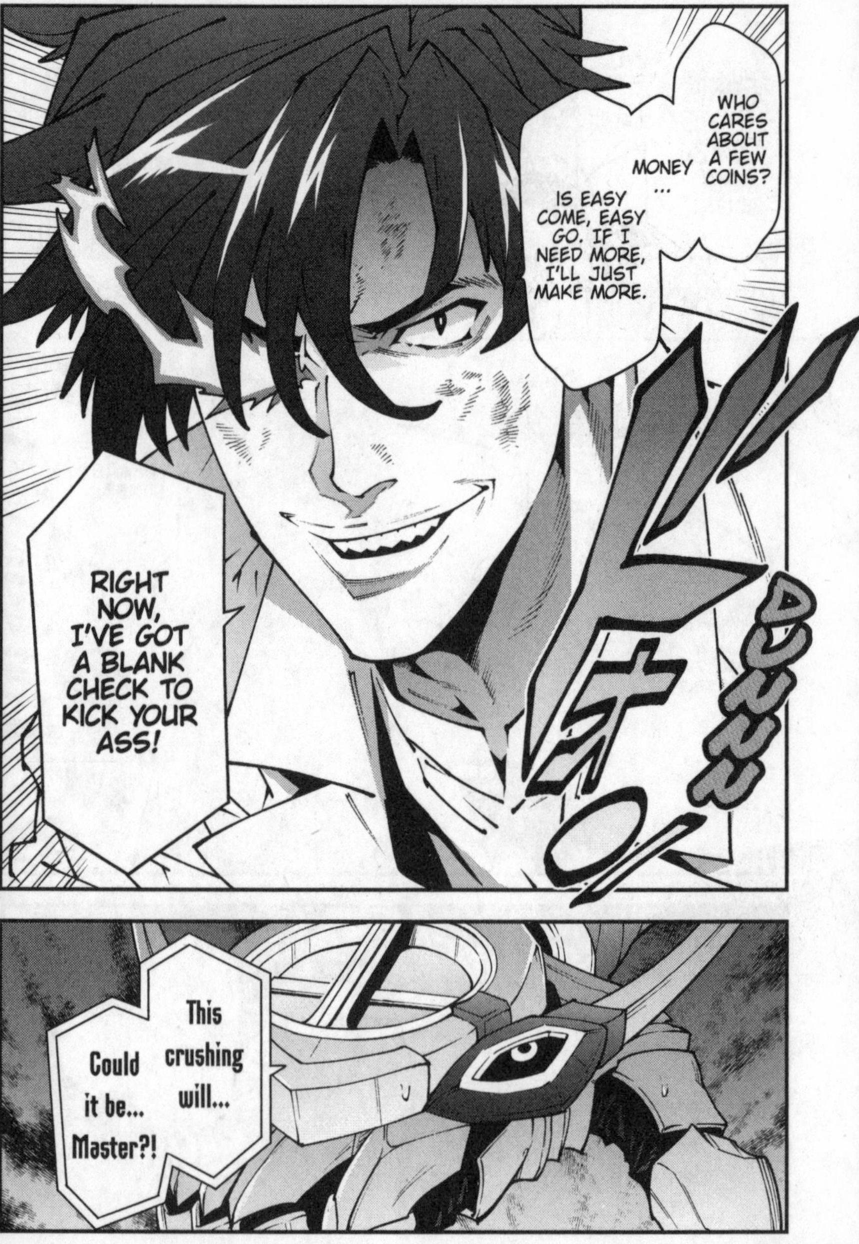
WHO CARES ABOUT A FEW COINS?
MONEY ...
IS EASY COME, EASY GO. IF I NEED MORE, I'LL JUST MAKE MORE.
DUNNN
RIGHT NOW, I'VE GOT A BLANK CHECK TO KICK YOUR ASS!
This crushing will...
Could it be... Master?!

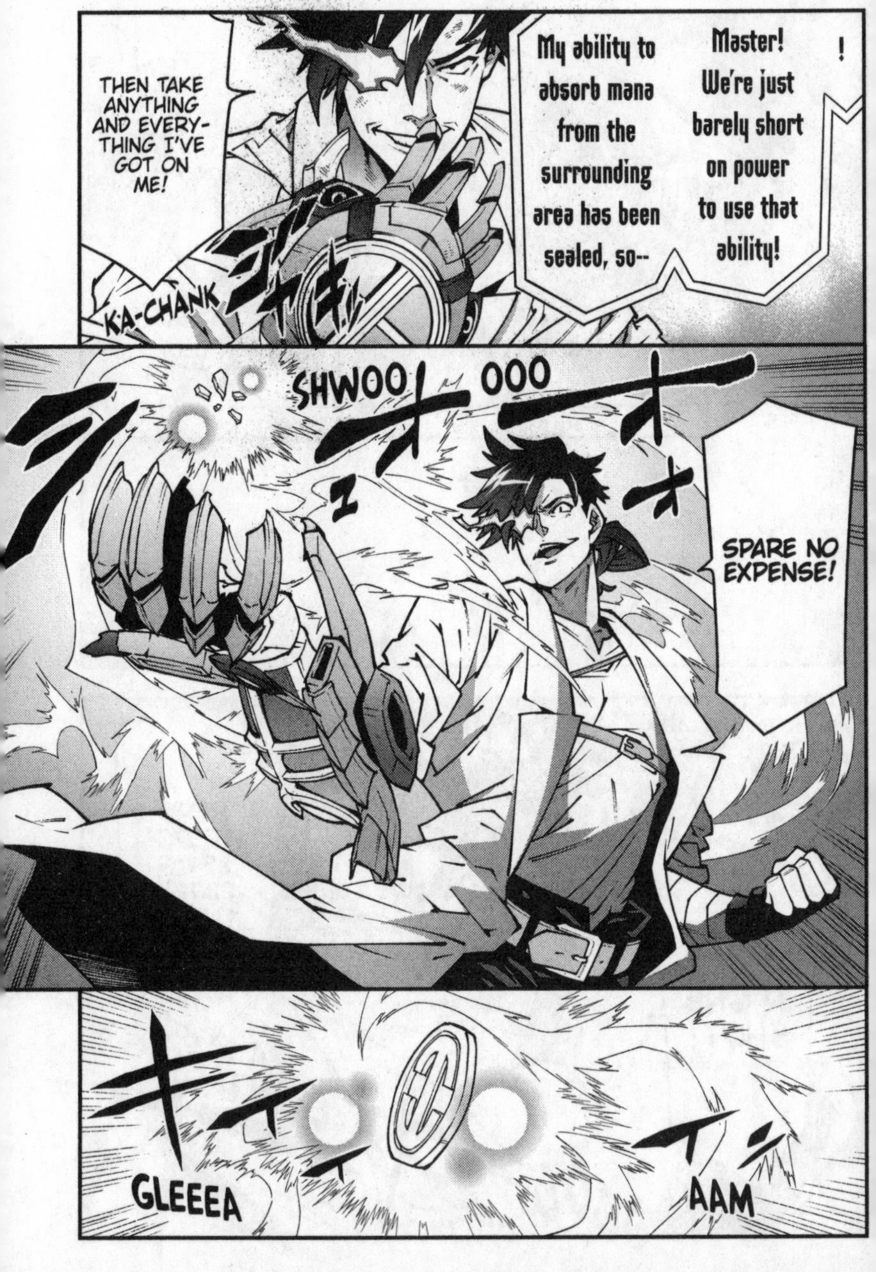
!
Master! We're just barely short on power to use that ability!
My ability to absorb mana from the surrounding area has been sealed, so--
THEN TAKE ANYTHING AND EVERY-THING I'VE GOT ON ME!
KA-CHANK
SPARE NO EXPENSE!
SHWOO OOO
GLEEEA AAM

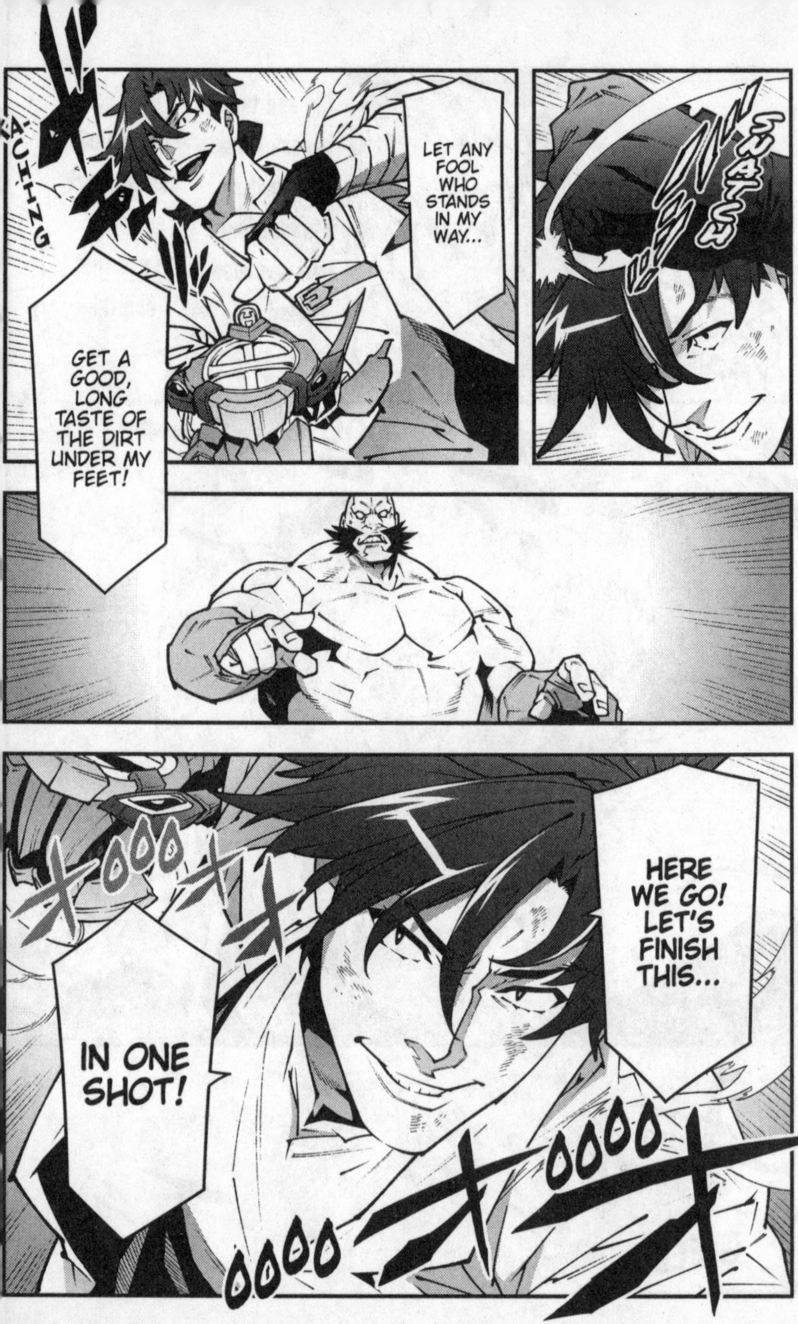
SNATCH
LET ANY FOOL WHO STANDS IN MY WAY...
GET A GOOD, LONG TASTE OF THE DIRT UNDER MY FEET!
KACHING
HERE WE GO! LET'S FINISH THIS...
IN ONE SHOT!

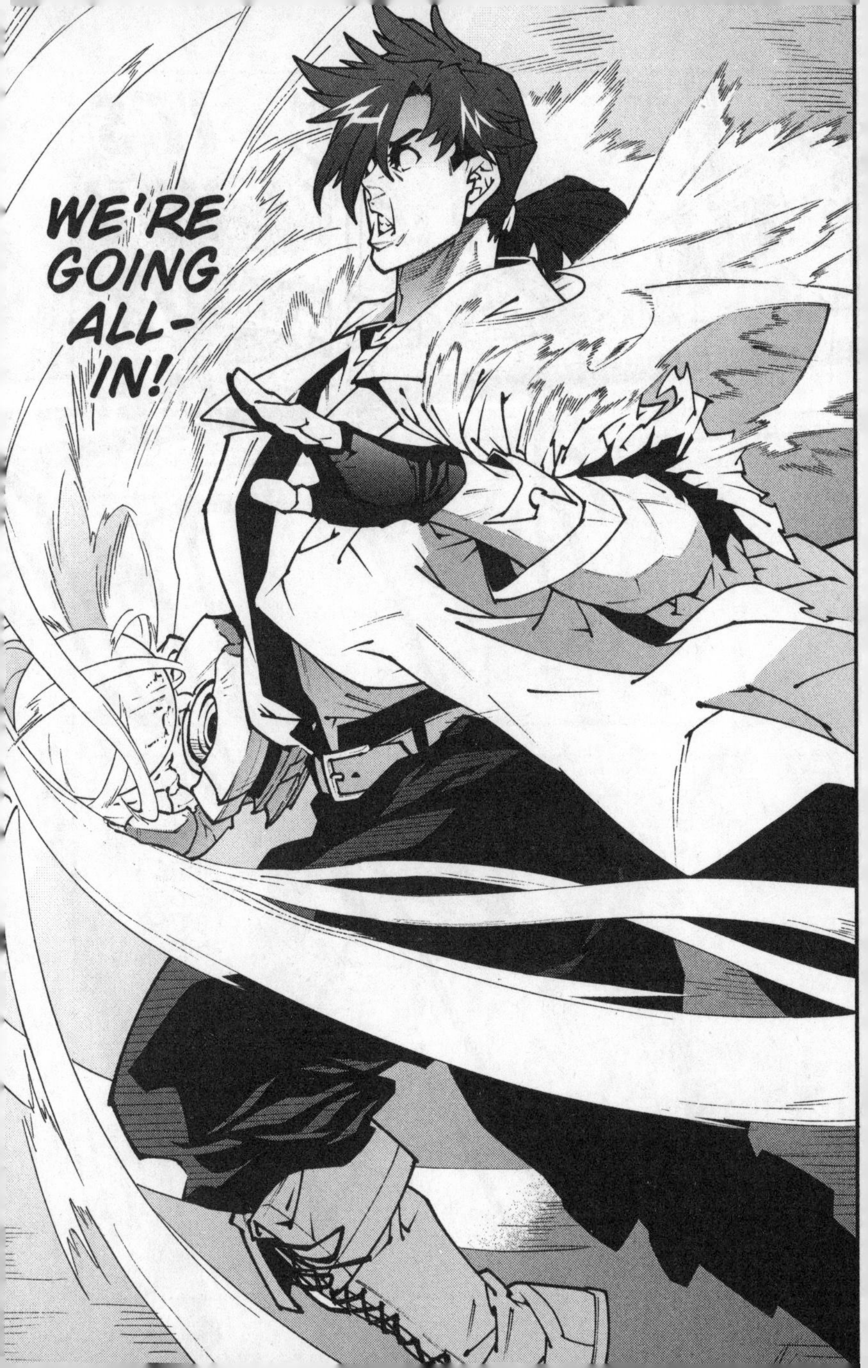
WE'RE GOING ALL-IN!

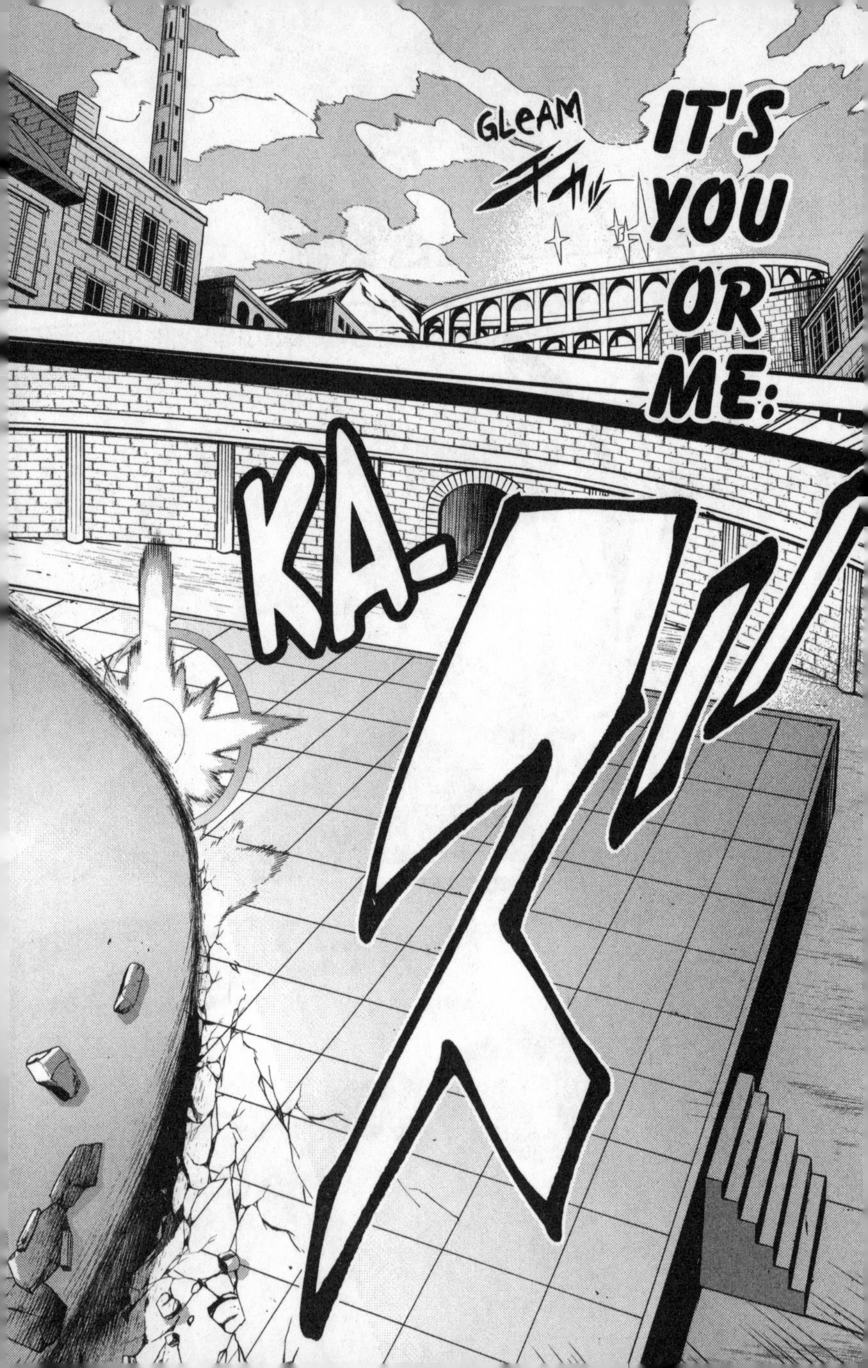
IT'S YOU OR ME:
GLEAM
KA-

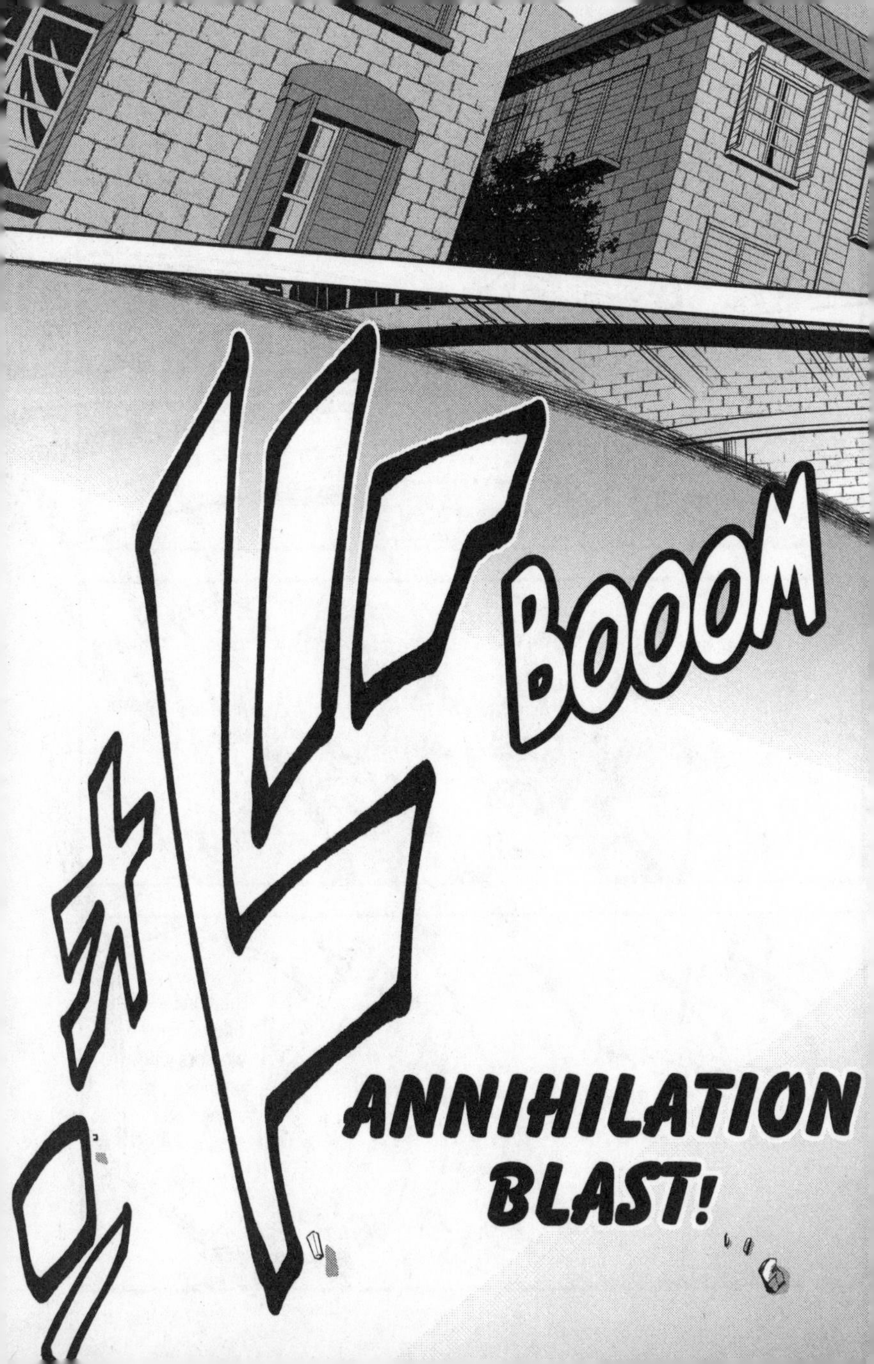
BOOOM
ANNIHILATION BLAST!

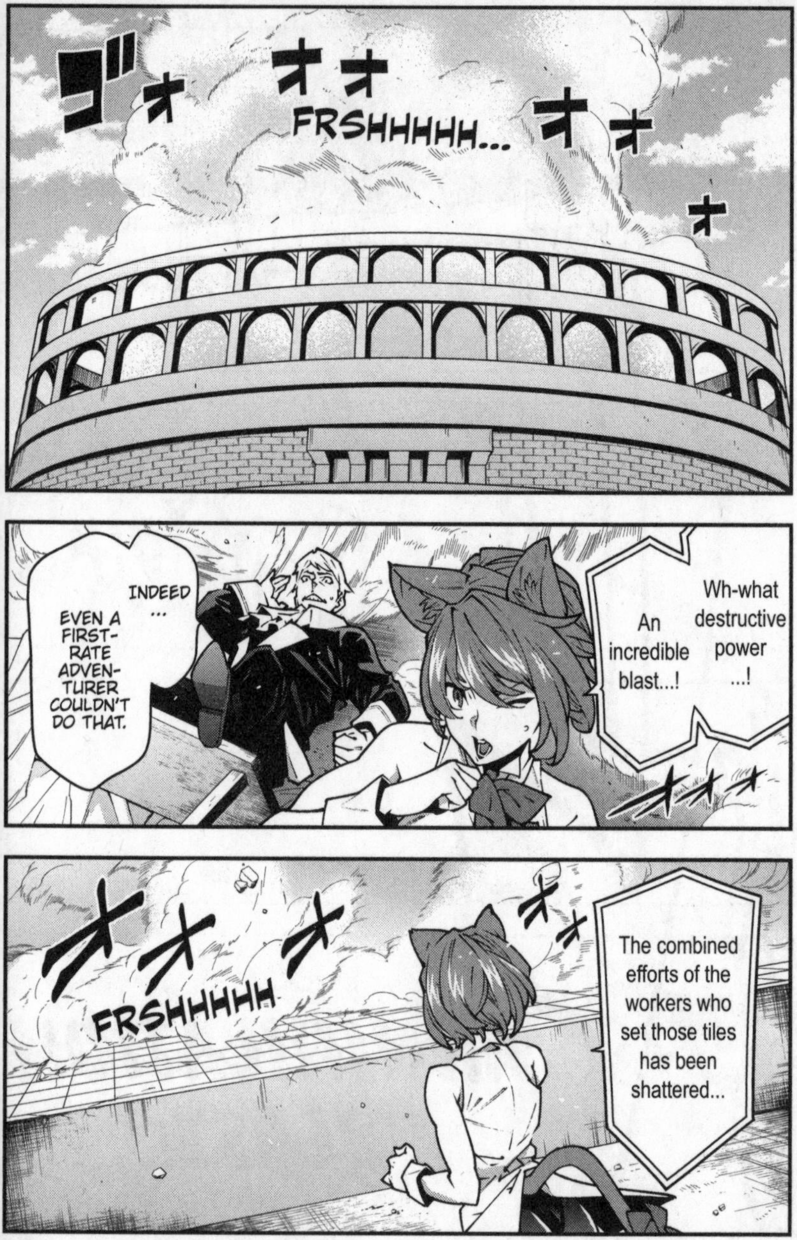
ゴォ
オオ
FRSHHHHH...
オオ
ォ
Wh-what destructive power ...!
An incredible blast...!
INDEED ...
EVEN A FIRST-RATE ADVENTURER COULDN'T DO THAT.
The combined efforts of the workers who set those tiles has been shattered...
FRSHHHHH

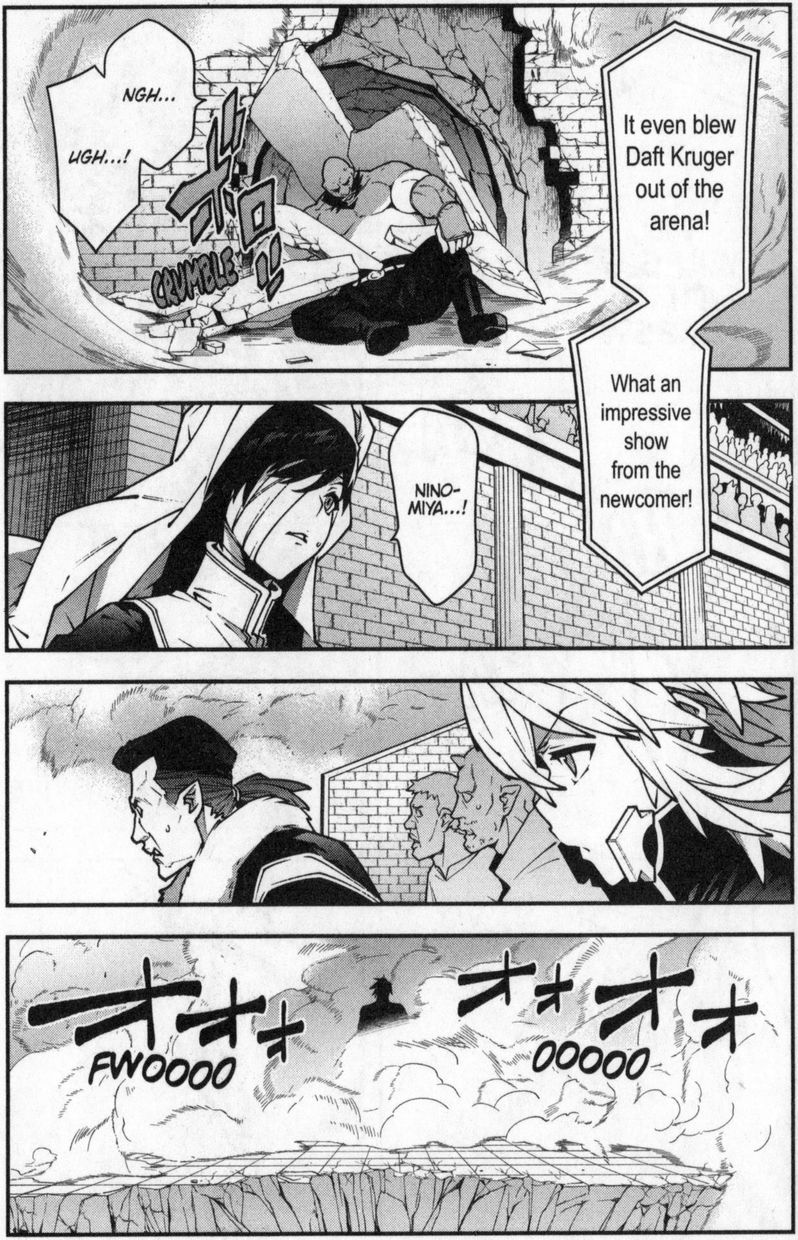
It even blew Daft Kruger out of the arena!
NGH...
UGH...!
CRUMBLE
What an impressive show from the newcomer!
NINO-MIYA...!
FWOOOO
OOOOO

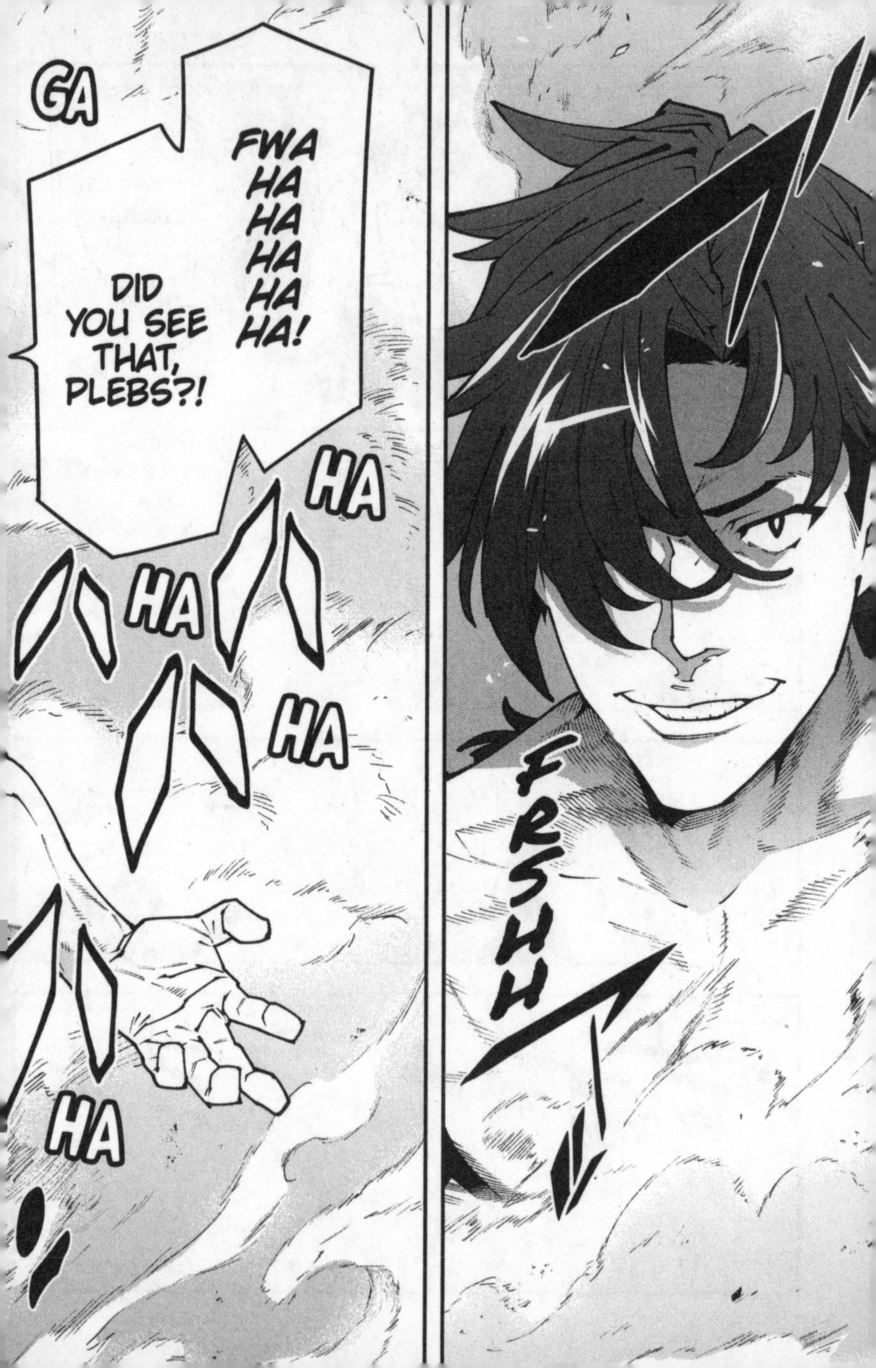
FRSHH
FWA HA HA HA HA HA!
DID YOU SEE THAT, PLEBS?!
GA
HA
HA
HA
HA

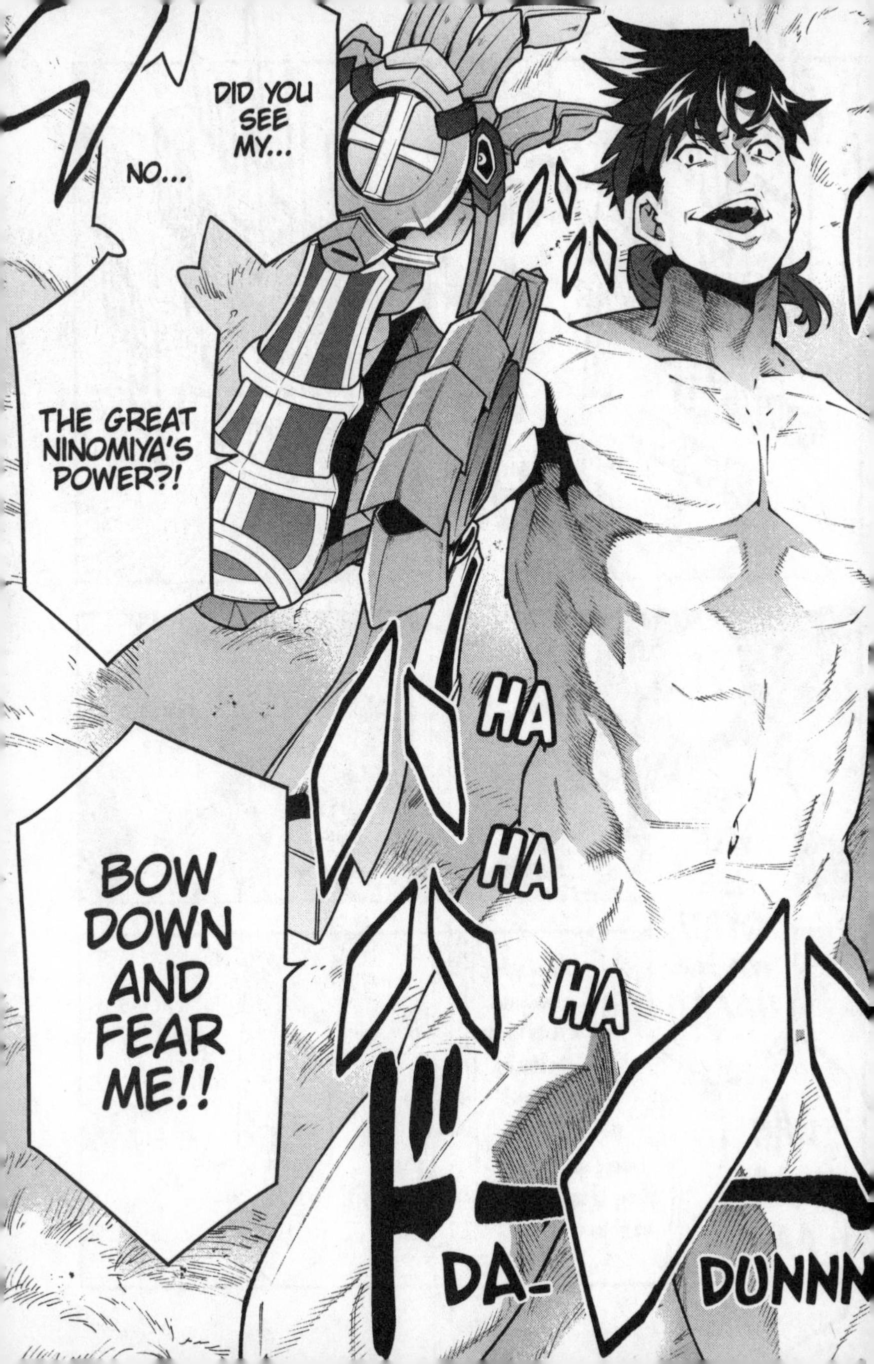
DID YOU SEE MY...
NO...
THE GREAT NINOMIYA'S POWER?!
HA HA HA
BOW DOWN AND FEAR ME!!
DA-DUNNN

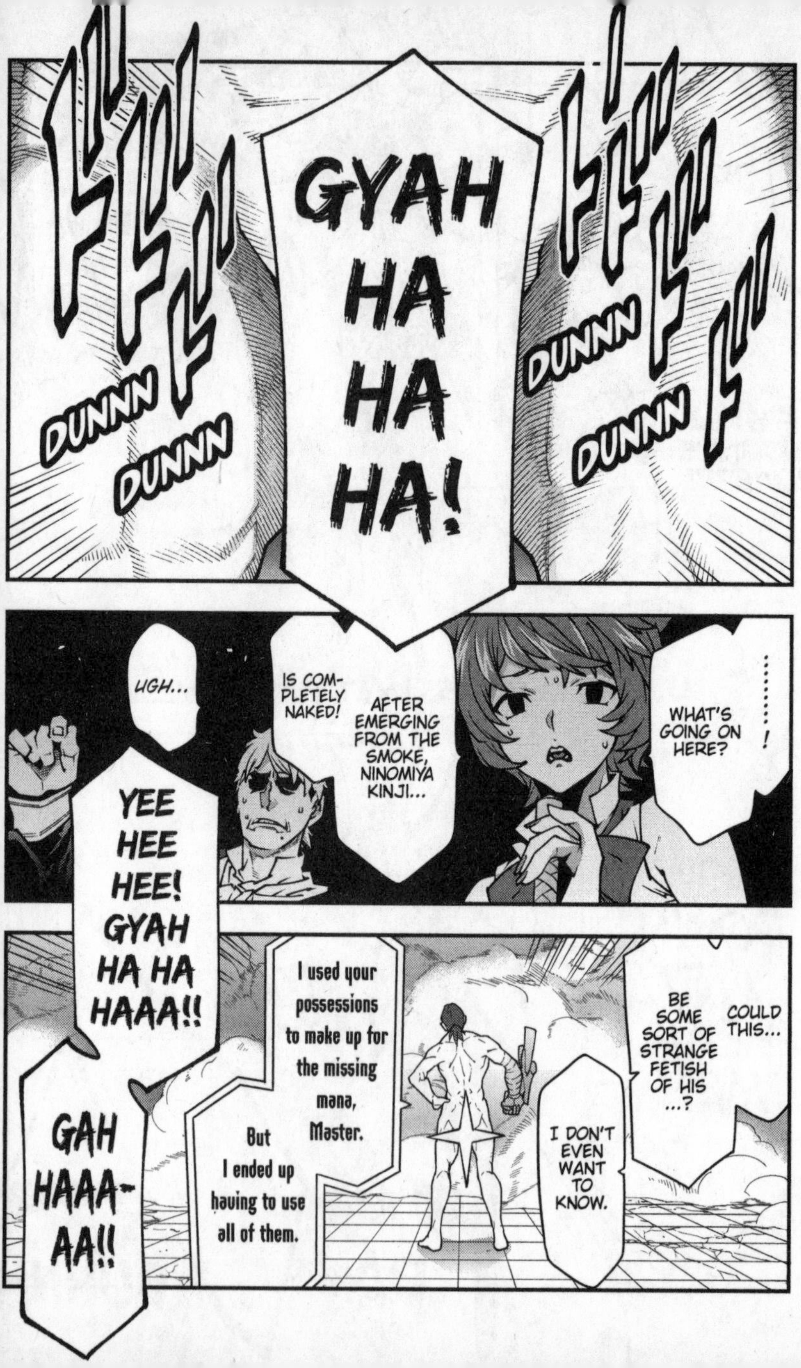
DUNNN
DUNNN
GYAH HA HA HA!
DUNNN
DUNNN
......!
WHAT'S GOING ON HERE?
AFTER EMERGING FROM THE SMOKE, NINOMIYA KINJI...
IS COMPLETELY NAKED!
UGH...
YEE HEE HEE! GYAH HA HA HAAA!!
COULD THIS...
BE SOME SORT OF STRANGE FETISH OF HIS ...?
I DON'T EVEN WANT TO KNOW.
I used your possessions to make up for the missing mana, Master.
But I ended up having to use all of them.
GAH HAAAA-AA!!

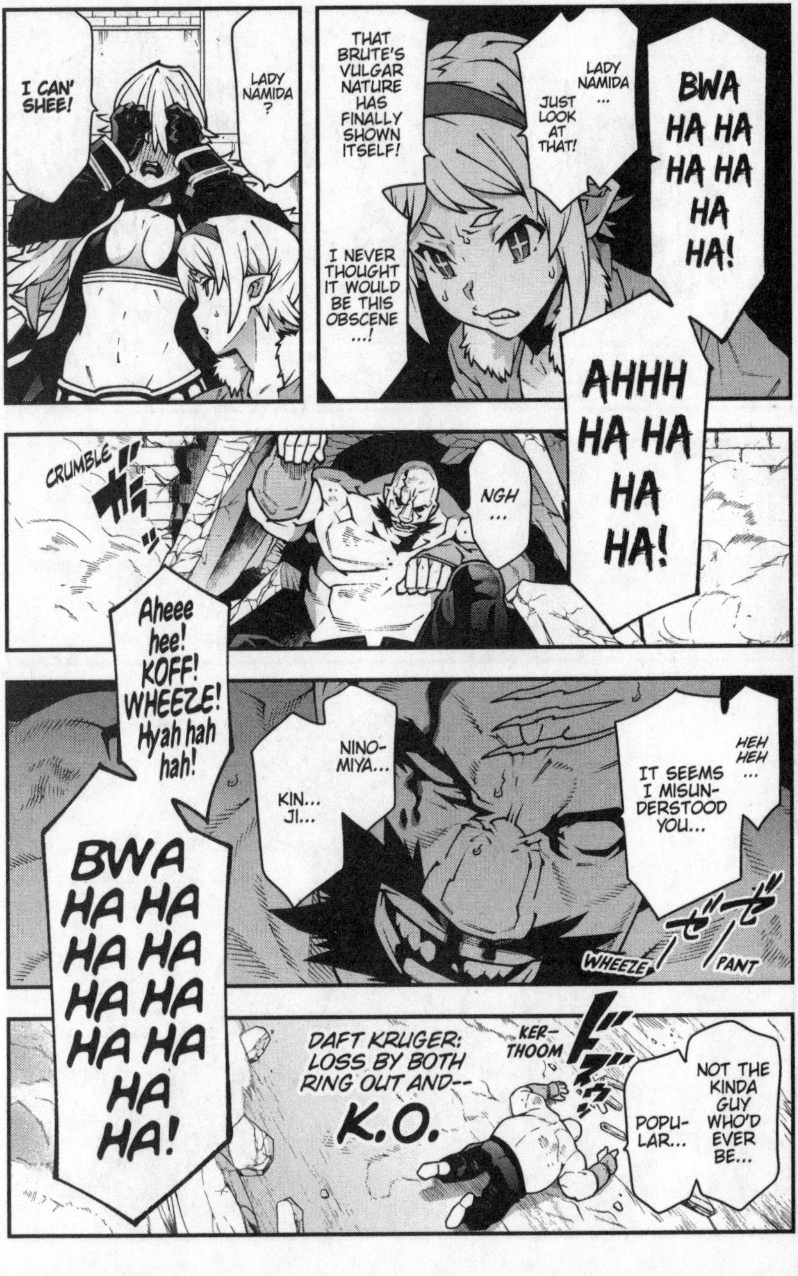
BWA HA HA HA HA HA HA!
LADY NAMIDA... JUST LOOK AT THAT!
THAT BRUTE'S VULGAR NATURE HAS FINALLY SHOWN ITSELF!
I NEVER THOUGHT IT WOULD BE THIS OBSCENE...!
LADY NAMIDA?
I CAN' SHEE!
AHHH HA HA HA HA HA!
NGH...
CRUMBLE
HEH HEH...
IT SEEMS I MISUNDERSTOOD YOU...
NINO-MIYA...
KIN... JI...
Aheee hee! KOFF! WHEEZE! Hyah hah hah!
BWA HA HA HA HA HA HA HA HA HA HA HA HA!
WHEEZE
PANT
NOT THE KINDA GUY WHO'D EVER BE...
POPU-LAR...
KER-THOOM
DAFT KRUGER: LOSS BY BOTH RING OUT AND--
K.O.

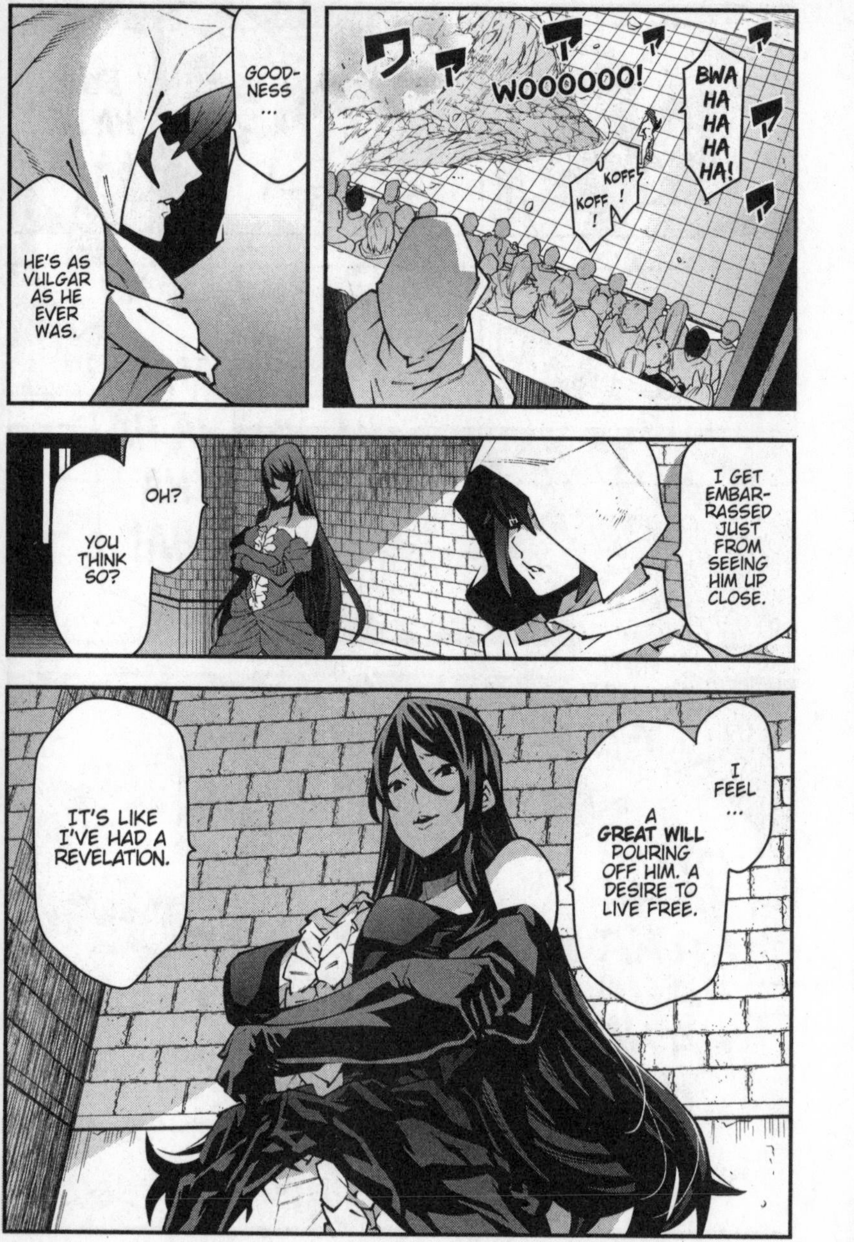
WOOOOOO!
BWA HA HA HA HA!
KOFF! KOFF!
...
GOOD-NESS ...
HE'S AS VULGAR AS HE EVER WAS.
I GET EMBAR-RASSED JUST FROM SEEING HIM UP CLOSE.
OH?
YOU THINK SO?
I FEEL ...
A GREAT WILL POURING OFF HIM. A DESIRE TO LIVE FREE.
IT'S LIKE I'VE HAD A REVELATION.

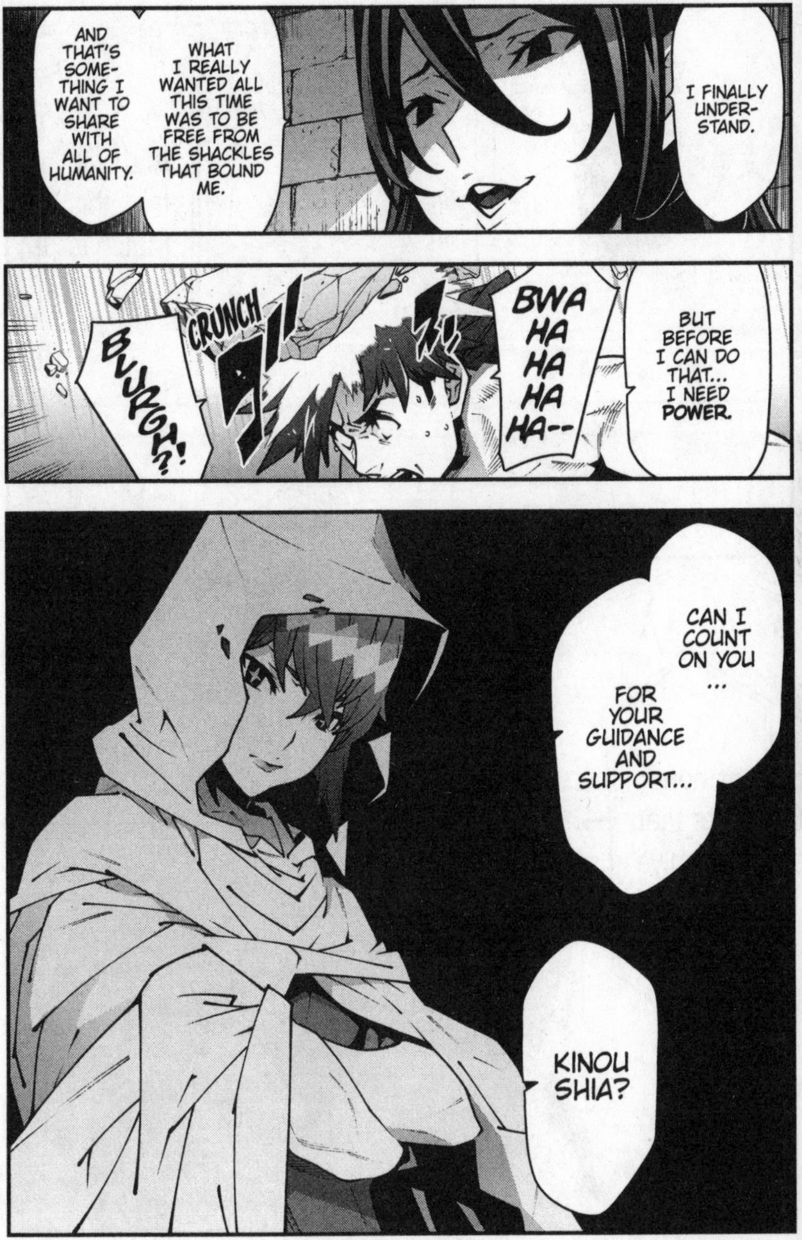
I FINALLY UNDERSTAND.
WHAT I REALLY WANTED ALL THIS TIME WAS TO BE FREE FROM THE SHACKLES THAT BOUND ME.
AND THAT'S SOMETHING I WANT TO SHARE WITH ALL OF HUMANITY.
BUT BEFORE I CAN DO THAT... I NEED **POWER.**
BWA HA HA HA HA--
CRUNCH
BLURGH!?
CAN I COUNT ON YOU ...
FOR YOUR GUIDANCE AND SUPPORT...
KINOU SHIA?

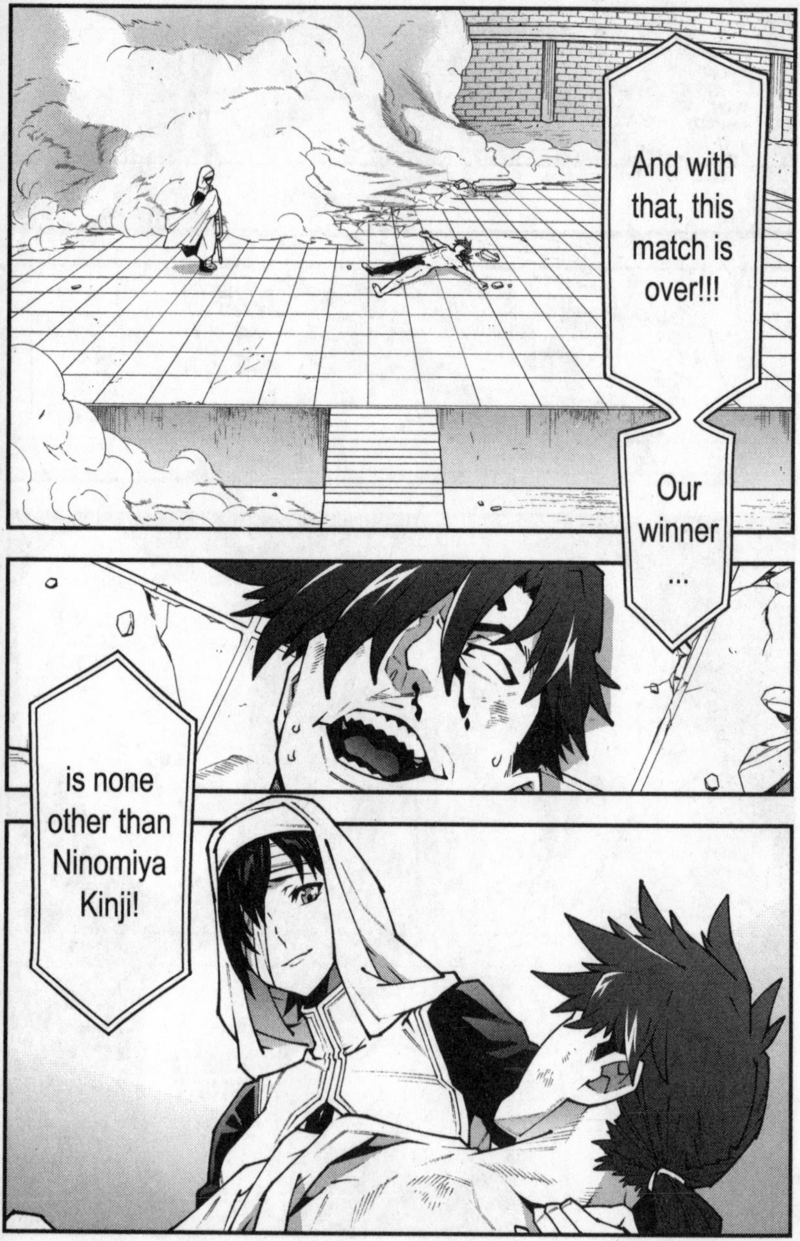
And with that, this match is over!!!
Our winner ...
is none other than Ninomiya Kinji!

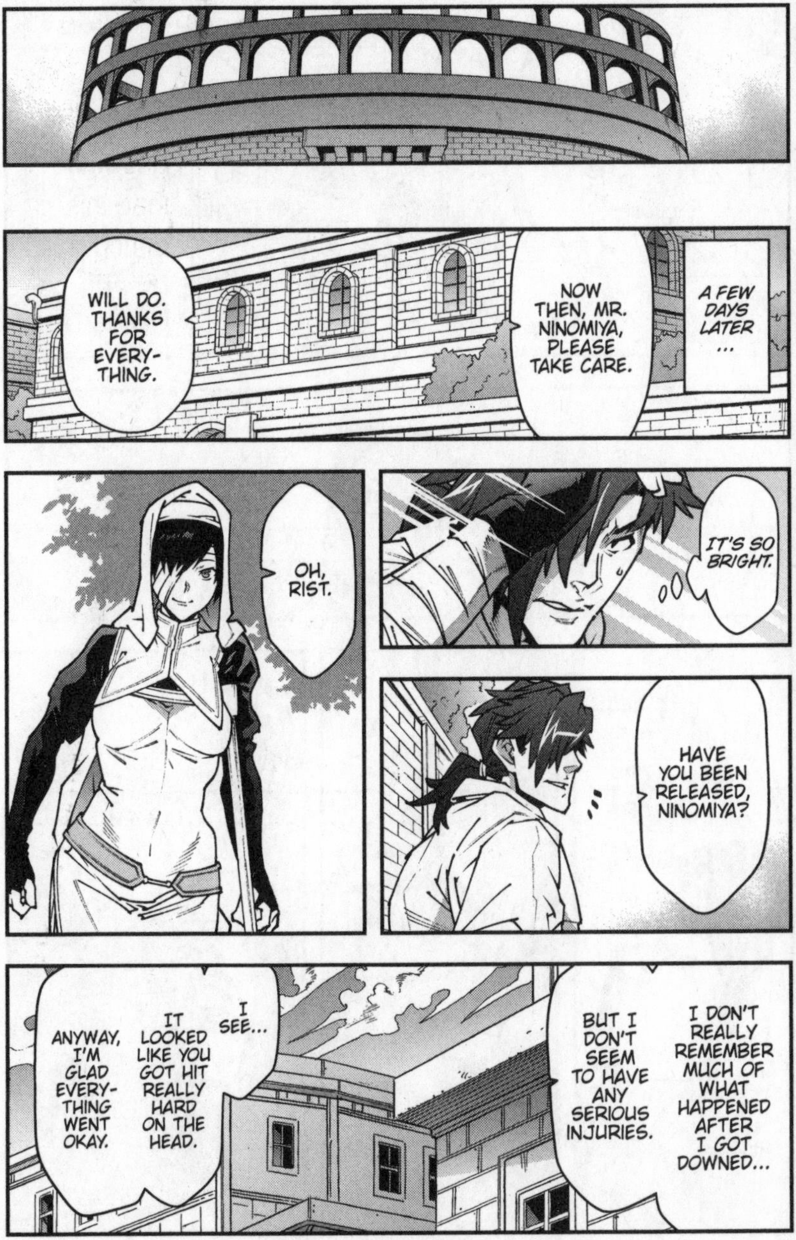
A FEW DAYS LATER...
NOW THEN, MR. NINOMIYA, PLEASE TAKE CARE.
WILL DO. THANKS FOR EVERYTHING.
IT'S SO BRIGHT.
HAVE YOU BEEN RELEASED, NINOMIYA?
OH, RIST.
I DON'T REALLY REMEMBER MUCH OF WHAT HAPPENED AFTER I GOT DOWNED...
BUT I DON'T SEEM TO HAVE ANY SERIOUS INJURIES.
I SEE...
IT LOOKED LIKE YOU GOT HIT REALLY HARD ON THE HEAD.
ANYWAY, I'M GLAD EVERYTHING WENT OKAY.

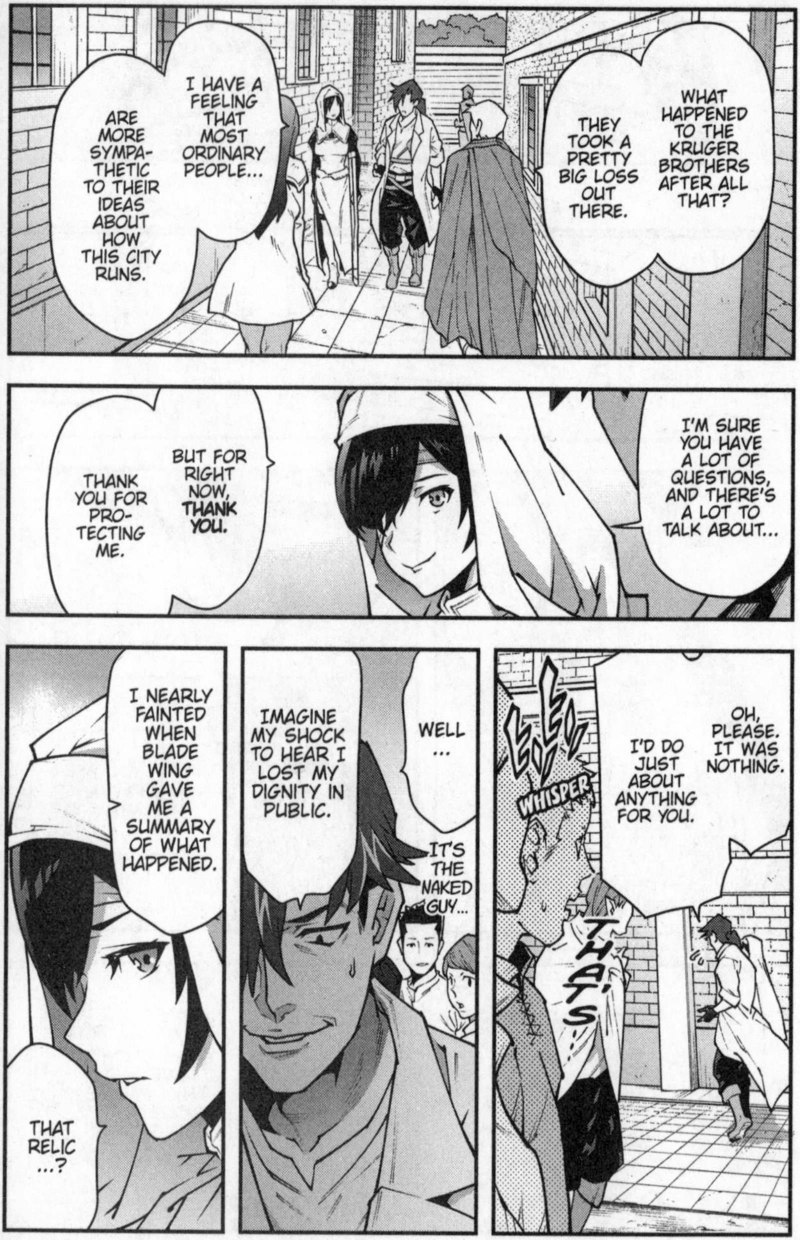
WHAT HAPPENED TO THE KRUGER BROTHERS AFTER ALL THAT?
THEY TOOK A PRETTY BIG LOSS OUT THERE.
I HAVE A FEELING THAT MOST ORDINARY PEOPLE...
ARE MORE SYMPATHETIC TO THEIR IDEAS ABOUT HOW THIS CITY RUNS.
I'M SURE YOU HAVE A LOT OF QUESTIONS, AND THERE'S A LOT TO TALK ABOUT...
BUT FOR RIGHT NOW, THANK YOU.
THANK YOU FOR PROTECTING ME.
OH, PLEASE. IT WAS NOTHING.
I'D DO JUST ABOUT ANYTHING FOR YOU.
WHISPER
THAT'S...
WELL...
IMAGINE MY SHOCK TO HEAR I LOST MY DIGNITY IN PUBLIC.
IT'S THE NAKED GUY...
I NEARLY FAINTED WHEN BLADE WING GAVE ME A SUMMARY OF WHAT HAPPENED.
THAT RELIC...?

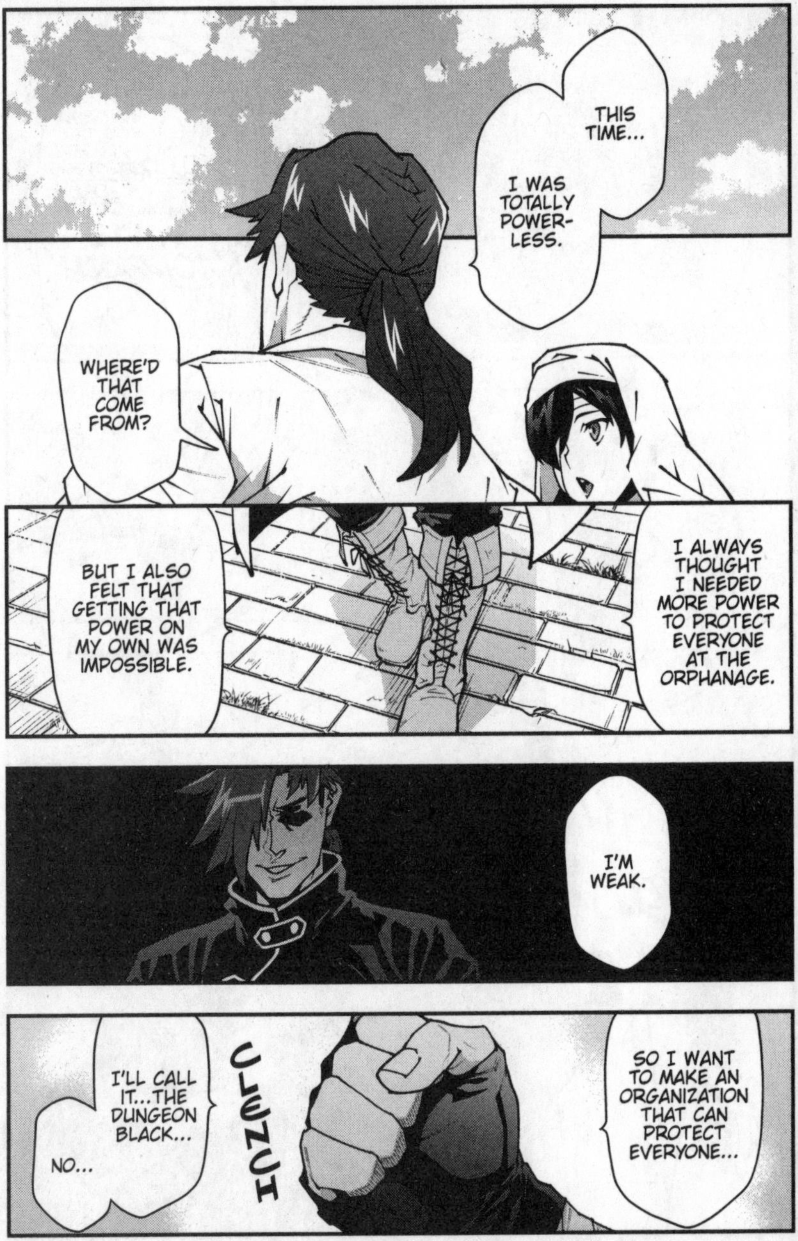
THIS TIME...
I WAS TOTALLY POWER-LESS.
WHERE'D THAT COME FROM?
I ALWAYS THOUGHT I NEEDED MORE POWER TO PROTECT EVERYONE AT THE ORPHANAGE.
BUT I ALSO FELT THAT GETTING THAT POWER ON MY OWN WAS IMPOSSIBLE.
I'M WEAK.
SO I WANT TO MAKE AN ORGANIZATION THAT CAN PROTECT EVERYONE...
CLENCH
I'LL CALL IT...THE DUNGEON BLACK...
NO...

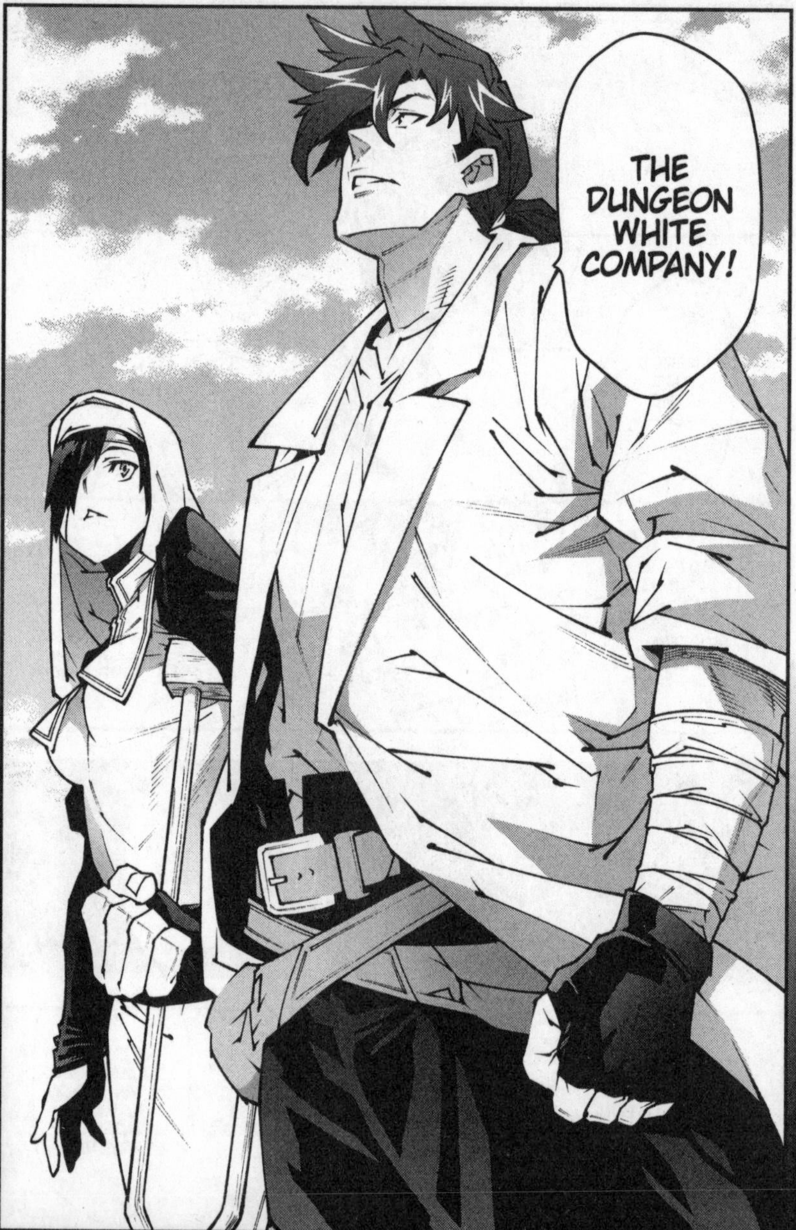
THE DUNGEON WHITE COMPANY!

DAFT KRUGER

| PRETTY BOY KILLER | HOLD ← THEN PRESS → AND PUNCH |

| DROP KICK TO HELL | ROTATE THE STICK ONCE WHILE NEAR OPPONENT + PUNCH |

| SPECIAL ATTACK: WILD SKIES BEAM | ROTATE THE STICK TWICE WHILE NEAR OPPONENT + PUNCH |

THE DUNGEON OF BLACK COMPANY

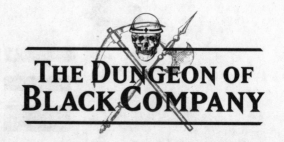

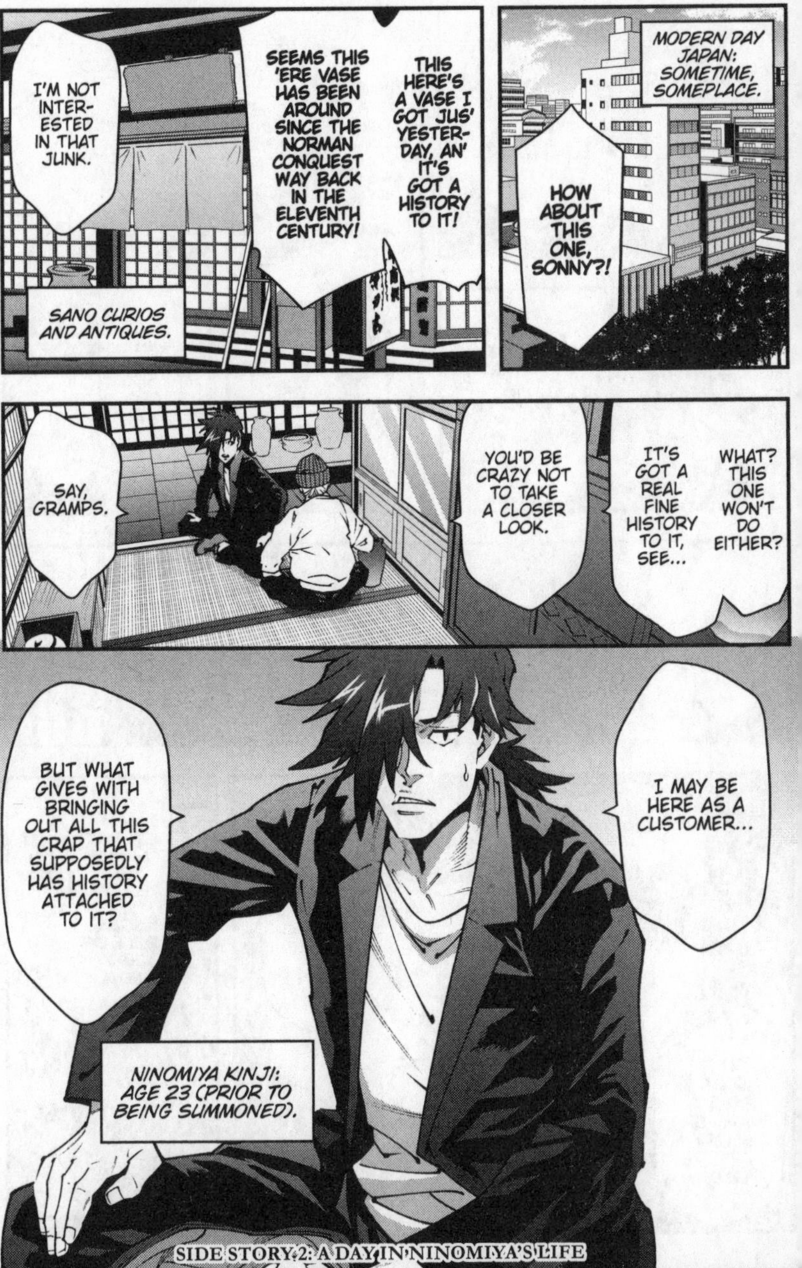
MODERN DAY JAPAN: SOMETIME, SOMEPLACE.
HOW ABOUT THIS ONE, SONNY?!
THIS HERE'S A VASE I GOT JUS' YESTER-DAY, AN' IT'S GOT A HISTORY TO IT!
SEEMS THIS 'ERE VASE HAS BEEN AROUND SINCE THE NORMAN CONQUEST WAY BACK IN THE ELEVENTH CENTURY!
I'M NOT INTER-ESTED IN THAT JUNK.
SANO CURIOS AND ANTIQUES.
WHAT? THIS ONE WON'T DO EITHER?
IT'S GOT A REAL FINE HISTORY TO IT, SEE...
YOU'D BE CRAZY NOT TO TAKE A CLOSER LOOK.
SAY, GRAMPS.
I MAY BE HERE AS A CUSTOMER...
BUT WHAT GIVES WITH BRINGING OUT ALL THIS CRAP THAT SUPPOSEDLY HAS HISTORY ATTACHED TO IT?
NINOMIYA KINJI: AGE 23 (PRIOR TO BEING SUMMONED).
SIDE STORY 2: A DAY IN NINOMIYA'S LIFE

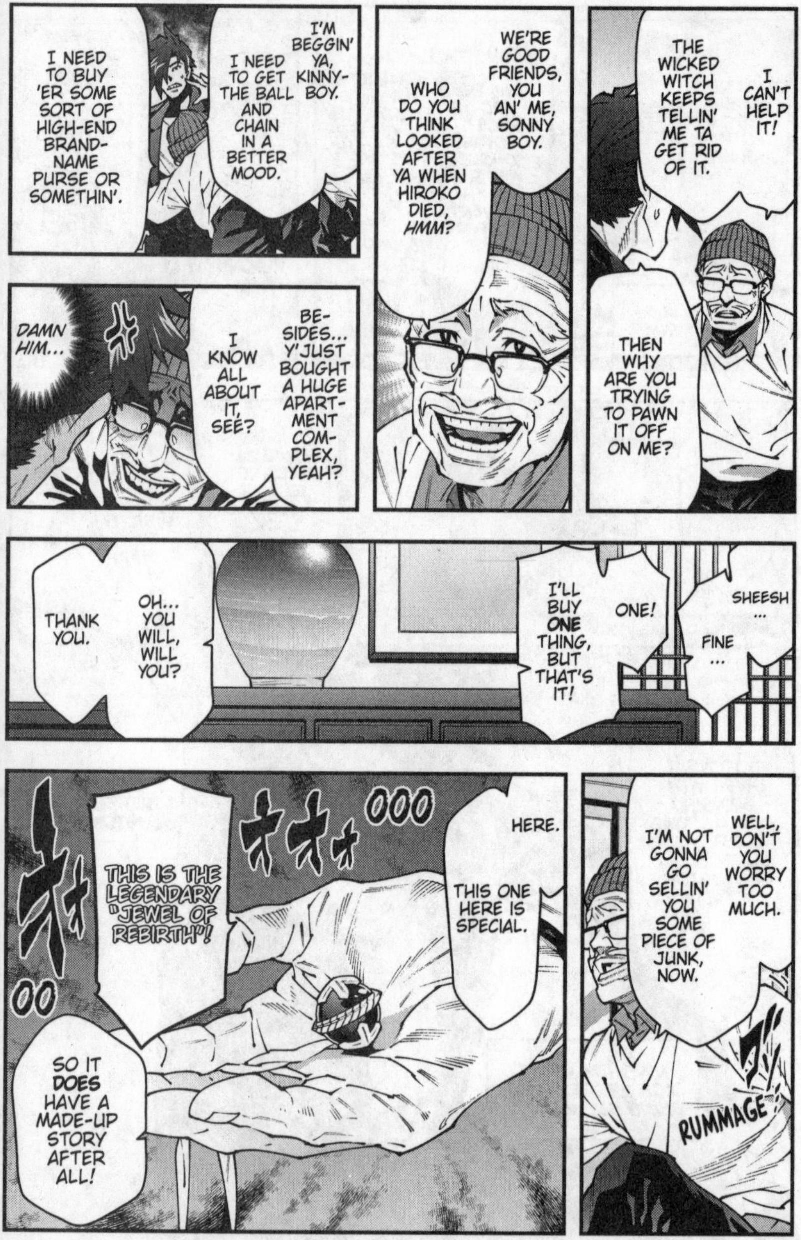
I CAN'T HELP IT!
THE WICKED WITCH KEEPS TELLIN' ME TA GET RID OF IT.
THEN WHY ARE YOU TRYING TO PAWN IT OFF ON ME?
WE'RE GOOD FRIENDS, YOU AN' ME, SONNY BOY.
WHO DO YOU THINK LOOKED AFTER YA WHEN HIROKO DIED, *HMM?*
I'M BEGGIN' YA, KINNY-BOY.
I NEED TO GET THE BALL AND CHAIN IN A BETTER MOOD.
I NEED TO BUY 'ER SOME SORT OF HIGH-END BRAND-NAME PURSE OR SOMETHIN'.
BESIDES... Y'JUST BOUGHT A HUGE APARTMENT COMPLEX, YEAH?
I KNOW ALL ABOUT IT, SEE?
DAMN HIM...
SHEESH... FINE...
ONE!
I'LL BUY **ONE** THING, BUT THAT'S IT!
OH... YOU WILL, WILL YOU?
THANK YOU.
WELL, DON'T YOU WORRY TOO MUCH.
I'M NOT GONNA GO SELLIN' YOU SOME PIECE OF JUNK, NOW.
RUMMAGE
HERE.
THIS ONE HERE IS SPECIAL.
OOO
THIS IS THE LEGENDARY "JEWEL OF REBIRTH"!
OO
SO IT **DOES** HAVE A MADE-UP STORY AFTER ALL!

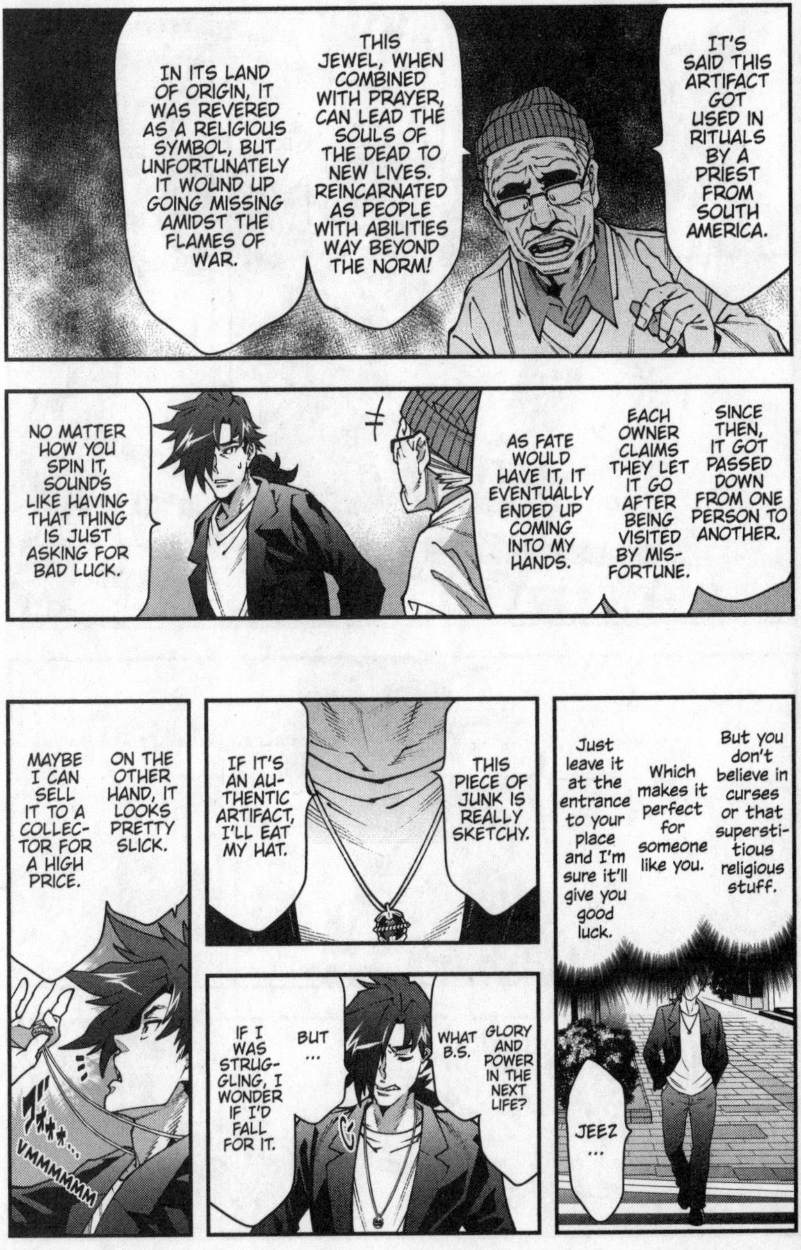
IT'S SAID THIS ARTIFACT GOT USED IN RITUALS BY A PRIEST FROM SOUTH AMERICA.
THIS JEWEL, WHEN COMBINED WITH PRAYER, CAN LEAD THE SOULS OF THE DEAD TO NEW LIVES. REINCARNATED AS PEOPLE WITH ABILITIES WAY BEYOND THE NORM!
IN ITS LAND OF ORIGIN, IT WAS REVERED AS A RELIGIOUS SYMBOL, BUT UNFORTUNATELY IT WOUND UP GOING MISSING AMIDST THE FLAMES OF WAR.
SINCE THEN, IT GOT PASSED DOWN FROM ONE PERSON TO ANOTHER.
EACH OWNER CLAIMS THEY LET IT GO AFTER BEING VISITED BY MIS-FORTUNE.
AS FATE WOULD HAVE IT, IT EVENTUALLY ENDED UP COMING INTO MY HANDS.
NO MATTER HOW YOU SPIN IT, SOUNDS LIKE HAVING THAT THING IS JUST ASKING FOR BAD LUCK.
But you don't believe in curses or that supersti-tious religious stuff.
Which makes it perfect for someone like you.
Just leave it at the entrance to your place and I'm sure it'll give you good luck.
JEEZ ...
THIS PIECE OF JUNK IS REALLY SKETCHY.
IF IT'S AN AU-THENTIC ARTIFACT, I'LL EAT MY HAT.
GLORY AND POWER IN THE NEXT LIFE?
WHAT B.S.
BUT ...
IF I WAS STRUG-GLING, I WONDER IF I'D FALL FOR IT.
ON THE OTHER HAND, IT LOOKS PRETTY SLICK.
MAYBE I CAN SELL IT TO A COLLEC-TOR FOR A HIGH PRICE.
VMMMMMMM

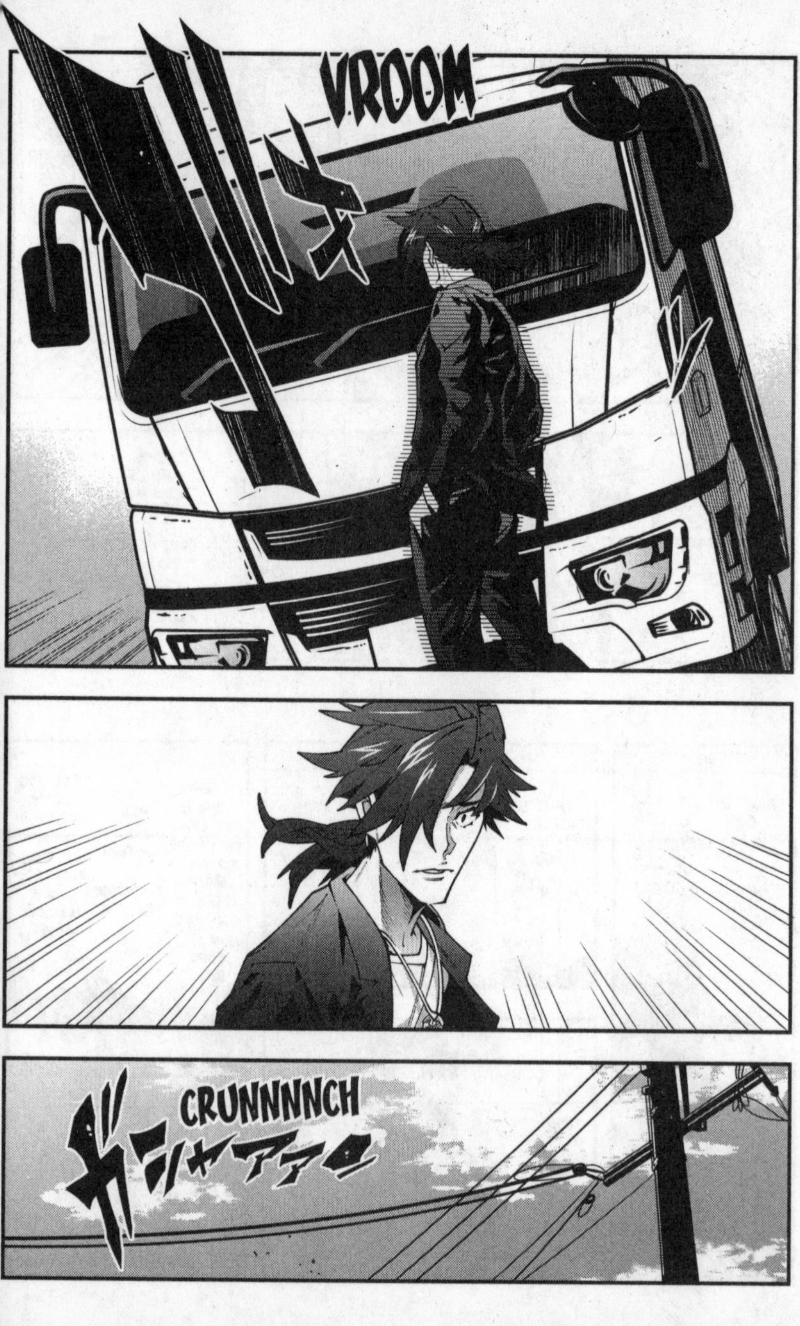
VROOM
CRUNNNNCH

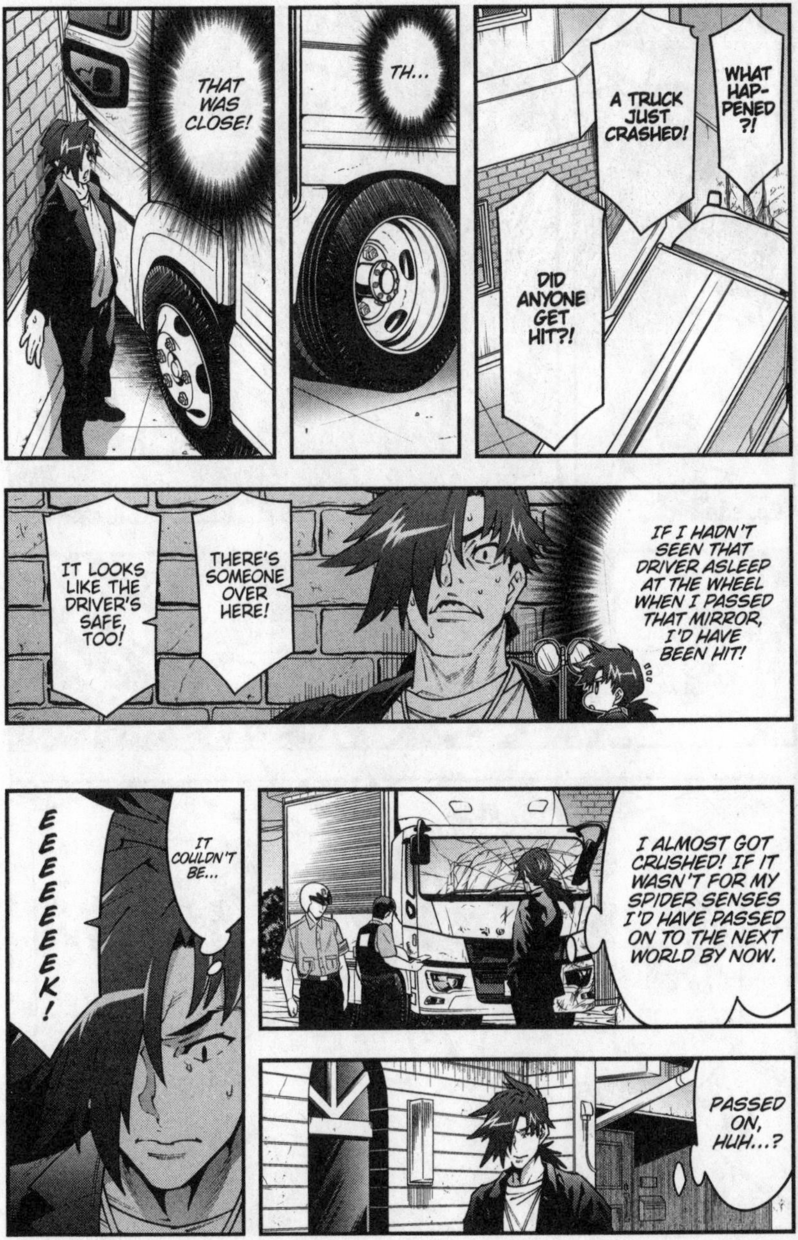
WHAT HAP-PENED ?!
A TRUCK JUST CRASHED!
DID ANYONE GET HIT?!
TH...
THAT WAS CLOSE!
IF I HADN'T SEEN THAT DRIVER ASLEEP AT THE WHEEL WHEN I PASSED THAT MIRROR, I'D HAVE BEEN HIT!
THERE'S SOMEONE OVER HERE!
IT LOOKS LIKE THE DRIVER'S SAFE, TOO!
I ALMOST GOT CRUSHED! IF IT WASN'T FOR MY SPIDER SENSES I'D HAVE PASSED ON TO THE NEXT WORLD BY NOW.
PASSED ON, HUH...?
IT COULDN'T BE...
EEEEEEEEK!

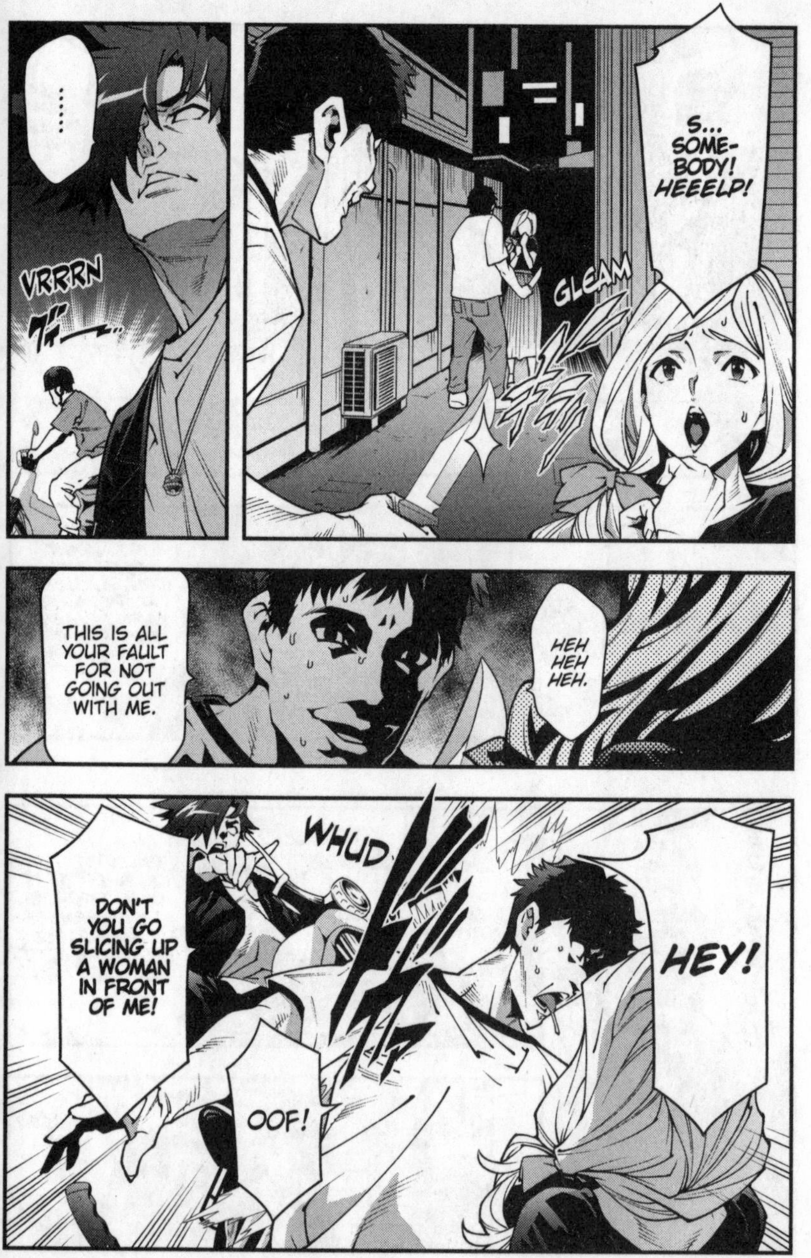
S... SOME-BODY! HEEELP!
GLEAM
......
VRRRN
HEH HEH HEH.
THIS IS ALL YOUR FAULT FOR NOT GOING OUT WITH ME.
HEY!
WHUD
DON'T YOU GO SLICING UP A WOMAN IN FRONT OF ME!
OOF!

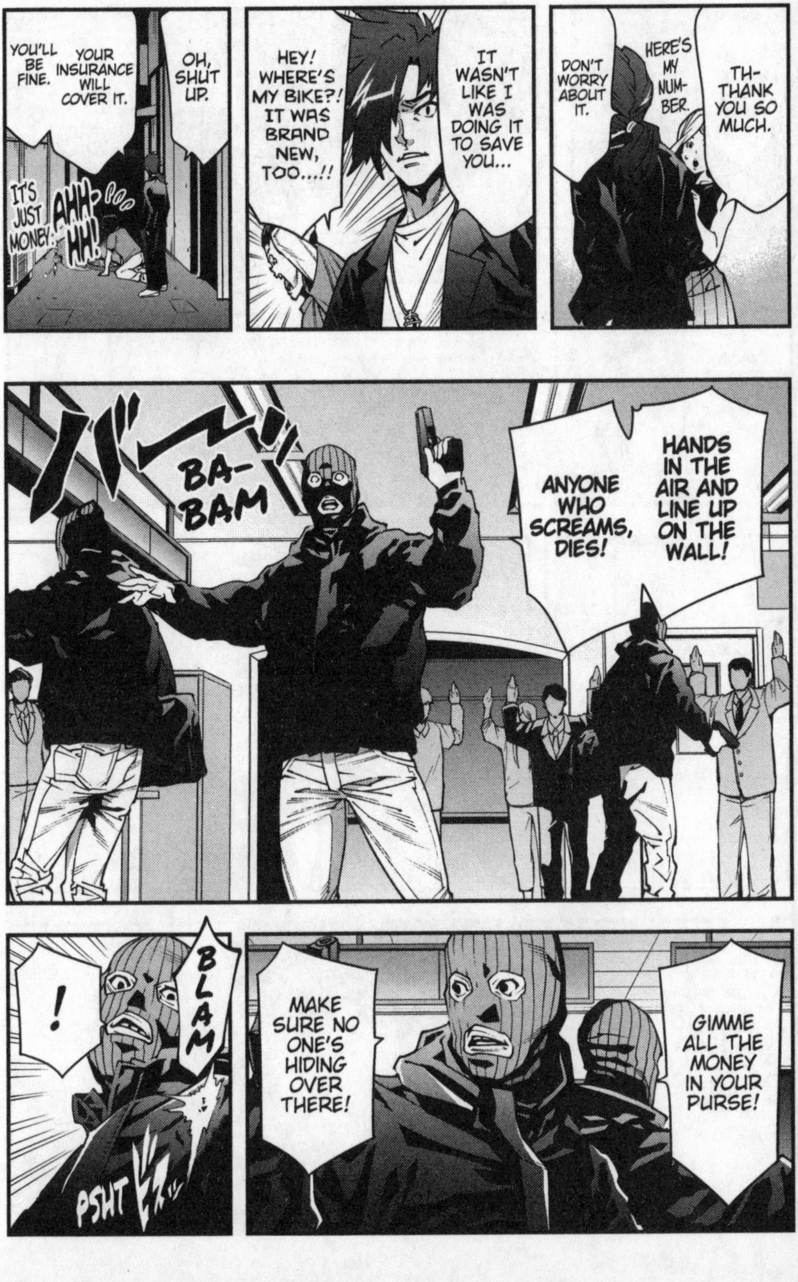
TH-THANK YOU SO MUCH.
HERE'S MY NUMBER.
DON'T WORRY ABOUT IT.
IT WASN'T LIKE I WAS DOING IT TO SAVE YOU...
HEY! WHERE'S MY BIKE?! IT WAS BRAND NEW, TOO...!!
OH, SHUT UP.
YOUR INSURANCE WILL COVER IT.
YOU'LL BE FINE.
AHHHH!
IT'S JUST MONEY.
HANDS IN THE AIR AND LINE UP ON THE WALL!
ANYONE WHO SCREAMS, DIES!
BA-BAM
GIMME ALL THE MONEY IN YOUR PURSE!
MAKE SURE NO ONE'S HIDING OVER THERE!
BLAM
!
PSHT

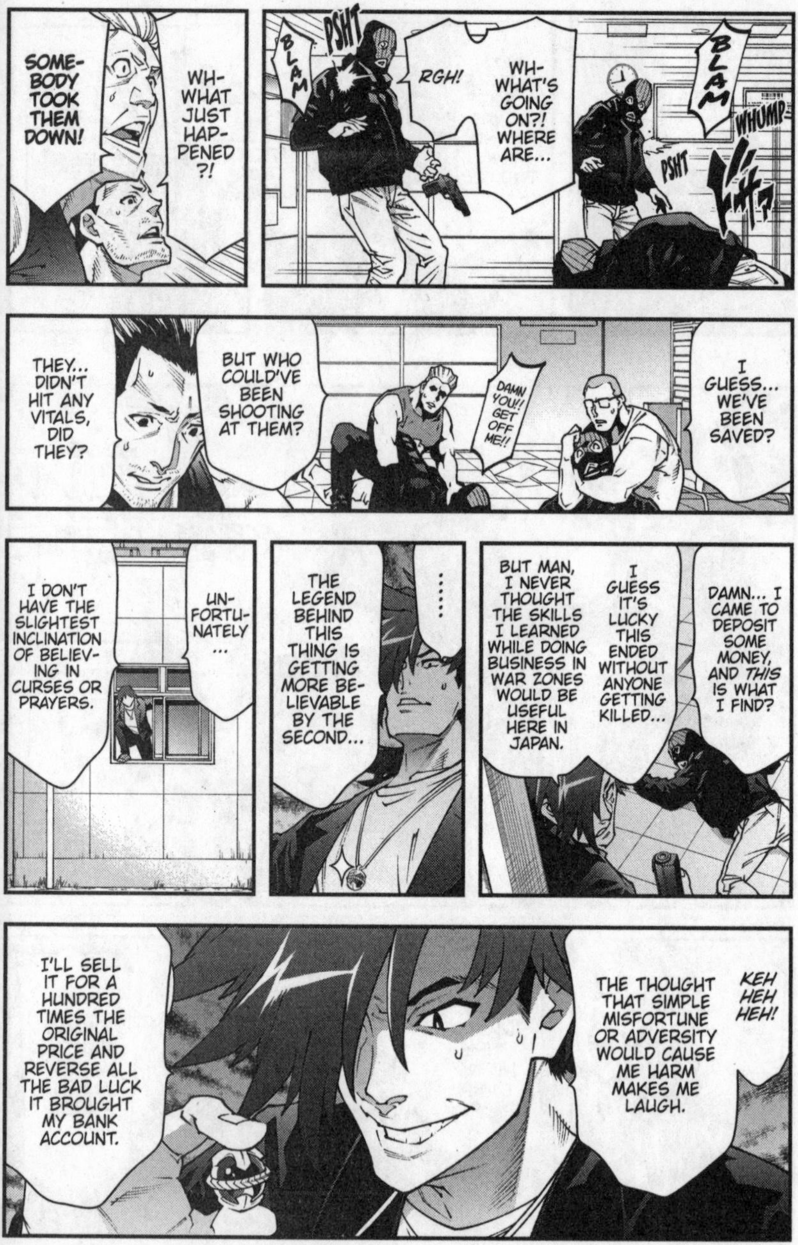
BLAM
WHUMP
PSHT
WH-WHAT'S GOING ON?! WHERE ARE...
RGH!
PSHT
BLAM
WH-WHAT JUST HAP-PENED?!
SOME-BODY TOOK THEM DOWN!
I GUESS... WE'VE BEEN SAVED?
DAMN YOU!! GET OFF ME!!
BUT WHO COULD'VE BEEN SHOOTING AT THEM?
THEY... DIDN'T HIT ANY VITALS, DID THEY?
DAMN... I CAME TO DEPOSIT SOME MONEY, AND THIS IS WHAT I FIND?
I GUESS IT'S LUCKY THIS ENDED WITHOUT ANYONE GETTING KILLED...
BUT MAN, I NEVER THOUGHT THE SKILLS I LEARNED WHILE DOING BUSINESS IN WAR ZONES WOULD BE USEFUL HERE IN JAPAN.
......
THE LEGEND BEHIND THIS THING IS GETTING MORE BE-LIEVABLE BY THE SECOND...
UN-FORTU-NATELY...
I DON'T HAVE THE SLIGHTEST INCLINATION OF BELIEV-ING IN CURSES OR PRAYERS.
KEH HEH HEH!
THE THOUGHT THAT SIMPLE MISFORTUNE OR ADVERSITY WOULD CAUSE ME HARM MAKES ME LAUGH.
I'LL SELL IT FOR A HUNDRED TIMES THE ORIGINAL PRICE AND REVERSE ALL THE BAD LUCK IT BROUGHT MY BANK ACCOUNT.

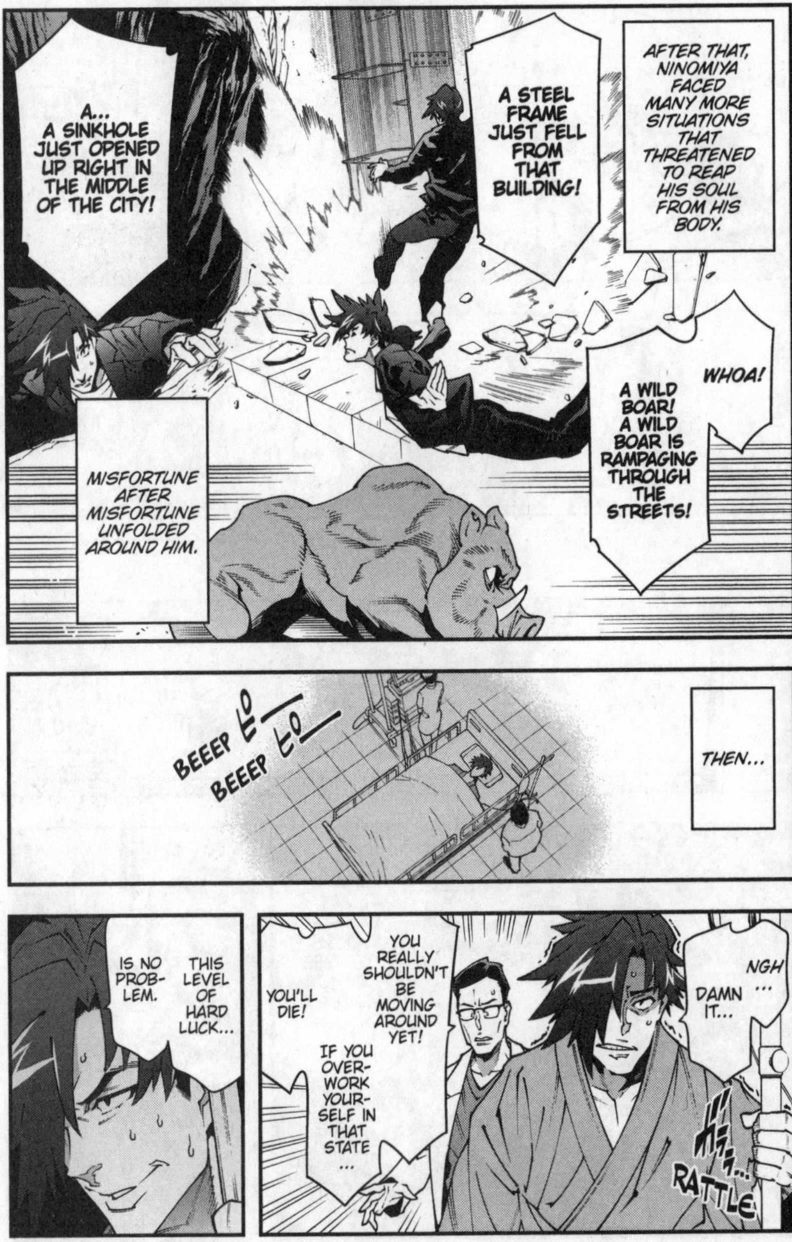
AFTER THAT, NINOMIYA FACED MANY MORE SITUATIONS THAT THREATENED TO REAP HIS SOUL FROM HIS BODY.
A STEEL FRAME JUST FELL FROM THAT BUILDING!
A... A SINKHOLE JUST OPENED UP RIGHT IN THE MIDDLE OF THE CITY!
WHOA!
A WILD BOAR! A WILD BOAR IS RAMPAGING THROUGH THE STREETS!
MISFORTUNE AFTER MISFORTUNE UNFOLDED AROUND HIM.
THEN...
BEEEP
BEEEP
NGH ...
DAMN IT...
RATTLE
YOU REALLY SHOULDN'T BE MOVING AROUND YET!
YOU'LL DIE!
IF YOU OVER-WORK YOUR-SELF IN THAT STATE ...
THIS LEVEL OF HARD LUCK...
IS NO PROB-LEM.

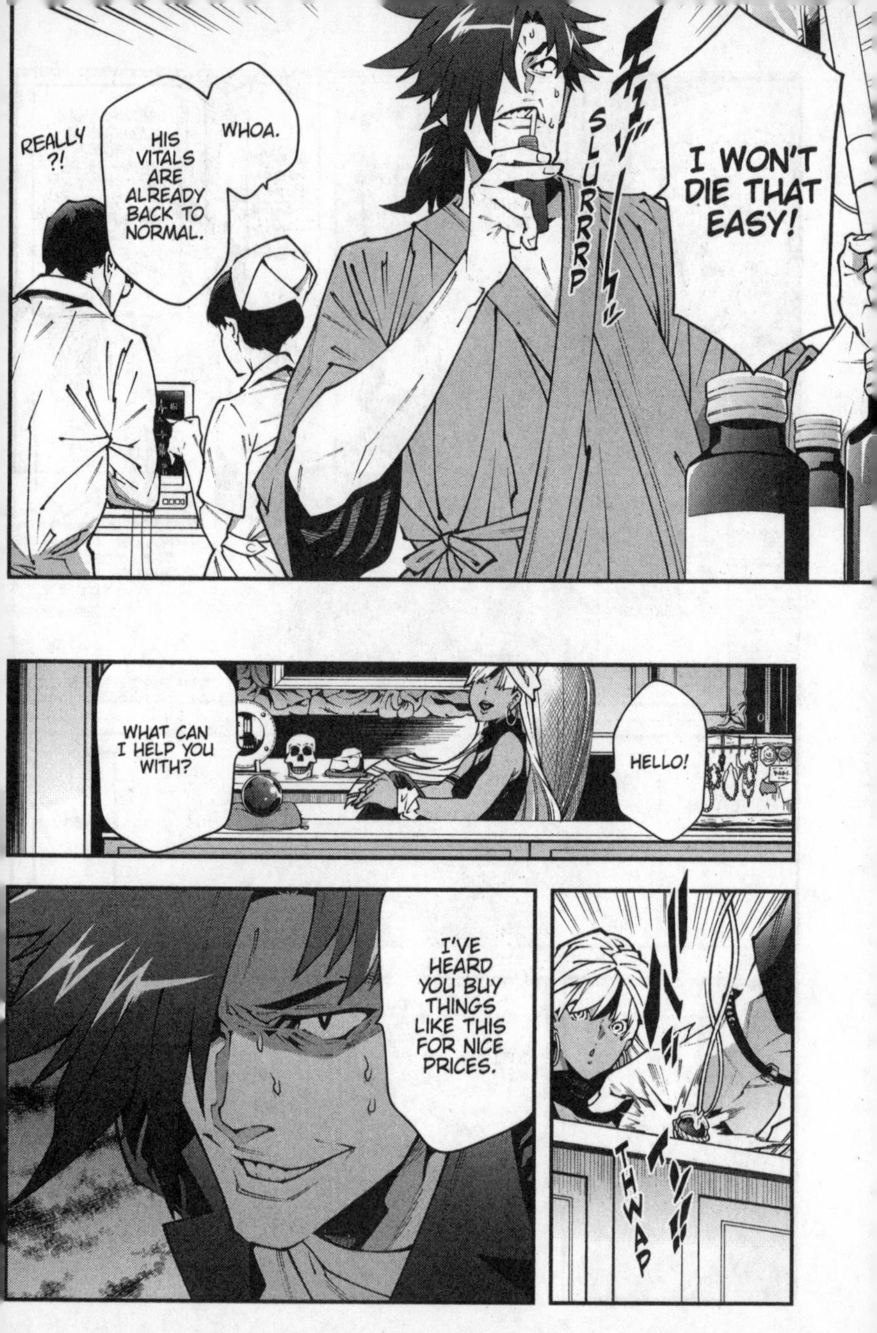
I WON'T DIE THAT EASY!
SLURRRP
WHOA.
HIS VITALS ARE ALREADY BACK TO NORMAL.
REALLY?!
HELLO!
WHAT CAN I HELP YOU WITH?
THWAP
I'VE HEARD YOU BUY THINGS LIKE THIS FOR NICE PRICES.

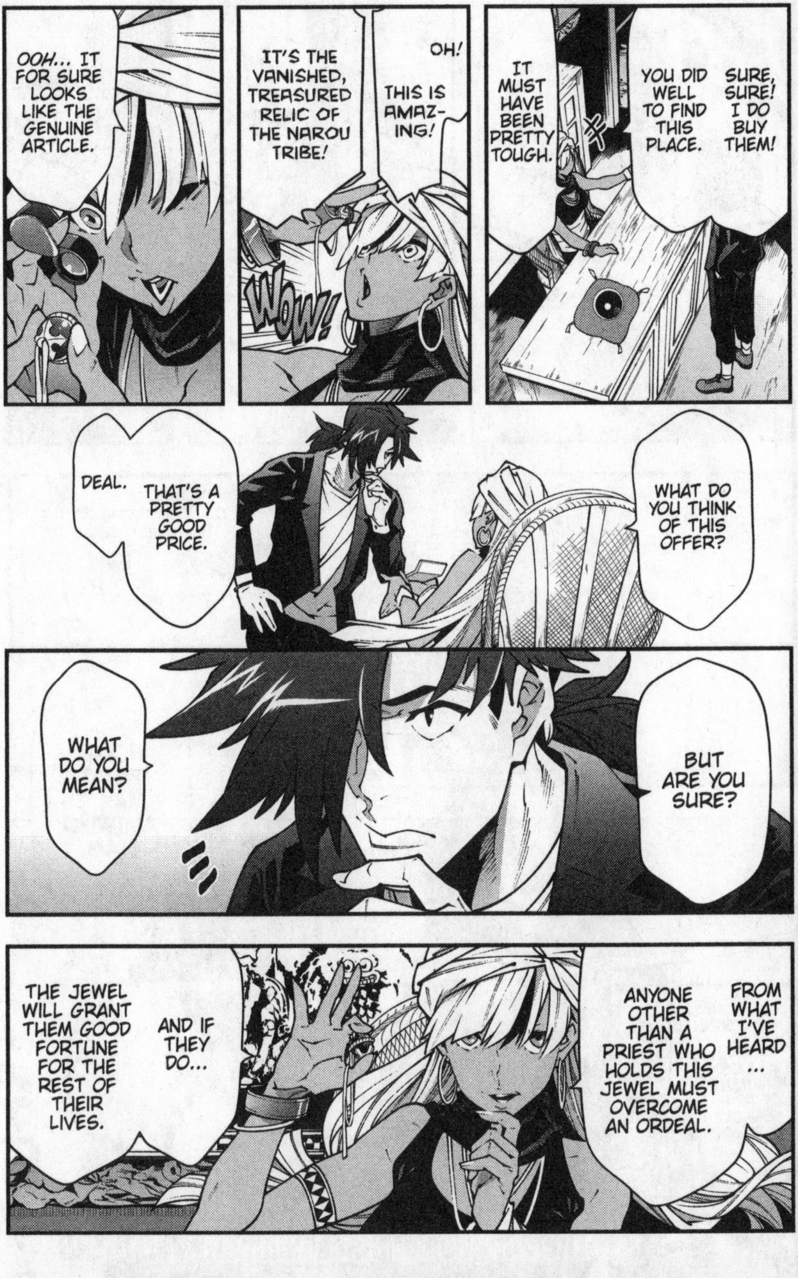
SURE, SURE! I DO BUY THEM!
YOU DID WELL TO FIND THIS PLACE.
IT MUST HAVE BEEN PRETTY TOUGH.
OH!
THIS IS AMAZ-ING!
IT'S THE VANISHED, TREASURED RELIC OF THE NAROU TRIBE!
WOW!
OOH... IT FOR SURE LOOKS LIKE THE GENUINE ARTICLE.
WHAT DO YOU THINK OF THIS OFFER?
THAT'S A PRETTY GOOD PRICE.
DEAL.
BUT ARE YOU SURE?
WHAT DO YOU MEAN?
FROM WHAT I'VE HEARD...
ANYONE OTHER THAN A PRIEST WHO HOLDS THIS JEWEL MUST OVERCOME AN ORDEAL.
AND IF THEY DO...
THE JEWEL WILL GRANT THEM GOOD FORTUNE FOR THE REST OF THEIR LIVES.

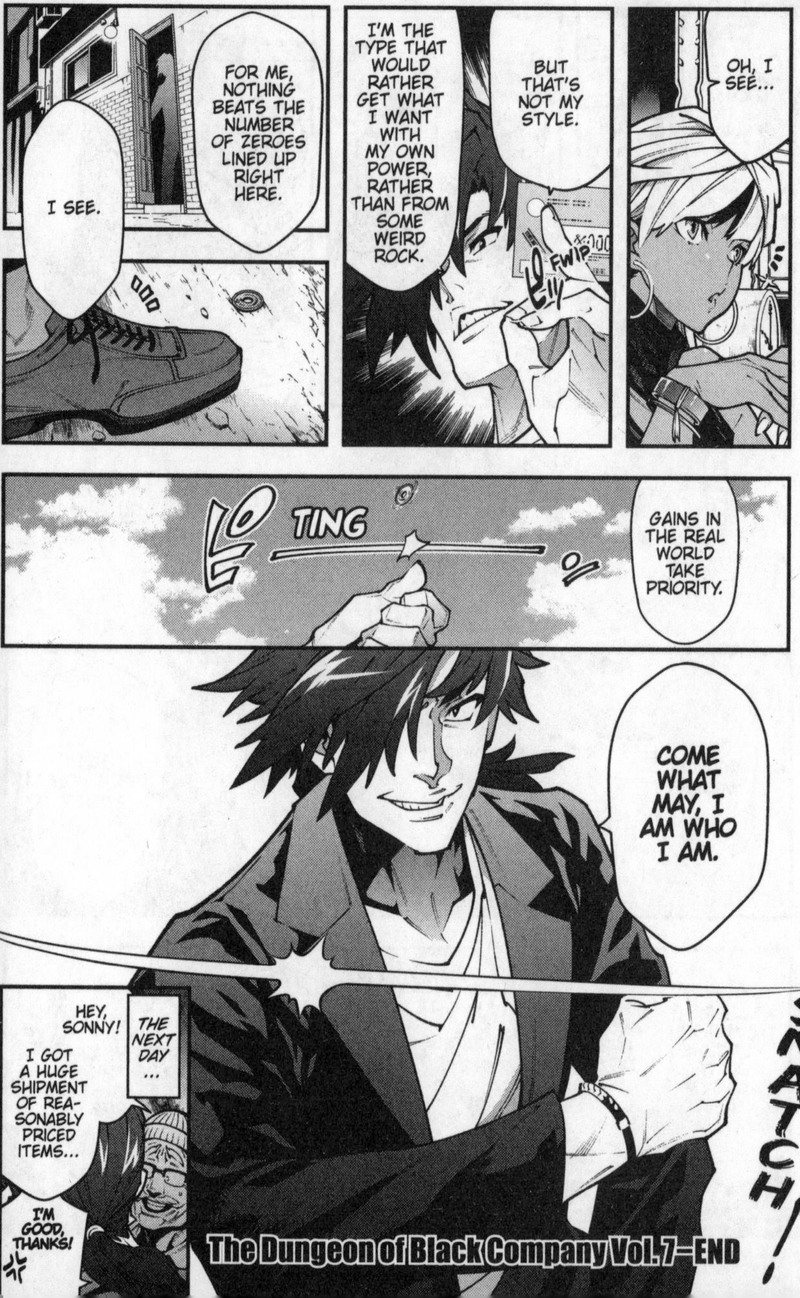
OH, I SEE...
BUT THAT'S NOT MY STYLE.
I'M THE TYPE THAT WOULD RATHER GET WHAT I WANT WITH MY OWN POWER, RATHER THAN FROM SOME WEIRD ROCK.
FWIP
FOR ME, NOTHING BEATS THE NUMBER OF ZEROES LINED UP RIGHT HERE.
I SEE.
GAINS IN THE REAL WORLD TAKE PRIORITY.
TING
COME WHAT MAY, I AM WHO I AM.
SNATCH!
THE NEXT DAY...
HEY, SONNY!
I GOT A HUGE SHIPMENT OF REA-SONABLY PRICED ITEMS...
I'M GOOD, THANKS!
The Dungeon of Black Company Vol. 7—END

SEVEN SEAS ENTERTAINMENT PRESENTS

THE DUNGEON OF BLACK COMPANY Vol. 7

story and art by YOUHEI YASUMURA

TRANSLATION
Wesley Bridges

LETTERING AND RETOUCH
Rina Mapa

COVER DESIGN
Kris Aubin

PROOFREADING
Krista Grandy

COPY EDITOR
Dawn Davis

SENIOR EDITOR
J.P. Sullivan

PRINT MANAGER
Rhiannon Rasmussen-Silverstein

PRODUCTION DESIGNER
Christina McKenzie

EDITOR-IN-CHIEF
Julie Davis

ASSOCIATE PUBLISHER
Adam Arnold

PUBLISHER
Jason DeAngelis

Seven Seas press and purchase enquiries can be sent to Marketing Manager Lianne Sentar at press@gomanga.com. Information regarding the distribution and purchase of digital editions is available from Digital Manager CK Russell at digital@gomanga.com.

ISBN: 978-1-64827-467-1

Printed in Canada

First Printing: April 2022

10 9 8 7 6 5 4 3 2 1

FOLLOW US ONLINE: ***www.sevenseasentertainment.com***

READING DIRECTIONS

This book reads from ***right to left***, Japanese style. If this is your first time reading manga, you start reading from the top right panel on each page and take it from there. If you get lost, just follow the numbered diagram here. It may seem backwards at first, but you'll get the hang of it! Have fun!!

1
2
3
4
5
6
7
8
9

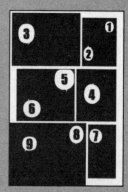